Prides Crossing

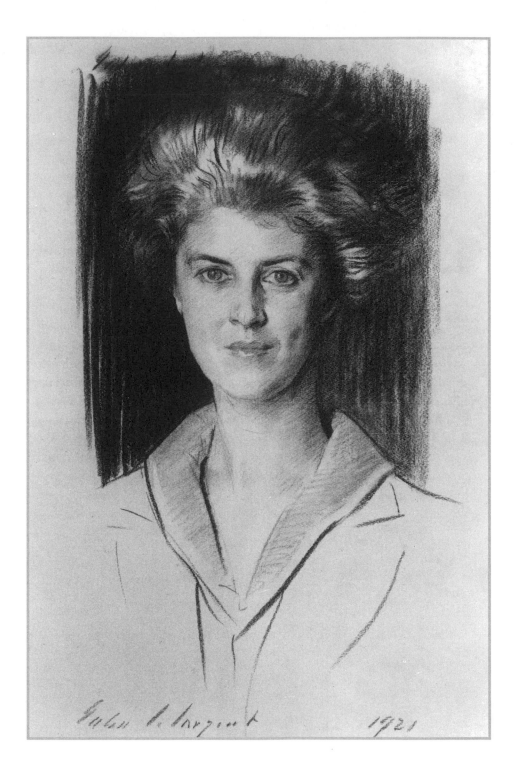

John S. Sargent 1921

Prides Crossing

The Unbridled Life and Impatient Times of Eleonora Sears

Peggy Miller Franck

Commonwealth Editions
Beverly, Massachusetts

Library of Congress Cataloging-in-Publication Data

Franck, Peggy Miller.
Prides crossing : the unbridled life and impatient times of Eleonora
Sears / Peggy Miller Franck.
p. cm.
Includes bibliographical references.
ISBN 978-1-933212-99-9
1. Sears, Eleonora Randolph, 1881–1968. 2. Socialites—United
States—Biography. 3. Horsemen and horsewomen—United
States—Biography. 4. Women athletes—United States—Biography.
5. Upper class—Massachusetts—Boston—Biography.
6. Boston (Mass.)—Biography. I. Title.
CT275.S2595F73 2009
974.4′61092—DC22
[B]   2009022585

Frontispiece: Charcoal portrait of Eleonora Sears
by John Singer Sargent, 1921 (Author collection)
Cover design by John Barnett
Interior design by Joyce Weston
Printed in the United States of America

Commonwealth Editions, 266 Cabot Street,
Beverly, Massachusetts 01915
www.commonwealtheditions.com

A loving salute to my father and mother

Contents

Sears, Eleonora R.—The Universal Female Athlete
— From *The Handbook of Pseudonyms and
Personal Nicknames*

If there are two words I can't stand, they're *resting*
and *tired*. They make me sick. . . .
— Eleonora Sears

Prologue

ELEONORA RANDOLPH SEARS had nearly everything worth having; she came to know nearly everyone worth knowing, and she did nearly everything worth doing. Eleo Sears was born to one of those old Yankee families whose names dot the map of Massachusetts, recalling the adventurers and dreamers who settled America when it was no more than a coastline. Eleo left her mark as the greatest pioneer in the uncharted territory of women's sports. She was reputed to be the most versatile female athlete in recorded history. Eleo faced off against the world like a gladiator, wielding her competitive skill, her wealth, and the force of her will to topple ancient and suffocating commandments. A bronze plaque commemorating this legendary Bostonian hangs quietly in a corridor in Beverly Hospital on Massachusetts' North Shore. The portrait of Eleo Sears on the plaque is based on a drawing by John Singer Sargent, but the bronze version has none of the vitality and charm of the original. The inscription is minimal and offers nothing of Eleo's bravery through the years, her obsessions, or the way she led generations of women to risk leaving the safe obscurity of the sidelines.

When the time came for Eleo to confront the ultimate dispersal of her money and properties, she assigned shares to friends, relatives, and her chauffeur. She saw to the upkeep of her family's chapel and, of course, she provided for her beloved horses. Honoring the civic-minded tradition of Boston's leading families, Eleo planned to give much of her fortune to local hospitals and open a medical center for children. My father encouraged her interest in making these gifts to future generations, as they combined tax benefits with credit from posterity. My father was Eleo Sears's business advisor, an accountant she elevated with the grand-sounding title "My Man of Business." In the spirit of the classic cowboy movies he loved, in which the hero saved the town and rode off gallantly into the sunset, Eleo's final legacy to expand medical horizons was a perfect last act for a life spent conquering social and athletic frontiers.

But from out of the shadows an unexpected opponent appeared, a cunning adversary with sinister ambitions who took Eleo down a darker road. In a heartbeat, in a shattering spiral of bitterness and suspicion, the trail was littered with broken promises and simmering resentments. Nobody would have believed the way it happened, had there not been so many witnesses. The modest bronze plaque marking Eleo's life was part of the deal the lawyers worked out eventually. This was not the way her story was supposed to end.

CHAPTER I

The Battles of Burlingame

S HE WAS GLORIOUS—tall and confident in the saddle, her face bronzed by the sun. Eleo stopped her horse at the edge of the Burlingame Polo Grounds and surveyed the chatty, handsomely dressed crowd filling the seats. Most were friends, but she knew there were some who would never take her side. They had all come to this exclusive enclave on the southern shore of San Francisco Bay to see a polo match between the Americans and the visiting British team. The afternoon of April 9, 1909, looked promising after a foggy start that had cleared during breakfast. Eleo turned her attention to the polo players congregating at the far end of the large field, and her eyes sparkled with the hint of mischief. She moved her horse smoothly into a canter and pointed him toward the group of sporting men and another quixotic foray into the primeval male kingdom.

Eleonora Randolph Sears, expert horsewoman, national tennis champion, formidable competitor in almost every other sport on land and sea, rode past the gallery along the polo field and acknowledged the scattered greetings from the audience. Her arrival anywhere was often the prelude to unpredictable and entertaining events. With her sun-streaked curls and unforgettable sapphire-blue eyes, Eleo Sears looked like a California girl, but she was only a visitor. She had come west out of "cold roast" Boston, backed by generations of good breeding and bushels of old money. From that safe harbor of wealth and position, she had chosen long ago to steer directly into roaring headwinds. Eleo's close West Coast friends called her "Searsie" and enjoyed the thought that it was they who were rescuing her from the prim conventionality of stuffy New England.

Twenty-seven-year-old Eleo Sears, born in 1881, had grown up in a time when great fortunes could buy an unburdened life of surpassing elegance. In the first blush of an exuberant new century, it remained a wonderful time to be rich. Immense wealth required no apologies, and a comforting clarity defined the roles that the men and women of the leisure class were expected to play in society's well-ordered tapestry. Men orchestrated the broad canvas. Women capably managed the details and avoided the world's glare under parasols and extravagant, flower-trimmed hats.

Polo was a man's game. This ancient "sport of kings" requires speed, precision, and aggression and has long been credited with fortifying the character of gentlemen. Playing polo is comparable to hitting a golf ball from the back of a galloping horse while being charged by a mounted foursome intent on slamming it out of reach. It was inconceivable that ladies, who rode sidesaddle in stately gowns and delicate veils, might think to participate.

The polo players at the Burlingame Club had good reason to be confounded by Eleo's arrival on the field. By the standards of the day, this memorably attractive young woman rode astride like a man, wore pants like a man, and liked to play men's games. With her deep suntan and long, belted jacket over men's-style riding breeches, Eleo Sears was not at all the vision of feminine horsemanship that most understood. Pants suggested unmentionable parts of the anatomy, and only women of the most common sort, those who worked in the world's oldest profession, were associated with such garments. The sight of a woman's legs straddling a man's saddle was startling, too, for what it suggested.

As she headed toward the home team, Eleo's path was blocked by Major Rotheran, a former cavalry officer in the English Hussars. "I would like to join you gentlemen," Eleo stated plainly to this warrior for His Majesty's Empire, and she thus provoked a confrontation that, as recounted by the *San Francisco Chronicle,* was comic on the surface. The major mumbled with distaste from under the brush of his large mustache, "How deucedly American!" To his teammate Frank Gill, the Irish polo ace, he added, "I wonder what the dickens she wears when she goes swimming." The Irishman was out of his depth in this new game, and, as he sought to commend Eleo's tailor, he stumbled, "I like the cut of your . . ." Eleo calmly appraised her perfectly cut twill riding pants and prolonged the man's discomfort before she finished his thought: "Trousers." Gill nodded stiffly and touched his cap. "Madame, I bow to you," he said before he rode off toward the middle of the field. With no warning, and probably intending no real harm, he swung his mallet and struck a backhanded blow that shot a ball breathtakingly close to Eleo and past her toward the gallery. Other riders on the field wheeled their horses and charged toward the audience in hot pursuit of the ball. The alarmed spectators fled to safety, the ladies gathering up their skirts as they ran. Above the commotion, Eleo's friend Harriet Carolan was heard to say to her husband as she watched Eleo gallop ahead of them, "That shows that even trousers have their good points. I'd give a new saddle at this instant to be wearing them instead."[1]

Not everyone was charmed by Eleo's brass, of course. Many were dismayed when she appeared at social functions in Boston and Burlingame in riding breeches, with a crop under her arm. No woman before her had ever played tennis on the courts of the tony Del Monte Country Club in men's flannel pants.[2]

In those early years of the twentieth century, there seemed to be a parade of unsettling new challenges to life's comfortable rhythms. Men by the thousands, clad in absurd-looking goggles and tentlike "dusters," had taken to driving belching motor carriages that scared the horses and threatened pedestrians. At air shows around the country, aviators gave demonstrations of flimsy-looking flying machines that rained destruction when they fell out of the sky. Rumbles of working-class discontent echoed across America's gilded landscape, and there were nagging political disturbances overseas. Although the consequences of these developments could not be foretold, they brought unease and a sense of loss. And then, along would come Eleo Sears, a fugitive from the Boston winter, blowing through this sleepy hamlet of adobe and palm trees, wearing mannish breeches and a tailored jacket, riding astride down Main Street.

During that summer of 1909, after Eleo arrived home in Boston, she organized her own polo team and enlisted women from among her most athletic society friends. Eleo studied the techniques and strategy of the best male players, and she coached her ladies to those standards. Their first crack at measuring their skills against a men's team came the following summer at the Point Judith Country Club in Narragansett, Rhode Island. An exhibition match held in the rain between Eleo's ladies and America's internationally renowned polo team, headed by the brilliant Devereux Milburn, proved to be the most entertaining sporting event of the season. The *New York Times* reported, with evident surprise, that the women acquitted themselves with distinction, despite the disadvantage that half of their team rode sidesaddle.[3]

Eleo returned to Burlingame in the spring of 1910, where the main topic of conversation was a sensational footrace between two men who had hiked from Burlingame down the Monterey Peninsula to Del Monte, a distance of 110 miles. Dr. William A. McEnery, a Britisher described as "a globe trotter and polo player," had outwalked one Percy Selby, covering the daunting route in an impressive 36½ hours. This considerable achievement was followed by much male self-congratulation about the fitness and stamina of their sex. All the chest-thumping incited Eleo to declare that a woman could also go the distance. Jennie Crocker, heiress to the Crocker railroad and banking millions, and her friend Mrs. Walter Martin promptly joined forces to bet Eleo $200 that she could not accomplish the feat in under fifty-five hours. Side bets multiplied, and in no time an additional $500 was wagered. Within the month, plans were made, the route was mapped, and on March 30 the journey was begun. It was a rollicking affair. The newspapers were abuzz with accounts of this "plucky" girl whom they dubbed the "Marathon Maid."[4]

Eleo departed from the Burlingame Hotel at 6:00 A.M. on the dot, the same time that had been chosen for the McEnery-Selby contest. Friends followed in two motor cars. The lead car, with Harriet and Francis "Frank" Carolan, was packed with refreshments and first aid supplies, including the essential flask of brandy. By 2:00 P.M., Eleo strode through the suburb of Santa Clara, and observers described her as "swinging along with the lithe grace of a thing of the wild."[5] Stewart Lowery was flattered that Eleo had let him join the adventure as her pacemaker. During the periods when Stewart hitched a ride in the Carolans' automobile, Eleo was paced by Jennie Crocker and Caro Crockett Scott, who had been granted a divorce only hours before in the courthouse in Redwood City and, henceforth, in accord with the etiquette of the time, no longer needed to be referred to as Mrs. Laurance I. Scott.

By 2:45 P.M., Eleo had reached San Jose, where at the Lamoile House she made a scheduled stop for lunch and a brief rest. She was given a rubdown, like a fighter being sent back into the ring. Jennie Crocker airily fielded questions from reporters and protected the venture with a misleading nonchalant spin, "No, she is not walking against time. . . . No, she is not trying to beat Dr. McEnery's time. I don't believe she even knows what it is." "No, she cannot be disturbed." One reporter's take on the scene is priceless: "Never was a Turkish maiden in the Sultan's seraglio guarded with more care than was she. Waiters and proprietor were as mummies as to the arrival of any such person as Miss Sears."[6]

Harriet Carolan, however, was handed the key to the inner sanctum as soon as she arrived, closely followed by Helene Irwin, heiress of a Hawaiian sugar fortune, and a half dozen other friends. All had a financial stake in this enterprise, and they were tickled to share in the excitement and gauge the prospects of their wager. There was much peeking through the curtained window at the reporters and the townspeople gathered outside. Feeling refreshed after a rest of two and a quarter hours, Eleo was off again, maintaining a pace of a bit over four miles per hour, passing through Edenvale and Coyote. Stewart Lowery was glad to be relieved of his pacing duties periodically by a succession of other men from the group, who promptly became known as "the Society Pacers."

The red evening sky faded to black as Eleo continued on through the Santa Clara Valley. Her pace slowed to three miles per hour as she paused more frequently to rest. Eleo reached Morgan Hill, fifty-three miles south of Burlingame, just before 11:00 P.M., and the outskirts of Gilroy, ten miles farther on, shortly after 2:00 A.M., and there the party stopped for the night. It was then that Stewart Lowery announced he would be unable to continue because, he said, he had urgent business back in San Francisco. There were those who thought that he pulled out of the venture because of exhaustion and sore feet, but whatever his reason, Eleo's friends prevailed on her to quit as well. Much of the remaining route was inaccessible to automobiles, and they feared for her safety if she continued on alone. Her companions also noted the physical toll taken on Eleo by the sixty-three miles she had already covered.[7] So the enterprise that had begun so brightly ended disappointingly short of the goal. And the worst part for Eleo was knowing that the failure would be seen as due to some weakness of hers, a failure that would undermine her assertion of the parity between the sexes. It was not a result she could live with.

Eleo's seasonal return to Burlingame in February 1912 was expected to include tennis and golf, parties, definitely polo, and quite possibly, knowing Eleo, some element of the unexpected. Her hosts during that year's western trip were Harriet and Frank Carolan. Harriet, who was the daughter of the railroad car magnate George Pullman, was deeply involved in the building of her new estate, Carolands, on a recently purchased 544-acre parcel of land in nearby Hillsborough. On the drawing board was a ninety-eight-room chateau, which Harriet intended to be the largest private residence ever seen west of the Mississippi. Frank Carolan took only minimal interest in his wife's project. He preferred polo and he played it well. For some years he had kept an eye on Eleo as she refined her polo skills, and he was happy to have her as a teammate. Eleo became the first woman to play competitive polo on a men's team.

Together with her longtime pal Jennie Crocker, Eleo rallied her West Coast equestrian friends to join her new polo team, which was welcomed in the 1912 Del Monte Club tournaments. Eleo's years of persistence, spiced by her snapping blue eyes, had parted the waters. The *San Diego Union-Tribune* noted that a number of athletic girls were now seen competing in "trouserettes" under knee-length skirts in imitation of Eleo, whose sporty attire was described as "advanced" by those wishing to be polite, and as "eccentric" or "freakish" by others.

In the flurry of excitement created by Eleo's visit, eight women signed up to ride with her in a genuine horse race, but on the appointed Monday morning only Lady Beatrice Herbert, wife of the 15th Earl of Pembroke, appeared on the racetrack at Coronado to face Eleo. During the weekend, the other expected contestants, counseled by their husbands and families, had rethought their participation. The large crowd that assembled to witness the spectacle would not go home disappointed. The race was on. A pistol shot rang out and Lady Beatrice, riding sidesaddle on Hawkeye, got off to a fast start and took the early lead. Eleo rode low over her horse with her stirrups high up like a professional jockey. She whispered urgently, "Come on Joe!" and with a flick of her crop Joe Ross surged ahead as they rounded the turn.

They crossed the finish line two lengths in front. Eleo continued around the track in a victory gallop, standing in her stirrups and beaming as the crowd cheered and whistled. Eleo definitely looked the part in peg-top knickers, leather leggings, and a plaid cap set backwards. She told her friends that she had "dressed to win."[8]

A mysterious phone call was received in the office of the *Burlingame Advance* on March 23, not long after the race. The caller alerted reporters to a proclamation that Eleo had just received in the mail. It read:

> Whereas, it has been brought to the attention of the Burlingame Mothers' Club that Miss Eleonora Sears has been parading through the streets of our city in the unconventional trousers and clothes of the masculine sex, contrary to the hard and fast customs of our ancestors; and whereas such a manner of dressing is in our opinion immodest and wholly unbecoming a woman, having a bad effect on the sensibilities of our boys and girls; now therefore, be it resolved that we hereby put ourselves on record as being strongly opposed to the unsightly, mannish garb worn by Miss Sears, and request that she restrict herself in the future to the normal feminine attire.

It was signed by Mrs. D. S. Harns, president of the Burlingame Mothers' Club and Mrs. Turner, secretary. This condemnation of Eleo's provocative behavior made for satisfying gossip at fashionable watering holes around California, and it disconcerted readers of Boston's newspapers. A brief search by local reporters did not turn up either Mrs. Harns or Mrs. Turner, which led to speculation that the proclamation was somebody's crude idea of a joke.[9] But a sympathetic chord had been struck, and Eleo's public immodesty became the basis of cautionary Sunday sermons from many pulpits. Eleo's celebrity grew and her friends enjoyed her even more for her notoriety. Eleo laughed with them. She had little patience for opinions contrary to her own. But still, it rankled. Her mother, she knew, would have gently agreed with the good women of Burlingame, and this thought hurt her but rarely stopped her.

Nearing the end of her seven-week sojourn in California during that spring of 1912, Eleo decided the time was right to make a second assault on the 110 miles that stood between Burlingame and Del Monte. The sting of failure from her aborted attempt two years before was still fresh, and the resentment shown by some in the Burlingame community only strengthened her resolve to take care of unfinished business. Eleo had been training for long-distance walking during the past two years, and Henry Lee, who had traveled to Burlingame with her from Boston, would make an ideal pacer and companion. Though Henry hailed from Boston, he had chosen a very different path from that of so many Harvard men of Eleo's acquaintance who had graduated to a life of relaxed gentility. Henry had not, in fact, gone to college at all. His father had been successful without attending college and advised him that it was a waste of time. Instead, Henry became a professional jockey and a horse trainer. He was a superb rider, competing in both steeplechase and flat racing, and he was a teammate of the celebrated polo player Tommy Hitchcock. Out of the saddle, Henry Lee held the record for running the half mile on an indoor track.[10] Eleo and Henry were seen so much together during this California trip that people began to wonder, with some concern, if they were "an item." Henry was dashing, certainly, but the expected alliance between Eleo and Harold Vanderbilt, the attractive son of one of the world's richest families, was a much juicier prospect and would generate much bigger headlines.

Eleo shared her plans for the monumental hike only with Henry Lee and the Carolans. At 6:00 A.M. on March 30, matching to the hour the start of her previous attempt, Eleo and Henry walked down the steps of the annex of the Burlingame Country Club and headed off on the road going south. Those few who saw them leave thought them a handsome pair. Eleo looked purposeful in a fitted jacket over a blue woolen skirt, a gray felt hat, and glowing eyes. By her side, Henry was also well turned out in his sporty belted tweed jacket and cap. With his dark looks and slicked-back hair, he was a ringer for Rudolph Valentino. Harriet Carolan provided the escort, her automobile filled with supplies, and Antelo Devereaux accompanied the group as starter and timekeeper. The morning was fair, with a brisk wind coming out of the northwest. Eleo and Henry kept the pace steady and fast, averaging four miles per hour, their arms and legs swinging in unison.

They arrived in San Jose, thiry-three miles out, by early afternoon. Reporters caught up with them, but the pair refused to be interviewed. Eleo and Henry reached Gilroy after midnight, and they stopped there for a few hours of sleep. They took off again as the sun rose. Families lined the route out of town to watch the adventurers pass by and waved them along with shouts of encouragement. Some nine miles farther on, Eleo decided to leave the main wagon road to follow a path along the railroad tracks, and she had Henry wait for her friends in the trailing auto so they would not be alarmed by her disappearance. Miles later, the Carolan auto caught up to her. The automobile stopped from time to time, and Eleo sat briefly on its wide running board. Antelo Devereaux traded his job as timekeeper to Henry Lee, and he took Henry's place as Eleo's pacer, but after a few miles a blister on his foot left him barely able to limp.

At Salinas, the ninety-one-mile mark, Eleo stopped for lunch and was met by a large contingent of friends that had converged from San Francisco, Burlingame, and San Mateo. Henry Lee told the well-wishers that Eleo was maintaining a nerve-racking pace. After a brief rest, Eleo was ready for the final push. The road wound west toward the Monterey Peninsula, past farms and groves of fruit trees guarded by low, rolling mountains, down dusty streets lined with Victorian frame houses, through dense green forests and sand-mounded dunes. As the sun set, the temperature dropped. Eleo turned her collar up and raced past twisted cypress trunks blasted a ghostly gray by the salt winds. At last she saw, with a surge of joy, a sign that read "Eight Miles to Del Monte." Eleo increased her pace, letting the pounding of her breathing and the rhythm of her arms and legs blot out the agony in her muscles. She began to sprint the final distance, counting the mile posts that she passed, not stopping to read them. Behind her the headlamps of the Carolan auto weakly illuminated the road ahead. Upon reaching the eighth post, dazed and trembling, Eleo read the sign that in the dim light seemed to bear precisely the same legend as the first, "Eight Miles to Del Monte." Eleo began to move forward, but she staggered and collapsed in the road. Her friends rushed to her. Gently, they lifted her head and revived her with brandy. It was then that Eleo learned she was within the Del Monte city limits and less than a mile from the hotel. She struggled to get up and continue, but she was persuaded by her friends that she had completed her task. She allowed herself to be helped into the auto for the short ride to the hotel. Eleo had been on the road for just over thirty-nine hours, and had proven her point.[11]

Eleo walked without assistance up the front steps of the palatial Del Monte Hotel, which was ablaze with lights at 11:00 P.M. She was physically drained but at peace with herself, at least for the moment, and she happily accepted the congratulations of the hotel guests. The house physician, Dr. Teaby, examined her and pronounced her fine, suffering only from exhaustion as a consequence of her exertions. Eleo explained what had happened during that last hour on the road, when she had misread the final marker: "I saw then I could not finish. I had traveled to cover just eight miles and had used up all my strength. And, besides, that signpost just seemed to take all the heart out of me. I just couldn't go a step farther at the time."[12]

CHAPTER 2

Back Bay Beginnings

~

"Y OU KNOW, IT'S FUNNY," said a younger friend of Eleo's while reminiscing about this extraordinary, precedent-setting sportswoman, "I never thought of her as having had parents."[1] Eleo Sears was a mercurial combination of both her parents, and she would come to resemble her father in ways she would not have thought possible.

As a young man, Eleo's father, Frederick Richard Sears, showed strong athletic tendencies. He rode horses and played baseball, cricket, and squash. Together with his cousin James Dwight, Frederick claimed the distinction of having played the very first game of lawn tennis in America. He dabbled in painting and had memberships in the best gentlemen's clubs in Boston. He was a man of impeccable beginnings.

The Sears family traced itself back to England in 1215, when King John put his seal on the Magna Carta and laid the foundation for constitutional government. The first Sears recorded in America was Richard Sares, using the original spelling, who arrived in Cape Cod in the 1630s. Later generations remembered him fondly as "Richard the Pilgrim."[2]

The Sears men prospered in real estate investment and trade with East India and China. By the mid-1700s, Eleo's great-great-grandfather, the first David Sears, was said to be the richest man in New England. With his marriage to Ann Winthrop, the Sears line doubled back to the Puritan founders of Massachusetts and to the first governor of the Massachusetts Bay Colony, John Winthrop. Early Puritan settlers held stern, uncompromising views of virtue, which in money matters meant living simply and spending carefully. These prescriptions retained a powerful, even bizarre hold on the generations that followed. Though it could never be said of well-to-do New Englanders that they hid their financial lights under a bushel, their display of wealth was tempered by a pervasive asceticism and a spirit of noblesse oblige. They distrusted big government–run charities and channeled their unsentimental efforts to improve the lives of the less fortunate through private organizations. The Boston establishment produced more than its share of prominent civic leaders and institutions, and no institution was more beloved than its local college, Harvard, which was an incubator for the city's intellectual and social elite. So many generations of the same families attended the school that they referred to it, proprietarily, as "the Family Seminary."

With the death of David Sears, his son David Sears II, Eleo's great-grandfather, inherited the largest fortune ever bequeathed in New England until that time. David II built an imposing gray granite mansion at 42 Beacon Street, then at the western edge of the city, and he moved his family there in 1821. Ten years later, after David II expanded his house at both ends to accommodate two of his daughters and their husbands, Bostonians knew it to be the costliest residence in the city. This property, which ultimately extended from 41 to 43 Beacon Street, overlooked the center of Boston Common and commanded, in effect, the fifty-yard line of what would become the most prestigious location in the city. Great-grandfather David showed extraordinary foresight when he chose the ground across from the Common barely two years after crowds viewed the last public hanging there. The fifty-acre Common had also been a staging area for British troops during the Revolutionary War and was still being used to graze cattle when David II began building his home. He furnished his Beacon Street mansion in the French Empire style favored by Napoleon. This was a departure from the standard New England preference, which placed a premium on English traditions. David Sears's admiration for the French emperor inspired his wife to name their six-hundred-acre estate a few miles outside Boston "Longwood," after the house on the island of St. Helena where Napoleon died. In proper Puritan tradition, David II used his wealth to leave a positive mark on his community. During the Civil War he gave generously to the Union Army and the soldiers of Massachusetts. He funded churches, libraries, and buildings on the campuses of Harvard and Amherst. The David Sears Charity, then the largest charitable trust of its type, was charged with providing support for "citizens or families who may have seen better days."[3]

David II's son, Frederick Richard Sears, was Eleo's grandfather. He married Marian Shaw, whose nephew Colonel Robert Gould Shaw is remembered for leading the all-black 54th Regiment during the Civil War.[4] Frederick and Marian had a daughter and a son, Frederick Richard Jr., Eleo's father. Unfortunately, Marian died shortly after the birth of her son. Frederick Sr. remarried two years later and sired five more children. Despite this apparent vigor, which lasted for eighty-four years, Frederick Sr. was said to have been in delicate health, and he never engaged in any profession. In this his eldest son followed his example. Eleo's father was one among fifty of the members of Boston's famously exclusive Somerset Club who listed his occupation as "Gentleman."

Frederick Jr. was a fine-looking man of set habits and formal manner. He made deep bows to the ladies, especially to very young ladies. At Harvard he played team sports and grew an impressive mustache, which added distinction to his long, straight-sided face. Following his graduation, he spent three years traveling the world. In June 1879, shortly after his return to Boston, Frederick married Eleonora Randolph Coolidge, a bright, sweet-natured twenty-two-year-old who was pleasant looking rather than pretty. Eleo's mother was known to family and friends as Nora. The wedding of Nora Coolidge and Frederick Sears at Trinity Church was witnessed by Boston's many distinguished First Families. It joined together two of the city's oldest families and biggest fortunes, and it was hailed as a most suitable match. Nora's father, the renowned Thomas Jefferson Coolidge, was satisfied, and Nora wanted very much to please her father. It is not known if she ever loved Frederick, or at what point she realized she had made a disastrous marriage.

The newlyweds took their place in the small, insular world of Boston society and moved into a town house at 122 Beacon Street, several blocks west of the Common. Twenty years earlier that section of Beacon Street would have been shunned as too close to the Back Bay, then a fetid area of mudflats and sewage that had been reclaimed from the Charles River. The residential area of early Boston was compact, and the narrow cobblestone streets were settled by generations of the same extended families, parents, grandparents, uncles and aunts, and cousins to the fourth degree. Tremont Street, then called Colonnade Row, was home to the Lawrences and the Masons. The Warrens lived on Mt. Vernon Street. The Amorys could be found on Franklin, the Gardners on Summer. The Curtises and the Lorings were on Somerset Street. And the Searses were on Beacon Street.

The ample, flat-faced house that Nora and Frederick occupied was set along a line of neat, narrow town houses that presented sturdy faces of gray stone and muted brick against the New England winter. Bow windows and tiny manicured yards fronted most of the houses and made a courteous gesture to the street. Whatever problems existed within those restrained exteriors, whatever the excesses, the illnesses, the heartaches, they remained enclosed amid rooms of dark carved wood and densely patterned walls hung with landscapes of Venice and gloomy ancestral portraits. From the street nothing was visible, but in that clannish world of First Families everything, eventually, was known. The families gathered together regularly for suppers, cards, and conversation. They celebrated holidays together. They vacationed together. They married each other. At family gatherings it was noticed, after a time, that Frederick paid special attention to the little girls. He would stoop down to kiss them, brushing their cheeks with his mustache, or lift them up in a great bear hug and reach under their petticoats to pinch their bottoms. This oddity was never spoken of, but Nora knew what they all thought. Frederick's cousin Dorothy Winthrop Bradford summed him up as being "the queerest man who ever lived."[5]

Frederick's life settled into strict daily routines that he interrupted for others' needs only rarely, when it suited him. He could be seen early every morning, tall and angular in a bowler hat, hiking through Beacon Hill and the Back Bay for his five-mile constitutional, his body inclined as if fighting an unseen wind. Bostonians have always been great walkers, their Puritan forebears whispering the need for a strong body and a disciplined mind. First Families did not allow money to make them soft or lazy. Regular exercise, preferably under harsh conditions, built character. For many years a group of businessmen, all in their eighties, walked from their homes to their offices through every season, a round trip of more than four miles. It was understood that wearing too heavy an overcoat would be bad form, a sign of weakness.[6] Frederick added an inexplicable twist to his usually solitary walks by always wearing rubber galoshes and often carrying an umbrella.

Frederick was well contented in his own world and could seem willfully unfamiliar with the world around him. He never managed to master the art of shaving, which he persisted in doing through his sixties without hot, soapy water to ease the path of the blade. His days were principally devoted to riding through the Fenway and playing racquet sports. After he became a father, Frederick sporadically turned his attention to family matters, and his two children might feel his firm hand on their bottoms for any misbehavior. Nora found corporal punishment distressing and she was relieved that Frederick took no sustained interest in the household.

The Sears home ran smoothly with Nora in charge of the traditionally female provinces of dealing with servants, planning meals, and organizing social engagements. Nora had great inner resources and rarely felt lonely. She was an ardent reader and she had close friends who shared her intellectual interests. The women of Boston's leading families, like their men, tended to favor activities that promised self-improvement. Nora and her friends took drawing classes to focus their powers of observation. They earnestly attended lectures about science and art. Harvard's distinguished Professor Louis Agassiz was a popular speaker who brought his European sophistication to discussions of the natural world. Boston women were stimulated by the professor's challenge to Darwin's theory of evolution, and by accounts of his expeditions to study glaciers, coral reefs, and the jungles of Brazil. When the sun shone, the young women explored nature with hikes and picnics. For pure fun, they piled into Cleopatra's Barge, a boat-shaped, horse-drawn wagon that was fitted with wheels in summer and runners in winter. Nora and other married matrons, all still in their twenties, were teased that they were invited along to chaperone the rides.

The world in those years moved at a more civilized pace. Businessmen often left their offices in the late afternoon and walked home through the Common to have a leisurely dinner with their families. Dinner was a formal affair that brought out the good china and the polished silver. Husbands, seated at the head of the table, carved the roast. After dinner they might return to their offices or head to their clubs to smoke cigars (cigarettes didn't yet exist) and read the evening papers. Frederick was a fixture at the Somerset Club, by this time headquartered in the granite mansion that his grandfather had built on Beacon Street. The club purchased the building from David II's estate in 1872. Of all the exclusionary clubs in Boston, the Somerset was the most notable for being a "sanctuary of the powerful and well-born."[7] Admission to this lucky sperm club was gained by pedigree, not by wealth alone. It was founded and strictly maintained as a social club and any mention of business within its walls would bring a waiter bearing a silver tray with a small card requesting the offender to refrain.[8] Settled comfortably around the fireplace, seamlessly juggling glasses of port, newspapers, and cigars, the members issued pronouncements in resonant voices about the prolific breeding habits of the foreign races and the dismal state of the world in general. Frederick dined often at the club and was an avid player of whist, the precursor of bridge, as was his grandfather before him. Frederick's companionship was sought out only reluctantly because he guarded his money as closely as he guarded his thoughts. When the opportunity came to pay for a meal or a round of drinks, it was said of Frederick that "he developed an impediment of reach."[9]

Nora Sears had been brought up in a time and place that valued duty and propriety above all else. Boston folk did not whine, nor did they contemplate divorce, which was rare and scandalous. One made do. Before her wedding, Nora had consulted the Bible, 1 Corinthians 7, "Directions Concerning Marriage." There she read the explanation of the conjugal rights shared by a husband and a wife, and there was the commandment to live together until parted by death. Nora had learned stoicism from her father. Thomas Jefferson Coolidge was a very principled and private man who lived a very public life. His parents were married in the drawing room at Monticello, the Virginia home built by his great-grandfather Thomas Jefferson.[10]

Young T. J. Coolidge saw early that money offered the smoothest avenue to social success, and after graduating from Harvard he set out, as he readily admitted, to "devote myself to the acquisition of wealth." He began as a clerk for the shipping company founded by Colonel Thomas H. Perkins, who had declined George Washington's invitation to become secretary of the navy for the new nation, noting that he already owned a fleet of ships larger than the navy. The up-and-coming T. J. Coolidge married Mehitable "Hetty" Appleton, whose enormously successful father, William Appleton, owned the Merrimack Valley Textile Mill. T.J. thrived in the textile business, and then in the banking business. He moved next to railroads, becoming president and director of the Chicago, Burlington and Quincy line. In partnership with Henry Clay Frick, T. J. Coolidge became the president and director of the Atchison, Topeka and Santa Fe Railroad. T.J. steadfastly refused to take advantage of his insider position at the company to act on information not known to all the shareholders. He resigned his presidency after a year and a half, having found the work to be "fatiguing" and, because of his excess of honesty, less profitable than he had expected.

T.J. shared the commitment to civic improvement that motivated many of his peers. As Boston's park commissioner, he worked with the landscape architect Frederick Law Olmsted to lay out roads and public greenways around the city. T.J. gave huge sums to build a physics laboratory at Harvard and a public library for the town of Manchester, but with typical New England reticence, he would not allow his name to be placed over either door. He devoted equal attention to self-improvement and kept a daily journal of his progress. Following the example of Benjamin Franklin, T.J. began a vegetarian diet, but he noted that he took it up not "as Franklin did as a duty, but to see if it would improve my mind and my temper." T.J. found the effort less helpful than he had hoped and he abandoned the diet after six months, though he continued to fret that he might have given up too soon. Also following Franklin's lead, T.J. kept a daily list of sins he had committed, which included "Pride, Want of Chastity, Temper, Meanness in Money Matters, Cowardice and Envy." T.J. was disappointed too in the results of this effort and he concluded, "as with my vegetarianism, . . . it did me less good than I expected."[11]

Though T.J. wrestled with his flaws, he had a clear-eyed appreciation of his strengths, and he shared the elitist views of his class. Thomas Jefferson had recognized the existence of a "natural aristocracy," comprising people of learning and refinement who earned their leadership authority through their accomplishments, not through their wealth alone. T. J. Coolidge was no fan of the direction being taken by modern democracy. He believed "the principle that the ignorant and poor should have the same right to make laws and govern as the educated and refined was an absurdity."[12] T.J.'s expectations of his associates and his family were equally demanding. His brother-in-law William Appleton Jr. observed, "I never knew him to do an unkind thing and never heard him say a kind word."[13] The quip is too neat to be entirely credible, but it suggests an atmosphere that offered Nora little emotional support during difficult times.

T.J.'s relationship with his wife, Hetty, was cordial but distant. He took the

"deepest interest" in the education of his children, however, and he determined that for his two youngest girls, Nora and Sallie, the public high school
in Boston would be more beneficial than a private girls' finishing school. He
ignored the advice of friends who "prophesied much harm would come" from
a public school education. On a family vacation in the White Mountains of
New Hampshire, T.J. spent "every minute of every hour . . . driving into their
little heads Latin grammar," and he was gratified when both girls easily
passed the two-day final exam.[14] Nora and Sallie remained in the public
school for three years, and T.J. was satisfied that they had acquired an excellent education and great self-reliance. It was the peculiar mixture of certainty,
self-righteousness, propriety, and self-denial exemplified by T. J. Coolidge
that Hetty's cousin Tom Appleton had in mind when he coined the phrase
"cold-roast Boston."[15]

On March 30, 1880, nine months after she was married, Nora gave birth
to her first child. To everyone's great delight it was a son, who was given his
father's name, Frederick Richard III. His godparents were Nora's father, T.J.,
and her sister, Sallie. Nora was a doting, attentive mother who lavished on her
baby all the affection she would have wished for herself. She carefully noted
the details of his small life, his weight, how he nursed, his first tooth, in a tiny,
green, leather-bound book, one of a set of three. That was when Nora first
began her journals, where she compulsively recorded the daily minutiae of
her life, the surfaces. Her most intimate thoughts would never be found on
those cramped pages.

CHAPTER 3

A Boston State of Mind

A<small>N OLD TOAST WAS</small> revised in 1910 to offer a gently mocking send-up of the rarefied, inbred world of Boston society that had taken root more than two hundred years earlier and was still flourishing well into the twentieth century:

> And this is good old Boston
> The home of the bean and the cod,
> Where the Lowells talk to the Cabots,
> And the Cabots talk only to God.[1]

Though the Cabots may have ranked first among the First Families, Boston's other Brahmin families had no doubt of their own honored place in the social firmament. In class-conscious Boston, where the aura of an old family name opened all doors, it was disingenuous of Massachusetts' august Senator Cabot Lodge to explain modestly when asked about his ancestors, "We do not talk about Family in this country. It is enough for you to know that your grandfather is an honest man."[2] Senator Lodge's family had coupled with the esteemed Cabots through the years and traced itself back to Chaucer.

Members of the "right" families were able to bypass many of life's inconveniences. Boston's merchants allowed First Families to run up tabs for years without pushing for collection. Trains waited for them. Judge John Lowell never missed the 8:25 A.M. commuter train, even when he arrived late to the station. The engineer held up the train, over the objections of other riders, until the judge was safely on board.[3] The women of Boston's First Families also expected and were generally given preferential treatment. Whatever complaints they might have about poor service went directly to the top and were likely to command immediate attention. Kate Winthrop was renowned for her sense of entitlement and for snobbery that was democratic in its disdain for both the ostentatiously vulgar rich and the slovenly vulgar poor. This story is told of her phone call to the Sanitation Department to complain about a discourteous garbage collector. "I am Mrs. Robert Winthrop," she announced, "and my garbage man is not a gentleman." "I'm sorry, Mrs. Winthrop," the official replied, "but it's very hard to get a gentleman to pick up your garbage."[4]

The early founding families were justified initially in their sense of entitlement. With awesome fortitude they tamed the hostile wilderness of the New World and built livable towns rich with civic and cultural amenities—hospitals, libraries, museums, symphony orchestras, historical societies, colleges— that flourished because of their sustained support. The founders developed thriving businesses, but they stressed the constraints of duty over the appetites of privilege. They managed the neat trick of living high on a low scale, toning down much of the excess found in the social capitals of New York and Newport. The working classes of Boston saw merit in the values espoused by the First Families and were too busy trying to emulate upper-class manners and fashion to resent them. Subsequent generations of those preeminent Boston families, however, caught themselves in a honeyed trap. Wanting to maintain their standards and their prerogatives, they walled themselves in behind a rigid barrier of social rules and narrow ideas. In this most judgmental of towns, the smallest distinctions determined who qualified as one of "us" and who was one of "them." Mere yards divided areas of exclusive Beacon Hill into "right" and "wrong" sides. Beacon Street and nearby Commonwealth Avenue were acknowledged to have a "swell" side, the water side, marginally nearer the Charles River. It was unlikely that anybody worth knowing would be found on the opposite side of the street.

Eleo Sears was born at home, on the water side of Beacon Street on September 28, 1881. Nora was very glad to have a daughter, and she shared her first name, Eleonora, with her baby. Eleo's middle name, Randolph, also came from Nora's side of the family. Nora had already produced a son to carry on the Sears family name, and Nora thought of this baby girl, who made her appearance three weeks after her 25th birthday, as a belated and perfect gift. Nora would teach her daughter how to behave and how to dress, and she would watch proudly as her little girl took her expected place in society. Nora approached motherhood with the steady, reasoned judgment she had learned from her father, and she adhered to the best advice available to manage her baby's development. Living in this eminently sensible community, Nora could expect that, if she followed the established rules, she could engineer the desired outcome. The small green baby book reveals the care Nora took when she weighed Eleo for the first time. Nora had estimated Freddy's net weight at birth after weighing him in his substantial Victorian infant gown. For her little girl, Nora wanted more precision, and she felt less constrained by the modesty required with a son. She weighed Eleo wrapped only in a flannel blanket, the weight of which she then subtracted. Nora concluded that this was the "fairest way of weighing." It is Nora's measure most of all that is to be found in this small detail.

Soon there was a test of wills between mother and daughter that hinted at what would come. In early July Eleo, then nine months old, pulled herself to a standing position, and Nora noted that this was "not allowed." Nora wrote on September 4 that she "cannot possibly keep [the baby] from walking beside furniture. She tries to walk alone and stand alone." On September 21, a week before Eleo's first birthday, Nora dashed off a brief note of surrender—"walks alone."5 Later Eleo would joke that she first began exercising when she fell out of her crib.

Eleo's brother, Freddy, despite his unruly shock of hair and a loopy "What, me worry?" grin, was growing up to be a tranquil and rather studious fellow. Eleo was an altogether different child. One of her proudest early achievements, which she displayed eagerly to her mother's unsuspecting visitors, was to walk down the staircase on her hands. In her journals, Nora would sometimes use a shorthand "E" to identify her daughter, but she could never bring herself to write the nickname "Eleo," which seemed as insubstantial as air. To Nora, her daughter was always "Eleonora," as if the gravity of such a proper name might call forth proper behavior.

Eleo, like her mother before her, grew up in a fond universe of extended family that watched over her and marked the boundaries of what was permissible with disapproving tut-tuts. She was schooled in the basics, Latin and French, literature and art, needlework, music, dancing, and deportment. Upper-class Boston girls were expected to make intelligent conversation and were encouraged to be well read. It was assumed that girls lacked physical stamina, but mild exercise like rhythmic movement, archery, croquet, and horsemanship was believed to be safe if pursued with care and restraint.

At children's parties given in homes around Beacon Hill, good manners were served with the tea and sweet punch, and sometimes welcome entertainments were included, such as jugglers and charades. Eleo was sent off to these parties wearing the requisite white gloves and ruffled party dresses that were lofted by four petticoats. Her wavy blonde hair hung below her shoulders and was controlled by satin bows that matched her dress. Nora learned quickly that Eleo would not be the child who sat primly on her hands. When Eleo returned home, breathless with the highlights of her afternoon, Nora could summon only mild exasperation with the disheveled state of her daughter's carefully chosen wardrobe. Young Eleo was not always a pretty child. In early photos her cheeks appear too full and her mouth a bit pouty, in apparent discomfort at having to remain quiet and still under the photographer's critical stare.

Eleo was happiest when she could escape from her lessons and social obligations and burst outdoors. She loved chasing friends around the Common, which in those days seemed like a private preserve for the families whose homes bordered it. Eleo's playmates were mostly cousins related in varying degrees in the convoluted way of Boston and included Amorys, Thayers, Winthrops, various Sears girls (Emily, Phyllis, and Evelyn), and several Gardner offspring. Eleo liked being a leader of this band of well-tailored urchins, laughing and yelling and always approaching any game with a plan to win. She had a knack for cajoling other children to join her in adventures, and she rounded up a group of girls to play football. "It took three of us," she recalled gleefully, "to tackle Alice Sargent." Whatever the dare or the bet, the youngsters knew that they could count on Eleo to try it. A favorite and risky game called "punging" sent children leaping onto the sides of tradesmen's wagons. If the driver was agreeable, five or six children could hang on for a ride. The real challenge and danger came when a passing tradesman urged his horses faster to thwart the hitchhikers. Eleo dragged Freddy along on many of her escapades. She had fond memories of the time they climbed onto the roof of their Beacon Street house and scampered across the line of rooftops, dropping into people's bedrooms through the skylights and leaving a trail of traumatized neighbors. Nora found raising her daughter to be a continual challenge, and every Sunday she took Eleo, hopefully, by the hand to church.

Youth can find pleasures even in foul weather. The winter of 1888 was memorable for the fierce March snowstorm, the worst in more than thirty-five years, that brought Boston to a standstill. Businesses remained shuttered until squads of Irishmen could dig them out and spread coal cinders over the ice-crusted sidewalks. The railroads were blocked. The telegraph between New York and Boston was knocked out, and communications had to be routed via London. Proper Boston girls abandoned their usual practice of keeping their hands still and warm in a fur muff and, away from watchful adult eyes, wiggled through secretly dug snow tunnels and tobogganed down the streets of Beacon Hill. The Charles River froze solid and six-year-old Eleo and her friends could skate on it without fear of falling through weak patches. Horse-drawn sleighs with their music of harness bells and hoofbeats muffled by the snow gave rides down the transformed expanse of Commonwealth Avenue.

Summertime sent Boston's brood away from the insistent clatter of the city streets to the fresher air and increased freedom of the country. In earlier times, the coastal areas north of Boston offered a refuge from the stench of the city's swampy Back Bay area. Steamboats and then the railroad opened up the coastline, and Boston's First Families headed beyond the shabby boardinghouses and bathing shanties that had sprung up along Revere Beach. They snapped up barren, unproductive stretches of land from the incredulous local residents. Along the treeless coves, seaside mansions sprouted up, their broad verandas overlooking private sections of beach. The chosen hamlets took on the status of the families who settled there. The area became popularly known as the Gold Coast, Boston's Riviera, and encompassed the mellifluously named villages of Beverly Farms and neighboring Prides Crossing, Manchester-by-the-Sea, and Magnolia. It was understood that "only the riffraff" would consider going beyond Magnolia.

David Sears II was among the first to build a summer residence up the coast on Nahant, a ragged, crescent-shaped promontory that, but for the slender, two-mile thread of rocky beach that attached it to the mainland, would have been an island. The coves and inlets of Nahant became a fashionable retreat for Boston's best families. These shrewd Yankee traders soon discovered it could be a tax haven as well. By declaring their country homes to be their principal residences, they could legally sidestep the city's higher tax on personal property.

The frugal Bostonians who summered along the Gold Coast were happiest when their vacations included some inconvenience. Stoically, they battled the battalions of blood-thirsty mosquitoes that raided the North Shore, and they delayed installing modern conveniences in their oceanfront estates, such as electric lights and telephones, because they thought their money could be put to better use. Nothing gave First Families more satisfaction than robust exertion in the great outdoors. Senator Henry Cabot Lodge, a Nahant resident, rated his skills as a sailor and a swimmer among the most satisfying accomplishments of his life. A plunge in the cold, choppy ocean along Massachusetts' rocky coast tested the most determined heart. The scratchy, full-body bathing costumes at the turn of the century were made of wool that stayed waterlogged and seemed designed to discourage swimming. For women there was the question whether it was healthful for them to enter the ocean at all. Those who were determined to risk outdoor bathing were advised to wade in gradually and close off their nose with their thumb and forefinger before attempting total submersion. Nora resolved the swimming controversy for her babies when Eleo was three and a half years old, and she recorded the milestone in the baby book: "Freddy and Eleonora bathed in ocean for the first time—July 18, 1885."

Occasionally, on the North Shore and on visits to Maine to see outlying friends such as the Lawrences and the Cabots, one encountered girls from New York and Philadelphia who walked along the roads swinging their arms. This tasteless display confirmed the view of Boston matrons that standards outside their town were disgracefully lax. New York had long been the focus of particular scorn as a hotbed of nouveau pretension and extravagance where people entertained too lavishly and drank too much. New York society, in turn, scoffed that Boston women were priggish and dressed badly. New York socialites accorded the Boston ladies grudging respect, however, because their families had been significant for centuries. For young Eleo, on whom the finer points of this regional friction were lost at the time, the casual freedoms enjoyed by girls from other parts of the Eastern Seaboard were seductively attractive.

The pleasure of riding horses on trails through Boston's Fenway area, which snaked along the city's western edge, paled in comparison to galloping across the fields of the North Shore. Horseback riding was an expected skill for upper-class girls and boys. Joan of Arc may have gone into battle astride her horse centuries earlier, but ladies ever since had ridden sidesaddle. The modern sidesaddle, with its pommel to anchor a woman's right leg, was an advance from earlier centuries, when women just sat sideways on a horse while someone else led it. A woman riding sidesaddle could control her own horse and even jump fences, but the position remained unbalanced and dangerous. One Boston mother, whose daughters were learning to ride sidesaddle, was so concerned that they might become "one-sided" that she had two different saddles made for their ponies. The girls alternated, riding one day on the right side of the horse and the next day on the left.[6] If her solution spooked the horses, it was not recorded.

Eleo credited one of her fondest memories to her father. She was just a toddler when Frederick took her to the stable and lifted her high up onto the saddle on his horse. Eleo held the horse's mane as it walked along, while her father stayed beside her holding the reins. Eleo never had the slightest fear, even this first time, as some children would, of an animal so large and so self-contained. Viewing the familiar scenery from the height of her father's horse, she felt the ancient thrill of exploring unmapped worlds. With gratitude and a sense of wonder, Eleo saw that a being of such great size and power submitted gently to a knowing and caring touch. She knew, too, that riding sidesaddle did not suit her at all.

It was with animals that Eleo was most comfortable in revealing her tender side. Horses and the family's dogs offered judgment-free affection that she returned in full measure. The dogs happily chased sticks thrown into the ocean, and on winter evenings they slept by the fire. The bigger dogs were sometimes hitched to two-wheeled carts to give Eleo and Freddy a ride down the lane. The fastest and flashiest horses followed the hounds on fox hunts and competed in horse shows, but there was always a reserve of older, patient horses that didn't mind pulling a fringe-topped surrey or a buckboard holding as many as twelve youngsters on a bouncy ride to a favorite picnic spot. The children knew to jump out and walk uphill to save the horses.

Horses powered all aspects of society, and their lives mirrored the world of their masters. Those horses belonging to the leisure class were clipped and brushed and worried over, but most were anonymous creatures that had to work hard for their rations. They hauled wagons carrying ice and produce and furniture. Teams of horses pulled huge commuter-packed omnibuses called hourlies, which made regular stops around Boston and across the river in Cambridge. In winter, straining to pull overloaded wagons, horses slipped and fell in the snow. A nightmarish scene that haunted Eleo and her young friends was all too common on the city streets. A small horse was hitched to a cart loaded with wood that had gotten struck in a rut in the road. The angry driver shouted oaths while furiously whipping the miserable fellow. A crowd of men, attracted by the noise, watched and did nothing as the little horse struggled beyond its strength to free the load.[7] It was a hellish sight that brought stinging tears of anger and helplessness to its small witnesses. Eleo was moved to spend a lifetime trying to make amends.

CHAPTER 4

Diplomacy and Fashion: Paris, 1892–1893

⟋

Lᴇᴏ's ɢʀᴀɴᴅғᴀᴛʜᴇʀ, Thomas Jefferson Coolidge, was surprised to read in the *Boston Transcript* early in 1892 that he had been nominated to be the next minister to France. The post was being vacated by Whitelaw Reid, editor of the *New York Tribune,* who was joining the reelection campaign of President Benjamin Harrison as the vice-presidential candidate. T. J. Coolidge had gained many admirers in Washington through his work to improve relations between the United States and its South American neighbors during the Pan-American Congress of 1889. Massachusetts Senators Cabot Lodge and Charles Hoar assumed correctly when they nominated T.J. for the key post in France that he would be unlikely to turn down such a prestigious position in such a desirable location.

The senators had indeed made a felicitous choice. Beyond the personal financial resources that the post would require, T.J.'s analytical temperament and wide-ranging business and civic experience left him superbly suited to represent his country in diplomatic circles. Enticed by possibilities both scholarly and romantic, T.J. always enjoyed the adventure of foreign travel. His Puritan side valued the intellectual stimulation that came from observing unfamiliar lifestyles. On a more primal level, he responded to the beauty of exotic landscapes, art, and women. T.J. had traveled by himself and later with his family throughout Europe, Egypt, and the Far East. He usually traveled in comfort in private railroad cars and first-class cabins, but he found even the inevitable difficulties of travel to be instructive and bracing, like a cold shower. In 1879 T.J. had combined business with pleasure on a journey that took him from one end of the United States to the other. He later recalled that 9,000-mile trip as an entirely positive experience, one with "not the least mishap or inconvenience."[1] This mellow assessment could be credited to his agreeable traveling companion, his then sixteen-year-old son, "Jeffie," Thomas Jefferson Coolidge Jr. Jeffie was endowed with a sunny disposition, and he shared his father's patrician good looks and his sense of fair play. Nora and her mother and two sisters loved to fuss over their handsome younger brother, and this was a big reason T.J. had been eager to take him off across the wide, rugged continent.

T.J. was quickly confirmed by the Senate as the new minister for France, and toward the end of May 1892 he and his wife sailed on the steamer *La Touraine*. On board with them were Nora and Frederick and their children, twelve-year-old Freddy and Eleo, age ten. The ship docked at the port of Le Havre during the first week of June, and the Coolidge and Sears families arrived in Paris in time to see the city bursting with spring. The sweet, pungent scent of lilacs was in the air, and stylishly dressed crowds strolled under the blooms of the chestnut trees lining the Champs Elysées. Regrettably, Mrs. Coolidge had become ill during the long voyage, and she was confined to the family's temporary lodgings in the Hotel Westminster on the Rue de la Paix, unable to fully enjoy the city. T.J. did not dwell on the loss of his wife's companionship. He enlisted Nora to accompany him to the many official and social functions that came with his new position.

Their first priority was to find living accommodations suitable for the new minister and his extended family. Nora and her father selected the sumptuous Montefiore House on the corner of Avenue Marceau and Rue de Bassano, which was convenient to T.J.'s post at the American Legation. T.J.'s bid of $15,000 (about $357,000 in today's currency), out of his own pocket, to rent the house for a year was promptly accepted, and within days the two families were installed in their new quarters.[2] As Eleo and Freddy wandered down the parqueted corridors of the Louis XV–era palace, they grew giddy with the realization of their good fortune. The paneled walls of the formal grand salon were gracefully carved and gilded and sparkled with mirrors and shimmering silk that billowed around the floor-to-ceiling windows. The library was two stories high and decorated with long Japanese scrolls depicting mystical landscapes. In the vast dining room twenty-four guests could be seated in comfort. The table was surrounded by classical scenes woven into acres of tapestries by French and Italian masters. The neat rows of gray stone town houses in Boston had not prepared the children for grandeur on this scale.

Ruling the awesome Montefiore House with shrewd and jealous majesty were its butler and head cook. They had reigned before the coming of the Coolidge-Sears clan and would continue to do so after they left. According to custom, the butler and the head cook were responsible for hiring the staff and for purchasing everything that would be needed to look after this distinguished household of six Americans. These two master servants lost no time in enlarging their domain and spreading the good fortune of their position among their countrymen. They engaged twelve more staff members, eleven men and a woman who was to serve as Mrs. Coolidge's personal maid. The butler and the head cook also controlled the account books. They compiled and submitted weekly purchase reports to T.J. for his approval and payment. Invariably, the accounts were submitted late and were shamelessly padded. With uncharacteristic forbearance, T.J. chose to consider this thievery as part of the price to be paid for such elegance and comfort. Perhaps there was magic in the Parisian air, because he would never have taken so expansive a view of larceny with his serving staff in Boston.

Within days of the move into Montefiore House, its population was delightfully expanded with the arrival of Nora's brother, Jeffie, and his new wife, the former Clara Gardner Amory, who was a not-too-distant cousin. The young couple had been married for less than a year, and they jumped at the opportunity to extend their honeymoon in their parents' splendid home, which bustled with servants and his sister's mischievous children. While Nora attended to official duties, Frederick joined the young couple on their excursions around the city and its environs, and they shared his box at the Grand Prix races.

T. J. Coolidge was a picture-perfect statesman, impeccably dressed in a silk top hat and kid gloves when he presented his diplomatic credentials to the president of France in a formal ceremony. After their own violent revolution, the French had continued their turbulent approach to government, and President Marie-François-Sadi Carnot was the fourth president of the Third French Republic. Carnot was captivated by the idea of American cowboys galloping across a vast, untamed landscape, and he had had the opportunity to live his fantasy when Buffalo Bill's Wild West Show came to Paris in 1889 while touring the Continent. Happy as a child, President Carnot had ridden in the famous Deadwood stagecoach as it escaped from a mock Indian attack. (This battered stagecoach had survived many authentic attacks by Indians and outlaws as it carried mail between Cheyenne and Deadwood, the most dangerous route in the West.) When T.J. presented his credentials to President Carnot, the French leader gracefully acknowledged the coincidence, of which T.J. himself was highly conscious, that his great-grandfather Thomas Jefferson had held the very same post of American minister to France one hundred years earlier.

President Carnot's government was far from secure, and Paris was serene only on the surface. The Third Republic had barely survived an effort by a promonarchist faction to topple it. In the year preceding T.J.'s arrival, the French government had faced a massive public demonstration by laborers demanding better working conditions. The demonstration had turned violent, and several people were killed. President Carnot's government was being rocked yet again, this time by scandal. Government officials had taken bribes from the now bankrupt company that had tried to build the Panama Canal. The scandal strengthened the growing socialist movement in the country and made T.J.'s job of representing his rough-and-tumble capitalistic young nation more challenging.

A seemingly petty problem of diplomatic protocol hampered and frustrated T.J. even more. The French diplomatic establishment, like that in other Old World states, clung to rigid, centuries' old etiquette that was immune to changing world realities. Diplomatic rank, with its attendant favors, courtesies, and proximity to power, depended on the title of the representative and the length of time he had been stationed in the host country. In the United States, foreign diplomacy was viewed as a temporary occupation, not as a career, and the players changed frequently. Each presidential election, especially when it put a new occupant in the White House, brought in a new cast. This practice ensured that American diplomats would always be the most recent arrivals. Protocol negotiated by the European powers during the Congress of Vienna in 1814 decreed that ambassadors outranked ministers. Thus, Minister Coolidge was, by every measure that mattered in Europe, the most junior statesman, and he was compelled to be at the tail end of all formal occasions. At state dinners T.J. was seated far from those most influential to America's interests. He complained bitterly in letters home to Senator Hoar that this intolerable circumstance forced "the minister of perhaps the greatest power on earth to sit below envoys of little Spanish republics or insignificant States." At T.J.'s urging, Senator Hoar proposed and Congress swiftly passed a bill that authorized the president to appoint ambassadors rather than ministers to head all future foreign legations. T.J. further recommended that the American government end its practice of staffing its overseas missions with people who were there primarily because of political rewards and payoffs. He argued that this left the United States at a perpetual disadvantage to countries like France, Germany, and England, whose diplomats were products of years of training and experience.

In the universe of diplomacy, work and play mingled almost indistinguishably. Discussions about trade and tariffs by day blended into opulent dinner and theater parties by night. T.J. attended a whirlwind of events with Nora on his arm, as she continued to stand in for her mother. Lord Dufferin, the English ambassador, could be counted on to entertain lavishly and often. His posting in Paris was the capstone of his long career in the British diplomatic service, during which he had served as the governor of Canada and as viceroy to India. Lord Dufferin enjoyed hosting garden parties for the diplomatic community on the lawn of his rented palace that had once belonged to Napoleon's scandalous sister, the Princess Borghèse. The palace had room for almost every human activity except the hanging of coats, so rows of footmen were employed to take visitors' outerwear as soon they entered. The garments were spirited away to a never-disclosed location. The new American minister and his engaging daughter were a novel and welcome addition to the Paris diplomatic community, and they quickly became a staple on everyone's A-list of guests. The wife of the French president, Madame Carnot, hosted Nora and T.J. at the Opéra soon after their arrival in Paris, and she became a special friend. The continental women were strongly attracted to T.J., who was a dashing and cultured gentleman, and he, in turn, had an appreciative eye for them. And Nora, seemingly in tune with the Parisian spring, bloomed with all the unaccustomed attention. Always gracious, Nora became increasingly poised in the diplomatic minuet of her new position. She had been carefully educated and was widely read, but more than that, people were enchanted by her lack of pretension and by her genuine delight in her surroundings. T.J. was immensely proud of his daughter, and he attributed the goodwill and kindness of the French people toward him entirely to her great charm. Such a warm judgment from her father, never a man to bestow accolades lightly, was high praise indeed.

Their intense schedule needed organizing, and Nora became T.J's. social secretary as well as his companion. She kept track of his appointments and acknowledged the constant stream of invitations they received. In a petite, leather-bound book she recorded the names and addresses of everyone of consequence they met during their time in France. Even in this extravagant setting, Nora remained the frugal Bostonian. The little book filled quickly with their new acquaintances, lords, ladies, counts, generals, and barons, and when she reached its last page, she turned the book upside-down and continued her record keeping on the reverse side.

Sojourns in Paris were de rigueur for the upper tier of international society, which flocked to the capital to soak up French culture and fashion. People from home were prominent on the Coolidges' social calendar. T.J. and Nora dined with their North Shore friends Susie and Caleb Loring and their Beacon Street neighbors Jack and Isabella Gardner, T.J.'s cousins by marriage. The Gardners were beginning to assemble an important collection of art and antiques, and they valued T.J.'s eye for quality. T.J. and Nora visited Mr. and Mrs. Edward Lee Childe at their château on 16,000 acres in the French countryside. The land was divided into farms rented by peasants whose children worked in the fields from eight years of age. T.J. observed that, though the people were poor, they were clean and happy looking.

American women were well represented in the French capital, owing to the decades-long custom of swapping plump American dowries for lofty European titles. T.J. abhorred this practice, but his assessment of the ennobled Americans they encountered was that most seemed content with their situation and, like the beautiful Countess d'Aramon (Blanche Fisher) and the Princess Brancaccio (Elizabeth Hickson Field), comfortable with their impressive new names. The biggest surprise was meeting Madame de Talleyrand, who had sprung from a branch of the Curtis family of Boston. She had left a respectable husband and a comfortable life in a New York mansion on Fifth Avenue to marry the Marquis de Talleyrand.

The French were unyielding in their pursuit of glamour, and their opulent wardrobes were hymns to fashion and to themselves. Gallic women made liberal use of rouge, powder, dye, and penciled beauty marks that lent an intriguing theatricality to even the plainest among them. In this glittering world Nora could not risk looking frumpy or provincial, and to be seen wearing the same dress twice was social suicide. With a daily round of tea parties, shopping excursions, dinners, dances, opera, and theater, an annual wardrobe of more than seven hundred dresses was not uncommon in the circles in which Nora now moved. Simple dresses for walking or traveling might be had for as little as a hundred dollars, but gowns for parties and receptions or for horse and yacht races could go as high as a thousand. The cost of a proper wardrobe, therefore, one that covered all likely occasions, could easily run as high as forty thousand dollars, a sum that, as the twentieth century began, equaled seventy years of wages for the average working man.[3]

Parisian fashion was evolving from a cottage industry sustained by talented private dressmakers to one dominated by big-name couturier houses that set the standard for dress in the civilized world. Carriages lined the Rue de la Paix, the "sacred" street, where doormen discreetly controlled the unassuming entrances to modest-looking shops where one could buy fantasies of satin, silk, taffeta, and velvet created by legendary designers, Doucet, Rouff, Paquin, Poiret, and, above all, Charles Frederick Worth. The English-born Charles Worth dominated the fashion world for decades with an arrogance born of his mastery of art and salesmanship. He had been the first to employ modern production techniques using standardized parts to create unique gowns of unparalleled cost. He was the first to put dressmakers' labels in his gowns. Worth required new customers to present him with a letter of introduction so he could judge whether to allow them the privilege of wearing his creations. His gowns came in delicious colors—primrose yellow, Devonshire cream, and cornflower blue. They were trimmed with fringe and ruffles and embroidered with glistening beads of gold, glass, or pearls. Nora's friend the effervescent Isabella Stewart Gardner had purchased her first Worth gown in 1867. The arrival of trunks from Parisian dressmakers packed with the latest styles was an occasion of supreme excitement, Christmas in any season, for upper-class American women.

Nora took pains not to betray her rush of elation and nerves the first time she entered the atelier at Number 7, Rue de la Paix, the House of Worth. Within, on the first floor, was an extravagant display of the smaller miracles, artful, intricately worked handbags and hats. In the salon above was another

Worth innovation, live models coolly showing off his clothes. One could also purchase expensive furs and lingerie that was more discreetly displayed. Eleo accompanied her mother for shopping and dress fittings and, to her surprise, she was fascinated by these missions. It was strange and pleasing to see her mother become the focus of attention, fussed over by seamstresses and salesmen. Eleo absorbed, almost in spite of herself, an appreciation of style and quality as she watched her mother's transformation into one of those tiny-waisted visions that strolled the avenues of Paris. A woman's waist was the demure focal point of feminine allure. The recently improved steam process for molding corsets permitted dresses to be fitted much more closely to the center of the body. A woman's shoulders were generously padded and draped, while cascades of lace or bow-studded brocade formed a generous train that guarded and swelled the derriere. The resulting silhouette mimicked the voluptuous curves of an hour glass. For formal occasions, fans made of feathers and a rainbow of gemstones completed this highly stylized picture. Nora's husband, Frederick, made his halfhearted contribution to the staggering cost of these necessities, but it was T.J., who was benefiting so significantly from Nora's company, who underwrote most of the expense for his daughter and for Eleo. As a young lady of quality who also represented the United States, Eleo, too, required appropriate dresses for special events.

Nora was honored with an invitation from a former queen, the exiled Isabella II of Spain, who had heard much gossip about the American newcomer and wished to satisfy her curiosity. The invitation was, in reality, a command to appear. Isabella was awesomely stout, and she rarely traveled beyond the confines of her palace. T.J. escorted Nora to her audience with the queen. Isabella loomed at the end of a long reception hall, her folds of flesh draped over a thronelike chair. T.J. and Nora had been advised of the exacting protocol required for this visit, and, though it seemed comical to these emissaries from the New World, they performed all the courtesies that the occasion demanded. As they approached the royal mound, T.J. bowed deeply many times. Nora executed three low dips as she approached the ex-queen and, after being looked over and exchanging pleasantries, three more while backing out.

President Carnot's wife invited the Coolidges and the Searses to join her group for the Bastille Day celebrations on July 14. Nora cautioned her children about behaving properly, and she leveled an especially piercing glance at Eleo, but she need not have worried. Eleo and her brother were quickly mesmerized by the masses of tricolor banners, the trumpets and drums sounding "The Marseillaise," and the foot soldiers in bright uniforms marching in precise rows. Cavalry soldiers, in brass helmets topped with fluttering plumes, carried lances and rode the most gorgeous horses. The parade climaxed with a thrilling display of fireworks. The explosions over the Seine silhouetted the

Eiffel Tower, a technological marvel of steel that, since its debut three years before, reigned as the world's tallest building.

Paris held many delights for the Sears children. Freddy and Eleo rode with their father through the Bois de Boulogne, cantering down the broad, tree-shaded paths alongside fine-looking ladies and gentlemen. They took their horses over low practice jumps while deer bounded away into the forest. Together with gaggles of French youngsters they laughed at the slapstick comedy of Punch and Judy puppet shows on the Champs Elysées. Freddy and Eleo fussed until they got toy sailboats, which they added to the armada that floated in the water basins in the formal gardens of the Tuileries. They galloped to waltz tunes on wooden carousel horses as the scene around them revolved with people strolling with their pets, nannies airing their little charges, and conveyances of every description—pony carts, barouches, victorias, and dogcarts.

Grandfather Coolidge was in command, so Eleo and Freddy could not escape their school lessons. Their education continued during their year abroad under the implacable eye of Mademoiselle Cogné. Mlle. Cogné's sterling reputation within the expatriate community had been secured years earlier when Alva Vanderbilt chose her as the governess for her daughter, Consuelo. Eleo and Freddy concluded that Mlle. Cogné was "pretty good" overall, though she refused to speak a word of English to them and in that way forced them to learn French.[4] Mademoiselle was determined to fulfill her mandate to educate these American youngsters, and she marched them through galleries in the Louvre that seemed without end. Eleo and Freddy much preferred racing their little boats in the basins against the Parisian children. When the devil-fidgets got her, Eleo discovered she could easily outrun Mlle. Cogné, and she would shoot off suddenly through the streets, taking refuge beneath parked horses, where she could watch Mademoiselle come puffing after her.

T.J. seized the opportunity to supplement his own education as well. He and Nora took French lessons to improve their already serviceable knowledge of the language. They studied the stylistic differences among the great periods of French furniture, the three Louises: XIV, XV, XVI, and Napoleon's favorite, Empire. T.J. was deeply interested in art and he toured all the important studios in Paris. Frederick often joined him. The two men visited the studio of Jean-Léon Gérôme, a noted painter and instructor who had taught the young Thomas Eakins. Gérôme was the president of the Jury de Contrôle, which awarded scholarships to promising American art students to study in Paris. The scholarships were funded by donations from art patrons in New York and Boston, and T.J. was responsible for evaluating the program and the quality of the work produced by the students who depended on those stipends.

In August 1892 the Searses and the Coolidges attended a large gathering in the Tuileries to raise money to aid starving peasants in Russia. Russian farmers were second only to American farmers in their production of wheat, but a severe drought across the vast Russian steppes, exacerbated by government ineptitude, caused a catastrophic failure of their crop. The French, who were allied both militarily and emotionally with Russia, sent substantial aid. Additional help came from England and from the fledgling American Red Cross. American farmers were desperate to find an outlet for their excess production and gladly provided tons of surplus wheat. Despite all the aid, more than 400,000 Russian peasants perished.

Toward the end of August Paris was terrorized by a cholera epidemic that swept west from Russia and the Middle East, where it killed hundreds of thousands. T.J. remained at his post in Paris, but he packed his wife and his daughter's family off to Geneva for the protection of the cooler Swiss climate. Eleo and Freddy returned to Paris in winter and rejoined their friends for ice skating in the Bois de Boulogne. In the spring, as angry workers rioted in cities across the Continent, a mass uprising of workers shook the French capital. On March 30, 1893, the French government fell, and foreign diplomats scrambled to realign their dealings with the incoming regime. T.J. and Nora were deeply concerned for the safety of their friends, the now ex-President Carnot and his wife.[5] But political instability and the lingering risk of cholera did not deter American society women, who returned in great numbers to the shops of Paris's top dressmakers. *Vogue* magazine, in its April 1893 issue, marveled that "Dame Fashion has prevailed over the fear of cholera."

On the first of May, angry workers again marauded through the streets of Paris, and a mob surrounded Nora's carriage as its drove down the Place de la Concorde. The coachman was barely able to steady the horses and race back to the safety of Montefiore House.

In the United States, Grover Cleveland was elected president over the incumbent Republican, Benjamin Harrison, and a new man, former Louisiana Senator James B. Eustis, was on his way to France to represent America. T.J. remained in Paris until Eustis had been officially installed as the first American ambassador.[6] The Coolidge and Sears families sailed for home on the *Bourgogne* on May 27, 1893. They reached New York on June 4 to find panic on Wall Street. Years of overproduction from farms and factories, financial speculation, and a sudden drop in the national gold reserve had combined to roil the economy. Frightened citizens hoarded gold as they watched the price of silver fall by half. Banks, mills, and railroads were shuttered and their workers thrown into the streets. In Chicago failed banks and railroads led to suicides among the directors. The huge General Electric Company was saved from collapse by the courage of its major shareholders, who pledged additional money for shares of the company's nearly worthless stock. Three years would pass before public confidence was restored and the country emerged from this bitter depression.

With their country in turmoil, it was doubly hard for the Coolidge and Sears families to let go of the mostly idyllic interlude of their year in Paris. Eleo and Freddy returned to their friends and their pets, but for Nora, especially, the familiar was a mixed blessing. In September, three months after they returned home, the two families reunited to travel to Chicago for the grand World's Fair of 1893. Officially known as the Columbian Exposition, the event celebrated the four hundredth anniversary of Columbus's great discovery. Chicago had beaten out New York, St. Louis, and Washington, D.C., for the honor of hosting the fair. The city was bursting to show itself off, having been completely rebuilt after the Great Fire that leveled it in 1871.

Spread over 633 acres of reclaimed swampland along Lake Michigan, lushly landscaped by Frederick Law Olmsted, the World's Fair brought together presentations by fifty-two countries, including the Sandwich Islands, the independent nation of Hawaii. The exposition was so large that it took two weeks to see it all properly. It was so beautiful that visitors likened it to a vision of Heaven, and many were moved to tears. General admission cost fifty cents for adults and twenty-five cents for children. Initially, crowds were small as the country wrestled with the depression, but word spread quickly that the fair was a must-see event. During the six months it remained open, the Columbian Exposition attracted 27,539,000 visitors from across America and Europe, a number that was nearly half the population of the United States. Many fairgoers dipped into their life savings to make the trip. One elderly couple was well satisfied with their visit. "Well, it paid," the old gentleman said to his wife, "even if it did take all the burial money."[7]

Eleo and Freddy were intoxicated by the sights and the crowds. The mile-long Midway brought to Chicago the exotic range of humanity, from African headhunters to Eskimos and Lapps. In the Turkish village (one dollar extra) you could ride in sedan chairs carried by natives. Visitors were lured to the naughty street in Cairo (another dollar) by cries of "Come, handsome infidel strangers."[8] There they could ride camels and watch snake charmers and belly dancers. T.J. and his wife and Nora and Frederick were borne along by the children's excitement. They floated in gondolas through a maze of canals and lagoons and rode on the elevated electric railway. They marveled at the way even food was made to perform wonders as they walked respectfully around the 22,000-pound cheese that sat in the Wisconsin State Pavilion. They admired the detailed copy of the Venus de Milo that was sculpted in chocolate and the life-size medieval knight on horseback made entirely of prunes. Equally impressive was the giant map of the United States made of pickles. Rising majestically above the fair, in a conscious effort to rival the Eiffel Tower that had starred in the Paris Exposition of 1889, was a revolving wheel designed by George Ferris. It was capable of lifting more than two thousand people at one time in railroad-sized cars, a total weight of one million pounds, and swing them 264 feet into the air. At the apex of the wheel, halfway through its twenty-minute rotation, the view was so astounding that passengers were stunned into silence. To friends back in Boston, Eleo mailed picture postcards, a new idea from the U.S. Postal Service, that showed scenes of the glorious fairgrounds.

The Columbian Exposition introduced other firsts—a hamburger, Cracker Jacks, Juicy Fruit gum, diet carbonated soda, fingerprint identification, a transcontinental telephone call. But for all its magnificence and innovation, the 1893 World's Fair was essentially backward-looking. The heart of the Exposition was an idealized classical city. Enormous colonnaded palaces, inspired by ancient Rome and accented by Greek statues, were designed by the nation's foremost architects, led by Richard Morris Hunt, architect to the Vanderbilts. These ethereal palaces overlooked a man-made Venetian lake with a wooded island and giant fountains ringed by life-size, rearing horses. At night the scene shimmered as in a dream, illuminated by fireworks and hundreds of electric lights. It was a magical-looking metropolis that gleamed like alabaster, but it was molded out of plaster of paris. As the century neared its end, this shining white city was an homage from the New World to the Old, a summing up. The multitudes who came to marvel at the great fair's attractions believed it was a window on the future. In truth it offered barely a glimpse of all that was to come.

CHAPTER 5

Coming of Age in a New Century

AMERICANS WELCOMED the new century with typical optimism and bravado. They had flexed their muscles in 1898, galvanized by the sinking of the battleship *Maine* in Havana Harbor, and had won, with relative ease, a "splendid little war" with Spain. Teddy Roosevelt had led his Rough Riders into the hills above San Juan, and Spain had relinquished control of Cuba, the Philippines, and Guam. It had all taken only six months. In Boston crowds lined Beacon Street, joined by members of the Somerset Club, who stood on the club's front steps, to cheer the returning Sixth Regiment as it paraded through Beacon Hill. The suntanned soldiers may have looked thin and scruffy, but they marched with pride, and several carried green parrots perched on their khaki shoulders.

By 1900 economic prosperity had returned, warming the pockets of those who labored in the wheat fields in the Midwest and those who toiled in the canyons of commerce on Wall Street. The *Boston Herald* was of the opinion that "if one could not have made money this year, his case was hopeless."[1] American innovation was paving the way to an increasingly wise, happy, and humane future. The last century had seen sweeping technological advances—railroads, ocean liners, telegraphs and telephones, and electric lights—that propelled the country from an agrarian society to the world's foremost industrial powerhouse. With the past as prelude, it was widely assumed that even the nation's most intractable problems—child labor, immigrant slums, corrupt politicians, and ruthless corporations—would eventually fade away. The *New York Times* editorialized on December 31, 1899, that the nation and the world were about to "step upon the threshold . . . of a still brighter dawn of civilization."[2] It was a brief but golden interlude, this decade and a half preceding the First World War, a time of self-assurance, of progress, and of limitless horizons. Later it would be recalled, wistfully, as the Age of Innocence.

Eleo Sears was eighteen years old at the start of the twentieth century. She had become a strikingly attractive and vibrant young woman, well aware of her powers. Eleo had the slim, tight body of an athlete and the assured carriage of a princess. It would be said of her through the years that "she held herself proud." Though only a bit above average height, she always seemed taller. Her eyes were her most arresting feature, an intense, deep blue that appeared almost iridescent and lit her deeply suntanned face. At times Eleo's manner could seem unnervingly direct, but a softness was lent by the charming dimple in her left cheek. Behind her laughter one sensed a deeper reserve, but that elusive quality only added to her allure. When Eleo was pleased, you were rewarded with a merry grin that revealed a row of even, white teeth.

Eleo had made her formal society debut at seventeen. She did not have the huge party with a band, extra butlers, maids, and doormen that attended the coming-out affairs of debutantes in her set. Most probably, Eleo's father was unwilling to finance the event at the level considered appropriate in their social circle, though by the standards of New York or Newport, Boston debuts were skimpy affairs. Eleo certainly did not lack for activity during that whirl-wind year. Life during a debutante's "bud" year was full to bursting, and Eleo did not escape some of the less enjoyable social rituals of the time. On the list of excruciating must-dos was a large tea party during which a debutante was presented to all the women who were bound by blood or decades of friend-ship to her mother and grandmothers. The star of the occasion, imprisoned in a high-necked, long-sleeved, tight-waisted dress, in a crowded, overheated room, was expected to nod politely and offer bland replies whatever the provocation, while serving tea to her mother's guests. Sweet punch flowed along with the tea, and there were piles of petite sandwiches cut into imagi-native shapes and cakes and candies, but there was no musical entertainment and no male presence; not even Freddy cared to show his face. Propriety frowned on discussing any number of potentially interesting topics. It was vulgar to discuss money or what anything cost. Off-limits also was any men-tion of diseases, physical ailments, or their surgical remedies.[3] The paltry reward for such a deadening afternoon was the tight-lipped approval of the assembled matrons.

The young ladies in Eleo's circle were not destined for college or for careers in teaching or selling hats. Higher education for women was still a novelty, and those few jobs that were available for women were better left to poor girls who actually needed them. In any event, the year of one's coming out, especially if the debutante pool was large, was so concentrated that it was almost a full-time occupation. Particularly from December through

February there were nightly dances and afternoons filled with lunches, receptions, matinees, and concerts. Formal, sophisticated dinners were often held in private homes and began at eight o'clock. Most of the young men present had been plucked from the reservoir of Harvard sophomores. During the first half of the dinner the well-mannered deb was expected to converse politely with the gentleman seated on her right. The second half of the meal was devoted to the boy on her left. If the host's home did not have its own ballroom or a large enough parlor, the young people, splendid in evening dress, would head off to dance at the Algonquin Club on Commonwealth Avenue or to the Copley Square Hotel. The dances included a four-course supper and ended at midnight. Dances held at lesser hotels and followed by correspondingly meager suppers were labeled the "Cheap and Hungries."

The festivities concluded with a cotillion, which often lasted until three o'clock in the morning. Eleo was acknowledged to be a marvelous dancer, and the cotillion offered an appealing element of competition. Several pairs of the young men and women were summoned to the dance floor, where the cotillion leader handed little favors to the men. The couples waltzed a turn or two around the hall before separating. The men were then free to bestow their favors—boutonnieres, colorful ribbons bound with tinsel, or beaded necklaces—on the girls still seated along the walls who had caught their eye. The newly formed couples then danced together until the leader called other pairs to the floor. The prettier girls, like Eleo, were frequently favored and tucked their tokens under their chairs with a studied nonchalance, while those less sought after tried not to let their unhappiness show. When the dancers left for home in the darkness of early morning, they would sparkle as they passed beneath the street lamps with cascades of ribbons draped over their shoulders. Many of the girls also trailed the tulle ruffles that had torn off their gowns during the dancing, carrying them like a badge of honor to prove they had had an especially good time. The next day some "little woman" would appear at their homes to sew the ruffles back on the dresses, restoring them for a future entertainment.[4]

Dancing, like riding horses, was a required upper-class skill, and generations of Boston's young elite attended "Friday Evenings" and "Saturday Evenings" at Papanti's studio on Tremont Street. To Eleo and her neighborhood friends Papanti's was simply where everyone you knew would be, but it was a carefully vetted congregation. A subscription book was sent around to all the families considered eligible for the dancing classes and for the twice-yearly assemblies at Papanti's. Boston society was "stern about who should and who should not have their name on that sacred scroll."[5] The social importance attached to dancing classes retained its hold on proper Bostonians for many decades. The *Boston Globe* observed their predicament with amusement: "If you send your daughter to the wrong dancing school at the age of six, you don't recover for three generations."[6] Count Lorenzo Papanti had introduced the waltz to America in 1834, demonstrating a slow, gliding version that became known as "the Boston." As a dance instructor, the count would terrify his more recalcitrant students with the long bow of his fiddle. Gradually grown thin, bald, and ancient, he oversaw the teenagers' progress with fish-gray eyes. A mother of one of the girls actually organized the dances, where the youngsters learned social etiquette together with several versions of the waltz, the polka, "the German," and the Virginia reel. The boys, whether they attended Groton, St. Paul's, or St. Mark's, could be relied on to hang back sheepishly with their sweaty hands jammed in their pockets. The girls were just as happy dancing with each other, but no one ever forgot the magic of the unique, springy dance floor, which yielded beneath their feet "like a live thing."[7] Even when they themselves were old, they could recall dancing "The Boston" on that bouncy floor, "swooping and swinging around the hall in a delirium of delight."[8]

Eleo was an enthusiastic participant in another Boston tradition, the all-female theatrical productions that were organized by the Vincent Club. The Vincent Club had mounted its first show in 1892 to raise money for the newly formed Vincent Memorial Hospital, which cared for indigent women. The earliest Vincent Club fund-raisers were a series of all-female tableaux vivants that were staged in the drawing rooms of private homes. By 1902, when twenty-one-year-old Eleo joined the club, the show had grown into a full-scale musical production presented in a theater. Club members wrote song lyrics and dialogue, created the scenery and costumes, and played in the orchestra. Some of the young women, dressed in the club's colors of purple and yellow, worked the front of the house as ushers selling programs and flowers.

Eleo's first recorded appearance in a Vincent Club show came in the 1903 production of *The Rajah's Daughter*. From then on she was a regular in the Vincent Drill, a conceptual forerunner of Radio City Music Hall's Rockettes. The drill required months of practice and was the centerpiece of every show. Participation was considered a major honor. Sixteen women, with "proper carriage," wore colorful military-style uniforms and marched in complex, high-stepping patterns. Eleo wrote original songs and choreographed dances for several of the Vincent Club shows, and in two of them she rode a horse onstage. The hit of the 1907 show was the "Sporting Song" number, in which Eleo teamed with three friends, all of them dressed in formal men's foxhunting attire, to sing timeless lines like "The next horse I ride on I've got to be tied on." Eleo came onstage riding Alice Thorndike's pony, Jack Rabbit. It was widely agreed that Jack Rabbit was the true star of that show. Men were officially barred from attending the club's performances, though occasionally some of the ushers looked suspiciously solid in their ruffled purple and yellow frocks and luxuriantly curled hair and bore an uncanny resemblance to Harvard undergraduates.

As much as Eleo enjoyed her crammed schedule of social engagements, time with her horses was as necessary for her as breathing. Horses gave their affection without pretense, and with them Eleo was relaxed and gentle, forgiving and generous of spirit, by every measure her best self. She loved the way these large, muscled creatures leaned their great heads into her as she rubbed the small hollow behind their ears, the sensuous curve of their necks, and the tender, velvety area above their nostrils. Their large brown eyes watched her every move, unblinking, and sometimes she imagined they knew secrets. As a small child Eleo had been enthralled by the world behind the barn door. Along the walls, leather saddles and bridles hung in neat rows and storage cupboards yielded large collections of curry combs, brushes, sponges, and hoof oils. There were stacks of handsomely trimmed horse blankets and monogrammed sheets that buckled on to protect against the cold of winter and the dust and flies of summer. An assortment of boots and wraps protected delicate legs from swinging polo mallets and hard-edged jumps. Eleo loved even the musky perfume that announced the horse barn, where acrid droppings mingled with the sweet, earthy aroma of straw bedding and leather cleaned with saddle soap.

Most of the grooms and stable hands had worked for the Sears family for many years. They watched Eleo grow up and knew she was a rare young lady. They could count on her to appear at the stable every day, brightening and punctuating their routine. Eleo breezed in full of smiles, usually bearing gifts of apples, carrots, and sugar for the horses. All through her childhood she followed the men around as they did their chores. They showed her how to braid the manes and tails of the horses before a show and how to use a hoof pick to clean out the mud and stones that accumulated under their hooves. Eleo never tired of watching the essential artistry of the blacksmith, who pounded glowing iron into shoes of the ideal shape and balance to suit the special needs of each horse. Time and again he plunged the pulsing iron into a tub of water and brought it sizzling and steaming to life.

The stable men were devoted to Eleo. They were warmed by her unfailing kindness to them and they enjoyed their role as wise counselors. Eleo would lean amiably against a stall door and soak up their opinions on the benefits of boiled oats or barley with molasses for horses with digestive upsets. They debated the nutritional value of seed hay versus meadow hay and when to add alfalfa for extra protein. The younger stable boys learned quickly what the old-timers already knew, that Eleo could be an exacting mistress. When confronted with chores done haphazardly or with horses left untended, she could suddenly turn icy and explode with an oath that brought the startled offender immediately into line. Still, the grooms were more proud of their pretty, young mistress than scandalized when she showed up wearing the most improper men's-style breeches and rode off sitting astride on a man's saddle. They, after all, worked for the family where this notable behavior took place. When Eleo returned from her daily rides, before heading off to a sporting event or a debutante ball, if her horse happened to lift his tail and dump a pungent load at her feet, she was not above grabbing a pitchfork and heaving the steaming pile onto the muck heap.

When the horses played together in the fields or cantered across the hills with their manes and tails streaming, wondrously outlined by the sun, Eleo watched quietly, stilled by the inspired assemblage of angles and spheres that move sculptors and tempt poets.

Ethel Barrymore was full of admiration for the familiar and loving way that Eleo had with horses and she luxuriated in long, relaxing carriage rides through the North Shore countryside with Eleo at the reins. Ethel spent many summers with Eleo at the Searses' country home in Beverly Farms. Eleo's family practically adopted Ethel when, as a young actress, she appeared in plays that worked out their kinks in Boston before moving to the big time on Broadway. Ethel cherished her welcome into the Sears family, where Nora fussed over her in a motherly way. In Eleo she found a soul mate, and she became one of Eleo's lifelong and truest friends. Both girls had a quick, cutting sense of humor, and when Ethel confided in Eleo that she had always hated her first name, Eleo snipped off part of her famous last name and called her "Birry," said with a faux-British trill. The girls liked to walk to the gray clapboard farmhouse of Supreme Court Justice Oliver Wendell Holmes, who shared Ethel's love of detective stories. Eleo and Ethel gleefully joined in the Holmes family tradition of mocking upper-class pretensions. It was Justice Holmes's father, Oliver Wendell Sr., a retired doctor and anatomy professor, who first classified the generations of snooty, inbred New Englanders as members of the "Brahmin caste." When the residents of neighboring Manchester pretentiously renamed their town Manchester-by-the-Sea, Dr. Holmes began heading correspondence from his home near the railroad station "Beverly-by-the-Depot."[9]

Ethel Barrymore made her stage debut at the age of fifteen in a production with her uncle John Drew, and from then on she often led the vagabond life of an actor. Ethel's own family was theater royalty, the Drew-Barrymore acting dynasty. Ethel was third generation. She was essentially a shy girl, a middle child, born between two dynamic brothers, Lionel and John, but she had a passion for the theater and a determination to make her own place in it. Ethel was handsome and substantial rather than pretty, with the assertive Roman nose of her brothers and eyes like great dark ponds. She had a deep, smoky voice that gave her every utterance an air of authority. With her hair piled on top of her head, Gibson-girl style, Ethel could play the regal Catherine the

Great as convincingly as she could handle the sarcasm and silliness of light English comedies. Whenever Ethel played in Boston, she stayed with the Sears family. Nora and Eleo attended all her shows and enjoyed visiting her backstage after her performances. These outings were especially pleasant for Eleo and her mother because a love of the theater was one of the few enthusiasms that they shared. Eleo and Nora were an appreciative audience for Ethel's earthy reports of backstage intrigues and gossip.

During her long and distinguished career, Ethel Barrymore remained unimpressed by the billing she earned as the "First Lady of the American theater." She was similarly matter-of-fact about her cozy familiarity with presidents, prime ministers, and kings. Her friend Tallulah Bankhead made the admiring observation that Ethel "normally wouldn't cross the street to meet God." In Ethel's autobiography, *Memories,* which she wrote when she was seventy-five, she looked back over her more than half century of devoted friendship with Eleo Sears and asserted that Eleo "has more charm than anybody I ever met." Eleo's smile, Ethel said, was "devastating." As a girl, Ethel never seemed to mind all the evenings she spent playing the piano for Eleo's parents, while Eleo entertained her many attractive beaux outside on the porch. The boys were drawn by Eleo's smile and generous laugh, and they were intrigued by her interest in all the sports they played. She played them all well, too. Eleo could belt a baseball deep into the outfield; she boxed, practicing jabs and uppercuts; her accuracy with a rifle made her one of New England's top trap shooters; she handled a boat like a seasoned yachtsman. Though the times dictated high-necked dresses, the young men could appreciate Eleo's slender waist and her graceful, fine-boned hands. Among Eleo's gentlemen callers was the blue-blood John Saltonstall, whose family was already on the scene when the first Sears to come to America, Richard the Pilgrim, landed in New England. Two of Frederick Prince's sons, blond-haired, dimple-chinned Norman and his older brother Frederick Jr., enjoyed a playful rivalry as they both courted Eleo. Frederick Prince and his four brothers were nearsighted, and Frederick celebrated this trait when naming the sporting club that was developed on his property in Winchester, Massachusetts, the Myopia Hunt Club. Prince's sons were not so shortsighted, however, that they failed to appreciate Eleo's charms, and their father encouraged their interest. As ever, there were few prospects more agreeable than the mingling of good bloodlines and old money.

Among the girls approaching marriageable age, Eleo incited envy and grudging respect because she had the attention of so many of Boston's most eligible prospects. For the younger girls, not in direct competition with her, Eleo's blend of snappy coolness and physical competence inspired a kind of awe. As a child Eleo had ridden horses bareback to develop her sense of balance and now, increasingly, she showed up riding astride, "man fashion" or "cross-saddle," as it was then called, wearing male-inspired riding pants and jackets. It was tantalizingly improper and it put rebellious thoughts in the heads of many of the girls. Young Margarett Sargent liked to watch Eleo as she rode in the indoor arena of the New Riding Club, and Margarett, too, began riding astride on those rare occasions when she could get away with it. Margarett was very proud that the older girls appreciated her skill with horses. Eleo's good friend Alice Thorndike allowed Margarett to ride her pony, Jack Rabbit, in a show at the club, and Margarett won first prize. To mark the win, Alice gave her "the dearest pin." Margarett wrote in her diary that she was "smashed" on Eleo and Alice. She nearly swooned with pleasure when Eleo noticed her one summer during a seaside vacation and greeted her with a cheery "Hello, Freckletop."

It was not unusual for young girls to have crushes on girls they admired. They invited best friends to be their dates at school events or, depending on the season, for an afternoon of riding, tennis, or sledding. A girl would court her special friend, wooing her with favors, polishing her shoes, or leaving a bunch of violets and an affectionate poem at her door. Such attachments were thought to represent the highest ideals of friendship, a mutual appreciation based on shared intellectual passions for the arts or athletics. It was important, however, to guard against the excessive emotional commitments or jealousies that could arise, because when such friendships were broken off, the rejected girls suffered so intensely that they would be incapacitated for weeks. Despite that risk, the tender bonds that developed among women were far less fraught with moral hazard than friendships with boys. It was thought preferable to delay male-female relationships until a young lady was sufficiently mature and the proper introductions had been made.

Eleo was lavish in her attentions to people whom she liked especially, such as pretty Alice Thorndike, who shared her affection for horses and tennis. Eleo took delight in surprising her favorite people with gifts and mementos, and she could be extravagant when it came to showing them a good time. When Eleo went to the theater with friends, she bought an extra seat to give her companions a convenient place to put their coats. The social conventions of the time suited her ideally. Eleo's friends, both male and female, were good-looking, self-assured types who were likely to be among the first chosen on teams for games or sports. It was thrilling to be part of Eleo's bright circle, to be the one whom she leaned toward conspiratorially to share a joke or a secret. Boys liked being with her, and if she was "smashed" on some of her girlfriends, that too seemed harmless and did not set off any alarms. There was no requirement then that she make a choice.

By temperament and by circumstance, Eleo's mother moved more quietly through the world, keeping tight control of her emotions and her expenditures. Nora was given an allowance for her personal and household needs, and she was strict with herself about keeping within those limits. It mattered little that she had come from great wealth, or that her ungenerous husband, Frederick, was an heir to the Sears fortune. In her background also lurked the Puritan Bostonian commandments to live frugally and to focus on self-improvement. Nora was much influenced by her father, who had, earlier in his life, taken pains to identify and overcome his own character faults. T.J. detailed these struggles in his autobiography, which he distributed to his family and friends in 1902, when he was seventy-one years old. In this record of his life and work, T.J. displayed the restraint he thought fitting for a man who had led a life in public service. He confined his enthusiasm and passion to an elegiac discourse on the exhilarating and manly sport of foxhunting. T.J. devoted several pages of his autobiography to reliving invigorating rides in the chill air at daybreak, jumping fences and splashing through streams to follow the throaty howls of the hounds when they caught a scent. He noted appreciatively the steam that rose from the flanks of the horses, the colors of the leaves, and the admirably clever strategies of the fox. On the women in his life, T.J. was mostly silent. He was stoic about the typhoid fever that nearly claimed his daughter, Marian, and the death of his brother, allotting these events a single sentence.

Though not at all intending to, Nora wrote her own autobiography in a small, maroon, leather-bound book in which she kept track of her household accounts. On one side of the pages she listed the books she had read and the sermons given at Trinity Church that particularly appealed to her. Nora's literary tastes were expansive, ranging from biographies of famous women to poetry, religious philosophy, and French history. She read classic novels and those written by her contemporaries Henry James and Edith Wharton, which slyly skewered patrician Boston. On the reverse side of the pages in the little account book, in tiny writing, in airless columns going off to the left and right and doubling back, leaving no wasted space, Nora recorded the financial minutiae of her daily life. She bought soap and spools of thread and needles and stamps. Gone was the extravagant interlude of her triumph in Paris, as evidenced by the modest record of the clothes she bought and had altered. She oversaw all needed home maintenance. Painting the exterior of the house took fifteen and a half days and earned the painters $4.80 per day. Managing the household staff engaged much of her time. Nora recorded giving the chauffeur fifty cents for his lunch. She noted which servants "behaved badly" and who received commemorative pins to recognize their ten years of service to the family. From time to time she bought a book for Freddy. It was pointless, Nora had learned, to give novels to Eleo, who could be induced to read things only of immediate, practical use and who, in any event, found reading to be an unpleasantly solitary pursuit.

By far the largest portion of Nora's account record was devoted to her charitable donations, many of them solicited by friends who knew that she could always be counted on to support their causes. Nora kept track of her contributions, mostly five or ten and occasionally twenty dollars, in dense columns that were tidy at first and finally spilled into every available patch of blank page. Nora donated to the Infants' Hospital and to Animal Rescue and to the church. She bought theater tickets for her family from Ethel Barrymore in support of Children's Aid. She bought a bouquet of violets for seventy-five cents as a get-well gift for a sick neighbor, Mrs. Henry Wadsworth Longfellow.

Nora's closest friend, Gretchen Osgood Warren, was publicly accomplished in a way that Nora never was, but they had a deeply sympathetic appreciation for one another. They shared a passionate curiosity about the world, past and present, and a sincere religious conviction about the world to come. They could talk together about almost anything, though about the peculiarities of their difficult husbands they needed to say very little.

Gretchen's upbringing had been conspicuously intellectual. Her parents led her and her sister in rousing discussions of New Age spirituality and Oriental philosophy. After breakfast, the family sang four-part Bach chorales. Gretchen went on to study philosophy at Oxford and graduate with honors. She wrote poetry and essays on education and the spiritual nature of man, many of which were published.

Gretchen had been attracted to Frederick Fiske Warren, known as Fiske, precisely because of his idealistic commitment to utopian schemes and radical politics. Both Gretchen and Fiske were strong supporters of the Anti-Imperialist League, a movement centered in New England that touted peace and internationalism. Many upper-class Bostonians were sympathetic to the league's principal goal of thwarting American domination of the Philippine Islands. They considered empire building or any show of naked military power to be an exercise in bad taste.

Gretchen joined Fiske in many of his dietary experiments, such as swearing off meat and alcohol. When traveling, Fiske always bought a second-class ticket and brought along his own food in paper bags. He supported nudism and invented "reform" clothing such as "digitated" socks, which accommodated each toe separately. Some called him a visionary. Even people who liked him thought he was odd. Friends noticed that he and Gretchen began leading increasingly separate lives. Gretchen was delicately pretty and renowned as a brilliant conversationalist with a talent for mimicry that delighted her guests. The celebrated thinkers and statesmen who gathered around her dining table through the years studied the otherworldly shapes of her collection of exotic seashells that she had brought back from her travels. Gretchen's eclectic assemblage of guests was linked by a passion for social causes. She entertained the Chinese nationalist leader Sun Yat-Sen, the black educator Booker T. Washington, patriots from the Philippines, the defense lawyer

Clarence Darrow, and the poet Robert Frost. Gretchen was happy whenever Nora Sears could join her group. Nora's warmth and conversational wit had charmed dukes and countesses, and she more than held her own with this group of eminences.

Gretchen enlisted Nora's help to plan a surprise party for her other great friend, Isabella Stewart Gardner. In Boston society there were two ranking Gardner families. One clan spelled its name with an i and the other didn't. Boston joked about the "one-eyed Gardiners" and the "blind Gardners."[11] The New York–born Belle Stewart took on the difficult role of outsider when she married into the prominent Gardner family. Many Boston socialites resented the new "Mrs. Jack" for removing John Lowell Gardner Jr. from the marriage market, and Boston's upper crust made sure that Belle knew how unworthy she was. For three years Belle existed in a state of near collapse, suffering from what was called neurasthenia, a catchall diagnosis of "women's problems" that included generalized weakness and fainting spells. When Belle's depression finally lifted, she burst from the shadows and embraced all that life had to offer. She flouted society's rules and gathered Bohemian types as friends—artists, writers, musicians—many of whom were homosexual, like the interior design pioneer Elsie de Wolfe and the actress Sarah Bernhardt. Belle arranged for John Singer Sargent to paint the murals in the Boston Public Library, and her patronage helped to make him the most sought-after portrait painter of his time. T. J. Coolidge recognized Sargent's great talent when he was still a fledgling artist and T.J. purchased his evocative study of gypsy dance, *El Jaleo,* when it was exhibited in New York in 1882. Belle Gardner would spend the next thirty years trying to buy the picture from T.J., but he put her off with vague assurances that one day he would sell it to her.

John Singer Sargent, the celebrated portraitist of Boston and Newport society, turned away commissions from people who didn't interest him. Belle Gardner was most eager for him to paint her dear friend Gretchen Warren. Gretchen contrived to sit next to the artist at a party, taking care to spread out her green dress, which had been specially chosen to complement her rosy porcelain complexion. Sargent was struck by Gretchen's artistic potential, but he hated the dress. He decreed that she must wear pink for her portrait and all her friends set to work finding a suitable pink dress for her petite form. The painting that resulted, *Mrs. Fiske Warren and Her Daughter,* is a gorgeous psychological study of the poised, apple-cheeked Gretchen contrasted with her more ethereal, dreamy-eyed twelve-year-old daughter, Rachel, a portrait of the ebb and flow of generations.

Belle Gardner's own appearance was less appealing. She was a short woman with tight, narrow lips, but she won men over with her quick mind, her lovely arms, and tiny waist. She accentuated her positives with daring, décolleté gowns from Worth. The sparkle of Belle's lively wit was almost a match for her astounding jewels. Belle bought herself an $11,000 ruby solitaire ring, which her adoring husband supplemented with a $55,000 nine-carat ruby ring and a string of pearls. Belle and Jack Gardner began to build a serious art collection, many works bought with guidance from the art critic and historian Bernard Berenson. Berenson's appraisal of Belle was that she lived "at a rate that makes other lives seem pale, thin and shadowy."[12] In 1898, as Belle's art collection grew beyond the confines of her double-wide Beacon Street town house, she bought land in a developing area in the Fenway, across from a park being laid out by Frederick Law Olmsted. The acclaimed Boston architect Willard T. Sears, a distant relative of Eleo's family, drew the plans for Belle's fifteenthth-century Venetian-style palace. Belle closely directed the construction, even climbing scaffolding and dabbing on paint. T. J. Coolidge was one of the few people she invited to see her work-in-progress. On New Year's Day 1903 Belle Gardner opened Fenway Court to the public. She treated the crowd to Champagne, doughnuts, and a concert by the Boston Symphony Orchestra. It was the hottest ticket in town.

Schoolchildren who visited the Copley Square Zoo were sometimes fortunate to see Belle Gardner, draped in a long mink coat and her face veiled against the sun, walking an old, toothless lion named Rex on a leash. Fifteen-year-old Eleo Sears watched with fascination as Mrs. Gardner returned home to Beacon Street one day with two lion cubs in her open carriage. Belle had borrowed the six-week-old cubs from the zoo for the afternoon. She tied a pink bow around the neck of the female, and immediately it was dubbed "Mrs. Jack." The cubs became a huge draw for the zoo, especially the one wearing the bow, which "let the world know it was a society lion."[13]

In a time and a place that preferred its women to be anonymous, Isabella Stewart Gardner and Gretchen Warren were outspoken, artistic, and eccentric. These ladies dismissed the standard choices that were offered to them and charted their own way in the world. Their mutual friend Nora Sears took a more traditional path. She was, by nature, gentle and prudent. Nora willingly subordinated many of her own needs and desires to what she believed was a greater good. Eleo loved her mother deeply, but she had no wish to be like her.

CHAPTER 6

Tennis Queen of Newport

ONTROVERSY SPRANG UP later over who had, in fact, played
the very first game of lawn tennis on American shores, but at the
time, Eleo's father, Frederick R. Sears, and his cousin James
Dwight had every reason to believe that the distinction was theirs. Sports historians have since uncovered other contenders for that historical marker,
including a woman from Staten Island who imported a tennis set from
Bermuda, and a lieutenant who played while stationed at Fort Apache in Arizona. In any event, it is certain that Fred Sears and Jim Dwight own the title
of being the first players in New England.[1] In August 1874, on a level patch
of lawn at William Appleton's summer home in Nahant, the two young men
marked out service lines and strung up a net imported from England, where
a game called *sphairistike* (Greek for "ball game") was the rage. The equipment included light, spoon-shaped racquets and bouncy children's-style rubber balls. Playing "sticky" looked like promising entertainment, but Fred and
Jim soon found that trying to swat the erratically bouncing balls over the net
and keeping them within the end lines was much harder than it looked.
Before long, they gave up in frustration and "voted the whole thing a fraud."[2]
Weeks later the racquets were brought out again, this time with more success
and, newly smitten with the game, they played all afternoon in the rain in
rubber coats and galoshes.

During the summers that followed, Fred and Jim attracted friends and relatives to the game. Fred's three teenage half brothers from his father's second
marriage, Richard Dudley and the twins Philip and Herbert, were talented
recruits. Fred got first crack at the rubber balls that his stepmother stitched
around with pieces of old flannel shirts to give the balls more weight, after
which Richard Dudley and the twins got them to practice with against the
barn door. Fred and Jim bested fifteen entrants in the first handicap tennis
tournament held in the United States, in Nahant in the summer of 1876. The

two men faced off in the finals, which Jim won. Many people huffed that lawn tennis was just an effete "seaside pastime," unlike the more substantial sports of football and rowing. This perception was not helped by the starched white outfits that the players wore or by the scoring that began not with zero, but with "love." Despite these affectations, the lawn tennis craze grew, and tournaments sprouted along the East Coast.

A section of the six-hundred-acre estate owned by David Sears II was taken over for the formation of the Longwood Cricket Club, and soon gentle-manly contests of cricket and lawn tennis covered its grassy expanse. The sporting equipment and scoring came from England, as did the aristocratic notions of chivalry and fair play, of being "cricket." Upper-class New Englan-ders had always shared the English reverence for exercise as a builder of char-acter through discipline and collegial competition. Lawn tennis had codes of honor and dress that endeared it to the amateurs who played purely, as intended by the Latin root *amare,* for the love of the sport. Bostonians were not alone in their perception that a debilitating softness was creeping into modern life, and sports were seen as an antidote. Vigorous athletic competi-tion trained future leaders and was thought to promote virility.

Lawn tennis, during its infancy in America, was more rough-and-ready than the English version, and visiting players were appalled. British teams judged the playing conditions at Longwood to be "abominable"—the grass on the courts was too high, the nets held up by sagging guy ropes were disgusting, the balls were "awful, . . . soft and motherly." In sum, they saw the Longwood setup as "a disgrace to civilized lawn tennis."[3]

While Frederick Sears soldiered on as a competent recreational player, his half brothers began earning national recognition. The twins were regional intercollegiate champions. Above all the Sears brothers was Richard Dudley, who became the brightest light of the Sears tennis dynasty. Dick Sears won America's first National Singles Championship in 1881, and he retained the championship through 1887. He was an unlikely-looking sports star—lightly built and wearing eyeglasses—but he was quick, agile, and observant. Dick Sears pioneered the tactic of rushing the net, and he confounded his oppo-nents with his ability to flick their shots off to the right or left at will. He also won the U.S. Doubles Championship for six years running, 1882–87, in part-nership with his cousin Dr. James Dwight and his classmate Joe Clark.[4] In their Longwood black-and-white-striped cricket jackets and caps, Dick Sears and Jim Dwight sailed to England for the championships at Wimbledon, the first Americans to play on that storied ground.

It was common wisdom, when ladies began taking to the lawn tennis courts, that light exercise in the open air was salutary for females. Women rode horses and practiced archery. They played golf and croquet. The empha-sis was not on success in those endeavors, but on their cautious and judicious pursuit. "Caution" and "Moderation" shielded the participants against a loss of womanliness. The fear was that strenuous athletic activity would damage female reproductive capacity and lead to a variety of nervous conditions, including unmentionable erotic impulses. Athletic competition for women was never contemplated as a training ground for warriors or leaders. Educators agreed that exercise for females, when pursued in moderation, promoted "judgment, . . . self-control, and harmonious working with others."[5] Friendly athletic interaction between men and women strengthened the bonds of family. These presumed benefits came first to women of the upper classes, who had the leisure to devote to such pastimes and the money to buy the latest in outdoor sports apparel.

When Eleo Sears first strode into the sporting arena with her uncommon sense of purpose, the female jock was a new and puzzling concept. Female athletes were admired, on the one hand, as symbols of the "modern woman," but they could meet with sharp disapproval when they strayed too far and adopted a "manly role" that blurred natural, "God-given" gender differences. Female athletes were then too few in number to be seen as a threat to the men. Ladies and gentlemen from the upper social ranks were disposed to give each other extra latitude. Eleo's early successes were unique, both in their constancy and variety, and for the most part they brought her admiration. Sports reporters called her "a busy and tireless example of the up-to-date society girl."[6] Eleo often spent four hours a day on horseback, joining in fox hunts and practicing for horse shows. Those who watched her demonstration of "whirlwind polo" came away convinced she could give even the best male players "a good run for the honors."[7] Eleo played softball wearing buttoned-up knickers and a newsboy's cap. She could drive a golf ball two hundred yards despite the stiffer clubs and balls that were then state-of-the-art. Eleo sometimes played, and walked, as many as forty-five holes of golf in a single day, but she found the standard game too slow to give it her full attention. In everything Eleo did, she cared more about winning than became a lady, but because she was pretty and popular with both sexes, because she carried herself like a lady and looked reassuringly feminine in evening clothes, she was hailed as "a thoroughly womanly woman [who] loves everything that every woman of good taste should love."[8]

Few women of Eleo's social class took sports competition seriously enough to train for and achieve a level of excellence that commanded attention. Sporting contests were tailored to a woman's presumed lack of stamina. Women's lawn tennis competitions were decided in two sets of three, whereas men had to win three sets of five. Female combatants faced off across the tennis net in ruffled dresses and bonnets that looked more appropriate for an afternoon tea party. They put the ball in play with an underhand serve, in part because their corsets and cumbersome tight-waisted dresses did not permit more determined action. In mixed doubles they paired with genial young men, themselves smartly groomed in starched white flannel shirts and trousers and sturdy leather shoes, who gallantly made up for the shortcomings of their female partners. An atmosphere of goodwill pervaded the sport. Clever shots by opposing players were saluted, and players were often the first to call missed points against themselves. The great charm of the lawn tennis scene derived as much from this code of sportsmanship as from the graceful inefficiency of its dress.

Imposing clubhouses with long, columned porticos offered a picturesque backdrop for the game. The audience, mostly friends and relatives of the players, arranged itself around the grass courts on short benches and wooden folding chairs. Men in straw boaters and ladies in white linen summer frocks and broad-brimmed bonnets encouraged and applauded all the players. For a long while, even as the decades passed and styles relaxed, lawn tennis, as played in the protected setting of the country club, exuded the "wonderful sense of leisure being used with good taste and decency."9

It is not surprising that Eleo became a tennis star, given her family's close identification with the sport. Buoyed by youthful exuberance and the challenge to her skill and strength, Eleo thrived on the atmosphere of athletic competition—the focused exertion of the practice sessions, the tingle of nerves as the contest began, the drama that unfolded before an aroused audience, and the comradeship of the postgame social events. Eleo preferred the men's fast-paced, aggressive style of play, and she was driven to test herself against them. She practiced their method of serving, throwing the ball up and whacking it overhand. She liked the way male players "chopped" the ball, sending it off with slices and sly cuts. It was a risky tactic but, when it worked, it yielded a quick and decisively won point.

In 1903, at the age of twenty-one, Eleo dominated women's lawn tennis on the East Coast. She had found her calling—competitive sports—but her athletic attire showed that she was not yet ready to flout all the conventions of the time, or to display the full range of her other, as yet unacknowledged, inclinations. Through her early twenties, Eleo appeared on the courts at the Newport Casino wearing fetching sporting costumes with skirts that reached within inches of her ankles. Skirts with modestly shortened hem lengths were known as "health skirts." For most female players, their long skirts gave them less trouble than their floppy, flyaway hats. Eleo's innovation, quickly copied by other socialite players, was the "grandmother veil," which she created by tying a length of white chiffon around a small sailor hat that she anchored jauntily under her chin with a large bow. In this ornamental chapeau Eleo conquered the top female players from Massachusetts, New York, and Maryland, as well as many of the better male players. Eleo took particular pleasure in playing mixed doubles, and she was offended by men who softened their shots because ladies were present. She didn't need such help, as she proved in win after win with her male partners. The *Boston Globe* highlighted Eleo's sports accomplishments and, because she was a girl, they also graded her appearance. Eleo won their approval by being "extremely handsome . . . the perfect type of a blonde," and the paper proclaimed her "the tennis queen of Newport."[10]

It was a heady time to be part of the Newport social scene, where Gilded Age fortunes minted in New York, Philadelphia, and Baltimore came together for brief summer seasons of giddy and absurd extravagance. Wealth beyond dreams had been amassed by visionary, audacious, and insatiable men who built industrial empires largely unencumbered by laws or taxes. These titans of oil, railroads, and finance brought their competitive drive to Newport, spending tens of millions to build ravishing summer "cottages," styled after the châteaus and palazzos of Europe. The front gates of these behemoths studded Bellevue Avenue and Ocean Drive like exclamation marks, and their manicured rear lawns overlooked the Atlantic Ocean. Their interiors were decorated with the choicest treasures, paintings, sculptures, and altars, which were shipped home from the Old World by the boatload. Platoons of household staff and groundskeepers earned their livelihoods by caring for these tycoons and their possessions.

The main business of the Newport season was the giving and attending of parties where the expectation was for conspicuous spending and unflinching creativity. The festivities might include dining on horseback or fending off roving packs of monkeys. The job of Society Hostess was not for the faint of heart. She needed the managerial skills of a field marshal to organize and direct the designers, dressmakers, gardeners, housekeepers, musicians, chefs, and serving staff that her entertainments required. It helped also to have the hide of an elephant, because everywhere lurked crevasses of envy, contempt, or pity. One's friends were always alert to pounce at the first sign of weakness. In this hotbed atmosphere, Harry Lehr, the calculating pet of society matrons, could say with only a trace of humor to the prominent Mr. and Mrs. Stuyvesant Fish when they rose to leave early from a party, "Sit down, Fishes, you're not rich enough to leave first."[11]

Masquerade balls were a staple entertainment, much as they were for the English aristocracy who the New World lords so admired and worked so hard to emulate. The guests impersonated the gamut of European royalty, but the American moneyed class could never quite manage the stultifying formality that was embedded in the English psyche and that defined Victorian society at the turn of the century. The Newport revelers behaved more like spoiled, wide-eyed children loose in a toy store where nothing was out of reach. One Newport hostess was concerned that the backdrop for her upcoming garden party offered nothing but a placid expanse of ocean and sky. She arranged with the Department of the Navy to borrow decommissioned battleships, which made an impressive statement as tugboats pulled them back and forth across the horizon. Yet another hostess indulged her guests with a favorite game of childhood. She had them tunnel merrily through a deep layer of sand that was spread over her dining table, digging with small sterling silver garden tools for their party favors among $10,000 worth of buried precious gems.

Proper Bostonians looked down the coast at these revelers and turned up their noses, repelled by such goings on. Eleo's great-grandfather David Sears II had been among the first to recognize the scenic pleasures of Newport and to appreciate its deep harbors. He built a three-story, English-style mansion on a promontory off Old Beach Road and kept his yacht in the harbor. Few of Boston's leading families followed him, choosing instead to migrate north along the shores of Massachusetts and Maine, thus ceding the field to the barons of business from the Middle Atlantic states. The old-line New England aristocrats failed to appreciate that the world of this newer breed of the "merely-rich" was bounded by rules that were every bit as demanding as those that governed their own.

One might disdain the excesses of the Newport playground, but who, if offered a chance to join in the fun, would really turn down the invitation? For the younger set, which placed no value on understatement, Newport was an irresistible draw. Well-connected youths flocked to this crossroads of summer pleasure to play sports and pair up. For Eleo, who had often felt stifled by the pinched rectitude of Boston, Newport offered happy times, and its summer residents were delighted to have her as a guest. Eleo's brash sense of humor and imaginative escapades were like a refreshing breeze during the frivolous season. July might find Eleo staying at Tower Top, the estate owned by the New York banker William H. Sands, as a guest of his daughter Anita. After winning the Women's Singles Lawn Tennis Championship, Eleo joined forces with Anita's brother, Harold, and won the Mixed Doubles title as well. Eleo was a regular guest also of the Widener family, well-known art collectors and horse-racing enthusiasts, who controlled the trolley car business in Philadelphia.

Alice Roosevelt, the president's famously headstrong daughter, loved the life and the people of Newport for exactly the reasons that her father loathed them. Alice had lost her mother just days after she was born, and she had grown up feeling neglected by her father and resented by her stepmother. Alice fought back with bratty, attention-getting stunts. She smoked in public, danced until the sun came up, played poker with congressmen, and jumped fully dressed into a shipboard swimming pool. The president was often forced to deflect criticism of his eldest daughter's antics. He explained that he could either run the country or control Alice, but he "couldn't possibly do both." Alice was well suited to the lavish, madcap nonsense of the Newport scene.

Though she was not able to participate on an equal financial footing with the flashy young crowd, they offered her the acceptance and attention that she craved. If she embarrassed her father by cavorting with the children of the very business monopolists he was targeting, so much the better. People across the nation adored this unruly, dark-eyed beauty who liked to practice looking sultry, and they thought of her as their American princess. Women named their babies Alice and ordered gowns in "Alice blue."

As a child, Alice Roosevelt had found a brief but loving refuge with her maternal grandparents at their Boston home on Beacon Street, where she played with her Cabot family cousins and first got to know Eleo. The two girls were well matched, both daredevils and determinedly independent. They grandly dismissed the pampered young men in their set as "mollycoddles." Eleo may have intimidated some in their crowd, but not Alice, who observed that Eleo "snarled a lot, but with great wit." Eleo, she said, "couldn't have been more fun."[12]

Another of Eleo's unconventional Newport friends was sparkling Nancy Langhorne. Alice Roosevelt thought Nancy was a showoff and confessed to jealousy because Nancy could turn cartwheels with ease. Nancy Langhorne was one of five comely sisters from Virginia, and one of the four who joined the northward stream of poor Southern girls who hoped to marry Yankee money. At the age of eighteen Nancy rushed into a brief marriage with Eleo's cousin Robert Gould Shaw II, a noted playboy, polo player, and drinker. Nancy obtained a judicial separation from Robbie in 1901, and a divorce two years later, citing his adultery. The Boston crowd, always slow to let down the bar to outsiders, was not kindly disposed to this Southern belle who had divorced one of their own. They also disapproved, with good reason, of Nancy's erratic mothering of her young son. Nancy sailed off to England, where she enchanted titled society with her elegant looks, needle-sharp sense of humor, and fearlessness in the saddle.

Eleo was admired and courted by many eligible young men, but Harold Stirling Vanderbilt, who had grown up in the social vortex of Newport, was her most determined suitor. His friends called him Mike, though he always remained Harold to his mother and sister. Mike Vanderbilt loved adventure at breakneck speed, and at the age of twelve he had captained his own yacht, but he was more complex and serious-minded than that would suggest. He was so analytical and rigorous in his interests that his mother nicknamed him "Professor." Mike was three years younger than Eleo. The tall Harvard freshman was still a bit gangly, but that he would become a handsome man was unmistakable. Eleo was flattered by his interest, but his attentions were premature and she didn't take them seriously. Mike's family credentials, however, were most impressive and of particular interest to Eleo because the Boston crowd viewed the Vanderbilts as New York upstarts with a shady past. Mike's father was the astonishingly wealthy William Kissam Vanderbilt, a mild-mannered grandson of "Commodore" Cornelius Vanderbilt. As a young man, the Commodore had piloted a ferryboat between Staten Island and the Battery. Though lacking education and social graces, he parlayed the ferry boat into a fleet, then into a railroad, and amassed a fortune of $105,000,000, which, at the time of his death in 1877, was the largest estate in American history.

One source of Mike Vanderbilt's infatuation with Eleo set him apart from her other admirers. Mike had learned at a tender age, from watching his mother's fierce manipulations, that great misery could be meted out to gentle souls by more domineering ones. Eleo's self-confident, independent nature was for him uniquely reassuring. He understood that Eleo would never allow herself to be under anyone's thumb, not even his.

Mike's mother, Alva Vanderbilt, was a dynamic woman of shrewd intelligence and towering ambition. She also had taken notice of Eleo and had begun to look on her as a potential daughter-in-law. Alva's own family, the socially prominent Smiths from Mobile, Alabama, had been thrust into genteel poverty after business reversals and losses in the stock market crash of 1873. Alva marched north and avoided a precarious future by marrying Willie Vanderbilt. The marriage went sour on their wedding night. Alva thereafter comforted herself by using Willie's money in a coldly calculated, and ultimately successful, climb to the pinnacle of New York society. In her youth Alva had fought with boys who laughed at her for being short and pudgy. She choked them and punched them when they taunted her for being unable to run fast or climb trees because she was only a girl. Later she would use other weapons to wring respect from the hard-core arbiters of New York's social caste system, who dismissed the Vanderbilts as boors and their fortune as nouveau.

Fiercely guarding the gates to New York society was Caroline Astor, who had whittled down the number of people she considered acceptable to four hundred. Alva Vanderbilt was nowhere among them. Mrs. Astor might have had the Vanderbilts in mind when she explained her refusal to receive a wealthy businessman in her home, "Just because I buy my carpets from him, does not mean I have to invite him to walk on them."[13]

Alva Vanderbilt hired the architect Richard Morris Hunt and together they designed an entrancing limestone château, which they plunked down in the heart of Manhattan, at 660 Fifth Avenue, diagonally across from St. Patrick's Cathedral. Alva's home put Mrs. Astor's narrow brownstone in the shade, but Mrs. Astor would not capitulate. Alva plotted her next move with her closest friend, Consuelo Yznaga, who had shared Alva's girlhood as a ruffian in Mobile. Known now as Lady Mandeville after her brilliant match with the eldest son of Britain's seventh Duke of Manchester, the former Consuelo Yznaga was the toast of New York society. Alva and her friend hatched a crafty plan for a medieval costume ball to mark the formal opening of Alva's mansion. Their audacious guest list of twelve hundred included all the cream—the formidable Four Hundred. Alva promoted this brazen move with the cunning of a seasoned public relations tout. Soon the entire city was speculating about the medieval ball and the splendors inside her white château. Then, when anticipation had built to a fever pitch, Alva let it be known that no invitation to Mrs. Astor's daughter, Carrie, would be forthcoming. Carrie and her friends were already practicing to dance in the Star Quadrille, a prominent feature of the ball. The girl was devastated. The battle was over. Mrs. Astor sent her coachman around to the Vanderbilt mansion with an invitation to call.

On March 26, 1883, the day after Easter, New York police cordoned off the huge crowds that crammed every vantage point along Fifth Avenue to watch the parade of carriages carrying the astonishingly costumed partygoers to the Vanderbilt mansion. The lavishness of the display incited little envy or resentment from the public, which was thrilled to be a peripheral part of the spectacle, like fans watching the glitterati arrive for a Hollywood awards ceremony. The Vanderbilts' guests were ushered into the Great Hall by footmen in powdered wigs. The upstairs maids were dressed as French peasants. Alva Vanderbilt, resplendent as a Venetian Renaissance countess, presided over the orchestras, the banquet, and the midnight supper. After that night, no major social enterprise in the city was undertaken without consulting her. People would nod to each other knowingly as the Vanderbilts' gleaming, maroon-lacquered carriages rolled by, leaving a tingle of excitement in their wake. Nor was this the last time Alva would reveal that within her "cute Pekingese" exterior there beat "the heart of a pit bull terrier."[14]

Alva was strict with her three children. They spoke only French with their parents, and they felt the sting of Alva's riding crop across the backs of their legs if their behavior deviated from her commandments. Alva's emotional strength was matched by her physical courage. She did not hesitate to throw herself in front of a runaway pony cart that was carrying her nine-year-old daughter.

Alva's first-born, Consuelo, was named for Alva's esteemed childhood friend, and it was this slender girl who bore the brunt of Alva's fierce temper and iron will. From the moment of Consuelo's birth, Alva was determined that her daughter would marry foreign nobility, and she molded Consuelo into a consort fit for royalty. To develop aristocratic bearing, Alva forced her to wear a metal back brace that attached around her forehead. Consuelo said later that her mother controlled the family like pawns on a chess board. At seventeen, Consuelo was married off to the ninth Duke of Marlborough. The ancestral home of the Marlboroughs, Blenheim Palace, was one of the grandest of England's stately homes, but it cried out for maintenance. The duke

Sears family gathering, circa 1893. Eleo is at left end of back row. Freddy is in front of her in second row. Her parents are fourth and fifth from left in back row. Uncle Richard Dudley Sears is second from right in back row. Grandfather Fredrick is in center. (Sears family archive)

Eleo with her mother in Paris, circa 1894.
(Sears family archive)

Portrait of Eleo in Paris, age thirteen, by John White Alexander.
(Author collection)

Eleo's uncle Richard Dudley Sears, America's
first national tennis champion, 1880s.
(Sears family archive)

Lawn tennis at Newport Casino, 1891.
(Wimbledon Museum, reprinted in *American Lawn Tennis*)

Beacon Street after a snowstorm, 1901. (The Bostonian Society)

Eleo's grandfather Thomas Jefferson
Coolidge. (J. Linzee Coolidge)

Eleo in June 1901.
(Burt and Kathy Goldblatt)

Another portrait of Eleo in June 1901
(Library of Congress)

The Marble Mansion on Coolidge Point. (J. Linzee Coolidge)

Eleo relaxing at home in Beverly Farms, circa 1905. (Sears family archive)

On the beach with friends, Coronado, California, February 1905. (Sears family archive)

Cast members of the 1905 Vincent Club show featuring *Alice in Wonderland,* left to right: Bettina Parks as the White Rabbit, Eleo as a Huzzar, Colette Dumaresq as Peddie Perkins, and Elizabeth Porter as the Mad Hatter.

Eleo at a costume party with
Harold "Mike" Vanderbilt, circa 1906.
(Sears family archive)

Eleo with her doubles partner Marion Fenno (left) after winning the singles and doubles titles at the Pennsylvania and Eastern States Championships, Merion (Pa.) Cricket Club, 1908. (*American Lawn Tennis*)

"Miss Sears wants to play polo," Coronado, California, circa 1910. (Library of Congress)

Claude Grahame-White in his monoplane above the Brockton, Massachusetts, fairgrounds, 1910. (Author collection)

Learning to fly with Claude Grahame-White, 1910. (Author collection)

Eleo wins riding sidesaddle at a horse show, 1911. (Boston Public Library)

Eleo on Radiant, circa 1911. (Sears family archive)

With Henry Lee (left) and Francis Carolan in Burlingame,
California, 1912. (Henry Lee Jr.)

Skating with Princess Patricia of Connaught (left),
1912. (Sears family archive)

A style all her own, 1912.
(Sears family archive)

Eleo behind the wheel of a new Simplex, winter 1913. (Henry Lee Jr.)

Eleo driving four-in-hand at Rockmarge, August 22, 1914.
(From *Boston Sunday Post*)

Outside Congressional Union headquarters in Newport, 1914. Alva Belmont is in second row, second from left. (Sewall-Belmont House and Museum)

resigned himself to a match with the Vanderbilt heiress, following in the footsteps of his forebears, who had also found wealthy American wives to keep their patrimony afloat.

By the mid-1890s, some five hundred American families had auctioned their daughters off to impoverished European lords. New World fortunes had eclipsed the vanishing glory of the titled families of Europe. In proportion to their decline, the Europeans viewed these rich colonials with barely veiled contempt. Both sides, though, were willing to strike a deal. To pay the tax collectors, the threadbare royals sold off the contents of their family estates. Next came the sale of their lineage to American would-be princesses with fat dowries. The mothers of these heiresses, the wives of America's industrial empire builders, were intent on making the ultimate purchase, the respectability that Old World families had taken centuries to develop. Some Americans would not compromise their standards. In their quest to ally their daughters with the peerage, they would accept "no one beneath an Earl." European royals were less picky, if one can judge by the impressive marriage made by the unfortunate-looking daughter of the shady financier Jay Gould. Framed by Paris gowns and viewed through the prism of her father's vast fortune, Anna Gould could charitably be called "plain." She made a glittering, though ultimately unhappy, marriage with the French Comte de Castellane.

Alva Vanderbilt kept Consuelo locked in her room at Marble House, the Vanderbilts' summer home in Newport, until the teenager tearfully agreed to the arranged marriage. The duke's attorney drew up the contract, which specified an initial settlement of $2,500,000 in stock, $1,600,000 in cash, and an annual payment to the duke of $100,000. In 1895 America was mired in a three-year-long depression and the Vanderbilts received hate mail from people fearful of so much money leaving the country. The duke told Consuelo on their wedding night not that he loved her, but that she was "a link in a chain." Her eleven-year-old brother, Mike, observed sadly to his big sister, "You know he's only marrying you for your money."

What from a distance seems like breathtaking cruelty was for Alva Vanderbilt merely common sense. By marrying into British royalty, Consuelo would not have to fight for social standing, as her mother had done. An impressive marriage gave a woman the platform so crucial to the Victorian upper classes. Such a woman was taken seriously. Her opinions mattered, and the way was open for her to live an interesting and useful life. Alva believed that Consuelo would eventually see her marriage in that light and would thank her. These were ironclad assumptions at the time, but change was in the wind—and Alva herself would lead the crusade to change them. In the midst of negotiating the terms of Consuelo's marriage, Alva began divorce proceedings against her own husband of twenty years. She charged Willie Vanderbilt with adultery, of which he was many times guilty, though it was widely believed that Alva was not blameless on that score, either. Alva was one of the first women of prominence to risk the scandal of divorce, and many friends turned their backs on her. Alva hardened herself to ride out the storm, and the coup of having a daughter marry into the House of Marlborough helped insulate her and her family from the maelstrom of scorn she unleashed upon them.

CHAPTER 7

Of Motor Cars and Militants

⌁

BATTLING STRONG September winds and crashing waves, Eleo dove into the ocean off Bailey's Beach at the end of Cliff Walk. A small group of friends stood vigil on the gray sand as Eleo pulled away from the shore. Her arms and legs churned strongly as she fought against the tide that surged relentlessly against her and past her to devour the beach. Eleo's friends had learned to expect from her a determined recklessness, and she did not like to disappoint them. Weeks earlier, she had challenged Newport's rocky coast with a swim from Bailey's Beach to Easton Beach, a distance of some four and a half miles. Today's opponent was the weather. Many of Eleo's friends, including her hosts in Newport, Mr. and Mrs. Joseph Widener, had warned that the stormy weather would make the swim too dangerous, but she had laughed off their concern.

The young ladies who clustered together on the coarse, damp sand stood sideways to reduce the force of the wind, which flung their dresses about them. Eleo's receding form disappeared completely in the valleys of the ocean between the dark swells and reappeared, ever smaller, on the crest of the blue-black waves. Her bathing costume, knee-length black wool edged in white and black stockings below, was a daringly streamlined version of the poufy bathing dresses worn by most of the girls in 1904, which billowed around them like halos as they bobbed near the shore. Eleo's swim dress gave only a hint of her slim-hipped, small-breasted figure as it hung heavily with water and dragged against her every stroke.

Some of the fellows on alert from the beach prepared themselves for action by taking off their shoes and socks, and they stood barefoot in the nippy sand. They did not relish the idea of having to attempt a rescue under these conditions, but they were honor-bound to try. The gloomy sky parted briefly to show a weak snatch of blue that was quickly overwhelmed by great, gnarly storm clouds. For long, anxious minutes the group scanned the throbbing sea. They had completely lost sight of Eleo. Then, to their relief, they saw her, a speck standing on a raft anchored a mile out in the ocean, waving at them with both arms.

Eleo sat for just a few minutes on the raft in the chill air, as the platform bucked in the ocean. She spit up the sea water she had swallowed. She would have liked to lie flat on the wooden boards for a long while and rest and let the sea rock her, but her friends were waiting. She made a long, flat racing dive back into the sea and headed toward the shore. She didn't have to fight nearly as hard in this direction, and she enjoyed trying to match her stroke to the rise and fall of the waves that were bearing her home. The waiting young men mobilized. They hitched up their trouser legs and waded out into the foaming surf to meet her. Eleo was draped with blankets and hugs. Her friends among the twenty-something set were thrilled with yet another "Eleo story" they could tell. The older folks shook their heads, not knowing what to make of her. Eleo always bristled at criticism of her athletic ability that came from some quarters. "They've made me out a sort of Amazon, which isn't true," she complained, sounding truly wounded, "I'm only a girl who likes fun."[1]

When the future came rolling in on the thin, flimsy tires of the "horseless carriage," Eleo was one of the first women anywhere to drive an automobile and learn to do basic repairs. Undeniably, the automobile was a mechanical wonder, exhilarating in motion, but maddeningly difficult to keep in motion. Eleo was not deterred by the difficulty or the mess or the prevailing view that operating an automobile was wholly unsuitable for ladies.

The horseless carriage made its debut at the great Columbian Exposition in Chicago in 1893. The intriguing new machine was little more than an open wagon powered by a crude electric motor, but the crowds that surrounded the exhibit were fascinated. Many autos at the start of the twentieth century ran on steam, taking their cue from the locomotives that chugged across the continent. Stanley Steamers had single-cylinder engines that were fired up with acetylene torches that heated water in asbestos-covered boilers. Motorists or bystanders could suffer severe burns when the pressurized steam shot out or the pressure gauges exploded. On most autos a hand crank below the front grille started the process. It was sweaty and uncertain work, and a sudden backfire could spin the crank with enough force to break an arm or a jaw. The first automobiles were steered with tillers, and then with a wheel on the right side of the machine that required considerable arm strength to control. Companies that manufactured automobiles sent a representative along with each car sold to instruct the new owner in its use. The hazards of automobiling remained daunting, especially for older buyers. People who could afford such toys generally employed chauffeurs. Many of the most skillful drivers were French.

The few automobiles built for racing had bursts of speed reaching eighty to ninety miles per hour, but most had top speeds of less than fifteen miles per hour. Speed limits through towns along the North Shore were set at eight miles per hour, and violators were chased down and caught by policemen on horseback. Higher speeds were not always desirable, given the bone-jarring cobblestone streets in the cities and the unpaved roads beyond the city limits that enveloped travelers in clouds of dust. Intrepid female passengers looked ghostly as they sat huddled under shapeless linen dusters, with their hats tied down and their faces wrapped like mummies. Even canine passengers were outfitted with protective goggles.

Motorcars were extravagantly expensive as well as tricky to operate, and egalitarian-minded folks condemned them as playthings for the rich. From the perspective of those first years of the twentieth century, they undeniably were. When a workingman could purchase a nice sofa for less than ten dollars and a pound of corned beef for eight cents, and send a letter off with a two-cent postage stamp, automobile tires cost a formidable forty dollars apiece. The narrow tires, easily punctured and supported by fragile spokes, required constant patching and frequent replacement.

Carriage horses were given the generic name Lizzie, and before long the sputtering horseless carriages were dubbed Tin Lizzies. A horse was a far more dependable means of transportation. Automobilists expected their vehicles to break down and carried with them all manner of emergency equipment—shovels, air pumps, wrenches, and axes. Hazards in the early days of automobile travel were abundant and exotic. Angry citizens pursued invading autos on horseback, shouting oaths and shooting at the drivers. Farmers resented the city dudes who raced their machines down quiet country lanes on weekends, fouling the air and scaring the livestock.

Horses and automobiles coexisted uneasily for decades. In rural Pennsylvania farmers formed the Anti-Automobile Society and succeeded in passing an ordinance that required drivers of automobiles that frightened their horses to disassemble the vehicles and hide the pieces behind a bush until the horses had safely passed by. Autos were banned entirely along great swaths of Massachusetts' North Shore, where old-line families owned large estates and controlled miles of roads. In 1906 the great steeplechase horse Land of Clover was being exercised by a groom along a road in Manchester when he was struck by an automobile driven by C. S. Houghton of Coolidge Point. Clover was so badly injured that he had to be shot. As a lasting memorial, his distraught owner had two of Clover's hooves cut off and made into ink stands.

Many politicians and private citizens denounced the automobile and the chaos it brought, but there were those seers who cheerfully prognosticated that motorcars, being so much more compact than the horse-drawn trolleys that clogged the streets, would eventually reduce traffic congestion. This prediction, alas, proved to be no more accurate than earlier warnings that the ever-increasing use of horse-drawn vehicles would leave city streets paved knee-deep with manure.

Mike Vanderbilt's older brother, William K. II, was one of the earliest and most zealous auto enthusiasts. In Newport in 1900 he was hauled into court for continually violating both the town speed limit of six miles per hour and the ten-miles-per-hour limit in the surrounding countryside. Automobile devotees as a group viewed speed limits as a personal affront. Willie K. had two goals in mind when he organized the Vanderbilt Cup Race, America's first great international automobile race. He was keen to promote the sport of automobiling in general, and he wanted to encourage American automakers who were lagging behind their counterparts in Europe.[2] Fifty thousand spectators converged on Long Island at six o'clock in the morning on October 8, 1904, for the 28.4-mile race, which was won by an American driver who bested the seventeen entrants in a French-built car.[3]

Mike Vanderbilt shared his older brother's fascination with automobiles. Mike owned several enormous open touring cars and some relatively more compact racing models. He had sped through his undergraduate studies at Harvard in three years and immediately began working toward his law degree. His principal release from the pressure of his studies came from driving his cars at eye-popping speeds along narrow dirt roads that had been laid out with only horses in mind. Eleo was equally in love with cars and speed and she was one of the few people willing to risk riding in a car with Mike. Mike and Eleo raced autos around Willie's racetrack on Long Island. They discovered they were a comfortable fit on many fronts and increasingly they were seen together. All Newport held its breath as Eleo led Mike through what appeared to be a series of tests. She had him diving with her from cliffs and swimming the mile and a quarter from Misery Island to Beverly Beach on the North Shore. He raced her on horseback, staying in the saddle from five o'clock in the morning until Eleo was ready to go in for breakfast at nine. He was with her on the ocean in good weather and bad, adding his extensive knowledge of sailing to her already considerable skill. Mike was her partner for hours of golf and tennis, and then in the evenings they danced until the small hours. Mike was unshakable through it all, and he steadily earned Eleo's respect and affection.

At the costume balls that Mike's mother still loved to host, Mike might arrive in flowing satin robes, looking like a supersized Lawrence of Arabia, with Eleo by his side, laughing in her multicolor jester suit and large ruffled collar. It was at costume parties that Eleo displayed her taste for the absurd and a self-deprecating sense of humor that was unexpected and disarming. To a costume party that Mike and Eleo attended early in their relationship, Mike dressed as a barefoot country gent. Eleo came as his chauffeur in a shapeless duster that she fastened at the neck with tiny flowers. She blackened her face with what looked like road dirt and topped off this odd vision with Mike's oversized straw boater.

Eleo could switch easily into her glamour mode when the occasion demanded it. For Newport's over-the-top parties, or for the evening events that followed the weeklong horse shows at Madison Square Garden, a continual parade of new outfits was expected, and Eleo excelled at competitive dressing. She was dazzling in cutting-edge gowns that she wore with confidence, with her hair swept up to dramatize her eyes. Her arrival at a party added a spark to the occasion, and she seemed to have a light around her. The California-born tennis star May Sutton, who over many years was both Eleo's opponent and partner on the tennis court, admired Eleo's sense of style and proclaimed her "the most attractive and best-dressed woman in Newport."[4]

Crucial to Mike's budding courtship of Eleo was the consent of Mike's mother. Had Alva stood against them, it is unlikely that Mike would have persevered in his pursuit. Alva heartily approved of the outdoor diversions that Eleo dreamed up for her son, whose innate studiousness and sensitivity she had always considered inadequate preparation for a harsh world. Alva believed that Mike would benefit immensely from Eleo's brand of toughening up. On paper, from Alva's side, a prospective alliance with Eleo Sears looked only modestly advantageous. Compared to the wealth of the Vanderbilts, the Sears millions were small potatoes. Alva had established the Vanderbilt family as a major power in New York society. She had engineered a divorce, persevered through disgrace, remarried well, and married her daughter off to a duke. Eleo's ties to the First Families of New England, though desirable, were unlikely to be of much use to her. Yet Alva felt a true kinship with this bold girl who so often defied society's expectations and who daily was a reminder of the strength and capability of the modern woman. For many years Alva followed Eleo's progress with the greatest interest and admiration.

Eleo became increasingly serious about refining her tennis skills, and she soon discarded bows and lace, first for a simple white linen dress, and then for a boy's button-down white shirt, a skirt that stopped just below her knees, and a long, dark, sleeveless tunic which she called (and it probably was) "grandfather's vest." In June 1908 Eleo won the Singles Championship of Pennsylvania and the Eastern States in the tournament held at the Merion Cricket Club in the Philadelphia suburbs. Eleo and her reliable tennis partner, the pretty, doe-eyed Marion Fenno, captured the doubles title as well. Always deeply tanned, Eleo squinted resolutely into the sun as she faced off against her opponents, her dark blonde hair tied back and her sleeves rolled up. She was agile and outspoken, and her play was frequently brilliant, but she lacked the patience to maintain long, grinding rallies. Eleo hit hard and liked to try daring but low-percentage "chop" shots that led, all too often, to unforced errors. (As one tennis father cautioned his son, "The way of the chopper is hard.") Even when she lost, Eleo seemed to be in command of the court. "It is a pleasure to watch her," Alva wrote in her diary; "her individuality is so marked and so unusually attractive."[5] Alva saw herself as a Woman of the Future, and she came to see Eleo as her surrogate daughter. Both women felt an almost mystical bond from the coincidence that both Eleo and Alva's daughter, Consuelo, were schooled, years apart, by the same governess in Paris.

The "new" Alva Vanderbilt carved out a leading role for herself in the fight for women's suffrage, a direction she took not long after her ruthless union of Consuelo with the Duke of Marlborough and her own divorce. Both of those transactions were finalized in 1895. Within months Alva was married to Oliver Hazard Perry Belmont, formerly a close friend of her ex-husband. Alva shuttered Marble House, except for its laundry facilities, where she continued to send her washing and ironing, and moved two blocks away to Belmont's baronial mansion, Belcourt. Alva's divorce was surely stain enough on her reputation, but much about her new husband riled her peers. On the plus side, Belmont was a successful financier and horse breeder, but he had also been a Democratic congressman from New York, and there were whispers of a Jewish branch on the Belmont family tree. In relaunching herself as Mrs. O. H. P. Belmont, Alva faced another avalanche of scandal and gossip that this alliance provoked.

From this storm, too, the unsinkable Alva emerged triumphant. Her influence remained intact—she could still make or break an aspiring entrant into New York society with a nod. It was the sameness of her life in the aftermath of the cataclysms she had wrought that changed Alva. She saw with new clarity the way she had shaped her own destiny by hurling her will against the world. Alva had always been clear about what she wanted, and she had taken what she wanted without waiting for permission from any man. Women around the globe were awakening to the reality that, though they might be at times the "power behind the throne," they were second-class citizens with no political voice. In most parts of the world, women had no right to own property, no right to keep their own earnings, and a less than equal chance to retain custody of their own children. Women began organizing and petitioning, then marching and demanding, that the male ruling class grant them the right to vote. Alva had always been offended by the idea of second best, and she became a leading and tireless crusader in the battle for women's suffrage.

Already decades old at the dawn of the twentieth century, the state-by-state struggle of American women for the right to vote had yielded meager results. Resentment built as women saw that Negro men, foreign immigrants, and Indians were being given a right that was denied to them. A powerful collection of "wet" business interests (those engaged in the production and sale of alcohol) were forcefully arrayed against the suffragists. The strident pro-Temperance faction of the women's suffrage movement provoked the realistic fear that the ladies would use their vote to banish alcohol. It was this fear that delayed voting rights for women for generations.[6] Siding with the liquor industry were tobacco manufacturers, railroad men, ranchers, and the hotel industry. These opponents liked to define a suffragist as a woman "who has ceased to be a lady and not yet become a gentleman."[7]

Opposition came also from women of the Massachusetts upper class. This influential group was centered in conservative Boston, where the Association Opposed to Suffrage for Women was formed in 1890. It was not that these well-educated females, known as the "Anti's," were pleased with male rule, but rather that they were more distrustful of the judgment of ordinary women. As one Boston gentlewoman put it, women's suffrage meant "no more than adding one quart of muddy water to another quart of muddy water. You get two quarts, but it's the same kind of water."[8] They worried too that they would be net losers in the trade-off between the privileges they already enjoyed and the rights they stood to gain. Suffragists dismissed these women, who were content to be cared for and governed by men, as clinging vines.

On a pleasantly cool spring day in 1909, Eleo Sears was in Burlingame, California, dressed impeccably in male-inspired polo attire, when she challenged a group of American and British players to include her in their polo match. Weeks later, Eleo traveled to London with Alva Belmont to attend the International Women's Conference. The keynote speaker, Carrie Chapman Catt, had succeeded Susan B. Anthony as the president of the National American Woman Suffrage Association. Mrs. Chapman Catt had signed a prenuptial agreement with her husband in 1890 that allowed her to devote two months in the spring and two months in the fall to suffrage work.

Mrs. Chapman Catt and the speakers who followed her denounced the routine male claim that the act of voting would cause women to "neglect the interests of maidenhood, of wifeliness, of maternity."[9] The conference leaders reproached the international community for foot-dragging. Only in Australia and Tasmania did women have full voting rights. Eleo listened to the speakers predict the certain end of centuries of "sexual serfdom" and proclaim that no "*human* power, no university professor, no Parliament, no government, can stay its coming."[10] These declarations gave form and context to the ideas that Eleo had begun acting on in recent years. The English suffragettes also advised women to resist paying taxes to any government that denied them the vote. Their rallying cry was "No Vote, No Tax."

Consuelo, the Duchess of Marlborough, introduced her mother to the more militant women's movement in England, which had taken root there shortly after it had surfaced in the United States. Consuelo was now formally separated from the duke. During the eleven unhappy years that Consuelo and the duke had been "condemned" to live together, Consuelo had large floral centerpieces placed on the dining table at Blenheim Palace, so that she did not have to watch her husband eat. She satisfied her part of the marriage bargain by bearing the duke two sons, "an heir and a spare," as she wryly noted. Consuelo moved out of Blenheim with relief, convinced that the vast gloomy pile did not contain one livable room, but Alva, assisted by Oliver Belmont, continued faithfully to upgrade the palace through the years, as they had agreed. Despite all that had passed between them, Consuelo and her mother began a gradual reconciliation, especially after Oliver Belmont died suddenly in 1908 and left Alva grief-stricken. In the end it was Alva herself who enlisted the help of Winston Churchill, a cousin and confidant of the duke, to convince him to grant Consuelo the annulment she longed for.[11]

Inspired by the International Suffrage Conference that Alva attended with Eleo, Alva hosted a fund-raising event for the women's movement at Marble House. On August 24, 1909, a large crowd of committed suffragists and the merely curious swarmed over Alva's property, paying one dollar to walk about the grounds and listen to prosuffrage speeches, and five dollars to tour the mansion itself. Twenty-five-year-old Mike Vanderbilt was embarrassed by the spectacle his mother was making of herself and he declined to participate.

Mike did come chivalrously to Eleo's defense not long after. In October 1909 Eleo was summoned to appear at the Police Court in Quincy, Massachusetts, to answer a speeding charge. She was the first woman in the country known to fight a speeding ticket. Mike was a month into his third year at Harvard Law School, and he volunteered to be Eleo's defense counsel. Eleo and Mike took the train from Boston to Quincy, where Mike's mother met them. Alva sat in the back of the courtroom and watched her son handle his first case. Mike began by advising his client to enter a plea of not guilty. Police Officer William S. Fallon testified that on October 7 he witnessed a big touring car, which reached speeds of up to forty miles per hour, racing through the streets of Milton. He followed the car for a mile and a half before he was able to overtake it and bring it to a halt. The driver was wearing a man's black derby hat, a long overcoat, and riding boots. Officer Fallon was amazed to discover that the driver was none other than Miss Eleonora Sears. When the officer left the stand, Mike leaned over and whispered to Eleo. She stood up and explained lamely to the judge, "Your Honor, I was going no more than thirty miles an hour." Judge Avery banged his gavel and ruled, "You are fined $15, Miss Sears."[12] The judge accepted Mike's offer of a plea of nolo contendere. Eleo tried to look repentant as she paid the fine.

CHAPTER 8

Wedding Bells and Porcellian Blues

AMERICA WAS FAIRLY bursting with the news that Alice Roosevelt was to be married at the White House. The entire country was infatuated with this irrepressible daughter of a dynamic and popular president, and no detail of her upcoming nuptials was too trivial to report. Alice's wedding dress was known to involve twenty-six yards of white satin brocade, but the pattern was a closely guarded document and the weavers were sworn to secrecy. Wedding gifts poured in from around the globe. The Dowager Empress of China sent jewels and silks and ermine robes. The Cuban National Congress voted to spend $25,000 for a pearl necklace. A friend sent a Boston terrier puppy from champion bloodlines. The puppy, named Fashion, came with a gold and jeweled collar, a sterling silver comb-and-brush set, and a sweater knitted in Alice blue.

Alice Roosevelt's intended, Ohio Congressman Nicholas Longworth, was fifteen years older than Alice and famously bald, but he was smart, self-assured, and entertaining, and Alice never had any patience for boys. To the nation generally Nick Longworth appeared to be "a sturdy and good-humored fellow," and he was embraced in a countrywide bear hug as the national bridegroom. Nick had an undisguised fondness for wine and women, and he had been engaged before, to a sister of Alice's friend Nancy Langhorne, but Alice was not deterred.[1] She was primed for marriage and eager to escape her quarrelsome life at home. She may have behaved as if she wasn't afraid of the devil, but she was sensitive to society's subtle pressures. Alice was approaching her twenty-second year, and by common consent, she had already passed her peak marital moment. Conventional wisdom predicted, Alice noted with gallows humor, that if you had been "out" for two or three years and were still not married, "you ended up with a thermos of tea in your room alone."[2]

Eight hundred guests crowded into the sun-flooded East Room of the White House on February 17, 1906, for the fifteen-minute ceremony. Most of those invited were dignitaries from home and abroad, but Alice insisted that her friends from New York, Boston, and Newport be included. Eleo Sears was on the coveted guest list, as were the Vanderbilts, Astors, Fricks, Whitneys, Saltonstalls, and Ethel Barrymore, who was an old friend of the groom. The Marine band played and Alice cut her wedding cake with a sword. Bells rang out in churches and courthouses across the land to mark the glorious day. The Roosevelt-Longworth wedding was considered by many to be an act of God. A New York lawyer missed a trial date to attend the ceremony, and opposing counsel demanded compensation. A justice of the New York Supreme Court held that attendance at the wedding was a justified excuse.

Alice's father, Theodore Roosevelt, was riding high as he presided over his daughter's wedding. He had been reelected by a landslide to a second term as president, after landing in the top job by the back door when he finished the term of the slain president William McKinley. At the time T.R. had been just forty-two years old, the youngest man to occupy the White House. Teddy's swaggering style and progressive ideas upset many career politicians, and when he was tapped to be McKinley's vice president, Republican Chairman Mark Hanna exclaimed, "Don't any of you realize, there's only one life between that madman and the Presidency?"[3] His alarm seemed prophetic later.

President McKinley was shaking hands in a receiving line at the Pan-American Exposition in Buffalo in September 1901 when a Polish anarchist pumped two bullets into his stomach. The president was rushed by electric ambulance to the nearby home of the director of the exposition, where a hastily assembled medical team botched the operation to remove the bullets.[4] Gangrene set in, and over the next eight days the doctors helplessly charted the president's decline and death. The haphazard, rudimentary medical technology that contributed to McKinley's death seemed to underscore his place as the last president of the nineteenth century. Teddy Roosevelt, boyish and bursting with energy, personified the vigorous young country as it began a new century.

From Roosevelt's vantage point, Nicholas Longworth was all he could have hoped for in a son-in-law. Nick was on the cusp of a great political career, and the president looked to Nick's age and experience to provide a counterweight to his wayward daughter. Nick and his well-established family hailed from America's heartland, and T.R. detested the trans-Atlantic trade of wealthy American girls for European titles. Topping the inventory of Nick's virtues was his membership in the Porcellian Club. Nick's new wife liked to describe Harvard's most exclusive social club as "the biggest snob thing you could imagine," where the members called each other "Brother," sang patriotic songs, and "drank each other under the table." The insignia of the Porcellian Club was the head of a wild boar. Eleo's father was a "Porc," as was her brother, her grandfather, and many of her uncles. Other noted members of the Porcellian Club, besides Theodore Roosevelt, were Oliver Wendell Holmes (both father and son), Henry Cabot Lodge, and Owen Wister, the author of the first great western novel, *The Virginian*.

Theodore Roosevelt was the role model for another, younger Roosevelt—Alice's cousin Franklin. Franklin attended Alice's wedding with his mother. His own bride, Eleanor, was six months pregnant with their first child, and, having entered her period of confinement, she remained out of the public eye. Franklin Roosevelt and Eleo Sears had known each other for many years and had ridden together in Central Park. Eleo had also been to a luncheon at Franklin's Hyde Park home at the invitation of his devoted mother, Sarah.

Franklin was a freshman at Harvard when his recently widowed mother moved to Boston to be near him. He was not getting on well with his schoolmates, and his mother's proximity added weight to their charge that he was a momma's boy. Franklin's smooth, pretty-boy looks and his fluttery mannerisms made him the target of picturesque taunts, such as "Rosey Roosevelt, Lily of the Valley."

Franklin was active in the Republican Club at school to support his cousin Teddy's political career, but his bid to impress his cousin foundered when he failed to win a place on Harvard's football team. Franklin set his heart too on joining the Porcellian Club, the ultimate bastion of belonging. His own late father had been a Porc, and preference was usually given to legacy candidates. Franklin was devastated when the club did not offer him a place, and the rejection left a lasting wound. To his roommate Franklin lamented that he never was chosen for the best things. Later he confided the depths of his disappointment to Eleanor, who always believed that this blow left Franklin with an inferiority complex.

At Alice's wedding Franklin endured further humiliation when the president retired to his private dining room with a contingent of his fellow Porcs. The select group included Teddy's new son-in-law and the Reverend Endicott Peabody, the headmaster of Groton, Franklin's alma mater. Peabody had officiated at Franklin's wedding to Eleanor the year before, and T.R. had given the bride away. But now, from the wrong side of the dining room door, Franklin could hear this chosen band of Porcs singing club songs, smoking cigars, and drinking toasts to Brother Longworth and Brother Roosevelt. Decades later Franklin had not forgotten his hurt, and he admitted that his rejection by the Porcellian Club was "the worst disappointment" of his life."[6]

The wedding guests pelted the newlyweds with rice as they sped away from the White House. Their getaway car was the French-built electric car that had won the first Vanderbilt Cup race and had since been enlarged as a limousine. Alice and Nick traveled to England not long after their honey-moon and were the guests of honor at a reception given by Ambassador Whitelaw Reid. Alice found herself seated between King Edward VII and the Duke of Marlborough. The king was said to have been charmed by Alice's dignity. The duke enjoyed Alice's irreverent commentary. Alice remembered him as "a bad little man, rather mean but amusing." The duke invited the Longworths to lunch at Blenheim Palace, where he began quizzing Alice, "Do you know Eleonora Sears?" He shared his suspicion that Eleo was working hard to catch a Vanderbilt. Eleo's growing attachment to Consuelo's younger brother was a topic of interest among England's best families. With the duke's marriage to Consuelo dissolving, he thought it prudent to keep track of any-one who might make a claim on her family's money. He assumed that Eleo's interest was as mercenary as his own.

While their relationship was being discussed on both sides of the Atlantic, Eleo and Mike Vanderbilt settled into a comfortable companionship. Mike was attractive, highly intelligent, and, most critically for Eleo, steadfast, and he had emerged from the pack of Eleo's suitors to stake something like a claim on her. The press identified him as a "quiet and studious young millionaire" and assessed his potential inheritance at $100 million.[7] Marriage to such a well-endowed man would catapult Eleo to the top of her rarefied social circle.

Soon after Alice's wedding, another of Eleo's friends made a notable match. Nancy Langhorne wed Waldorf Astor, of the English branch of the New York Astors. As a wedding gift, Nancy's father-in-law gave the couple Cliveden House, a forty-six-bedroom baroque palace overlooking the Thames. Cliveden House also boasted a covered tennis court that Eleo enjoyed playing on. The elder Astor later gave the Waldorf-Astoria Hotel in New York to his son as a birthday present.[8]

The stream of friends entering wedlock kept marriage very much on Eleo's mind. She was drawn, intermittently, to the idea of a home and a family of her own, but her nature was driven by different forces. And warring too with the image of cozy domesticity in palatial homes was the specter of stifling rou-tine, of family-imposed obligations, of keeping track of her life in account books. Mike Vanderbilt, for reasons of his own, appeared content with the parameters of their relationship, which was clearly, though loosely, commit-ted. Their long-standing friendship had not been without its bumps. Mike and Eleo were both legendarily stubborn, strong-willed people, and Mike's view of a woman's proper place was less expansive than Eleo's. Their dis-agreements sometimes boiled over into loud, angry arguments. For days after a blow-up, they would refuse to speak to one another directly. During those long silences, their mutual friend Richard Kaswell acted as a go-between, relaying their thoughts back and forth, until a truce was arranged and their relationship got back on track. Over the years Eleo and Mike were willing to give one another the space they each needed, but neither was willing to let the other go entirely.

Mike graduated from Harvard Law School in 1910 and went to work as a legal assistant for the New York Central Railroad. Within three years, aided by Vanderbilt magic, Mike was made a director of the railroad, replacing the banker J. P. Morgan. Eleo cruised through her twenties, followed closely by a clutch of sports and society reporters who continually looked for a change in the marital status of Boston's courageous "society bachelor girl," a girl so fearless that in 1910 she prevailed on the Admiral of the Pacific Fleet to let her explore the ocean's depths in a submarine. Marriage was a finish line everyone understood, and it would be the crowning jewel of the trailblazing career of this often paradoxical young woman. That Eleo would settle down with any one of the nice young men who came to call had always been her mother's fond wish. Nora had a mother's pride in her daughter's achievements and popularity. Her love for Eleo never wavered in the face of all the detours that she had taken. And yet . . . The cultivation of the family's good name, through good works, religious observance, and quiet fortitude came naturally to Nora. She could not always curb the frustration she felt with what appeared to be Eleo's reckless disregard of that precious commodity.

CHAPTER 9

Thoroughbreds, Yachts, and Aeroplanes

A WAGER WAS MADE AMONG THOSE spending the season in Newport that Eleo, as celebrated as she was in so many sports, was no match for Alfred Gwynne Vanderbilt on the high seas. Mike's attractive older cousin was an accomplished sailor, and his yacht *Walthra* was one of fastest ships in Newport Harbor. It was the type of challenge that Eleo loved, but she would have to meet it with a borrowed yacht. She arranged to skipper *Mirage,* a beautiful boat belonging to Paul Rainey, the explorer, philanthropist, and big-game hunter who had come to Newport from his 11,000-acre spread in Mississippi. Eleo's name had been sporadically linked with Rainey's and reporters from as far away as San Diego contended that a union with the Cleveland-born adventurer was likely. The Newport summer crowd was riveted as Eleo set the straighter course for *Mirage,* caught the stronger wind, and sailed across the finish line well in front of *Walthra.* Reporters rushed to print their newest speculation, that it was now Eleo and Alfred Vanderbilt who were talking engagement.

Alfred's first marriage had ended in divorce in 1908. His wife accused him of having an adulterous liaison, in his private railway car, with the wife of a Cuban diplomat whose life he had saved. Alfred had an old-fashioned sense of chivalry, and when Mary Ruiz went screaming toward disaster on a runaway horse, Alfred rode to her rescue. The subsequent alleged infidelity in the railway car brought Alfred and Mary only misery. Mary's husband divorced her, and she never recovered from the scandal. Six years later she committed suicide in a hotel room in London, a tragedy that haunted Alfred for years.

Alfred Vanderbilt earned his place in history as the guiding light of the National Horse Show, the pivotal sporting event that annually graced Madison Square Garden. Alfred was the president of the association that produced

America's most prestigious horse show. Knowledgeable horsemen across the United States and Europe valued Alfred's imaginative and honorable leadership, and the respect they had for him personally added to the prestige of the show. Alfred organized the first international jumping competition ever held in the United States when he convinced five British cavalry officers to undertake the long, expensive journey across the Atlantic to compete at the Garden in 1909.

The social calendars, of "everyone-that-one-knew" were governed by the dates of major sporting competitions. Horse-related events took precedence over all others. November belonged to the National. The country's most serious horsemen and most distinguished horses came together at the National. Owners were eager to compare the contents of their stables, and their wives and daughters were keen to compare the creativity and expense of their wardrobes.

The architect of Madison Square Garden, Stanford White, had designed a noble venue for the indoor show, a vast, graceful Italianate building with a tower, inspired by the Giralda of Seville's cathedral, rising at one end. Flowers billowed from window boxes and bronze nymphs romped along the exterior walls. Stanford White topped off his building with a weather vane sculpted by Saint-Gaudens, a lithesome, nude figure of the huntress Diana with her bow and arrow aimed in the direction of the wind. This undraped female form, the most highly positioned sculpture in New York City and the first to be electrically illuminated, set off a storm of protest over its very public indency. In the men's club across the street, telescopes were lined up along the windows that faced the Garden.[1]

The interior of the Garden was organized like a grand opera house, three tiers of seating encircling the manicured center arena. The audience sat between white columns that were cheerfully linked by striped banners. The arena and the spectators sparkled in the light of more than two dozen crystal chandeliers. During the National the box seats were occupied by the great sporting families, the Whitneys, Belmonts, Wideners, Clothiers, du Ponts, Dodges, and Cassatts, who had held those seats since the 1890s. The sumptuously dressed audience did justice to the setting, with its splendid horses and valorous riders.

Nothing, however, before or since has equaled the excitement and glamour of the evening performance of the National in 1895, which was attended by Consuelo Vanderbilt and the Duke of Marlborough a few weeks after their marriage. A tide of humanity swept into the Garden, shoving and straining for a vantage point along the wood-floored promenade that surrounded the arena. It seemed as though the entire world had come to gape at what one newspaperman called "the Duke Show." The pressroom overflowed with reporters, all wearing tuxedos for the occasion. The duke's twenty-three-year-old nephew, Winston Churchill, accompanied the celebrated couple. Young

Churchill was a dedicated horseman who believed firmly that "No hour of life is lost that is spent in the saddle."

The Chicago native William H. Moore owned a controlling interest in the National Horse Show Association. Judge Moore, using an honorific that more than likely signified his sharp eye for evaluating horses rather than any accomplishments at law school, compiled a remarkable blue-ribbon record at the National that spanned more than two decades. For several years the gorgeously produced National ran at a deficit. Judge Moore made up the substantial difference from his own pocket, thereby ensuring the show's survival.

Eleo competed regularly at the National, with notable success in the driving competitions. In 1909 she won the blue ribbon in a daring race against the clock. Driving a phaeton coach, she dashed around the arena, guiding her horses around the turns with only inches to spare.

Until 1915 female riders who competed at the Garden were required to ride sidesaddle.[2] In 1899 eighteen-year-old Eleo astonished the crowd by riding into the arena sitting astride her horse, the first woman to do so at the Garden.[3] In the years that followed, rather than risk disqualification, Eleo obediently rode sidesaddle, but she sent a mixed message by wearing a slim-fitted jacket with velvet lapels and a man's bowler hat. She adhered to an inner timetable that dictated when she would conform to preset standards and when she would not. Eleo knew and respected several women who could cover long distances and jump sizable fences while riding sidesaddle, but this type of seat made it harder to control a headstrong horse, and it rapidly strained back and leg muscles.[4] Eleo was conflicted. She was well aware that she looked regal, gracefully draped down the left side of a horse, yet she resented being obliged, by rules decided by men, to do what they themselves would never consider doing. She claimed, with false bravado, that she actually preferred riding sidesaddle when she played polo because it made the game more dangerous.

Following a tradition that began in 1892, the third week of January found Boston's leading families at the New Riding Club at the intersection of Norway Street and Hemenway. Nora Sears was there to watch her husband compete in the Hunter and Park Hacks divisions, though Frederick was rarely in the ribbons. With becoming modesty, Nora enjoyed the congratulations that came her way through her often successful daughter. Eleo rode Grey Friars in the Jumper and Hacking divisions and little Vera in the Pony classes.

During the weeklong show, one afternoon was always set aside for gymkhana events for the youngsters. These contests sparkled with so much merriment that many of the riders kept pushing back the age of their retirement and continued to participate well into their twenties. For many years Eleo, together with such friends and cousins as Alice Thorndike, the Forbes and Thayer girls, the Saltonstalls, and Norman Prince, rode with deliberate haste toward the finish line while cradling an egg teetering on a spoon. In the Shirt Waist race, the boys dismounted midway across the arena, put on girls' clothing, and then remounted and raced back to the starting point. Most boys tried to enter the ankle-length skirts from the top and ended in a tangle. The observant fellow who knew to slip the skirt neatly over his head was the one who rode to victory. Boys and girls were paired for the Suffragette race. The boys saddled their ponies in the middle of the ring, swung themselves aboard, and let the girls tow them to the finish line.

Society snowbirds, who decamped in February for Palm Beach, or Aiken, South Carolina, or Pau in southern France, returned at the end of April in time for the beautiful Boston Horse Show. The interior of the Mechanics Building on Huntington Avenue was festooned with flags and banks of hothouse flowers and provided a haven from the often blustery Boston spring. All the prominent families were in more or less continuous attendance during the week of the show. Eleo and Freddy visited with friends around the gallery and watched the show from their parents' box in the grand tier. Next to the Searses' box were the Thayers, who were hosting the Joseph Wideners from Philadelphia. Near them, the Herbert Sears family, including Eleo's cousins Phyllis and Lily, chatted with Mr. and Mrs. Rudolph Agassiz. Nora Sears looked fine in conservative black velvet and lace with a bright splash of red roses on her hat. Sitting companionably together, Nora and Frederick Sears looked much like their friends, prosperous and congenial. Eleo chose simple dresses for the daytime events, but she never looked ordinary. Her deep suntan and sapphire-blue eyes made a striking contrast with her white chiffon and lace dress, which she paired with a small black hat accented by a single black ostrich feather.

The Boston show attracted horse enthusiasts from New York and Pennsylvania and as far away as Virginia. The southerners brought along retinues of black grooms and jockeys to tend to their show horses. This cultural peculiarity baffled the New Englanders who, by long-standing preference, hired only help who came from Northern Europe, particularly from the "desirable" countries of Ireland, England, and France.

Reginald Vanderbilt, Alfred's younger brother, came from New York with his beautiful young wife to watch their horses compete. They took rooms at the Somerset Club for the week of the show. One reporter covering the fashion angle of the horse show made the stinging suggestion that the women of Boston ought to be grateful to the lovely Mrs. Reggie Vanderbilt for the education in couture that she provided daily by appearing in two, and often three, extraordinary new outfits. All of Mrs. Vanderbilt's ensembles—confected of pompadour chiffon or champagne voile and silk, her hats cunningly trimmed with ribbons and wreaths of flowers, her lace stockings and jeweled buckles on her shoes—offered, the reporter enthused, "some new feature to be absorbed by the feminine multitude."[5]

The show's Hunt Club competition provided a spectacle of color and sound that was always a crowd favorite. New England's three most renowned foxhunting clubs, Myopia, Norfolk, and Middlesex, maintained a sharp but friendly rivalry among themselves, but they presented a united front against their mutual archrival, the Meadowbrook Club of Long Island. Each club was represented by its Master of Fox Hounds and two Whips, who paraded into the ring riding handsome, seasoned hunters and wore brilliant scarlet coats. Scores of hounds followed, each the pick of the litter, each introduced by name. Encouraged by the Master's call, "Hip, hip," and the crackling sound of the whip, the dogs demonstrated their ability to travel together as a pack and track a scent, nose to the ground. Many of the hounds howled their excitement, and their cries sent a tingle up the spine.

Smaller regional shows were sprinkled all though the warm outdoor months, in places like Newport and Magnolia, where Eleo could often be found as an exhibitor and observer. The pride of Brockton, Massachusetts, was its annual fair, which attracted eminent horsemen like the Vanderbilts, the Whitneys, and Judge Moore and his family. Eleo gave a blue-ribbon performance there in 1909 in the Jumping class for horses over 15.2 hands. The win was especially gratifying because the ringside boxes were filled with friends. Few people watching Eleo circle the arena with the blue ribbon fluttering from her horse's bridle could imagine that she was ever prey to fear of any kind. In fact, when she jumped horses over high fences in competitions or fox hunts, she often fought a knot of fear in her stomach, but she preferred to keep such weakness to herself.[6]

The Brockton Fair sprawled over fifty acres and offered competitions for breeders of every variety of animal—cattle, sheep, horses, pigeons, and children's pets large and small. Huge crowds watched track-and-field events and high-wire circus acts. The bravest visitors ascended above the fairgrounds in a hot-air balloon. The fair's organizing committee proudly advertised the "eating tents," which could be found throughout the grounds. "The great majority," ran the glowing testimonial in the commemorative program, "will give you a real meal for real money, and not a horrible roast either."[7]

In August North Shore society converged at Judge Moore's estate in Prides Crossing for his annual horse show. Three hundred invited guests settled along the shaded hillside at Rockmarge that overlooked the large, beautifully appointed arena. Many of them had driven from Boston, and the stream of automobiles was directed into rows near the entrance to the property by off-duty policemen the Judge had hired. One hundred workers readied the horses and hitches and kept the tan bark in the ring clean and raked. After the show, tea was served on the terrace.

Judge Moore's horses were considered the finest private collection in the world. Wearing a black top hat, he personally drove several of his prize-winners around the track to enthusiastic applause. He enlisted horsemen he admired to exhibit his other beauties. Eleo's cousin Phyllis Sears expertly showed the Judge's trotters. Eleo drove the Judge's four-in-hands, which was her specialty. It required skill, strength, and nerve to control four horses at a gallop from atop a bouncing coach, with only long reins and a primitive brake to slow it down.

The fame of Judge Moore's horses increased after they triumphed at the International Horse Show in England in 1910, where he sent forty-nine of his finest steeds. The Judge was victorious also in the twenty-five-mile coaching marathon that ran between Windsor Castle and the Olympic Arena in London. The sport of coaching, a favorite activity of the upper classes in the United States, England, and France, featured handsome Regency-style coaches called "tally ho's" and teams of carefully matched horses. Tally ho's often dashed along the back roads of the North Shore carrying uniformed grooms and a horn player hanging on at the back to sound warnings of their approach around corners and at crossroads.

Judge Moore and his friend and business partner Henry Clay Frick were among the most wily and notorious of the Robber Barons, those cunning men with gamblers' instincts, heedless power, and creative vision who flourished from the last quarter of the nineteenth century through the first quarter of the twentieth. Judge Moore was a genius at identifying and seizing business opportunities. He controlled the Rock Island Railroad line and specialized in company takeovers and corporate mergers. His outsized business manipulations placed him "among the most brazen and astoundingly successful stock-waterers in American finance."[8]

Henry Clay Frick was born humbly in a mining town near Pittsburgh, Pennsylvania. A compactly built man, Frick had the deceptively benign look of an indulgent uncle. By dint of hard work, intelligence, and cast-iron nerves, he built a coal empire during the Panic of 1873. Henry Frick ran the Atchison, Topeka and Santa Fe Railroad, a venture that was briefly joined by Eleo's grandfather T. J. Coolidge. Frick achieved notoriety as manager of the Carnegie Steel Company during the violent Homestead Strike in 1892, when union workers were killed by strikebreakers he had hired. Frick was later shot and wounded by a disciple of the anarchist Emma Goldman.

The noisy arrival of Henry Frick and Judge Moore on the North Shore in the early 1900s was greeted frostily at first by the Bostonians who had built their summer homes there decades before. Frick purchased a landlocked property in Prides Crossing and offered a million dollars to Katherine Loring, the granddaughter of one of the area's earliest residents, for a right-of-way across her property to the beach. She put him in his place. "Why, Mr. Frick," she said, "what would *I* do with a million dollars?"

Frick called his country manse Eagle Rock. The grand brick and stone

Georgian-amalgam on Hale Street dwarfed all that had come before. In a labor reminiscent of the pyramids of Egypt and the palaces in Newport, three hundred groundsmen sculpted thousands of yards of topsoil brought in by chartered train. Scores of European craftsmen were imported to work on the interiors. Frick ensured that his horses and carriages were housed in similar comfort. He built an almost equally grand Tudor-style stable across the road and surrounded it with a handsome eight-foot iron fence set between stone pillars. The fence alone was said to have cost $100,000. Frick began to assemble a masterful collection of paintings that he intended to donate to the public after his death. Most of the art hung in his New York mansion on Fifth Avenue, but he brought a selection of paintings to Eagle Rock for the summer. This rival collection so intrigued Isabella Stewart Gardner that she motored up to Prides Crossing to inspect it. Judge Moore also chose Hale Street to build his competing homestead, Rockmarge. It rose to four stories and was lined with balconies and arches, part Italian villa, part French-Quarter New Orleans, all American audacity.

One mark of the eventual assimilation of these two outsiders into the North Shore community was their admittance to the ranks of the Myopia Hunt Club. The bar to membership at Myopia was set high, and the club retained its allure precisely because so many ached to join this mighty group of "those who matter"—and so few were chosen. President William Howard Taft, Teddy Roosevelt's hand-picked successor, was a member. The English critic Henry Leach observed that it was "easier to become president of the United States than to become a member of the Myopia Hunt Club. It is therefore all the more to the credit of Mr. Taft that he is both."[9]

When the Myopia Hunt Club outgrew its original site on Frederick Prince's land, T. J. Coolidge offered the club a section of his Manchester farm, but the club chose the hospitable pine forests on the outskirts of Hamilton, about twenty miles north of Boston. The headquarters of the lofty Myopia Club were three very modest frame bungalows set at right angles to each other like an arthritic letter S. The club's dining facilities were housed in one building; the Ladies' Annex was in the bungalow about twenty-five yards beyond, and the men claimed the sacred structure in the center. The ladies were under strict orders not to venture onto the men's porch, and certainly not to use it as a shortcut, even in damp weather. From Myopia's earliest days, the clubmen looked forward to sitting outside on the cramped front porch of their small cottage to sip their drinks and observe the women stepping into and out of their carriages in the tight turning circle off the main road. Lounging contentedly on their porch of an afternoon, these gentlemen nearly dropped their drinks in their laps when Eleo Sears and her cousin Margaret Winthrop came crashing past on their horses, both riding astride, on a quiet Sunday.

The air of rustic simplicity and the plain-jane look of Myopia's cluster of clubhouses were themselves a kind of snobbery. The members did not need more. They were who they were, and that was sufficient. Of course, given the club's august roster of names, it could easily have built something palatial, but the everyday lives of the members were already of such comparative ease, their homes so lavish, so filled with every comfort, that they found it salutary to escape to a rougher place when they played. They were of Puritan stock, after all—they had not gone soft.

Even Henry Frick and Judge Moore fell in step with the Boston instinct for understatement, though they could not entirely resist making improvements. Frick gave Myopia its high-ceilinged Men's Locker Room, and he and Judge Moore shared the cost of realigning the main road leading to the clubhouses, which allowed for easier automobile access and an improved layout for the golf course. Henry Frick took up golf rather late in life, and he played rain or shine, but never particularly well. Myopia was his favorite course, and whenever he was playing, other golfers on the course indulgently spread the word, "Look out, Mr. Frick's coming."[10] Myopia was renowned for foxhunting and polo, and a smattering of the club's space was allotted to lawn tennis, but golf was its fastest-growing activity. Its difficult course was enhanced when Frick dug a pond at the ninth hole and Mike Vanderbilt financed the remodeling of the third hole. Mike and Eleo made up one of the club's most formidable golf duos. They were challenged regularly by the competitive Frick and his daughter Helen. Helen was nine years younger than Eleo; she had a birdlike delicacy, but she was a very determined girl and a competent golfer. Helen was troubled by the reputation for ruthlessness that trailed her father, and she envied the self-assurance that seemed so effortless for Eleo. Helen Frick would remain Eleo's friend through even the most trying times.

The Myopia Hunt Club was President Taft's favorite golfing venue. He was as large as he was jovial, standing just under six feet and often weighing over three hundred pounds, the heaviest man ever to occupy the White House. For one so portly, Taft was surprisingly agile, and he played and walked a golf course so rapidly that he wore out his caddie. Taft's military aid, Major Archibald Butts, whom he had inherited from Teddy Roosevelt, was a frequent golfing partner. Taft disregarded advice that he should avoid being seen with the controversial Frick, and when the president played golf with Frick, the press marked it against him. During Taft's first two summers as president, in 1909 and 1910, he set up a Vacation White House on the North Shore, in a rambling cottage near Beverly Cove that he rented for his family. President Taft was the first president to own a motorcar, and he loved taking his guests on "automobile parties."

President Taft almost became the first president to ride in an airplane. The famed English pilot Claude Grahame-White, winner of the world's first long-distance airplane race, offered to take Taft up in his plane during the historic airplane contest in September 1910, hosted by the Harvard Aero Club.[11] Eleo Sears attended this spectacular nine-day aviation event, and she came away captivated by the idea of flight. The *Boston Post* headlined the matchup of the world's greatest flyers: "Master Birdmen to Clash." Twenty-two airmen competed in twenty-four independently built biplanes, many barely ever tested. In 1910 the fragile aircraft all shared essentially the same body type, two sets of white canvas wings that were stiffened with a paste of flour and water and stretched over artfully arranged wooden struts. The delicate construction resembled a row of coat hangers sandwiched between a pair of starched pant legs. At the time it was widely acknowledged that the Europeans had taken the lead in the development of airplane motors.

Grahame-White was the audience favorite. "Claudie" had the tall, sturdy good looks one wants in a hero. He had been inspired to become a pilot after watching a flying demonstration in France given by Wilbur Wright.[12] The Wright brothers sponsored their own air team at the Boston meet—the duo of Walter Brookins and Ralph Johnstone, who were to pilot a biplane that the brothers had spent more than a year redesigning in secret. Ralph Johnstone had been a trick bicyclist in vaudeville shows until shortly before he became a pilot.

On the opening day of the Boston contest, the band played the "Star-Spangled Banner" for the American pilots and "God Save the King" in honor of Claude Grahame-White. Most of the spectators were seeing airplanes for the first time in their lives, and they were enthralled as the flying crates soared and swooped above them. Automobile enthusiasts in the crowd envied the freedom of the air, where there were no speed limits and no police enforcers. The aviators vied with each other in tests of speed, altitude, and distance. There was a bomb-throwing contest in which pilots pushed weighted blocks of plaster-of-paris out of their planes while flying over a tennis court–sized target marked off with lime. On the eighth day of the meet, President Taft arrived with his family, and Grahame-White offered to take him flying. The president declined, perhaps out of concern that the slightly built biplane might not be able to lift a passenger of his bulk. The ride went instead to Boston's mayor John "Honey-Fitz" Fitzgerald, grandfather of the future president John Fitzgerald Kennedy. A sobering reminder that flying was an experimental sport came when the Farman biplane flown by the New York millionaire Clifford Harmon plunged to the ground. Miraculously, Harmon crawled out from beneath the wreckage in the eight-foot-deep pit, dazed but barely hurt. At the conclusion of the flying contests, Claude Grahame-White claimed the highest point totals and the winner's purse.

When Grahame-White returned to Boston ten days after the Harvard event, he was greeted by a wildly enthusiastic crowd of 23,000. Claudie soared seventy-five feet above the spectators, pretending to charge the grandstand, and at the last moment tilting his body and swinging the plane around. The crowd rose repeatedly to its feet to cheer the man and his flying machine.

The famed aviator consented to take three women up in his plane that day. The modestly veiled Dorothy Jordan, a popular member of the Vincent Club, was the first to ride. Next was Mrs. James Barr, whose husband insisted that she try it. Both ladies reported themselves very pleased with their brief flights. A vivacious young woman in a black-and-white tweed suit introduced herself enigmatically as "Miss Brown." Grahame-White had little difficulty in discovering that "Miss Brown" was actually Eleonora Sears. Eleo's alias was likely her halfhearted attempt to conceal her interest in flying from her strongly disapproving family. Eleo laughed excitedly as she climbed into the plane behind Grahame-White. She had hungered for this moment since she had seen him perform at the Harvard Aero Club contest. At her signal the biplane took off and Grahame-White shot up quickly to nearly 150 feet. Eleo waved delightedly to her friends watching from the ground. She was not content to be just a passenger, and Grahame-White, yelling over the noise of the engine and the wind, began to teach her about the controls of the plane. He liked having someone with him who was as enthusiastic about being in the air as he was, and he kept Eleo up for more than twelve minutes, far beyond his usual time for passengers. It was the longest flight made, until that moment, by a female passenger, and when Grahame-White swung the plane out over the battleships berthed in Boston Harbor, Eleo became the first woman to fly over water. After a series of banks, rolls, and figure eights, they descended to the field in a steep dive. Grahame-White touched the wheels down neatly and rolled almost to a stop before taking off with Eleo again for another great loop in the air. Eleo was ecstatic about her experience, which she described as "soaring" and "floating." "I wouldn't take a million dollars for that trip," she declared.[13] The only drawback, she acknowledged, was the deafening roar of the motor. In answer to a reporter's question, Eleo asserted that she never had the slightest worry about the danger; her only fear was that the ride would end.

At the Brockton State Fair during the first week of October 1910, flying exhibitions by Grahame-White were the featured attraction. Claudie's rich contract for $50,000 called for daily demonstrations for the duration of the fair. The air route chosen by the organizers went directly over the grandstands for maximum effect, but no thought had been given to safety. Graham-White refused to fly until full insurance coverage was bought for him and the spectators. A mob of 120,000 people converged on Brockton to see this world-renowned aviator, but wind and drizzle conspired against any takeoffs until the end of the week. During the frustrating delay, Eleo kept Grahame-White company and introduced him to her friends. The spectators who waited out the bad weather came away well satisfied with Grahame-White's efforts. Despite his abbreviated schedule, the flyer was deemed to have earned his entire fee.

Grahame-White followed his success at the Brockton Fair with a public relations stunt on October 14, 1910, in the skies above Washington, D.C. Clifford Harmon arranged for the necessary clearances for Grahame-White to fly over the city and land next to the White House. The seat of government came to a standstill as workers charged out of their office buildings to catch a glimpse of Claudie and his Farman biplane sailing over the Capitol. Crowds lined Pennsylvania Avenue and cheered as he soared above them and touched his plane down on Executive Avenue. President Taft was not in residence at the time, but Grahame-White was greeted by Admiral Dewey of the navy and two generals representing the army. At the National Press Club dinner given in his honor, Grahame-White spoke about the possible military applications of aircraft, a topic that was receiving little attention from the American and British governments but was of considerable interest to the French, Germans, and Russians. General James Allen of the Army Signal Corps voiced his remote concern that a fleet of foreign aircraft could, theoretically, invade the skies over Washington, D.C., at night. "This city has positively no defense against them," he observed."[14] Grahame-White believed that the devastating potential of airplanes to make war would ultimately ensure peace. "Civilized nations," he said in a later interview, "would recoil in horror before such possibilities of destruction."[15]

A month after Eleo made her first flight, she traveled to New York, the site of the next major air show, the Gordon Bennett Trophy Race at Belmont Park. The flight course was again set over major population centers, areas dense with people and telegraph poles, and over pine forests dense with trees. No provision had been made for emergency landings, and no American insurance company was willing to write a policy under those conditions. The entire event was in jeopardy until Lloyd's of London agreed to provide coverage.

News of Eleo's plan to fly again with Claude Grahame-White reached Beacon Street with the morning newspapers. Eleo's family, Nora especially, was horrified. The flyboys were a reckless lot. Several had well-earned reputations for drunkenness, and none would be mistaken for a gentleman. Grahame-White summed up his interest in etiquette by observing that "only show-offs drink more than one bottle of Champagne before breakfast."[16] The Sears family was fearful of more than mere social impropriety. Flying was, fundamentally, an unnatural human activity, and the danger was appallingly obvious. As more people took to the skies, reports of airplanes somersaulting to the ground and injured pilots came with increasing regularity. Nora sent off an impassioned telegram to Eleo in New York, commanding her to "stay on earth." Eleo telegraphed back that she wanted to take "just one more flight."

The anxiety in the Sears household was so intense that Eleo's brother was dispatched to New York to stop her. Freddy met Eleo at the hangars out at the airfield, just after she and Grahame-White had finished flying three great circles over the Belmont Park racetrack and around the Statue of Liberty. Freddy conveyed to Eleo in the strongest terms the family's opposition to her perilous and totally unacceptable new interest. Grahame-White was no help. "Really, Miss Sears is her own mistress," he said. "I may take her up tomorrow if she wishes." Eleo was more conciliatory, but no less definite: "I am not sure but what the temptation will prove too strong. I never enjoyed anything so much in my life as my flight today."[17] Not long after this confrontation, during his descent at the end of a race, Grahame-White misjudged his landing and ended upside down in a field. He was lucky then to be thrown clear of the wreck and was not seriously hurt.

Weeks later, in mid-November, twenty-four-year-old Ralph Johnstone was killed when his plane failed to recover from a steep dive during a flying exhibition in Denver before a crowd of 10,000 people. He had been part of the nine-man traveling team that the Wright brothers assembled to demonstrate their planes, and he was the first American pilot to die in an airplane crash.[18]

On December 3, 1910, Eleo placed an order to have her own biplane built. The thrill of flying trumped the wrath of her family. Claude Grahame-White agreed to be her instructor, and her plan, which she announced enthusiastically to family and friends, was to participate the following year in an aviation meet in San Francisco. In England on December 18, Grahame-White's plane crashed into a stone wall during takeoff, and this time he was badly injured. Days later, during another flying contest, five planes were destroyed and one of the pilots died. These terrible events alone were not enough to discourage Eleo. Once she had publicly declared her intension to begin a new venture, even when she herself might have had second thoughts, it was practically impossible to persuade her to reverse course. She preferred to plunge ahead stubbornly rather than risk being branded a clichéd weak-willed female.

During the first week of January 1911, Eleo was invited to attend the International Automobile and Aviation Show in New York at the Grand Central Palace on Lexington Avenue. Eleo's interest in flying and her order for a new plane were widely known, and she was presented as a guest of honor on Aviation Day. Later Eleo attended a pilot-training school in California that was set up by Glenn Curtiss, the holder of pilot's license number 1, issued by the American Aero Association. While there, Eleo flew in a biplane with Raymond Morris, an instructor, to an altitude of fifteen hundred feet. Morris considered her an exceptional student, on track to get her license.

No record has been found to show that Eleo ever obtained a pilot's license, though during those early days many people flew planes without bothering with the formal paperwork. Nor is it certain that Eleo took delivery of the plane she had ordered. Eleo's unorthodox interests had discomfited her family often over the years, but nothing before had provoked Nora to such vehement and tearful opposition. The intensity of Nora's feelings about the airplane led to violent disagreements and, possibly, threats to withhold Eleo's funds. Whatever the final arguments or tactics, it appears that Eleo was sufficiently impressed to give in finally to her family's insistence that she remain grounded.

CHAPTER 10

A Titanic Year

B Y 1911 NEWPORT FIRMLY BELIEVED that Eleo had finally been caught by Cupid, and friends and family on the more skeptical North Shore were increasingly convinced. The relationship between Eleo and Mike Vanderbilt, which had spanned so many years, certainly did seem to have reached a more intimate level. The press took note and lusted after the pair, which they were delighted to describe as "the wealthy and athletic young woman from Boston and the scion of the rich New York family."[1] Every sighting of this high-profile couple was analyzed breathlessly. Eleo and Mike were seen emerging from a train at Boston's North Station after returning from an August visit to the North Shore. Then, together, they sped off in a taxicab. Great significance was read into Eleo's visit to Newport only days later to stay at Marble House as Alva's guest. Mike met Eleo at the Newport train station in his racing car. The *San Diego Union-Tribune* jumped the gun with a page 1 prediction on August 17 that Mrs. Belmont would announce their engagement in Newport two days later. Speculation about the couple was so intense that Eleo's family felt compelled to issue a statement. "There is no engagement; they are merely friends," Nora and Frederick stated flatly. Their denial served only to heighten interest in the long-running marriage mystery; it was especially baffling in light of Mike's response to friends who asked him, "May we congratulate you?" "Very many thanks," he replied.[2] Social columns on both coasts expressed the widely held sentiment that "Eleonora Sears had tried everything going, except matrimony," and now, they rhapsodized, it appeared certain that marriage would be her next daring feat.[3]

The football-themed dinner that Eleo gave for Mike at the Touraine Hotel in Boston on the night of November 25, after the Harvard-Yale game, cemented expectations. Eleo rented a private dining room and had it decorated in Harvard crimson. Bouquets of brilliant red chrysanthemums were set strategically around the room, and Eleo centered a large arrangement on the dining table. As if to underline the importance of the evening, Eleo oversaw the details of this dinner party with unusual care, in contrast, observers noted, to her signature simplicity—a "simplicity often verging on severity in dress, in manner, and in her entertainments."[4] Eleo's guests for the evening included Mike's cousin Reggie Vanderbilt and his wife, Cathleen, the Joseph E. Wideners, and the Harry Payne Whitneys. All were united in their understanding that this was a special occasion, and they offered their congratulations to the couple.

Eleo carried such a burst of positive energy into the New Year that her friends took it as still another sign that 1912 was definitely the year they would be hearing wedding bells. The year began with Eleo winning a twenty-five-dollar bet that she would not have the nerve to drive a four-in-hand down the entire length of New York's Fifth Avenue. By 1912 horse-drawn vehicles were losing their place to motorcars along the streets of the rapidly urbanizing metropolis. Cadillac had introduced an electric starter on its automobiles, after CEO Henry Leland learned that the wife of a friend had been killed while cranking the engine of her car. Eliminating the temperamental hand crank on the Caddie was a boon to motorists, but it was the little Model T that provided an affordable entry-level vehicle for the general public and captured its heart. Ford's motorcars were being sold for $575, in any color as long as it was black, and these basic runabouts could be repaired with inexpensive replacement parts, a muffler for 25 cents and a fender for $2.50.[5] People were very fond of their flivvers, though they lacked such niceties as windshield wipers and rearview mirrors because Henry Ford thought those details were appropriate only for frivolous people. In January in New York City, where a large stagecoach drawn by four powerful horses had never been part of the traffic mix, Eleo made quite a show as she rolled down Fifth Avenue alongside all the honking Tin Lizzies.

While in New York, Eleo stayed at the 660 Fifth Avenue apartment of Mike Vanderbilt's brother, Willie K., and his wife, Birdie, the former Virginia Graham Fair. Birdie's father, James Graham Fair, was an Irish immigrant who had made $200 million in Nevada's Comstock Lode, the richest silver find in history. Birdie's mother-in-law, Alva Vanderbilt Belmont, not a woman to leave anything to chance, had arranged for Willie to meet her friend's eligible daughter.

From New York Eleo headed to Ottawa at the invitation of Princess Patricia of Connaught. Patricia's father, the first Duke of Connaught, was the governor-general of Canada and the youngest son of Queen Victoria. Princess Patricia was an artist, specializing in watercolors of landscapes and flowers, but she also loved outdoor sports. By facing off against Eleo in ice hockey, she added zest to the long Canadian winter. The two women had gotten to know one another the previous summer during a tennis tournament at Niagara-on-the-Lake, Ontario, on the grounds of the Queen's Royal Hotel.

When Eleo returned home from Canada, the innovations in outdoor wear she had introduced with her "severely plain" skating outfit came in for scrutiny by the *New York Times*. Interest centered on her close-fitting, knitted wool cap, which incorporated ear flaps for warmth, a feature that had come in handy up north, and on the wool muff she used for her hands in place of the usual bulky fur muff. "The wool cap and muff," the article explained helpfully, "can be made in any color desired."[6]

Eleo's demonstrations of her latest interest, then called "fancy" skating, led to the birth of a skating club in Boston that met at the Arena Rink on St. Botolph Street. Eleo's performance on the club's opening day left its members "wild with delight," according to a special report in the *New York Times*.[7] Looking glamorous in a coonskin toque, Eleo first performed the Dutch roll and then, "like a writing master," cut precise figure eights into the ice. Eleo moved gracefully into a waltz with the new club's skating instructor, and finally she led a group in speed skating "when she cut loose and shot around the rink like a meteor."[8]

Weeks later Eleo traveled to California to stay with her friends Frank and Harriet Carolan in Burlingame. Nora gave her extra money for the trip. Eleo's schedule while in California remained disciplined. A typical morning included polo practice and an eight-mile walk before lunch. Later in the day she competed in tennis matches and cooled off with a long swim. To fill an afternoon, Eleo drove to San Francisco, where she appeared as a Gainsborough girl in a Vincent Club–style tableau vivant for a charity event.

The Burlingame Country Club opened its season on March 15 with a party that ended at dawn the following morning. While the other partygoers headed to their beds, Eleo changed from her dancing shoes to her riding boots and set out on her morning ride over the mountain to Half Moon Bay. A blinding rainstorm caught her at the top of the mountain, but instead of turning back she continued to the bay, thirty miles away. In what was whispered to be a high-stakes craps game, Eleo won a polo pony from Mrs. Devereux Milburn, the wife of the polo great Dev Milburn, whose team had humbled the long-unconquerable British squad.

Residents of Burlingame were provoked to see Eleo ride her horses astride in public, "man-fashion," and by her masculine, oversized topcoats and trousers. A formal protest of Eleo's incendiary behavior, allegedly sent by the Burlingame Mother's Club, arrived in her mail on March 23. Word of the tempest reached Boston, and Nora bore with dignity the grim nods of condolence from her friends. Eleo answered the complaint the following week and redeemed a previous failure when she walked 109½ miles from Burlingame to the Hotel Del Monte, collapsing from exhaustion within sight of the finish line. Eleo was up and out the next morning at the polo field with Mrs. Milburn to root for Dev and his teammates. A reporter on the scene, aware of the ordeal Eleo had just endured, was amazed to find her "chipper as a bird."[9]

Eleo was barely back home in Boston to train for the new tennis season when the tranquility of the universe was shattered on April 14, the night the *Titanic* went down. This grandest example of a new technological age, the pride of the White Star fleet was considered by its builders to be "unsinkable," and the name of the ship had been selected to evoke the immensity of its creation.

The dimensions of the tragedy at sea became clear as the list of the lost and the saved unfolded. Of the more than 2,000 passengers and crew on board, only 651 survived. The losses fell heavily on working-class European immigrants and reached into the highest realms of American society. From first class, a Rothschild, a Guggenheim, and Sears family friends in the Thayer and Loring families were drowned. Eleo was close to the Widener family of Philadelphia, which lost its son George and grandson Harry. Major Archie Butts was returning home after delivering a letter from President Taft to the pope, and he helped a woman into one of the last lifeboats. He tucked a blanket around her and raised his hat in a final salute. "Luck be with you," he said. "Will you remember me to the folks back home?"[10] Major Butts was last seen on the boat deck arm-in-arm with John Jacob Astor as the band played "Nearer, My God, to Thee."[11]

The Sears family suffered still another loss that was related to the tragedy at sea only by the coincidence of occurring on the same day. Nora's younger brother, Thomas Jefferson (Jeffie) Coolidge Jr., died suddenly. He was just forty-nine years old and left a wife, Clara, two small sons, and a magnificent oceanfront home on Coolidge Point in Manchester-by-the-Sea, which he had modeled after Monticello, the house built by his great-grandfather Thomas Jefferson. Though Jeffie had become diabetic early in life, he had worked diligently as president and chairman of the board of the Old Colony Trust Company, which he had founded with his father. From boyhood Jeffie had been adored by his sisters and his mother, and he was the light of his father's life. Jeffie's father had written in his autobiography in 1902 that the death of his mother from pneumonia was the "greatest misfortune" of his life. T. J. Coolidge understood now that, in the earlier ranking of his misfortunes, he had been naïve. The Coolidge home was draped in black and the families gathered to mourn. With daily headlines blaring the details of the last moments of the doomed *Titanic,* the misery of this family seemed but a small wave as it joined the worldwide ocean of shock and grief.

Overshadowed too by the scale of the *Titanic* disaster was the achievement of Harriet Quimby. On April 16, piloting an unfamiliar airplane and relying on a compass she had just learned to use, she flew fifty-nine minutes through fog across the English Channel and landed safely near Hardelot, France. Harriet's interest in flying had been sparked at the great Harvard Aero Meet in 1910, which had also captivated Eleo, and Harriet became the first American woman to obtain a pilot's license. She traveled the country giving flying exhibitions in her trademark purple satin flying suit. Her history-making flight as the first woman to fly across the Channel was greeted by cheers from the locals in Hardelot, who hoisted her on their shoulders, but poor timing denied her the international acclaim she deserved.

The loss of the *Titanic* was the beginning of the end of many things. Never again would people accept without question the infallibility of technology and the assurances of company "experts," nor would there be quite the same complacency about the protection provided by money and privilege. Yet after even the most stunning tragedies, life pauses, is altered slightly, and then resumes, as it did for Eleo's family and friends. Eleo's routine of daily exercise and competitive sports focused her and channeled her energy. As it always had, it made her feel alive and helped keep disquieting thoughts at bay.

In May Eleo organized a new polo team of women from Boston and Brookline to challenge the Meadow Lark team of Long Island, which was the first female polo team in the nation. The benignly named Meadow Larks were a hard-fighting group whose captain was the formidable Louise Hitchcock, the wife of the great Thomas Hitchcock, a teammate of Dev Milburn. Louise Hitchcock was remembered by many people as being the very first woman to ride "cross-saddle." Eleo was appalled when asked whether she and her teammates would be wearing skirts during the matches against such first-rate opponents. "I should say not," she snapped back. "It would be as much as your life was worth to wear skirts in polo."[12]

Also in May an army of suffragists in New York went ahead with their planned parade up Fifth Avenue. The marchers included more than eight thousand women and as many as one thousand sympathetic men. The vast crowd watching the parade was divided in its support. Some cheered the idea of female equality. Many jeered the marchers and wondered aloud whether the gallantry shown by the men on board the *Titanic,* who put women into the lifeboats first, had been misplaced. Lida Stokes Adams, one of the marchers, offered her opinion that an equal number of men and women should have filled the boats.

At the end of the month, Eleo took part in an unprecedented occurrence in the history of the Devon Horse Show, the prestigious annual event in Devon, Pennsylvania. One of the four days of the competition was designated Ladies' Day and intended as an all-female enterprise; the contestants were women, and women filled the executive positions, handled the judging, and managed the ring. Even the veterinarian on the show grounds wore skirts. Eleo competed in several of the riding and driving classes. The unusual show attracted the support of women from across the country, and the novelty of the concept drew a large crowd of men. The day's scheduled events went without a hitch, and the men were fulsome in their praise of the way the feminine sex had mastered the situation. The experiment proved such an unqualified success that more horse shows by and for women were expected.[13]

During that eventful summer there was a halfhearted attempt to inject the titillation of a catfight into the sporting world. In a tennis match at the Essex County Club, Eleo lost, quite unexpectedly, to her pretty seventeen-year-old cousin Phyllis Sears. Phyllis was known to be a talented horsewoman and a graceful swimmer, but her victory over Eleo in the Ladies' Singles final seemed to come out of nowhere. Phyllis represented a new generation of society women who coveted the distinction of "lowering the colors of Eleonora" and supplanting her as the daring queen of sports.[14] Snide comments advised Eleo to "look to her laurels" lest her crown be snatched from her by these challengers from her own exclusive set. Left unmentioned was the fact that Eleo's exploits a decade earlier had opened the door for these eager young upstarts to compete with such breezy self-assurance. Phyllis's victory over Eleo was not repeated, and harmony returned to the heavens.

The premier tennis event of 1912 was the National Tennis Championships at the Philadelphia Cricket Club. Eleo made it through to the championship round of the Ladies' Singles competition. In the finals she met a Los Angeles native, Mary K. Browne, winner of the Pacific Coast Championships. Brownie, as her friends called her, was making her first appearance in an East Coast tournament, and she felt she was carrying the honor of all California tennis players on her shoulders. Because the weather in California was too dry to support the manicured lawns found at the country clubs in the East, West Coast players developed their skills on hard-surface courts of cement or asphalt, where balls bounced higher and moved faster. The California women, in general, hit harder, volleyed more, and followed their shots to the net better than their eastern counterparts. From out of the West came other legendary players, such as the sturdy Sutton sisters and Hazel Hotchkiss, who had teamed with Eleo the previous year to win the National Doubles Championship. In the Ladies' Singles final of 1912 Eleo faced Mary Browne, who was invariably described as "a little slip of a girl" and "a wee whiffet of a girl," but Brownie won the title in straight sets.[15]

Later that same afternoon, Eleo met Brownie again in the final for the mixed doubles championship. Eleo's partner for that contest was her long-time friend William J. Clothier. Bill Clothier was exactly one day older than Eleo, and for years they shared "Age before Beauty" birthday humor. Bill was the son of an old Philadelphia Main Line family. He had gone into the coal business rather than follow his family into the Strawbridge & Clothier department store chain. Bill Clothier was a member of the U.S. Davis Cup Team in

1905, and in 1906 he became the number one–ranked tennis player in the United States. When he clinched that title with a victory in Newport, Eleo rushed onto the court with Bill's wife, Anita, whom she embraced with such exuberance that they both landed in a heap on the ground.

Eleo and Bill Clothier had been a successful tennis couple for many years. Their wins together included the Mixed Doubles Championship of Pennsylvania and the Eastern States in 1910, but a much hoped-for national win had so far eluded them. After mighty battles in the previous four years, their names had been engraved on the silver trophies for the runners-up.[16] Observing Eleo and Bill play together was a lesson in contrasting styles. Eleo, in the heat of a game, hid little of her emotions; the tide of battle, whether high or low, was always evident in her eyes. She loved dashing off to make a shot and she was always alert to return the ball at a sly angle or to try to make a kill with an overhead smash. Bill Clothier's style of play matched his looks, smoothly elegant and austere. He crafted his game with cool deliberation. His strokes were powerful and methodical, and he wasted no energy. He came to the net often, but his game offered no spectacular runs or lunges, and after a match his opponents could never figure out how they had been beaten.

Mary Browne met her doubles partner, twenty-one-year-old Richard Norris Williams II, for the first time at this Philadelphia tournament. Dick Williams was another Philadelphia native. He was a player of consummate grace who had made a name for himself by winning the French indoor championship the previous year. All four of the players had worked hard to reach this mixed doubles final, but Dick Williams had made the most astonishing journey. Two months earlier, to take his entrance exams for Harvard, he had sailed home from Europe with his father on the *Titanic*. After the ship collided with the iceberg, Dick and his father stood together in the bitter cold on the boat deck and experienced the strange sensation that the ocean was rising, not that the boat sinking. The *Titanic*'s forward funnel collapsed and crushed Dick's father and other passengers standing near them. Now alone, Dick jumped clear of the ship into the ocean fifteen feet below. He was surprised to find himself face-to-face with a prize bulldog belonging to a first-class passenger, Robert Daniels. Someone on board had thought to go below deck and release the dogs from their kennels. Dick discarded his waterlogged fur coat and shoes and swam to a raft that already had thirty people hanging onto its sides or sitting on top, waist-deep in the water. From there Dick watched the *Titanic* break in half, the stern rising up 150 feet into the clear, star-flecked sky before it disappeared. "Then came the terrible part," Dick shuddered as he remembered, "hundreds and hundreds of people in the water crying for help, and there was nothing to do!"[17] Most did not drown in the inky black water, but died from the cold. Dick and his companions could do little but endure as twenty of them froze to death. After six hours in the water, the survivors were picked up by a lifeboat sent out from the *Carpathia*. Dick's legs were so badly frozen that the surgeon on board the *Carpathia* advised amputation, but Dick refused to give his consent. He forced himself to walk back and forth in his cabin through the entire night, despite unbearable pain, until circulation returned. And now, two months later, he was playing in a tennis final.

The threatening clouds that had hung over Philadelphia since early morning yielded a drizzle by midday, and the grass was slippery. In 1912 tennis tournaments were not usually halted by wet weather, nor were the contests spaced over days to allow players in multiple matches time to recuperate. All three championships for women—the Ladies' Singles, the Ladies' Doubles, and the Ladies' and Gentlemen's Doubles (mixed doubles)—were decided on the same day. Mary Browne, the winner of the singles title in the morning battle with Eleo, had prevailed as well in the Ladies' Doubles match. By the start of the mixed doubles contest, the drizzle had become a steady rain. The pockmarked grass court looked as if it had been hit by exploding shells. Eleo and Bill Clothier won the soggy first set, 6–4.

Brownie got into her rhythm. She was a terrific volleyer, and that was the only way to keep the ball from landing and dying in the soaked ground. Her new colleague, Dick Williams, was impressive, too. His shots looked effortless, and yet they sped across the net with machine-gun regularity. Rain poured on the four drenched players, whose limp pants and skirts were coated with mud. The footing was so precarious that sometimes when a player tried to hit an overhead ball, he or she was left swinging at the empty air. It looked so ridiculous and the conditions were so impossible that the quartet was immobilized with laughter. Brownie and Dick recovered first and took the next set. After every third game, the sodden balls were replaced. The wooden tennis racquets, strung with gut, became increasingly mushy. The final set ran for twenty games, each side staying alive by winning its serve with furious volleys to keep the ball from landing in the mud. In the end, Brownie and Dick prevailed, 11–9.

After the Philadelphia tournament, many of the players converged in Newport for more tennis and for the other pleasantries offered by this Queen of Watering Places. In a burst of good fellowship, the Newport Golf Club and the Bailey's Beach Bathing Association opened their facilities to the visiting players. Their hospitality included the loan of bathing suits to those who arrived unprepared. The players returned this generous reception by sharing playing tips with local tennis enthusiasts. One Newport hostess, Mrs. Lorillard Spencer Jr., organized a dance and called it, appropriately, a Tennis Ball. The Beach Club hosted a swim and clambake for members and visitors and set out tables groaning with refreshments.

While in Newport, Eleo was again invited to stay at Marble House. Eleo and Mike Vanderbilt were very much at home in this resort town, where the atmosphere was charged with laughter and friendship. Through the years Eleo and Mike had come to know each for better and for worse, and being together felt like second nature. The world considered them to be formally engaged, and if Eleo, at the age of thirty, was inclined to marry anyone, Mike was exactly the person she would choose—he was tall and ruggedly handsome, athletic, smart, and he had more than ample money of his own. Here, in this lighthearted town with the endless ocean stretching before them, she could imagine them having a future together. Eleo and Mike left Newport in Mike's large, powerful touring car, a brand-new 1912 Simplex built in New York City and rated at 50 horsepower. With Eleo at the wheel, they roared up to Beverly Farms, where Mike stayed at the Searses' country home. When Eleo was asked, as she frequently was, if the engagement rumors were true, she responded with a "rippling laugh" and turned the discussion to the fine weather they had enjoyed during the weeks they spent in Newport, and the tennis tournament, and the baseball game she'd played in, but she didn't deny it. Eleo's family was very fond of Mike, and Nora made sure he understood that. No date was set, but Nora was content to see that Eleo, at long last, seemed headed down the right path.

Nora showed Eleo a disturbing news article that summer that reported the death of Harriet Quimby at an aviation meet in Quincy, Massachusetts. Harriet had been one of the headliners, and her appearance fee was reported to be $100,000. The cause of the disaster was never pinpointed. Harriet was circling Dorchester Bay with her passenger, William A. P. Willard, the organizer of the event, when the plane began to pitch violently and Willard was thrown from his seat. As Willard fell to earth, Harriet struggled to regain control of the aircraft, until she too was thrown from the plane. Nora Sears took grim satisfaction from this distressing confirmation that her caution had been justified. If people had been meant to invade the sky, the Lord in his wisdom would have given them wings. Her daughter, at least, would be safe.

Dominating the national news in the fall of 1912 was the gathering battle for the White House, which featured the return of Teddy Roosevelt. T.R.'s friend and successor, William Taft, had been buffeted by entrenched politicians and had pursued few of the reformist, trust-busting policies that T.R. had championed. T.R. broke with his own party and ran under the third party banner of the Progressive "Bull Moose" Party. The party adopted its colorful name after T.R. was shot by a madman channeling the ghost of President McKinley's assassin. Teddy survived the attack and declared, "It takes more than that to kill a Bull Moose."[18]

The 1912 election was shaped by social unrest. Union workers battled big business for a living wage and better working conditions. A record number of voters were attracted by the antiestablishment rhetoric of the Socialist Party candidate Eugene Debs. As Roosevelt plotted strategy one afternoon on the porch of his home on Oyster Bay, Long Island, the talk about shaking up the establishment turned to his daughter's friend, Eleo Sears. Like T.R., Eleo had never shied away from defying conventional wisdom and imposing her personal vision on the landscape. T.R. knew Eleo to be a prime example of the independent, energetic, modern woman. "Let me tell you something," T.R. predicted, "this girl will be one of the best known women in America in the next twenty years. If you see her, remember me to her."[19]

The weekend before the election, Boston was fixated on the fortunes of Harvard's football team. The team was in the middle of a three-year, thirty-three-game winning streak, and the city swelled with pride in its young gladiators. Eleo, an experienced quarterback and fullback on her own local team, was a fervent supporter of the Harvard squad and a friend to many of the players. The game was still thrilling despite the rule changes that followed the gruesome season of 1905, when 18 college players were killed and 159 seriously injured. Teddy Roosevelt had called representatives of the colleges together at the White House and urged them to find ways to increase player safety. One result of that meeting was the forward pass, a play that was first used by Yale to crush Harvard in 1907.

Eleo invited nine couples to help her cheer Harvard on in the 1912 edition of its annual war with Princeton. After the rousing game, in which the Harvard team steamrolled Princeton, Eleo and her friends went to the Copley Plaza Hotel to continue their celebrating. The hotel was bursting with people in town for the game, but Eleo had rented the State Suite for her group and hired a piano player so they could dance. Shortly after they arrived, Eleo had a brief whispered conference with Reggie Vanderbilt, and suddenly the pair whirled onto the dance floor in a fast, high-stepping number that Eleo had invented. Eleo called her new dance the Chicken Flip. It was described by those privileged to witness it as a combination of the Turkey Trot and the Grizzly Bear, but more fun and more daring than either. Eleo and Reggie taught the steps to the others in their party, and they danced long into the night.

Two days after the football game, Princeton had its revenge. Woodrow Wilson, past president of Princeton University and a former student-manager of the football team, was elected the twenty-eighth president of the United States. Teddy Roosevelt's candidacy had split the Republican vote and handed the election to Wilson, the first Democrat to be elected in sixteen years. The political revolution extended to both houses of Congress, which went Democratic by wide margins. President Wilson demonstrated his intention to set a high moral tone by canceling the traditional Inaugural Ball.

Though most of the American public was dazzled by the adventures of the superrich, Wilson always had an academic's disdain for the upper classes. In 1905 he declared that "nothing has spread socialistic feeling in this country more than the automobile. . . . To the countryman they [the automobilists] are a picture of the arrogance of wealth, with all its independence and carelessness."[20] The idea of redistributing all this careless wealth appealed very strongly to Wilson. Republicans, in a bid to silence those trying to whip up class animosity, proposed the Sixteenth Amendment, which invited the federal government's hand into every pocket. A national income tax had been imposed during the Civil War, but it had been suspended after that conflict. Though the Republicans never really expected the amendment to pass, it was ratified in the waning days of the Taft administration and took effect a month after Wilson was inaugurated.

The countdown to Christmas that began in December 1912 added its increased holiday preparation to routine household tasks. Nora Sears bought stamps for Christmas cards and the usual soaps, and she mindfully entered those purchases in her small account book. She decided against attending a lecture with friends because she had developed an inconvenient cough, which would be annoying to others in the lecture hall. Nora's housekeeper assured her fondly that the house would continue to run smoothly if she wanted to remain in bed, and since Nora was feeling warm, possibly with a slight fever, she decided to let her chores go for a bit. She enlisted Eleo and Freddy to attend to the errands that would not wait. Secretly, Nora was pleased to have the extra time to finish reading the fascinating book that all of her friends were discussing, *The Loss of the Titanic,* a meticulous eyewitness account by a survivor, Lawrence Beesley.

The family's physician, Dr. Ellis, came to check on Nora when her temperature rose. He advised rest and liquids, and Nora paid him five dollars. She was too ill to record his visit the following night. The servants knew, as they watched Dr. Ellis come down the stairs from Nora's bedroom to confer in hushed tones with the family, that it was serious. The doctor had detected an inflammation of the lung. Pneumonia. Nora died a few days before Christmas. Her funeral service in Trinity Church was filled with many of the same people who had attended her wedding there thirty-three years before. Nora was remembered for her support of countless charities, for the love she had given so generously for fifty-six years to family and friends, and for the dignity with which she had faced disappointment. She had been, her friends all said, "a saint on earth."

Nora's obituary in the *Boston Globe* noted that "to the public at large she was little known, save as the mother of Miss Eleonora R. Sears."[21] Eleo was caught off guard by the well of feeling she had for this good and quiet woman. Nora had made it a point of honor to live within the boundaries set by others and, as befitted a lady, her name had appeared in the newspapers only three times, at her debut, when she married, and at her death.

CHAPTER 11

Warrants and War Clouds

ORA'S CASKET WAS PLACED in the simple brick vault reserved for the immediate family in the basement of Christ's Church Longwood following a private memorial service in the imposing stone chapel that David Sears had built.[1] Though Eleo's relationship with her mother had often been strained, she fully appreciated that Nora had been, in Eleo's own words, a "wonderful" wife and mother, and that she herself had been a fortunate daughter. It was Nora who had made the Sears household a family. For Eleo, Nora had been a moderating influence, like a mile marker signaling when her daughter had gone too far. Nora's grown daughter admitted, publicly, to having been a disappointment to her "poor dear darling mother" because she had never been very good at her school lessons—that one fault apparently standing in for all the others.[2]

Time-honored rituals of grief organized and clarified the way that daily life continued after a loss. As prescribed, the Sears family entered into a yearlong period of mourning. Initially, Eleo "put on mourning" in the expected way, wearing a somber black dress and hat to the church services. Thereafter, she slipped a black armband of the type traditionally worn by men over the left sleeve of her everyday clothes. Nobody expected Eleo's father, who had been to this point a disengaged and haphazard parent, to take renewed interest in his offspring, so Eleo's friends rallied around her with all the sympathy reserved for an orphan. Nora's closest friend, Gretchen Warren, stepped warmly into the role of surrogate mother. As a small girl, Eleo had been attracted by Mrs. Warren's sense of fun and impressed by the breadth of her intellectual interests. Now they were united in sorrow. Gretchen Warren took Nora's place beside Eleo for evenings at the theater. Gretchen's grandchildren rode Eleo's ponies and scampered through her stable in Beverly Farms, helping to brush the old, abandoned horses that Eleo had given refuge.

In the month following his daughter's death, T. J. Coolidge set up a trust fund for his grandchildren. The world that he had known felt as though it was ending, and he wanted to ensure that, at the very least, his grandchildren would have a secure financial future. The looming national income tax threatened those few who fell within its grip. Personal exemptions, set at $4,000 (equal to $85,000 today), protected more than 99 percent of the population.[3] The new federal tax would take 7 percent of one's income above $500,000. T. J. Coolidge felt no compulsion to give away to strangers what he had earned and, after suffering two body blows in a single year with the loss of two of his children, the income tax piled insult on injury.

T.J was left to ponder how fleeting life and joy could be, and perhaps that was why he was agreeable when Isabella Stewart Gardner asked to borrow his painting *El Jaleo* by John Singer Sargent for an art exhibition she was planning. For thirty years Belle had coveted that painting and pestered T.J. with requests to buy it, and she had had ample time to imagine a setting worthy of it. Belle hung Sargent's majestic eleven-foot-wide portrait of a passionate Spanish gypsy dancer at the end of a hallway at Fenway Court. She surrounded the painting with a custom-built Moorish stone arch that was edged with mirrors. On the floor in front of the painting she placed musical instruments and footlights so that the dancer glowed with life. When T.J. saw the showcase that Belle had created, he gave the painting to her.

For the entire year following her mother's death, Eleo did not enter any tennis tournaments or any horse shows, though she did not remain cloistered. She crewed on a yacht and continued with her extensive sports schedule. When Mike Vanderbilt sailed off to the Mediterranean in the early fall, he left one of his brand-new automobiles in Eleo's care. Eleo took the auto out for a test drive, racing it around her Beverly Farms neighborhood and up through Manchester, and thus she came to the attention of the Beverly police. Eleo was charged this time not for excessive speed, but for driving a car that was not registered in Massachusetts. Mike's automobile, it appeared, carried papers that were valid only in New York. The summons that required Eleo to appear at the Salem County Court House contained a spelling error. It had been issued to "Eleanor Sears," and Eleo returned the document to the Beverly chief of police with the notation that she did not know anyone by that name. Chagrined and annoyed, Chief S. Walter Woodbury took personal charge of the case and delivered a new, corrected summons to the home of "Eleonora R. Sears."

To Eleo it was a continual a source of annoyance to see her name (which was also her mother's name) spelled creatively, either with too many A's or too few. She and her family had lived in the Beverly area for many decades, and she expected the Beverly police to know better. No less irritating to Eleo was the general confusion of herself with her tennis-playing cousin, Evelyn Sears. Evelyn had won the U.S. National Singles Championship in 1907, and she and Eleo had alternated winning the big annual tournament at the Country Club in Brookline (Evelyn in 1909 and Eleo in 1910), which only added to the mix-up. Reports of tennis matches often assigned the wins and losses of each Sears girl seemingly at random. It was Eleo's unshakable conviction that anyone who didn't care enough to get the details right was either hopelessly inept or a fool. In either case, no attention need be paid.

Three times in the courtroom in Salem the clerk called out, "Eleonora R. Sears," and was met only with silence. Eleo had chosen to ignore the summons. Knowledgeable onlookers were not surprised by her high-handed behavior and they whispered darkly that, as they had suspected, "she intends to do as she pleases." The presiding judge, aptly named George B. Sears though he was no relation, was not amused. He issued a warrant for Eleo's arrest, and he ordered Chief Woodbury to find her and bring her to justice. At this point, reporters jumped delightedly on the developing story of the Boston socialite who drove an unregistered "high-powered" automobile all over the North Shore, said automobile belonging to Harold Vanderbilt, who was known to have been showering her with attention.

The initial problem that confronted Chief Woodbury was how to locate Eleo. On October 1 she had decamped from her summer home in Beverly Farms and returned to her winter residence at 122 Beacon Street. A reporter from the *Boston Traveler* had no trouble tracking her down. The maid who answered the door of Eleo's Boston town house told him that Miss Sears was, indeed, at home but would not give him a statement. The newsman was surprised to find the fugitive making no attempt to conceal her whereabouts and was "calmly awaiting arrest." "At the young woman's home this morning," the reporter wrote with evident disappointment, "there was nothing to indicate that she shares in the slightest degree the interest shown by other parties to the case."[4] Eleo was not secretive when she left her house later, in a "nonchalant *I should worry* manner," to attend a horse show at the Brockton Fair. Poor Chief Woodbury, supposedly out looking for her, was plainly uncomfortable with his options. To actually arrest this high-profile young woman would be undignified and would serve only to fuel the growing and unwelcome media attention. Such an arrest would also antagonize Eleo's influential friends who lived in Beverly. Not a wise career move. Chief Woodbury was an officer of the court, however, and he had a court order to enforce. Judiciously, he chose a wait-and-see approach while talking tough: "I'll see that she is in court all right."[5]

In the Salem courtroom on the third day, Eleo's name was called again, and still there was no response. The idea of seeing just how long she could string out this cat-and-mouse game strongly appealed to her. Eleo's attorney,

John P. Wright, was more practical, and he convinced Eleo that she needed to appear in court voluntarily and soon. Wright had a long conference with Judge Sears, who was increasingly impatient with Eleo's disregard of his authority. The judge was working himself up to make an example of her, and if she waited until Chief Woodbury was forced to march her into the court-room, the consequences would be severe and expensive.

On the fourth day Eleo drove up alone to the Salem County Court House in "a big, luxuriously-fitted limousine," arriving minutes before the court opened at ten o'clock. She wore a simply tailored jacket and skirt of dark blue and a black hat with a heavy dark veil that dramatically hid her face. Eleo was the only woman in the nearly empty courtroom, and she seated herself at a desk beside Probation Officer Hart. Associate Judge E. C. Battis was now presiding, and Eleo's lawyer, knowing her penchant for stirring the pot, advised her to let him do all the talking. Eleo followed his advice literally, and when her name was called she stood in front of the desk with her arms folded, but she did not utter a sound. She was seen chatting away afterward with Probation Officer Hart. Attorney Wright vigorously presented her case: Miss Sears had at first been improperly summoned and had stood on her technical rights; an attempt had been made to register the car, but for some reason that had failed; the issuance of the warrant had created unnecessary publicity that prevented her from appearing in court sooner. And looking con-trite, Eleo's lawyer offered a plea of nolo contendre. Judge Battis conferred with Chief Woodbury, who couldn't wait to get this problem off his plate. Wright paid the twenty-five-dollar fine that was handed down and Eleo quickly slipped out of the courtroom. When Mike returned from his trip to collect his automobile, he was heartbroken to have missed all the excitement. He suggested that if Eleo was going to persist in living on the wrong side of the law, she should consider keeping him on retainer.

Eleo's friends waited in vain for the wedding announcement that always seemed to be just over the horizon. Eleo was now thirty-one, well past the age that respectable girls married. Boston matrons shook their heads. They had prophesied that no good would ever come of letting a girl focus so much on athletics. But Eleo had always been a willful child and, Heaven knew, Nora had done as much with her as any mother could. Eleo had had her pick of eli-gible young men years ago, but these days she could count herself lucky that Mike Vanderbilt still seemed interested. For Eleo marriage was never an urgent desire, and, now with her mother gone, it was even less a priority. It is appealing to speculate about the path Eleo might have taken if her mother had not died just when marriage rumors about the pair were at their height. Responsibilities, appearances, and conventional happiness were important to Nora, and though Eleo was always reluctant to subordinate her interests to anyone else's, she had cared about not disappointing her mother. But Nora did die, and the presumed engagement progressed no further. The year of mourning that followed Nora's death came and went. Mike remained a dear friend, and he and Eleo continued to be each other's most entertaining playmate. And gradually speculation about the couple's intentions withered.

Eleo kept her tennis skills sharp during her yearlong hiatus from the tennis circuit, and she met with great success when she returned to competition in the spring of 1914. A national ranking of women players had begun in 1913 after Maud Barger-Wallach spearheaded the drive for a system modeled on the one used to rank the men. The Sears family was in mourning during 1913, so Eleo was not listed in the rankings. Upon her return to lawn tennis competition, Eleo won the women's singles title at the Country Club in Brookline against Mrs. Barger-Wallach, who remained a dangerous opponent despite her use of an increasingly archaic underhand serve. Eleo was victorious too in the tournament at the neighboring Country Club, where she beat the defending singles champion, her cousin Evelyn Sears. Eleo then took the singles title from her longtime friend Alice Thorndike at the Montserrat Club in Beverly. Among all female players in 1914, Eleo was ranked number six nationally.

Eleo returned to the horse show world in Judge Moore's annual show at Rockmarge in the summer of 1914. Heavy rains throughout August, culminating with a downpour the day before the show, seemed to conspire against the much-anticipated event, but on show day the sun came out. All Saturday morning and through the early afternoon, scores of workmen furiously raked the tan bark on the pathways and in the large show ring at the driving park. By the start of the show at three o'clock that afternoon, only a damp patch at the north end of the track betrayed the weeklong deluge. A fine crowd gathered along the shaded bank overlooking the track and thumbed through their hardbound copies of the program, which listed the scheduled classes and the tea and sweets to follow. Among the spectators were Frederick Prince and his two sons, Norman and Frederick Jr., Mr. and Mrs. Rudolph Agassiz, the Neal Rantouls, and the former ambassador to Russia, Curtis Guild. On the hillside made green and lush by the summer rains, the well-groomed families presented a graceful tableau in their flowered hats and summer flannels under the warm, blue, cloud-flecked sky.

A young coach bugler called the audience to attention. Freddy Sears joined the vigorous applause that greeted his sister's return to the show ring as Eleo guided two of the Judge's champions around the track in the tandem class. Excitement built when Eleo reappeared high atop a gleaming open park coach, deftly handling four sets of reins and four charging horses, which she drove around the track at a gallop. Two top-hatted footmen hung on for dear life at the rear of the coach. Eleo's cousin Phyllis Sears drove the Judge's high-stepping international champion Lady Seaton to much acclaim. The

Judge's two grandchildren made their first appearances in this show, adding their youthful charm to the blue-ribbon afternoon. The prizewinning horses exhibited at the show had all just returned from competitions in England. Fortunately, this precious cargo arrived home only days before war was declared in Europe.

Far from the North Shore, in a remote and rather grubby-sounding region called the Balkans, a toxic brew of nationalistic ambitions and regional antagonisms had been percolating for centuries. Exotic armies of Serbs, Bosnians, Bulgarians, Croats, and Slovenes invaded one another periodically, and the battles were joined variously by the Russians, Turks, Austrians, Albanians, and Montenegrins. In the Balkans in 1912 a smallish war had broken out, followed by a second Balkan war in 1913. By 1914 Americans would surely have suffered from crisis fatigue if they had given any thought at all to that part of the world. A foreign problem of far more compelling interest to many Americans had nothing to do with the Balkans. It seems that all five of the princesses of Bavaria, daughters of King Ludwig and Queen Marie, had reached marriageable age without any of them having had a serious suitor. The five lovelorn royal daughters seemed doomed to spinsterhood.

After the Austrian Archduke Franz Ferdinand and his wife were assassinated on June 28, 1914, as they drove through the streets of Sarajevo, Austria promptly declared war on Serbia and on its protector, Russia. In a spreading tangle of military alliances and old resentments, the Great War began. The war fever that gripped the people and the thrones of Europe had no equivalent hold on their brethren on the other side of the Atlantic. Bostonians shared the countrywide view that America was an innocent among the royal jackals on the Continent. "Peace-loving citizens of this country," declared the *Chicago Record-Herald,* "[should] tender a hearty vote of thanks to Columbus for having discovered America."[6] This sentiment from the heartland was echoed by the *Wabash (Indiana) Plain Dealer:* "We never appreciated so keenly as now the foresight exercised by our fathers in emigrating to America."[7] President Wilson's proclamation of American neutrality in "this war with which we have nothing to do" was in harmony with the feelings of the American man on the street, even though the president's phrasing reflected an elite education that still revered the language.[8]

For years, as the small nation-states of Europe picked away at each other like irritant scabs, their diplomats spent companionable summers in Newport and on the North Shore. The vast, turreted Oceanside Hotel in Magnolia played host to ambassadors from Russia, France, England, Germany, Turkey, and several Latin American countries. This rainbow of foreign dignitaries took meals together in the glass-enclosed dining room that ran half the length of a football field. The ambassadors and their staffs played tennis on the hotel's grass courts and took bracing dips in the ocean. They sprinkled their

Old World charm on the hotel's other guests, such as Mrs. J. P. Morgan, Mrs. Ulysses S. Grant, and Alice Roosevelt Longworth. They discussed current events with Major Douglas MacArthur when he dropped in to visit his aunts. In the evenings they gathered to enjoy concerts given by the hotel's twenty-three-piece orchestra under the baton of another guest, the March King, John Philip Sousa.

Older residents of the close-knit North Shore communities were incensed by the summertime liberties taken by members of the foreign diplomatic corps. The boorish Russian ambassador and his friend from the German embassy were known for wearing their tennis whites both on the courts and on the beach. Then they turned up at lunch in the same attire. In Newport, where codes of dress and manners were more relaxed, these same men were thought enchanting. The broadest source of international friction was the special "D" license plate issued to diplomats beginning in 1909. Residents resented the ability of the foreign vacationers to ignore local speed limits without consequence.

As the world spun toward an unknown destination, old-timers grumbled about the general collapse of standards. Young women, in the grip of new fashion fads, affected a "careless" look as they went about town. Most of the offending girls played tennis, and they spent the entire day wearing casual summer flannel. Eleo had defied the stricter standards of an earlier decade and risked harsher condemnation when she first appeared in her "mannish" tennis clothes. These days, as Eleo hiked through downtown Newport in her tan Norfolk jacket that was part of her tennis costume, some residents conceded that the jacket did look becoming on her. As she drove along Bellevue Avenue in her gray racing car, many admired the way "she maneuvered [her auto] with the dexterity of a professional chauffeur."[9]

At first, as war swept across Europe, daily life changed little in the United States, but on the North Shore the conflict did not pass unnoticed. The summer season was measurably more subdued with the absence of Madame Dumba, the popular and socially prominent wife of the Austro-Hungarian ambassador. The official line was that she had decided to "take the cure" at a spa on the Continent, but it would have been politically unsupportable for her to enjoy a leisurely summer in America while her country was at war.

In Newport on July 25, 1914, war or no war, Alva Belmont staged her spectacular Chinese Ball in honor of her daughter, the Duchess of Marlborough. Alva transformed Marble House into a Chinese pavilion, complete with pelicans. The guests, all wearing oriental costumes, dined in groups at several homes in the summer colony before the evening's climactic dance in the Gold Room at Marble House. Alva, Mike, and Eleo were in the group that dined at Crossways, the home of Mr. and Mrs. Stuyvesant Fish, which had been made over as the "Temple of Heaven," the summer palace in Peking.

Eleo's delicately embroidered silk robe, which she had ordered from China, harmonized well with the costume of her dinner partner, the German ambassador, who was dressed as a Chinese emperor.

Slowly but inexorably the war abroad did alter life in America. French chauffeurs and Italian gardeners left their posts Stateside to return to their countries to fight. In Newport Harbor the big steam yacht *Josephine,* owned by a member of the Widener family, was sitting at anchor. It was being readied for a rescue mission to England to retrieve Mr. and Mrs. Joseph Widener and their friends, who were stranded there when war was declared.

In December 1914 Eleo attended the Red and White Cross Horse Show at Madison Square Garden. This charity event was a scaled-down substitute for the National, which had been canceled because of the war. The thrilling international jumping competition initiated by Alfred Vanderbilt was impossible now. Nevertheless, the rainy two-day event was supported by all the usual horse show faithful. The show cost $100,000 to produce (more than $2 million today) and was completely underwritten by Judge William Moore so that all the proceeds could be donated to the Red Cross and other war relief organizations.

CHAPTER 12

The Great War: From Fox Hunts to Fox Holes

CHORUS: [accompanied by a jaunty piano]

I didn't raise my boy to be a soldier,
I brought him up to be my pride and joy,
Who dares to place a musket on his shoulder,
To shoot some other mother's darling boy?
Let nations arbitrate their future troubles,
It's time to lay the sword and gun away,
There'd be no war today,
If mothers all would say,
"I didn't raise my boy to be a soldier."[1]

I DIDN'T RAISE MY BOY TO BE A SOLDIER" was one of the biggest hit songs of 1915. On the cover of the sheet music was a tender sketch of a white-haired mother clutching her soldier son to her bosom. Above them floated ominous rows of rifle-bearing lads with bombs bursting around them. As Europe slaughtered its young men, the mood of the American public remained resolutely against getting sucked into the mess "over there."

From a reassuring distance Americans sympathized with plucky France and stalwart Britain. They hissed the Germans who carried out the first air-raid attack in history, using Zeppelin airships to drop bombs on London. In Belgium, at the Battle of Ypres, the German military continued to innovate and unleashed a terrifying new weapon, poison gas. Idealistic, adventurous American boys with romantic notions of war rallied to the stirring cry "Tout et tout pour la France," and they sailed to France to give their all. They offered their services as ambulance drivers and pilots. Some fought in the trenches with the French Foreign Legion.

Against the strong opposition of his parents, Norman Prince, the younger of the Prince brothers and Eleo's fond childhood friend, left his law practice in Chicago to join the battle in France. Norman and two friends had a vision of an All-American flying squadron that would fight the Hun in the air. Norman's affection for France and its people had its roots in the lovely summers he had spent at his family's estate in Pau, with its extensive stable of horses. Norman had always preferred foxhunting and flying to lawyering, and it was widely predicted that the war would be over by Christmas. He and the other lads needed to hurry if they were to see any action at all. The first battle Norman and his friends fought was with the French military bureaucracy. The French high command maintained that it did not need outside help and preferred to scatter the American volunteers anonymously among its own fighting units. Norman resisted this solution. His dream of a cohesive, distinctly American contribution to the defense of France attracted more than thirty American pilots, including some former Legionnaires. After months of frustration, Norman and his comrades were allowed to form l'Escadrille Américaine under the command of the French captain Georges Thenault. The boys flew N-124s, appealingly named Nieuports, the lightest and fastest planes available. William K. Vanderbilt, Alva's ex-husband, underwrote the cost of maintaining the Escadrille, and he paid the passage of many American volunteer pilots who went to France.

The accumulating shocks of entering an uncharted era grew more personal for Americans at home when an unarmed British passenger ship, the HMS *Lusitania,* was torpedoed by a German submarine on May 7, 1915. Of the 1,198 people who died in that attack, 128 were Americans. Though the *Lusitania* carried an adequate number of lifeboats, the ship sank in twenty minutes, before many of the boats could be launched.

The beautifully appointed *Lusitania* was the fastest passenger liner in service: it crossed the Atlantic in less than five days. One passenger, Alfred Vanderbilt, planned to chair a meeting of the International Horse Breeders Association in London, and then buy a fleet of hospital wagons for the Red Cross and offer himself as a driver. On the morning of the *Lusitania*'s departure, New York newspapers carried a message from the German embassy that warned Americans against traveling on Allied ships. That same morning Alfred received a strange telegram: "THE LUSITANIA IS DOOMED. DO NOT SAIL ON HER." It was signed, "MORTE."[2] Alfred laughed off the melodramatic cable. Toward the end of the comfortable sea voyage, Alfred attended a party given by Charles Frohman, the theatrical producer and manager who had guided Ethel Barrymore's career and whom she thought of as a second father. That night Alfred attended a benefit concert for the Seaman's Charity and paid five dollars for a ten-cent program. "There," he said to the young lady selling programs, "that's for your lovely smile."[3]

After a German torpedo hit the ship, Alfred and his valet, Ronald Denyer, ignored the deck steward's warning, "Hurry, Mr. Vanderbilt, or it will be too late," and both men continued to seek out and assist women and children into the lifeboats. Alfred thought it was bad form for a man of his position to panic. He was last seen putting a lifebelt around a woman's shoulders. Alfred himself had never learned to swim.

Alfred's wife, Margaret, offered a reward for the recovery of his body, but it was never found. Eventually, most of Alfred's horses and cars were sold. Alfred's devoted chauffeur, Thomas Greene, and Thomas's wife and young son found themselves suddenly adrift. Eleo invited Thomas and his family to come and work for her. Thomas would remain with Eleo for fifty years.

Officially, the United States was neutral in the conflict, but the uneasy blend of war and peace was evident even in the pages of the *American Lawn Tennis* magazine. Advice on building regulation-size dirt courts and the insight that gut strings of tennis racquets, though called "catgut," were in fact lamb intestines, seven of which were needed for one tennis string, shared space with articles on European players now fighting in Germany and France. From northern France came word of the first death in the tennis community. Gone was Anthony F. Wilding, the Australian who was the Men's Singles Champion of 1910 and a member of their fine Davis Cup Team.

Tennis officials sought advice from international experts to resolve vexing issues of protocol and sportsmanship. A written query went to the German tennis champion Oscar Kreuzer, who was then residing in a prisoner-of-war camp in England. Some of the forty questions posed to Kreuzer were deeply philosophical—under what circumstances is it honorable for players to take advantage of their opponents? Kreuzer's response reflected modern realities. "Everything is fair in love and war," he wrote back; "press your advantage where you see your chance."[4] Overburdened censors delayed Kreuzer's letter, fearing that his answers might be some kind of code. It took fourteen weeks for his reply to reach New York.

Philadelphia in June 1915 was the site of two of the most significant tournaments in lawn tennis. Again, the Merion Cricket Club hosted the Pennsylvania and Eastern States Championships. As before, Eleo and Bill Clothier were a strong mixed doubles team, but they failed to repeat their previous victories. Eleo took a special interest in the matches played by Edgar Scott, who turned in a respectable performance. Years earlier, when Edgar was a boy, Eleo had saved his life. The story of the rescue was handed down from generation to generation in the Scott family. Edgar and his mother had stopped in Boston on their way to deposit him at his school in Groton, and Eleo visited them at the Copley Plaza Hotel. The two ladies were deep in conversation, and the thoroughly bored Edgar watched them from his seat on the windowsill. The window screen suddenly gave way and Edgar fell backward toward the plaza below. Eleo sprang forward, grabbed his legs, and pulled him back up. Edgar remained grateful and intimidated by the lady who had kept him, as the Scott family put it, "from being splattered."

The national tennis tournament that was forerunner of the U.S. Open began the following week at the Philadelphia Cricket Club. Young Bill Tilden pulled together his gifts of speed, height, and long reach to win the Men's Singles competition. In the fifth round of the Ladies Singles contest, Eleo lost to Hazel Hotchkiss Wightman. Hazel had recently returned to competition after a three-year hiatus that included marriage to George Wightman and motherhood. Later that same day, Eleo and Hazel joined forces and won their second National Doubles Championship together. The crowd was on their side throughout the match. Diminutive Hazel was a master of court tactics, and she directed the play like a "little general." Eleo obeyed her without hesitation.

A new star on the American tennis scene, recently arrived from Christiana (Oslo), Norway, was Anna Margarethe Bjurstedt, or "Molla" for short. Molla Bjurstedt was Norway's national tennis champion, and she had won a bronze medal at the 1912 Olympics. When Molla first appeared on American tennis courts, sports reportage billed her as "the Norwegian girl," as much to avoid grappling with the complexity of her name as to reference her exotic birthplace. Molla looked more exotic still. With her blunt-cropped hair that hung straight and dark to her chin, her narrow dark eyes, and her nut-brown complexion, Molla resembled more the nomadic peoples of Eastern Europe than she did a girl from Scandinavia. Molla was a trained masseuse, an occupation that was popular at the time with Norwegian girls. While working in England, Molla learned decent English and excellent tennis, and she began to dream of playing tennis half of every year and working the other half to pay for it. There was little opportunity for tennis in war-racked Europe, so Molla moved to Canada. She was working for a family there when she visited New York for the first time in 1914. She decided then that America was the place to be.

Molla's hard-hitting style on the tennis court, the wide grin that frequently lit her sturdy face, and the grace with which she accepted victory or defeat quickly won her many fans. For a girl so widely traveled (she had learned German in boarding school and French in Paris), Molla was absurdly superstitious. She was afraid to play in a tennis match without an admittedly "ugly" rectangular Japanese brooch pinned on the front of her tennis dress. And always, whenever Molla encountered two white horses, she made a wish.

In the Women's Singles final at the Philadelphia tournament, the three-time title holder Hazel Wightman was the sentimental favorite. Molla Bjurstedt was the largely unknown foreign challenger. Molla drove the ball relentlessly from corner to corner. Her mighty topspin forehands and back-hands were propelled by arms and shoulders strengthened by her work as a masseuse, and she exhausted her worthy opponent. Molla believed her win was preordained. The night before the match, she had wished on a falling star. This victory was the first of Molla's eight national singles titles, a record that remains unequalled.

It says a great deal about both Molla and Hazel that, in the highly competitive world of tennis, they emerged as friends. Molla observed with regret that it was difficult to form many real friendships in tennis because women lacked the "give-and-take spirit" of men and resented players better than themselves. Molla was equally critical of European and American women, too many of whom could not shrug off the emotion of the contest and shake hands and mean it. Molla saw how losing female players sometimes started a nasty buzz about their opponents to detract from their rivals' victories. This jealousy kept many women from assisting less skilled players with their game.

Eleo Sears was not petty like that. She enjoyed mentoring younger players. She was a fierce competitor, but she had a realistic view of her abilities and genuinely admired players of superior talent. Far from disparaging people more gifted than she, Eleo sought them out, believing that her own star was enhanced rather than diminished by their success. Eleo took an immediate liking to the plain-spoken, fun-loving Norwegian girl who wasn't afraid to laugh out loud or get a freckle or two in the sun. On the court Molla was as stealthy and as focused as a panther, but after-hours she loved to let loose and dance and smoke, and she did not like to leave a party early, even the night before a match. Like Eleo, Molla had "no patience with the languishing, made-up beauty," who Molla considered to be "not much more than a dressmaker's dummy."[5] The trio of Eleo, Molla, and Hazel could often be found holding court in the bar after tournaments in Philadelphia, the West Side Tennis Club in New York, or the Casino in Newport. Their cheerful table was always surrounded by players and friends who stopped by to joke, analyze the matches, and gossip.

Molla selected her doubles partners with great care. Her favorite partners were Hazel Wightman, Mary Browne, and Eleo Sears. Molla felt that these three women were the best in the nation when playing at the net, and that they had the mental and physical endurance to sustain championship-level play throughout a tournament. Above all, these three women shared a willingness to suspend their individual ambition and play, instead, for the good of the side. Molla pinpointed Eleo's chief fault to be her overreliance on the short, quick chop shot, which she used to the detriment of her otherwise strong game.

In June 1916 at the Philadelphia Cricket Club, Molla and Eleo captured the National Doubles Championship. Earlier in the day Molla had also won the Women's Singles title. She had known she would win because, before the match, she found a four-leaf clover and placed it solemnly in Eleo's hand for safekeeping.

Many players of the top rank like Molla and Hazel devoted all their energy to tennis, but Eleo's interests were always too wide-ranging for such narrowly focused dedication. She rarely followed the game to backwater venues such as Pittsburgh or Mexico, and she would choose to miss tournaments, even at her beloved Longwood Club, if the timing of an important horse show conflicted and she could find no way to participate in both events. Eleo used part of her time away from the tennis circuit to win the badminton sectional championship. Eleo's absence from one tennis tournament at Longwood was noted and lamented by a reporter for *American Lawn Tennis* magazine: "One missed the jovial, gay atmosphere always surrounding Miss Eleonora Sears, who was busy winning another half dozen blue ribbons at that time. She seems to have the happy faculty of giving others just as good fun as she herself enjoys."[6]

Eleo initiated Molla in many of the invigorating pastimes of her adopted country. In something akin to a baptism, Molla joined the group of liberated men and women who played tennis in their bathing suits on New York's Brighton Beach and jumped into the ocean at the end of the game. On winter afternoons Eleo took Molla ice skating at the Boston Arena. Eleo introduced Molla to her favorite home away from home, the suburban Philadelphia estate of Bill and Anita Clothier, which was often filled with friends in the tennis and foxhunting worlds. During the disheartening years of the war, the hospitality of the Clothiers and the gently rolling beauty of the Pennsylvania countryside seemed, more than ever, like a refuge.

The Clothiers' informal stone home, known as the Lodge, was in Phoenixville, two miles west of Valley Forge. It rambled along the crest of a hill at the end of a long driveway that wound its way up from Clothier Springs Road. Bill and Anita encouraged friends to come and go as they pleased, and they left the front door unlocked.

The Clothiers' grass tennis courts were across the circular driveway from the main entrance. Bill and Anita had started with one court, but they soon discovered that a second was needed to accommodate all their tennis-playing guests. The greatest champions in the history of the game played on those courts. The players answering to the name Bill alone could fill a Tennis Hall of Fame roster. There was "Big Bill" Tilden and his rival "Little Bill" Johnston, and Bill Clothier's closest friend, Bill Larned, who was a top-ten player for nineteen years, which would probably have extended to twenty years if he hadn't spent the 1898 season with Teddy Roosevelt's Rough Riders.

The Clothier home offered four-season fun for children of all ages. There were ponds for fishing, swimming, and ice hockey. Sections of fence leading to the pastures below the main house were removed in the winter to allow for sledding and cross-country skiing. After the Clothiers added a baseball diamond and a basketball court for their two children, Eleo rounded up her housemates to join her in running bases and shooting hoops. At day's end, everyone looked forward to cocktails on the stone-paved terrace that offered sweeping views of the Clothiers' 850-acre Valley Hill Farm. Horses grazed peacefully in the white-fenced paddocks. In the distance was the piggery, with its shaded outdoor runs, and a two-hundred-year-old complex of barns, which housed the dairy herd that produced rich, grade-A milk for sale along Philadelphia's Main Line.

Cascading canine howls floated up to the main house from the foxhound kennel at the bottom of the hill. The racket was stilled instantly by the steadying commands of Orville E. Roberts, the huntsman who handled the breeding and training of the pack and recognized each hound by its voice. Sharp, well-mannered hounds were an essential part of any fox hunt. Those hounds that were habitually noisy, who "gave tongue" for no good reason while out on the trail, were known as "babblers," and babblers soon lost their place in the pack.

Bill Clothier established the Pickering Hunt and presided as M.F.H. (Master of Fox Hounds) for forty consecutive years. The Pickering Hunt ranked with the nearby Radnor Hunt and New England's Myopia Hunt as among the best in the nation. The territory of the Pickering Hunt crossed several counties and covered more than twenty-five square miles. Bill Clothier was sensitive to the fact that the sport he loved depended on the benevolence of a great many farmers and property owners who allowed the hunt to cross their land.[7] To ensure the continued friendship of his neighbors, Bill organized thank-you breakfasts for them and "Farmers Day" competitions for working farm horses ridden by the farmers and their children. Each Thanksgiving Day the Blessing of the Hounds was offered at St. Peter's Church, the little whitewashed chapel that stood like a beacon above a broad patchwork of fields. Bill Clothier added his own prayer to the service: "We thank you, Lord, for the opportunity given us to enjoy the goodwill and hospitality of neighbors and landowners, which make possible for us the enjoyment of our hunting."[8]

Alone among sports, foxhunting is wrapped in a hazy glow of romance and ancient tradition that was imported from Merrie Olde England. Certainly, the happy combination of spirited horses and tricolor hounds, radiant red jackets, polished hunting horns, and autumn leaves floating down sparkling streams makes it the most picturesque of sports. The scarlet coats worn by the principal actors for high visibility in the field are called "pinks" after the British tailor Thomas Pink. Following more than a century of tradition, riders are expected to lift their hats to the M.F.H. when he passes by in his blazing pink. To the M.F.H. falls the important job of planning the route for the hunt, taking into account the terrain, the wind, and previous fox sightings. Often, as was the case with Bill Clothier, the M.F.H. supplies the hounds and many of the mounts. The task of the huntsman is to oversee the hounds in the field and to sound the horn that helps direct the pack and alert the fox of their approach. Whippers-in assist the huntsman to sight the fox. All manner of noble purposes are claimed for this attractive congregation of humans and nature. Foxhunters are held up as men who love the land and who are more than commonly attuned to the values of duty, honor, courage, and loyalty. Self-mastery over sloth and fear is attributed to the requirement to rise early and go forth on freezing winter mornings to face danger. During the summer, the off-season for foxhunting, tennis is considered a good prehunt conditioner because sportsmanlike behavior, adherence to a dress code, and early rising are expected. Many of the high-minded values associated with foxhunting were transferred to the battlefield. Foxhunters and tennis players fought with Teddy Roosevelt as Rough Riders, and the First Troop of the Philadelphia City Cavalry, which saw action from the Revolutionary War through the First World War, was composed predominantly of foxhunters.

As for the dangers of foxhunting itself, there were plenty. During the six- to seven-month hunting season, one bed at Beverly Hospital was kept continually occupied by members of the Myopia Hunt Club. Painful falls into briar patches, crashes into trees, and tramplings beneath horses left riders with a string of torn ligaments, broken collarbones, and concussions. The death of at least one member of a major hunt club could be forecast each season. And then there was the danger to the fox, the object of all this obsession and pageantry, its fate to be torn apart by the hounds. Sections of the fox, the pads of its feet and its handsome tail or "brush," were awarded to the riders who achieved special distinction during the hunt. These grisly souvenirs live on as paperweights and letter openers.

In America, where there are fewer foxes than in England and where foxes are perceived as less of a nuisance, the death of the fox is not strictly necessary for a successful outing. Often, if a fox is sighted and an enjoyable chase ensues, the hounds are called off to let the good fellow escape to run again another day.

Eleo grew up surrounded by the mystique of foxhunting, a sport that her grandfather Coolidge had pursued with urgent devotion and described reverently in his memoirs. Eleo was not so enamored, though foxhunting, like tennis, offered the excitement and camaraderie that she craved. Indeed, any outdoor activity that combined horses and hounds was wonderful by definition, but she was never comfortable charging over ragged hedges and fences, and she took no pleasure in the occasional mutilation of the fox. Yet, if she was to do a thing she would do it well, and she was Puritan enough to want to keep her "courage muscle" well exercised.[9] Eleo was often the first to awaken on the cold mornings before a hunt, and she went about rousing other members of the group, who were still snuggled under the covers at five-thirty.

Eleo never minded that on many fox hunts she was the only woman riding. Occasionally, when Eleo rode with the Pickering Hunt, she was joined by Bill Clothier's wife, Anita, who rode sidesaddle throughout her life. Both women knew that, should they get banged up in the process, they could expect little sympathy from the stoic Bill Clothier. During his forty-plus years of foxhunting Bill suffered more than twenty-six major injuries, including fractures of both arms, ribs, and collarbone, yet in that time he never missed a hunting season. A revealing tale was told by Bill's friend Stanley Reeves about a fall Reeves took. Reeves came off his horse while going over a fence, and he was knocked unconscious. A rider following behind him dismounted and came to his aid. Bill rode by, observed the dazed but now conscious Reeves on the ground, and said only, "Be sure to put back that rail you knocked off," before he galloped away.[10] Anita knew what she was getting into when she married Bill Clothier. He had gone foxhunting the day before their wedding and had broken several bones when he was thrown from his horse. The wedding ceremony took place around his hospital bed.

Always lurking in the background of everyday pleasures was the shadow of the war that was supposed to have ended by Christmas. Instead, it continued to expand. Italy and Bulgaria jumped into the global fray. Norman Prince returned home for a Christmas visit, still shining with the novelty of his adventures. During a reception at Boston's Tavern Club, Norman spoke enthusiastically about sleeping in tents on stretchers that served as beds and of eating his meals in the horse shed of an old farmhouse. He told of flying his single-man plane in soaring aerial duels with his German counterparts, his left hand on the gas control, his right hand guiding the altitude lever and firing the machine gun. Norman described a harrowing descent after his plane was hit by German fire and his motor quit. He managed to outfox his pursuers by gliding his plane to safety over French lines. He landed in a graveyard planted with white crosses that marked fallen French and German soldiers from an earlier stage of the conflict. The romance of Norman's near-death experiences left his mother cold. She followed an inner voice and took him to New York to have his portrait painted.

In the fall of 1916 the Escadrille Américaine was assigned to Verdun, which was the scene of some of the most monstrous fighting of the war. After a mission in which Norman brought down his opponent, he swung his plane toward his home lines, flying through a thickening haze that made visibility too poor for further combat. He was staying low to get his bearings when he flew into a string of telegraph wires. His plane somersaulted when it hit the ground and crushed his back and part of his skull. As Norman lay dying in a

French hospital, the French government awarded him its highest military honors, the Croix de la Légion d'Honneur and the Croix de Guerre. Norman had compiled a fine record of 122 aerial engagements. He knocked out several observation balloons and was credited with five "kills" and four "assists," which earned him the designation Ace. Still, it was not the glorious death that Norman would have wished for himself. He would have preferred to die like his friend Victor Chapman, who had been shot down while attacking an enemy plane that was pursuing his friends. Till the very end Norman remained seduced by the poetry of the Great War, in which fallen warriors bled the "red / Sweet wine of youth" in a grand cause.[11] Within eight days of Norman's death, his brother Frederick sailed to France to take Norman's place in the squadron. The Escadrille Américaine was drawing so much worldwide attention that the Germans complained it was making a mockery of America's claim of neutrality. In December 1916 the corps was renamed the Escadrille Lafayette.

CHAPTER 13

Dry Socks and Ambulances

❧

UNDER ORDERS FROM DOCTORS worried about her blood pressure, Alva Erskine Smith Vanderbilt Belmont took a leave of absence from the clamorous world of war and need. After her husband's death, Mrs. O. H. P. Belmont, lioness of New York and Newport, had reinvented herself yet again. She was now "Alva E. Belmont—Woman of the People." With a banner across her bosom, Alva had led the shopgirl section of the great parade for women's suffrage up New York's Fifth Avenue to a rally at Carnegie Hall on May 4, 1912. Though Alva had looked as imposing as a battleship, she confessed later to Consuelo that she had been trembling as she marched, because parading in front of catcalling, curious crowds was so alien to a woman of her sheltered upbringing. Alva threw all of her awesome emotional and financial resources into the battle for women's rights, and she included in her sometimes stifling embrace legions of working-class foot soldiers for the cause. Alva set up soup kitchens and settlement houses for unemployed suffragists. She walked picket lines, lobbied Congress, and provided financial backing that kept Max Eastman's strident socialist magazine, *The Masses,* afloat. To raise additional funds, Alva wrote and produced an operetta, *Melinda and Her Sisters,* with music and lyrics by Elsa Maxwell that had a sold-out premiere at the Waldorf-Astoria.

In the summer of 1916 Alva leased a large, white, coal-fired yacht, a houseboat named the *Seminole,* from the horse breeder and financier Henry Phipps, and she plotted a leisurely monthlong excursion. As her doctors had recommended, Alva's sole and simple purpose would be to float, merely to drift, to cleanse the mind and renew the spirit. The planned route snaked along the eastern coastline, around Long Island, up past Connecticut, Rhode Island, and Massachusetts, with stops to take in local sights, pick up and deposit a changing cast of companions, and visit friends onshore. Alva had prearranged for Eleo to meet her party when the *Seminole* dropped anchor near Prides Crossing. Alva and her initial band of four men and one woman departed the narrow bay at Port Jefferson, Long Island, on July 1. She had made a solemn pact with herself to suspend all her usual impatience and severe judgments for the duration of the tour. She preselected the mood for the journey—tranquil and neighborly—and she intended that nothing, neither hell nor high water, would spoil her vision.

It was from the start a storm-tossed voyage. Wind-driven rain and tormented seas kept the travelers in their cabins. Alva remained resolutely cheerful. Her guests could read, and converse, and create their own "small spheres" of contentment. They dared not get seasick and throw up in her presence. Alva and her group of adventurers were forced to seek refuge from the storm on the very first night. They slept in a hotel onshore, and for entertainment they went to a picture show. Though Alva fought mightily against the impulse, she could not, in good conscience, deny that the hotel was one to avoid in the future, and that an extremely unpleasant odor pervaded the movie theater.

Day 2 was little better. Magnificent winds and temperatures that mimicked late October buffeted Alva and her companion, Elizabeth Shevlin, as they motored down to Southampton to lunch with friends at the National Golf Club on Peconic Bay. The large, open car that chauffeured them across Long Island would have been fine on a standard summer day, but on this day Alva and her friend sat huddled under a lap robe to avoid being pelted by road gravel and mud. As they did battle with their wind-tossed blanket, billowing skirts, and flapping hats, Alva watched their spattered but unperturbed driver, who was seated far in front of them. Alva snarled inwardly, "The law and custom allowed him clothes fitted to his form. How I envied him! How at each turn of the wheels I believed more and more in woman's suffrage!"[1]

Storms and fog followed the sailors up the coast to Vineyard Haven, and again they abandoned ship, this time at the New York Yacht Club. The cosmic unrest put Alva in a biblical fame of mind. She wondered if Mother Earth herself might have been born in a storm such as this, and she pondered the Bible's version of procreation, in which Woman begat Man, and Woman rejoiced and forgot her pain. Alva had no patience for this fable written by a man, "But no woman had a voice in those days, and so the man-world patted itself on the back and went on saying just what it liked to believe."[2]

A day of intermittently passable weather soothed Alva's snarly mood. The *Seminole* anchored off the ruggedly beautiful Massachusetts coast and the explorers from Manhattan went ashore to spend the day with Eleo. Alva continued to consider Eleo a kindred spirit who embodied her conviction that women and men deserved equal treatment. Alva encouraged Eleo to continue using Marble House as her local address when she registered for tennis at the Newport Casino. Eleo too placed great value on her friendship with Alva. She knew Mike's mother to be a person of uncompromising opinions and unsparing judgments. She was flattered by the older woman's approval and stimulated by her enthusiasms. Eleo treated Alva and her sailing companions to lunch at the Myopia Club. Despite the low-key atmosphere of the club's paneled dining room, Alva's hair-trigger sensibilities detected offense, though she kept her complaints to herself. The dining room was crowded with golfers, and Alva rated golf as an unproductive pastime pursued by idlers. In an analysis only Alva could have made, she contrasted the lunching golfers with King Louis XVI, Charles V, and George Washington. Alva ignored the failings of the French monarchs while applauding their pursuit of artful, result-oriented hobbies—one king had designed locks, the other tinkered with clocks. Alva credited the first president with working off his excess energy by chopping down cherry trees. Any of those activities was, to Alva's mind, preferable to "merely driving a ball over hill and dale."

Eleo took Alva and Alva's gentleman friend for a drive in her open touring car through the tree-lined countryside around Beverly Farms and Prides Crossing. Alva enjoyed the scenery, but she could take no holiday from her own exacting nature. The beauty of the landscape was marred for her by the large homes of Judge Moore, Henry Clay Frick, and Frederick Prince Sr., the McMansions of their day. Alva scorned their houses, all less than two decades old, as attention-getters that lacked the indefinable exclusivity found in more ancient dwellings. "Why do creations of new wealth miss this atmosphere?" Alva wondered in her diary with exquisite disdain, "Do they bespeak their owners?"[3] Conveniently forgotten was her own not-too-distant social-climbing past and her mansions, refined though they were by the architect Richard Morris Hunt, which had been conceived as "look-at-me" creations.

During Alva's monthlong voyage, she arranged several opportunities to link up with Eleo. When Eleo came to dinner on board the *Seminole,* Alva sent word to her son to join them. Mike had just won a yacht race from Bar Harbor, Maine, to Marblehead, Massachusetts, on his boat *Vagrant,* and the cozy dinner became a celebration of his victory. Eleo brought armfuls of flowers to decorate the houseboat. By now, Alva knew that Eleo and Mike would never be more than friends, but "She-Who-Could-Arrange-Anything" seemed frustrated that she had been unable to orchestrate a more permanent attachment between them.

Days later Alva and her traveling companions relaxed at a charming club and watched Eleo compete in a tennis match. Alva was gladdened by the sudden warmth of the afternoon and by the opportunity to observe Eleo's display of talent and dash. Still, Alva was deeply into her Joan-of-Arc phase and, though she could never bring herself to fault Eleo, Alva lumped tennis into the same dilatory category with golf, another pointless activity with a ball. Alva noticed two men digging with shovels on the other side of a fence and she contemplated these laborers with remorse. Drawing no connection between them and her servants at home, Alva wondered how these two workmen felt as they toiled for their meager living, while nearby others were chasing after balls.

These days Alva was bonding with working-class hearts in many unexpected places. While having tea on the piazza of a hotel in Magnolia, Alva sensed something special about her efficient waitress and learned that the girl was indeed sympathetic to the suffragist cause. Immediately, Alva felt a kinship flowing between them and she was infused with the joy Christ's disciples must have felt when they encountered believers in remote villages. With renewed hope for the human race, Alva resolutely bypassed expensive clothing shops and reveled instead in a bookstore stacked with literary treasures.

Alva radiated goodwill for laborers who were mere cogs in the wheel of life. The same spark of recognition and fellowship, however, did not extend to every unsung worker who crossed her path. The *Seminole* docked near New Bedford, where Alva's party was met by a black porter who ushered them to their hotel. Alva found the porter's manner to be intrusive and unpleasantly "officious." Though Alva was progressive on any number of issues, she retained many of the social attitudes of her time, particularly regarding Jews and people of color. Those attitudes were not chosen, so much as they were breathed in with the atmosphere, a reflex that was as unexamined and unremarkable as table salt.

The weather gods were not yet finished with the *Seminole*. Until the end of the final week of the voyage, the houseboat was tossed about by dark storms and biting winds that forced further changes in plans and routes. Then, on July 28, the mariners were greeted by clear skies and calm water, and Alva exulted, "Let joy be unconfined!" The group lounged under the broad awnings that shaded the deck and savored the luxuries of sparkling sea and a sky that smiled, at last, with puffy white cheeks. The voyage ended on just the note of calm, jovial camaraderie that Alva had planned all along.

In the two decades since Alva had locked her daughter in her room to keep her from fleeing a hated royal marriage, Alva had come a long way. Though Alva was never inclined to serious introspection or self-doubt, and her patrician hauteur was often at odds with the plebian tastes of her newfound comrades, her struggle was redeeming.

In the fall of 1916 President Woodrow Wilson won his bid for reelection with the pacifist campaign slogan "He Kept Us Out of War." Lieutenant George Patton was frustrated that Wilson still clung to neutrality. The young lieutenant was impatient to do more than drill mindlessly and fight on the polo fields of Myopia. Patton complained in a letter to his father that President Wilson had "the backbone of a jelly fish."[4]

Barely three months into his second term, even Wilson had had enough. Before a special session of Congress on April 2, 1917, Wilson outlined the case for a declaration of war against Germany. Wilson was moved to action by Germany's "warfare against mankind," which targeted noncombatants—"men, women, and children engaged in pursuits which have always, even in the darkest periods of modern history, been deemed innocent and legitimate." Memories of the sinking of the passenger ship *Lusitania* were revived. There was also the matter of the intercepted telegram from German Foreign Secretary Arthur Zimmermann that offered to help Mexico reclaim its former territory in the United States, an area occupied by the states of Texas, New Mexico, and Arizona.

America lumbered to war. During the peacetime lull, the United States had allowed its military to wither until it had fewer men in uniform than the Belgian army. Supplies of gas masks to protect the troops had to be gathered from the French and English. American newspapers were soon filled with the names of the first half million men who were called to arms. To help finance the military buildup, cities around the nation competed with each other to buy the most Liberty bonds and Victory bonds. Everywhere there were drives to fund ambulances. Eleo was among the many Bostonians who donated some or all of the thousand-dollar cost of each ambulance. Brass plaques engraved with the names of the donors were fastened to the sides of the vehicles. The Great War was the first conflict to employ motorized transportation. Most of the thousands of ambulances that were eventually deployed overseas were built on top of the versatile Ford Model T chassis. The hooded crates on wheels were configured primarily to hold stacks of stretchers, but the ambulances used by the Ice Flotilla were insulated for daily ice runs to victims of fever and disease. The rickety ambulances and the corps of tireless drivers who hand-cranked their engines helped more soldiers survive more grievous wounds than had ever been possible before.

Americans no longer hummed "I Didn't Raise My Boy to Be a Soldier." Morton Harvey, the baritone who had recorded the popular song, had the misfortune of being closely identified with its suddenly inappropriate sentiments. Four months after war was declared, Victor Records stopped releasing Harvey's recordings, and he went back to working in vaudeville.[5] American homemakers boycotted sauerkraut and, instead, served steaming pots of Liberty cabbage. Their children became patriotically ill with Liberty measles.

"Keep the Home Fires Burning" was a wistful melody that had remained popular since its introduction in 1914, and women took its message to heart. Despite male misgivings that factory work would make them unfit for traditional family life, women signed up in large numbers for shifts in factories that produced railroad equipment and military uniforms. City girls worked on farms and helped bring in the crops. Across the nation, people were exhorted to save food and gasoline. Some families took a page from the recent past, and, rather than curtail their Sunday drives for lack of gasoline, they hitched horses to the front bumpers of their autos.

The fear that German U-boats might be prowling along America's Eastern Seaboard was no longer theoretical after German saboteurs blew up thirteen munitions warehouses on a small island off the New Jersey coast in July 1916. Shrapnel from the blast hit the Statue of Liberty. Massachusetts' North Shore residents took comfort from their rocky coastline, with its jagged offshore reefs. Behind this uncertain fortress, women met at the library in Beverly, where they machine-knitted socks for American soldiers overseas who cherished anything clean and dry. Gretchen Warren devoted a portion of her wartime efforts to the London-based Chelsea War Refugees Fund, which kept Belgian women employed in the knitting industry. Mike Vanderbilt became a navy lieutenant and used his nautical skill to chase U-boats from the coasts of England and Ireland. His brother, Willie K., also did sea duty, commanding the *Tarantula II,* a ship he bought and contributed to the war effort. Birdie Vanderbilt (Mrs. Willie K.) drove through shelling to the front lines at Vaulecourt to hand out cigarettes to the men, and then, as winter approached, she sent over a load of sheepskin coats that were received with grateful "hurrahs" from the drivers in the American Ambulance Corps.

Horses were crucial to the war effort, and an estimated six million served during the conflict. As they had for centuries, they ferried supplies and carried men into battle. This was the last war in which horses were used in such massive numbers. Cavalry units, the most elite of the fighting forces, constituted at least one-third of each nation's military, but barbed wire now limited the effectiveness of battle charges. The United States sent more than a million horses to Europe, but only a couple of hundred returned. Getting enough food to all the horses was a continual problem, and most had to survive on minimal rations. Often they were fed cakes made from sawdust, which provided bulk but no nutrition. The British military noticed that mules were sturdier and more sure-footed than their swift, handsome cousins, and they purchased two hundred mules from the U.S. Army. Neither the mules nor the horses stood a chance against machine guns or the mustard and chlorine gases. After even the smallest whiff of the colorless, sweet-smelling acid, they choked and dropped dead along the roads.[6] An estimated half million horses were lost on the British side alone.

To counter the devastation wreaked by machine guns, the British began sending out gasoline-powered tractors covered over with steel plates. Called "landships" and "Little Willies," these early tanks caused panic in the German ranks, though many of the tanks quickly broke down or got stuck in the mud. Attacks also came now from the air, and ambulances operating in the war zone were camouflaged with tree branches fastened to their roofs.

When American soldiers arrived in Europe they found the opposing armies had, quite literally, dug themselves in. The Europeans had spent nearly three years living, fighting, and dying in thousands of miles of trenches that zigzagged from the North Sea to the Swiss border at Alsace. The trenches that the British excavated along this Western Front were an extension of their belief that their troops needed to focus on attack, not on defense, and that British pluck and resourcefulness would see them through. Consequently, their trenches were temporary, squalid, mud-soaked pits, plagued with rats and lice, which the Americans called cooties. The trenches dug by the French army, in which African American soldiers shared space, were just as miserable as the British version, but from some of the French trenches enticing cooking aromas wafted over No Man's Land. The German army lay in wait on the other side of No Man's Land, the godforsaken, shell-pocked buffer that was blanketed by vicious tangles of barbed wire, which Americans had invented to corral livestock on their western plains. The German trenches reflected elements of their national character. They were clean and permanent and orderly. Many were furnished with bunkbeds, cupboards, mirrors, overstuffed chairs, and steel doors with doorbells.

The pervasive feeling of shared enemies and shared privation led to a spotty thawing in the perennially problematic area of race relations. Two African American soldiers, Henry Johnson and Needham Roberts, were presented with citations for bravery by General Pershing, and they received additional honors from France, becoming the first black men to be awarded the Croix de Guerre. Their fighting spirit was depicted on an American poster titled "Our Colored Heroes," which showed the two soldiers in a bloody, hand-to-hand encounter with the Hun on a moonlit battlefield in France. The poster acknowledged, in understated British stiff-upper-lip style, that all Americans were in this fight together, "The colored man is eager to show his mettle and do his bit."[7]

After America entered the war, the tennis world began a gradual slide into near oblivion. The scarcity of rubber for balls was the least of the problems. Many of the biggest names in tennis were fighting overseas. Dick Williams was a captain in the artillery; Bill Johnston was a navy ensign, Willis Davis was a lieutenant in the U.S. Air Corps. The public did not care to spend its time and money to watch mostly second- and third-tier players. The great players from California were either unwilling or unable to travel to East Coast tournaments. The national rankings were suspended. There were no foreign players. The Davis Cup matches were canceled, as were many club tournaments. The last National tournament before the end of the war was held at the Philadelphia Cricket Club in June 1917. Eleo and Molla Bjurstedt joined forces for their second National Doubles win together and took their bows holding large bouquets of American Beauty roses. In the two years since Molla had left war-torn Europe, she had become the reigning female player in America on both grass and clay courts. Molla learned the word *humdinger,* and she inserted it into her conversation at every opportunity. She acquired a tiny new friend, a terrier puppy whose fuzzy head peeked over the tops of her silver trophy cups.

After the Philadelphia tournament, the best tennis was played in "patriotic matches" that benefited the Red Cross. Karl Behr, a player often ranked in the top ten, conceived the plan of holding tennis exhibitions around the country to raise money to buy ambulances. Karl was another survivor of the *Titanic* disaster. He had escaped with his fiancée on Life Boat number 5, one of the first boats to cast off from the sinking ship, which left only half filled in the frenzy. Molla and Mary K. Browne turned Karl's fund-raising idea into a hugely successful venture. Between July and October 1917 their patriotic exhibition matches raised $100,000 for the Red Cross. The combined star power of Molla and Brownie, representing the East and West coasts, allowed them to recruit many of the best available players for the charity matches, and the crowds followed. Red Cross nurses dressed in white Florence Nightingale uniforms lined the entrances to the courts armed with baskets to collect donations from the spectators, who had already paid admission. Molla and Brownie were inexhaustible, traveling some six thousand miles and outlasting and outplaying many of the male players. Molla played in fifty-three exhibition matches, and Brownie played in forty-nine.

Eleo played in two of the matches, and then she went off to France to drive ambulances. It was a mission born of her love of automobiles and her fascination with the stories Bill Tilden told of his experiences driving an ambulance in France. Tilden was on hand to take Claude Grahame-White to Calais as the pilot was making his way back to England to recuperate. Grahame-White had been forced to ditch his plane in the English Channel in foul weather during an unsuccessful raid on German U-boat bases. He was fished out of the water by a French minesweeper; he had not drowned, as had been reported by London newspapers.

The Red Cross trained many women and sent them overseas to drive ambulances because of a shortage of able-bodied men. Some women of means paid their own way and bought their own ambulances, which undoubtedly is what Eleo did. The one undated photograph known to exist of Eleo as an ambulance driver shows her dressed for action: tweed cap, trousers, car coat with the collar turned up, her favorite plaid wool scarf, and a small leather case for carrying messages.[8]

When Helen Frick arrived home in the States after working for the Red Cross in France, she turned her energies to producing a movie she titled *Home Fires.* Helen planned to show the movie in military canteens in Europe to boost the morale of the soldiers. *Home Fires* had its premier screening at Eagle Rock, the Frick estate in Prides Crossing, before a large audience from the North Shore, where it was filmed. Helen's movie was a collage of scenes of things worth fighting for—parades; children in dancing classes and attending school in Manchester-by-the-Sea; women at work on farms, knitting socks, canning, and rolling bandages; foxhunts and golf at Myopia; and polo at Frederick Prince's estate, Princemere. Helen included a sequence showing a tennis match between Eleo Sears and Alice Thorndike. The benefit screening raised more than four thousand dollars for the Red Cross.

The tide of war was turning in the Allies' favor when President and Mrs. Wilson arrived in Magnolia on a special train in mid-August 1918. Eleo's aunt Clara, the widow of her Uncle Jeff Coolidge, lent the Wilsons the grand estate that Jeffie had built on Coolidge Point overlooking the Atlantic Ocean. In addition to giving the Wilsons the run of her 250-foot-long summer home known as the "marble mansion," Clara included the use of her household staff and automobiles. She moved into a smaller house on the property with her mother. The local police became wary when an unfamiliar man, tall and thin and wearing rimless eyeglasses, was seen wandering around the neighborhood. The policemen discussed their suspicion that this stranger might be a burglar with a man who happened to be walking behind him, who, to their great surprise, turned out to be a Secret Service agent. Thirty-three heavily armed Marines camped out on the grounds of the Coolidge estate, as the president and his friend Colonel Edward House discussed the expected end of the war and prepared a covenant for the League of Nations, which Wilson hoped would become a framework for mediating future international disputes.

The ghastly war came to an end three months later, on November 11, 1918. Thirty-one countries had joined the fighting, and worldwide casualties, dead, wounded, and missing, approached forty million. For the United States, which had been at war officially for nineteen months, the human losses from battle and disease exceeded 116,000. On the very day that the armistice was signed with Germany, the National Horse Show opened in Madison Square Garden, and the atmosphere was alive with joyous relief that had seemed unimaginable just weeks before. A huge banner marked with a giant red cross stretched over the vast ceiling of the stadium, as if to shelter the participants. The receipts from the show were earmarked for the United War Work Campaign, and society turned out in force. In her box on the north side of the arena, Alva Belmont hosted a group of friends. Eleo came down from Boston. To an earlier show Eleo had worn a black armband in memory of her friend Norman Prince. Today she sported a red, white, and blue boutonniere the size of a cabbage that she had pinned to the front of her riding jacket. Judge Moore's four-in-hand won the gold trophy cup for Best Road Team in the Alfred G. Vanderbilt Memorial Challenge.

Eleo entered the arena on her majestic chestnut horse Radiant to compete in the class for Ladies Saddle Horses over 15.2 hands. Thirty-seven-year-old Eleo Sears was the only female contestant to ride astride. Radiant was one of those creatures that God made to show off his best work—perfectly balanced, spirited, elegant. He held his fine head high, ears pricked forward, seeming to exist in a state of perpetual expectation. A white blaze, jagged like a lightening strike, ran from his forehead to his nostrils. Radiant had always been explosive and difficult to handle, but today he was on his best behavior. His glossy russet coat rippled under the lights as Eleo moved him confidently through the required sequences of the walk and trot, and, after his slight hesitation, into the canter. The audience members clearly loved the team and demonstrated their sympathies with vigorous clapping and shouting, oblivious to the risk that the commotion might spook the horse. Eleo and Radiant had chalked up many wins together, including a recent win over Twilight, the champion of the previous year's event. This time, though, it was not to be. Eleo and Radiant ended with a second-place ribbon. Eleo didn't really mind. Radiant was strutting, the crowd was smiling, and the world seemed suddenly shining and young.

CHAPTER 14

Roaring Twenties: Mixing Cocktails and Freud

THE WORLD'S FIRST four-way electric traffic light was hung at the intersection of Woodland Avenue and Fort Street in Detroit, Michigan, in the fall of 1920. Within eighteen months the few traffic signals in New York City that had ruled Fifth Avenue became a matrix of flashing lights throughout Manhattan, all operated from a single switch located in Times Square.[1] Traffic control had become a necessity for a nation of thirteen million automobiles, but the stoplight was not an apt symbol for America as it entered the Roaring Twenties. In reaction to years of sacrifice and pleas to cut back, the impulse was to cut loose, not to sit still. The nation's wealth more than doubled as factories turned swords into automobiles and household appliances. The public was hungry for new, life-enhancing products like washing machines, refrigerators, and radios. Mail-order catalogues brought these new inventions and fashions to America's rural heartland. More than two-thirds of these big-ticket items were bought on credit that was paid off with installment plans.

By the end of the decade, Americans would be rolling along in more than 26 million automobiles, one for every 4.6 persons, and some families would own two cars. While unionized workers staged hundreds of bitter strikes for higher wages and relief from twelve-hour shifts, Henry Ford kept his assembly line moving by paying his workers five dollars a day, twice the standard wage, and by introducing the forty-hour workweek. Ford began to expand his business to new markets overseas. Though England was the richest country in Europe, with an empire that covered one-quarter of the globe, only one Brit in a hundred owned an automobile. By 1927, when Ford's breakthrough car for the masses finally ceased production, half of the automobiles in the world were Model T's. The price of the little black runabout dropped to two hundred dollars, but its customers had moved on. They were driving nearly two hundred billion miles a year, and they wanted to do it in bigger, flashier cars with more up-to-date features.

Women entered the war years wearing corsets and high-buttoned shoes to hide their ankles. Modern coquettes in the 1920s favored short, boxy dresses and rolled-down stockings, a fad that left them exposed up to their knees. Girls invaded barbershops for short, boyish haircuts called bobs. The *Hartford Times* grumbled, "When Samson was shorn, they made him go to work."[2] The complete flapper look included an arrogantly long cigarette holder caressed between bee-stung red lips or held aloft with an air of cool ennui. The young moderns jitterbugged to jazz and drank bootleg whiskey in clubs below street level, and they experimented with other undercover activities like parking, necking, and petting.

The cigarette-smoking flappers stirred up the polarizing issue of "women and cigarettes," a subject that had long riled moralists. Eleo was outspoken in her support of the suffragists' position—if it was not immoral for men to smoke, it should not be counted against a woman's morals either. In 1910 Eleo had been the first woman to smoke at Boston's Copley Square Hotel. She had puffed up a storm there, refusing an order to surrender her cigarette because no similar demand was made of the men who were smoking. The police were called to escort Eleo out of the hotel to the station house jail, where she was given several hours to reconsider her behavior. In typical fashion, soon after Eleo had gotten her opinion on record, she gave up cigarettes, though for many years while she was relaxing at home she smoked a pipe.

Eleo was thirty-eight years old when this roaring decade began. Society commentators noted approvingly that Eleo did not bob her own abundant, wavy hair. It was not because she disapproved, but rather that she knew the look did not suit her features. She was amused by the devil-may-care high jinks of the era's young moderns. Her own outrageous stunts had already passed into legend. Eleo was remembered in Lenox, Massachusetts, for riding her horse inside the town's post office to mail a letter. In acknowledgment of Eleo's pioneering work in nonconformity, the editors of the *Schenectady Union-Star* called her the "First of the Flappers."[3]

Eleo had never been shy about setting trends, but she understood that "shocking" was not shocking once it became routine. In public these days she was seen in skirts, donning pants only when she was on horseback. She no longer cared to be deliberately provocative in that way, but she remained prickly and quick to strike out whenever she felt her freedom of action was threatened, as Patrolman Glidden of Beverly Farms learned when he ordered Eleo to get her horse off the sidewalk, where she was riding in violation of a city ordinance. The officer was unmoved by Eleo's insistence that the roadway was slippery and made the footing dangerous to her mount. The patrolman handed Eleo a summons. Eleo won no sympathy either from the Salem County magistrate. He dispatched her with a stiff fine and the warning that jail time would follow any future infraction.

Suffragists had battled for seventy-two years for recognition and the right to vote. After the Great War they were joined by women who had filled jobs vacated by their men in uniform and were unwilling to fade back into their subordinate, prewar roles. Voting rights for women remained a hard sell even when President Wilson pitched the concept as a vital war measure. Congressmen conjured nightmare scenarios of regional anarchy if states lost the right to select their voters. In the end, the fate of the Nineteenth Amendment depended on a single vote cast by the twenty-four-year-old representative from Tennessee, Harry Burns. In his pocket was a letter from his mother that urged him, "Don't forget to be a good boy. Vote for suffrage."[4] Though several southern states, joined by Vermont and Connecticut, refused to ratify the amendment, women marched triumphantly to the polls for the first time in the presidential election of 1920, and they helped repudiate the pinched morality of the Wilson years.

The bustling postwar period was racked by less positive developments. A creeping moral looseness, made visible in the skimpy styles of women's clothing, reflected a widespread feeling of disillusion and dislocation. The noble crusade to make the world safe for democracy had segued into a middle-class quest to own a new toaster. The wise, optimistic, humane world that seemed within reach of the last generation was nowhere in sight for the current Lost Generation. In the literature of the period, these sullen youths became T. S. Eliot's "hollow men," adrift in *The Waste Land*. They resided on Sinclair Lewis's *Main Street* among boorish George Babbitts. At mid-decade, F. Scott Fitzgerald contributed his knowing portrait of the national malaise and the corruptions of wealth with *The Great Gatsby*, a story of longing for an elusive dream that ultimately proved not worth the struggle.

The cocktail had its heyday in the 1920s. Mixed drinks helped to disguise the off taste of alcohol that was made illegally in bathtubs and backyard stills during Prohibition, America's thirteen-year-long "noble experiment" that began on January 20, 1920. The liquor industry had always feared the good intentions of the temperance ladies who sang and prayed in front of saloon doors. Their denunciation of Demon Rum was echoed by folks from areas that were rural, southern, and middle class, and by the industrial titans John D. Rockefeller and Andrew Carnegie, the carmakers Ford, Hudson, and Packard, and the American Medical Association. All were convinced that alcoholism was the root cause of most illness, Monday-morning laziness on the job, and the destitution of families who spent their rent money on liquor. Preachers sermonized that a ban on alcohol would empty the jails, the hospitals, and the poorhouses.

The continuing availability of spirits was unforeseen on the day Prohibition went into effect, a day marked by restaurant patrons in several cities who dressed in black tie and came together to mourn. They sat at tables draped in black next to coffins filled with liquor bottles. The nation suffered buyer's remorse almost immediately and devoted itself to subverting the new law. Fishing boats chugged up to Canada and returned with caches of liquor which were dropped into the sea under the cover of darkness for retrieval by men waiting at prearranged locations from New England to the beaches of New Jersey. Pharmacists wrote prescriptions for medicinal alcohol. Rabbis and priests distributed sacramental wine. College boys wore hip flasks. Women drivers blocked roads with their automobiles and feigned helplessness, so that their bootlegger boyfriends, driving getaway cars with booze stashed in spare tires or in false ceilings, could escape pursuing cops.

Major cities around the country became speakeasy meccas, none more so than New York City, with its estimated 32,000 illegal bars. It was impossible, it was said, to get drunk in that city "unless you walked 10 feet in any direction."[5] Eleo's favorite Manhattan speakeasy was the '21' Club, run by two cousins, Jack Kriendler and Charlie Berns. The club's elite clientele reveled in wild nights of drinking and dancing the Charleston and the foxtrot. Jack and Charlie supplied top-quality booze from their secret wine cellar, cunningly hidden in the brownstone next door. A two-ton cellar door that looked like an ordinary brick wall was activated by a meat skewer pushed through a hole in one of the bricks. The '21' Club was raided many times, but each time a system of pulleys and levers swept liquor bottles off the bar shelves and dumped the evidence down a chute into the New York sewer system. In 1923 a federal agent worked undercover in a number of cities and clocked the time it took him to make an illegal alcohol buy from the moment he arrived. In New York the agent scored within three minutes and ten seconds. In Boston he wandered thirsty for eleven minutes.

The gentlefolk raised in the old ways of privacy and discretion were fish out of water in this postwar world. There were many with older eyes who tried to hold the line against the gathering assaults on the social order. Helen Clay Frick opened the Frick Art Reference Library in New York City in 1924 to continue her late father's legacy to the art world. For nearly sixty years Helen remained the director of the library, until shortly before her own death in 1983 at the age of ninety-six. During that time, she required men seeking to use its resources to wear jackets and ties. Her long friendship with Eleo did not alter her insistence that no woman wearing trousers be allowed to enter the building.

As the founding generations faded away, they took with them memories of traditions grounded in an earlier time. In Boston, Thomas Jefferson Coolidge died on November 17, 1920, at the age of eighty-nine. He left his personal affairs in good order and his assets safeguarded in trusts. He had lived long enough to see his country graduate from its piddling seat at the international children's table, which had so irritated him when he was minister to France, to become the world's most dominant economy. He died before the foolishness and criminality of the Jazz Age reached full cry. His life had been rich with civic achievement and an array of enthusiasms and talents. A widower for decades, he had had mistresses. The greatest tragedies of his life were the deaths of two of his children, and from those he never fully recovered. Friends and grandchildren visited, but increasing deafness during his last years left him isolated. At his funeral, T.J.'s strength of character and fundamental decency were highlighted in the eulogy given by his friend John Morse, who noted that T.J. had never lost himself in the ethical fog that so often enveloped others in their scramble for wealth. Morse recalled that T.J. had always conducted his business affairs in "the honorable spirit of a gentleman for daily use in rooms where it did not habitually intrude."[6]

T. J. Coolidge had been among the first to recognize the artistic promise of the young John Singer Sargent, who eventually painted portraits of most of Boston's leading citizens. Sargent was a houseguest of the Montgomery Sears family, cousins of Eleo's, before he moved to Fenway Court at Belle Gardner's insistence. Sargent's oil portraits, done on location in clients' homes over several weeks, commanded as much as four thousand dollars. By the time of his sudden death in 1925 (which followed Belle Gardner's death by less than a year), Sargent's charcoal portraits were in great demand. These portraits were done during a two-and-a-half-hour sitting in his studio and cost a then formidable one thousand dollars. The price did not deter a steady stream of well-made men and women from visiting Sargent's studio to be immortalized by his hand. For every person Sargent chose to portray, he managed to uncover some elemental spark that made his subject look more interesting than he or she might actually have been. It disturbed the artist that so many people seemed to care more about "how well they looked in their *Sargent*" than in the quality of his work. In 1921 Sargent asked to do a charcoal portrait of Eleo. While Eleo posed for this large, bearded, blunt-spoken man, they no doubt spoke of Eleo's recently deceased grandfather T. J. Coolidge and of her mother's friendship with Belle Gardner and Gretchen Warren. Against a background of quick, dark chalk strokes, Sargent captured perfectly Eleo's unflinching gaze and the way her lively eyes dominated her handsome, well-proportioned face. The artist drew Eleo's long, aristocratic neck and the prominent dimple in her left cheek, all under a corona of shining hair. Eleo was delighted with this vision of herself. She rushed the portrait off to be framed at the Copley Gallery near Copley Square and ordered a stack of photographic copies to give to friends.

The tennis community reawakened after its war-induced slumber, but the peace treaties signed by politicians could not paper over lingering animosities. "Enemy players"—those who resided in Germany, Austria, Turkey, and Bulgaria—continued to be excluded from tournament play. When Julius Bajusz of Hungary, a steady though never brilliant player, became an American citizen after the war, he was lauded as being "an immigrant of the desirable kind."[7] Molla Bjurstedt had been just such a desirable immigrant since 1914, and after the war she too became a naturalized citizen. Molla was the top-ranked female player in the country when she married Franklin Mallory, a stockbroker, in 1919. She was listed in tennis programs after her marriage as Mrs. Mallory, and that completed her transformation in the public mind into an All-American champion. During the spring of 1921, with her ready smile and her chunky good-luck brooch pinned to the front of her tennis dress, Molla joined Eleo as a member of the American team when it traveled to Canada for the first time since the start of the war, and then went on to France. Eleo had been ranked among the top ten players nationally for three years, from 1914 through 1916. When the postwar rankings resumed in 1918, she was twelfth. By 1922 Eleo had dropped out of the national rankings and was sixth in the New England sectional ranking. She had never been faint-hearted in assessing her own accomplishments, and she was not now. When a young umpire chairing one of her matches at Longwood persisted in calling out the scores with a booming voice, Eleo set him straight: "You don't have to shout so, young man. Nobody gives a damn about this match."[8] Still, in several big tournaments Eleo reached the singles finals. More often, she was a contender in the quarterfinals, and she concentrated on playing in doubles matches. An inexorable crop of talented younger players, such as the pretty college girl Helen Wills, was moving into the spotlight and Eleo saw the writing on the wall. Eleo was plagued, also, by excruciating flare-ups of tennis elbow, a common tennis players' malady exacerbated by the heavy wooden racquets of the day. At times the pain forced her to keep her playing arm in a sling, though she prided herself on never giving in easily to injuries. Eleo sprained her ankle badly during a doubles final in Philadelphia when partnered with Hazel Wightman, and, rather than cause her side to forfeit, Eleo had the ankle taped up and returned to play. Though they ultimately lost the match, a sports reporter gave Hazel and Eleo kudos for pluck: "Mrs. Wightman and Miss Sears did everything that one able-bodied and one half-crippled player could do, and it was almost enough."[9]

Eleo was in Monte Carlo for the Riviera's annual Beausoleil Tennis Championship in April 1922. Americans tended to have a difficult time in European tournaments because the Continent used a heavier, slower ball that changed the pace of the game. Tennis balls were not standardized until 1925. Eleo was not the only player to offer little resistance to the French star Suzanne Lenglen. Lenglen went on to win the tournament without dropping a single set. Even Molla Mallory and Elizabeth "Bunny" Ryan, the stocky, hard-charging "Terror of the Riviera," ranked fifth in the world, went down in defeat before Mademoiselle Lenglen. The flashy fashion sense and high kicking athleticism of the hatchet-faced French champion would have made her a big draw on the tennis circuit even if she had been a lesser player. Lenglen's crowd-pleasing tennis outfits combined knee-length pleated skirts, sleeveless blouses, and colorful silk head scarves. When the first professional tennis match was played in Baltimore in October 1926, Lenglen was the headliner. During her tour of America's premier East Coast tennis venues, the temperamental French star voiced her countrymen's disdain—"ordinary locker rooms, impossible food."

Eleo made annual visits to Europe and no trip there was complete without a stop in Paris, where she could indulge her lifelong passion for shopping at the exclusive ateliers in the world capital of couture. While in Paris Eleo gave parties that people remembered for decades. Gertrude Stein and her companion, Alice Toklas, attended one party. Though the unapologetic intimacy of their shared lives resonated with Eleo, she was undoubtedly repelled by their bohemian style and by Gertrude's rotund, masculine physical presence. Women whom Eleo admired were invariably slim and feminine and lived fast-paced lives. Gertrude Stein enjoyed a placid existence as an expatriate, having chosen to remove herself from America's increasingly mass-produced culture. Despite Eleo's impatience with the decline in civility in her own country, her roots there went too deep for her ever to leave it for very long.

England occupied a special place in Eleo's heart. She played tennis there at Wimbledon in June 1922, following in the footsteps of her uncle, the tennis great Richard Dudley Sears, and her cousin James Dwight, the first Americans to play at the All England Club. The newly renovated courts reopened just in time for the famous fortnight in 1922, but the weather stayed chilly throughout and the grass courts were slick with drizzle and intermittent downpours. Their Majesties George V and Queen Mary frequently left the royal box to wait out the worst of the weather in the comfort of the Centre Court pavilion. The ordinary English fans were not deterred by the rigors of their climate, and most remained in their seats, determined to see all the matches they had come to see. British resolution and "fixedness of habit" extended to their afternoon tea, which they sipped on schedule at tea tables in the soaked garden under a "mushroom growth" of black umbrellas.[10] Two American men shattered precedent when they played with steel-framed, steel-strung racquets. Purists were relieved that the racquets did not appear to help their game and the scores of the two Americans improved only after they switched back to wood.

Forty-year-old Eleo lost in the second round of the Women's Singles matches, having had the bad luck to draw the British national champion, Kitty McKane. For the Women's final, Eleo joined all of America in rooting for Molla in her battle against Suzanne Lenglen. On the sea voyage over, Molla had suffered from a severe stomach virus, and she was not in peak form, but she played valiantly before losing to Lenglen. David Windsor, Prince of Wales and future king of England, was in attendance during much of the Wimbledon fortnight and avidly followed the women's play. In several fun tennis matches away from Centre Court, the prince was Eleo's doubles partner and they became good friends. The perennially boyish-looking prince had a knack for appearing both shy and sophisticated, a combination that women found irresistible. To Eleo's immense pleasure, David anointed her his "favorite tennis and dancing partner." Eleo left England that year with reluctance, sailing home with Molla on the *Homeric* at the end of July.

When Eleo visited England she often reconnected with Nancy Langhorne, who had passed her formative years in Boston and Newport. Nancy had prospered in England and was known now as the politically and socially prominent Lady Astor. In 1920 Nancy was the first woman to be elected to Parliament. When Nancy and Waldorf Astor embarked on a tour of the American continent, Eleo and Gretchen Warren sailed with them from England on the *Olympic*. Overheard was this exchange as Eleo speed-walked around the top deck. Lady Astor offered her old pal some free advice from her deck chair: "Slow down, Eleo. You're going to kill yourself." "Oh, shut up, Nancy," Eleo called back over her shoulder as she strode past without pausing.

Eleo was one of twelve American players to be formally presented to the king and queen at Buckingham Palace during Wimbledon 1923. Eleo adored English pageantry, with its jeweled tiaras and ancient costumes edged in gold braid. As Eleo performed the required curtsies before the royal couple, a memory came to her unbidden of her mother's account of curtsies she had made before the portly former Queen Isabella in Paris so many years ago. While Eleo was dipping solemnly before Queen Mary, sensitive to the honor of the moment, she felt a small smile escape.

Shortly before Eleo sailed for Wimbledon in 1923, she starred in a homegrown version of *Queen for a Day* when Barkley Henry invited her to the Harvard Junior Prom. Barkley "Buss" Henry, class of 1924, was one of the athletic young men Eleo regarded with particular favor and whom she liked to invite home for tea. Rather than select a girl from the pool of eligible debutantes, Buss asked Eleo to be his prom date. He loved making an entrance and he knew that his arrival would not go unnoticed if he walked in with Eleo on his arm. Eleo too appreciated the entertainment value of the idea. So off they went to Memorial Hall in Harvard Yard, Eleo dressed to the nines. They danced and drank punch and had a grand time. Eleo got on famously with Buss's friends and their dates who shared their box. Eleo, at the age of forty-one, was old enough to be the mother of the undergraduates there, but she was acknowledged by all to be the belle of that ball.

Eleo organized parties in Boston that were as memorable as those she hosted abroad. She liked to transform out-of-town visitors into guests of honor. For large dances she rented the ballroom at the Copley Plaza and hired Ruby Newman's orchestra. Proper invitations to such occasions were always handwritten. Only business correspondence was ever banged out on a type-writer. Eleo hired girls from Radcliffe College, "discreet" young women with good penmanship, to produce the invitations. Such jobs paid thirty-five cents an hour in 1922. So it was that eighteen-year-old Mildred Young, who had reg-istered with the college's Placement Bureau in the hope of earning extra pocket money, rang Eleo's doorbell on Beacon Street at one o'clock on a spring afternoon. Mildred later described the small side room where she was directed, and the writing desk on which a box of stationery and a guest list had been placed. Soon after Mildred had settled down to write out copies of the sample invitation, Eleo's housekeeper appeared bearing a tray with a pot of hot chocolate and a sandwich, explaining that Miss Sears was concerned that she might not have had lunch. At four o'clock a maid entered with more nourishment, a pot of tea and a plate of cream cheese and cucumber sand-wiches with the crusts cut off (the first Mildred had ever seen). Shortly before five o'clock Mildred did as instructed and rang the bell to signal that the task was complete. Eleo's housekeeper reappeared to convey Miss Sears's appreciation and give Mildred her pay envelope. Mildred was sitting on the train from North Station on her way home, dreamily recalling the unexpected hospitality, when she opened her pay envelope. She was thrilled to find two crisp dollar bills, a bonus of more than 40 percent.[11]

In May 1925 Eleo found herself in possession of a perfect party space when she got title to the old stable on Byron Street that had belonged to her grandfather Frederick Sears. Grandpa Sears had put the property in a trust in 1889 and named eight-year-old Eleo as the eventual beneficiary. Byron Street is a narrow thoroughfare, even by Boston standards, that runs for a few short blocks behind the Somerset Club. Originally, the street had been lined with stables, but the horses were long gone and their stalls had become prime real estate, home to automobiles on the ground level, and spacious living quarters above in the former haylofts. Eleo's town house at 4–5 Byron Street was the largest on the street. The residence had an inviting, three-story-high great room, where guests were welcomed by a fire blazing in the massive fireplace. Tall windows facing the street were hung with green and copper silk draperies, the edges heavy with fringe. Eleo set up the bar near the entrance. Close by, a glossy concert piano was surrounded with comfortable seating of Italian walnut. On the lid of the piano Eleo placed a framed photograph of the Prince of Wales that he had inscribed to her, "All my love, David." Eleo now had a place that was completely her own and she gradually moved in, leaving her father in command of 122 Beacon Street. The Byron Street pad was where Eleo hung her prized collection of autographed photos of circus clowns. It was where she installed glass-fronted cabinets for the sterling silver trophy cups and bowls, ultimately numbering some 240, that marked her achievements in a dazzling variety of sports.

As the nation tried fitfully to "dry up" during Prohibition, Eleo held firmly to her view that alcohol was a desirable social lubricant. She enjoyed surprising her guests with vintages that were expensive and rare. Eleo herself drank sparingly at parties, preferring to rattle the cocktail shaker. She did not like the feeling of losing control, and she had no patience for anyone weak-willed or ill-mannered enough to be a sloppy drunk. But like many private citizens who disliked the heavy hand of the law and the politicians who voted "dry" but stocked their bars at home, now that alcohol was illegal, Eleo drank with a sense of mission. She stockpiled liquor in her wine cellar on Byron Street. Bottled liquor purchased by individuals before the start of Prohibition was grandfathered and, within the privacy of one's own home, its consumption was legal. Eleo could easily have stayed on the right side of the law had she chosen to, but the restriction enticed her to public displays of contempt.

Boston's Somerset Club was risk averse in dealing with federal enforcement agents bent on closing down clubs and imposing fines and jail time for violations of the Volstead Act. The club was committed to a strict no-liquor policy, though it had no qualms about accepting dues from members whose money descended from merchant seamen who ran rum from the West Indies. Eleo needed no prompting from her forebears to try her hand at rum-running.

Following the common practice of men's clubs, the Somerset Club did not permit women in its large, sun-filled rooms on the main floor.[12] Women whose husbands or fathers were members in good standing were allowed to enter through a small side door that led to a warren of paneled rooms on the lower level. Eleo hosted a dinner party in the downstairs dining room and smuggled in several choice bottles of booze with subversive relish. The waiter assigned to Eleo's party that evening was an old-timer on the Somerset's staff. Eleo enlisted him in the conspiracy, overpowering his initial reluctance to uncork, supply glasses, and pour with her commanding tone and narrowed violet-flecked eyes. Unluckily for the waiter, his participation in Eleo's scheme and his failure to report the violation were discovered and led to an ugly scene. The club chose to make a great show of this transgression, but it shied away from prosecuting Eleo and her friends. The management nabbed instead the lowest rung on the ladder and fired the waiter. No amount of fury from Eleo or pleading from the waiter altered their decision. With the Somerset Club as his only reference, the hapless waiter had no prospects for finding other employment. Eleo's escapade had backfired and caused this poor man's desperate situation. She began to send checks to the waiter to cover his expenses, and she continued this support every month for the rest of his life. Through the years, whenever Eleo had entered the Somerset Club, she had felt a twinge of annoyance. This, after all, had once been the home of her great-grandfather David Sears II, and she was required to use the side door to the ground floor. After this latest insult, Eleo made a point of never setting foot in the building again.

Now that the beverages of choice were illegal, parties really did seem gayer and more glamorous. Eleo's cousin Vivian (Mrs. Dudley) Pickman set up a bar on each floor of her town house on Commonwealth Avenue and had her butler hand martinis to guests as soon as they passed through the front door. Eleo and her brother, Freddy, attended many parties at the home of the vivacious Vivian, as they had when Vivian was married to the late Alexander Cochrane, twenty years her senior, who had fathered her two beautiful, blonde daughters, Nancy and C.Z. Vivian Cochrane Pickman had once been a Ziegfeld chorus girl, and she was famous for her parties, which often lasted until dawn. Vivian added a risqué twist that was often missing from the usual Boston gatherings, where the guests merely drank more than was proper and called each other by their nicknames. After Vivian's guests were all pleasantly tipsy, she arranged herself on top of the grand piano and taught them bawdy numbers from her Follies days. For Freddy, Vivian's evening sing-alongs were among the highlights of his agreeable and unhurried life. Freddy seemed to live in his dinner jacket. An affable raconteur, he held forth daily at his clubs, and most evenings were spent at the homes of friends, where an entertaining, unattached gentleman was always welcome. Freddy maintained high standards of personal grooming. His hair was neatly pomaded and parted in the center; his high white collar was well starched, and his pince-nez were perched primly on his nose. He was a contented man, a man of no profession and no apparent goals. Fire and ambition seemed to have bypassed him in the womb and settled, instead, in Eleo. An observation made regularly by friends who knew them both was that the innards of this brother and sister seemed to have gotten reversed, that Eleo should have been the boy and Freddy the girl.

During the 1920s Sigmund Freud and his disciples provided tools that laymen could use to psychoanalyze one another and try to solve puzzles like Eleo. Newly popular psychoanalytic theory had uncovered disturbing erotic undercurrents in all human interactions. Assertive women who behaved "unnaturally," perhaps by working passionately for a cause in concert with other women, were seen as a threat to the social order. Their aggressiveness and their female friendships loomed now as ominous signs of "sexual inversion," a vile disorder that increased public concern about the kind of world that would emerge as women began to vote.

Eleo had started acting out her personal obsessions almost two decades earlier, when the gulf between men's and women's lives and clothing was intentionally vast and the tolerance for deviation was small. Beginning in her early twenties, Eleo had alternated between exquisite, feminine high fashion and tailored sports costumes that provocatively crossed the line into male territory. To have been with Eleo in those years, lounging by the seaside on a fall day with a group of female friends, she clad in jodhpurs and boots, a camel-hair greatcoat, and a jaunty tweed cap, and they in extravagant hats and voluminous dark gowns, was to know that it required all of Eleo's considerable psychic and emotional energy to withstand the curiosity and disapproval that her choices provoked. The news media, which loved to shadow Eleo's life and athletic career, often took notice of her "mannish" outfits, but all that was intended, early on, was a factual description. Eleo's tailored clothes were modeled on men's fashions, a style that was unquestionably practical and provided an edge for success in sports. Eleo had inherited her grandfather's refined eye for beautiful things. She enjoyed owning good jewelry and had the happy talent of looking soignée in bespoke clothing in the finest fabrics. It was reassuring that her evening gowns for formal occasions looked so becoming, and that the dimple in her cheek was so disarming. The total effect helped neutralize her more surprising and idiosyncratic choices. For a long time Eleo remained, in the view of her social set, balanced on the comfortable side of scandalous. The more damaging implication of Eleo's mannish clothing, as a sign of her likely deviant sexuality, did not surface until later.

The alternative meaning of the word *gay* to refer to a condition that was not merely cheerful, had been in use since early in the century. Like other pejorative terms such as *pansy* and *nancy-boy,* it was applied exclusively to men. During the 1920s the symbolism of clothes not just as marks of status but as indicators of sexual direction became readily apparent, though the relationship between behavior and sexuality was still only dimly understood. "Manliness was all the rage," said the British author and wit Quentin Crisp, who observed the heterosexual world from the outside. Most men of the time, Crisp went on to explain, "searched themselves for vestiges of effeminacy as though for lice. They did not worry about their characters but about their hair and their clothes. Their predicament was that they must never be caught worrying about either." "To wear suede shoes," Crisp noted, "was to be under suspicion," and to wear one's hair longer than was usual was to risk being considered "an artist, a foreigner, or worse."[13]

Two infamous causes célèbres gave both men and women a cautionary peek at homosexuality. The sensational sodomy trials of Oscar Wilde in 1895 ended with the imprisonment of the flamboyant playwright, husband, and father of two. Wilde emerged from prison broken and bankrupt. Women were able to ponder the fate of lesbians in *The Well of Loneliness,* the first novel to deal with female homosexuality. The book by Radclyffe Hall was published in

England in 1928. Hall put a sympathetic face on the "sexual disorder" of her heroine, an upper-class British woman named Stephen who had an affinity for riding and fencing. The novel called for understanding and tolerance, but the plot left Stephen tormented and alone. The pipe-smoking author was the incarnation of her fictional heroine. Radclyffe Hall wore men's suits, kept her hair close-cropped, and preferred to be known as John. The year after the book's publication, Hall stood trial for obscenity in a proceeding that attracted such literary lions as Virginia Woolf and E. M. Forster to the defense table. The chief magistrate pronounced Radclyffe Hall guilty and vented his particular disgust with the chapters that placed Stephen and her friends in the ambulance corps during the Great War. The judge believed such literary license stigmatized the "women of position" who had served in the corps. In the United States, where the book was similarly tried for obscenity and banned, the accompanying notoriety made it a best seller.

Through her twenties, Eleo thoroughly enjoyed her many courtships with young men from exclusive prep schools and colleges. Those ego-boosting flirtations offered her a way to keep score. Her friendships with women struck a deeper chord. Long after Eleo realized the implications of that fact, she chose to remain discreet about her preferences. Most certainly, the atmosphere of the time discouraged the unveiling of unorthodox sexual interests, and the upper classes placed great value on maintaining the boundaries of good taste. Eleo was keenly aware of the fate that befell those whose private lives moved into the public domain. Boston's communal First Families had always entertained themselves by tossing off startlingly frank observations about secret failings within their circle, while they served tea and pastries. Those revelations were often cushioned with indulgent humor, as they could be among friends and families that had been bonding for generations. Eleo had never been reluctant to compare notes on her quirkier neighbors—the rich tightwad who never parted with a nickel, the old gal who curled up in bed in the middle of the day with a teapot filled with dry sherry, the married sly fox whose "squash games" were actually backstreet rendezvous with a lady friend. Eleo's undercover life was exponentially more deeply personal and, should it be exposed to the eyes of the world, more grievous than these routine, risqué peccadilloes. To become a source of sordid speculation and twittering innuendo would have violated Eleo's sense of her own dignity.

Eleo also had no desire to put at risk her comradeship with her many male friends. She had always been at home in the company of men, fitting in easily with their conversation and pastimes. In sports played with men, she never had to endure any gentle fluff with a ball. Men hit hard; they talked sports, and horses, and politics. Women's conversation, more often then not, circled around topics less apt to sustain her interest—lectures they attended, the cost of the art they bought, the latest achievements of their clever children.

Tennis match at Philadelphia Cricket Club, June 1915; Eleo and Hazel Wightman
are in the far court. (*American Lawn Tennis*)

"Women Players in Action," by Julie Brown, 1918.
(*American Lawn Tennis*)

Molla Bjurstedt receiving the Wissahickon Challenge trophy at the Philadelphia Cricket Club, June 1918. (From *American Lawn Tennis*, courtesy Arthur Ashe Tennis Foundation)

Consuelo Vanderbilt, Duchess of Marlborough. (Library of Congress)

Alva Vanderbilt Belmont during an Atlantic crossing, circa 1920. (Library of Congress)

Clowning with Mike Vanderbilt before a costume party, 1920s.
(Beverly Historical Society and Museum)

Fast and steady, Eleo walks from Newport to Boston, February 1928.
(Leslie Jones photo/Boston Public Library)

Finishing a twenty-five-mile "Walkathon" in Maryland, October 1928. (International Newsreel)

Eleo watching a tennis match with Isabel Pell, 1930s.
(Associated Press photo, courtesy Boston Athenaeum)

Squash star of New England,
January 22, 1929.
(Leslie Jones photo, courtesy
Boston Public Library)

Eleo demonstrating squash technique to the U.S. Wolfe-Noel team in London, 1930s.
(Times Wide World Photo, courtesy Sears family archive)

Backstage with Tallulah Bankhead after opening night of *Private Lives*,
Marblehead, Massachusetts, July 1949. (Boston Public Library)

Eleo on her palomino stallion
Golden Flight at St. Paul's Horse
Show, Hamilton, Massachusetts,
July 4, 1949.
(Boston Public Library)

At a benefit dinner, November 1949. (Boston Public Library)

With Gabor and Elizabeth
Foltenyi on their wedding day,
December 13, 1954.
(Elizabeth Foltenyi)

Bill Steinkraus jumping Ksar d'Esprit.
(Burt and Kathy Goldblatt)

At a benefit for the Alvan T. Fuller Foundation with Holbrook Smith
and Tenley Albright, February 1959. (Boston Public Library)

William Miller with Sizzling at Burrland Farm, circa 1959. (Author collection)

Rock Edge, with Eleo's wood-paneled Mini Morris at left, circa 1960.
(William Miller photo, author collection)

With the vice-presidential candidate Henry Cabot Lodge Jr., September 1960.
(Boston Public Library)

Eleo's stable, Prides Crossing, November 1960.
(William Miller photo, author collection)

Eleo with the elegant Reno, Prides Crossing, November 1960.
(William Miller photo, author collection)

Prerace publicity for Rockingham Park, July 1963.
(Detail of Bob Coyne illustration, *Boston Sunday Advertiser*)

In the winner's circle, Rockingham Park, September 7, 1963, top panel,
left to right: Marie Gendron, Jimmy Rowe, groom Leo Hall, Eleo,
and jockey Jimmy Combest on Rough Note. (James Rowe)

Eleo's retreat at 200 El Bravo Way, Palm Beach. (Author collection)

Eleo's favorite group of young men belonged to Harvard's Porcellian Club, and the athletes among them enlisted eagerly in her adventures. After Eleo's sexual preference became widely known, some of the Brothers Porcellian looked back and reassessed their roles as mere window dressing.

After the Great War and throughout the 1920s, the vast numbers of maimed and displaced former soldiers overwhelmed the government's ability to care for them, and the private sector mobilized to help. Eleo was a principal sponsor of one such relief initiative, a benefit for the National Disabled Soldier Fund. Together with a friend, the gifted singer and comedienne Ethel Levey, Eleo coordinated a fund-raising evening of musical comedy on May 2, 1921. Ethel Levey's first husband had been Broadway's premier showman, George M. Cohan, the original Yankee Doodle Dandy. Ethel had joined his family's act onstage as the fifth of the Four Cohans, and she performed in several of his Broadway hits. After they divorced in 1907, Ethel became the wife of the pilot Claude Grahame-White. A bond with Cohan remained, and the benefit evening Ethel and Eleo organized took place in the legendary Cohan & Harris Theatre on 42nd Street, co-owned by Cohan and his partner, Sam Harris.

Eleo had always been more than a bit starstruck, and she loved nothing better than the exhilaration and glamour of an opening night. Though as a rule she preferred comedies and musicals to heavy dramas, she could be counted on to be front and center at any show that featured one of her friends. Eleo made her own theatrical debut in response to a hundred-dollar bet. During the second act of *The Yankee Girl*, a musical at the Majestic Theatre in Boston, Eleo vamped across the stage midscene, dressed in her fur coat. Her sudden appearance was all the more incongruous because the scene was set in the tropical South Seas. Eleo later recalled with a chuckle that she never did get paid for her walk-on bit. "That," she said, "was dirty business."

Eleo's friend Ben Ali-Haggin, society portrait painter and theatrical set designer, worked wonders as a costume designer for the Ziegfeld Follies. His designs for the minuscule outfits worn by Ziegfeld's beauties exploited a legal loophole that permitted partial nudity as long as performers remained motionless. For the Follies of 1917, Ali-Haggin staged patriotic tableaux with statuesque, micro-dressed starlets frozen in titillating tributes to Paul Revere and President Woodrow Wilson. President Wilson's idealistic proposal for a League of Nations never caught fire with the electorate, but Ziegfeld's "Legs of Nations" number in the 1920 edition of the Follies was the hit of that hugely successful production. Audiences loved the songs and antics of Fanny Brice, the irascible humor of W. C. Fields, the redoubtable Ethel Barrymore spoofing her famous family, and the homespun wisdom of Will Rogers, the cowboy who twirled his rope, scratched his chin, and hog-tied the political idiocies in Washington.

The criteria that Florenz Ziegfeld used for selecting girls for his chorus lines were simple and intuitive. That they must be beautiful was a given. Beyond beauty, they needed a certain indefinable something, a look, a move, a smile that sparked his interest. Everything else could be taught. Ziegfeld spared no expense in staging his shows, which were a sparkling showcase of legs, lingerie, and incomparable performers, and all of it was done with class. Ziegfeld's Midnight Frolics provided another venue for Ben Ali-Haggin's decorative talents. In this exclusive late-night cabaret on the rooftop of the New Amsterdam Theatre, overlooking the bright lights of 42nd Street, Ziegfeld's girls paraded on a glass runway suspended above the audience. The view was more implied than real, as the performers were well covered by ankle-length bloomers.

It was at an after-theater party hosted by Ali-Haggin at his New York apartment in 1917 that Eleo first met a young actress who would become a lifelong friend. Eighteen-year-old Eva Le Gallienne, a recent arrival to the Broadway stage, was brought to the party by the matinee idol William Faversham and his wife. The versatile London-born Will Faversham played Hamlet on Broadway and a cowboy in the first feature-length film ever made, Cecil B. DeMille's silent western classic *The Squaw Man*. Faversham and his wife were devoted to young Eva and her mother, who had been abandoned by her husband, the English poet Richard Le Gallienne. "Uncle Will" introduced Eleo Sears to his refined, delicate-looking teenage charge, and their attraction for each other was immediate. Perhaps because Eva's father had been so unreliable, Eva was always on the lookout for older role models. She drew strength and artistic inspiration from her friendships with Sarah Bernhardt and Eleonora Duse and Ethel Barrymore, with whom she shared the stage in a number of plays. Eva was thrilled and awed by her growing friendship with Eleo Sears. To impressionable Eva, who was burning to make her own mark, Eleo represented the truly emancipated woman that Eva hoped to become, and she took to heart Eleo's lessons on living her life unapologetically on her own terms. Eleo's patrician hauteur, her confidence that she was the equal of any man, and her talent for swearing like a truck driver without losing her dignity were all dazzling. Much to Eva's delight, Eleo called her "Le Gal" and undertook her sports education, playing tennis with her and riding with her through Central Park.

As a fledgling actress, Eva Le Gallienne began with conventional steps on the path to stardom. She modeled the latest fashions and gave interviews about her beauty secrets. But acting for her was a calling, not merely a job. She dreamed of developing a nonprofit repertory theater that would make the Broadway experience accessible to people in all walks of life. With backing from John D. Rockefeller, Ralph Pulitzer, and Mary Curtis Bok of the Curtis Publishing empire, Eva bought and rehabilitated a once-magnificent but dilapidated 14th Street playhouse, which she named the Civic Repertory

Theatre. An anonymous donor to the repertory theater project contributed $24,965, a very specific, idiosyncratic amount calculated to meet Eva's fund-raising goal. That anonymous donor was most probably Eleo Sears.[14]

Under Eva's direction, the Civic Theatre brought to New York, and on road tours to Boston and Philadelphia, critically acclaimed productions at ticket prices between fifty cents and a dollar and a half. Eva directed and acted in classic works by Shakespeare and Chekhov and staged her own translations from the Danish of Ibsen's *Hedda Gabler, Ghosts,* and *Master Builder.* Real-life dramas were also playing out in the small close-knit world of the Civic Theatre. The talented company began to develop a behind-the-scenes reputation within theatrical circles that discouraged a number of aspiring young actresses from joining its coveted apprentice program. The Civic was rumored to be a "lesbian theater." Eva lived in a rented apartment nearby that she shared with the actress Josephine Hutchinson, who left her husband for Eva. Several of the theater's female apprentices and the female set designer were involved with one another. The theater building itself was located in the wildly bohemian low-rent district of Greenwich Village, where such "inverted" behavior was common.

Suspicions about Eva's sexual leanings surfaced periodically throughout her career. Eva's response to probing questions from the press was never entirely dishonest, but it deliberately avoided candor. She enjoyed flirting with attractive young actors, which provided some light cover as well as an ego boost. Eva's fellow performers were certainly aware of her sexual preferences, and her wealthy society friends and backers either knew or assumed, but they were content to leave the ambiguity unexamined. It was not that Eva was ashamed of her lesbian relationships, which were accepted by her Danish mother and family with European nonchalance, but she knew the American theatergoing public was far less tolerant of sexual deviance. Eva herself was repelled by overt public displays of homosexuality.

Theater actors, including Eva Le Gallienne, looked down on the moving picture business in California. Eva thought movies were related to live theater as much as canned vegetables were to garden fresh. The film industry, from its flowering in Fort Lee, New Jersey, in 1910 to its consolidation on the alfalfa fields in Burbank in the 1930s, had never been about highbrow taste. It had always been primarily about car chases, mustachioed villains, and custard pies. In the 1920s the moral compass of the movie colony pointed toward the gutter. Though the locals claimed, "Hollywood at night is just like your New England village," it demonstrably was not so.[15] Two heinous, high-profile scandals put the spotlight on sex and sin in Hollywood and sent ripples down Ol' Broadway. The most notorious by far was the case involving Fatty Arbuckle.

Roscoe "Fatty" Arbuckle was a three-hundred-pound plumber who became a film star. He headlined Mack Sennett's delightfully nutty Keystone Cops series and played opposite other legends of silent film such as Buster Keaton, Charlie Chaplin, and Mabel Normand, who was a friend of Eleo's. At the height of Arbuckle's fame, Paramount Pictures signed a three-year deal with him for an unheard-of one million dollars per year. In 1921 Arbuckle was accused of raping Virginia Rappe, a model and actress, in a San Francisco hotel room during an alcohol-fueled orgy. Virginia died of a ruptured bladder and Arbuckle was indicted for manslaughter. Newspapers across the nation whipped up public outrage with lurid rumors tossed carelessly about like confetti, and a coalition of states and theater owners banned Arbuckle's movies. Ultimately, it mattered little that Arbuckle was acquitted and received an apology from the jury for the injustice he had suffered. Arbuckle's career never recovered, and he eked out a living as a director of minor comedy films and later as a tavern owner, but only after changing his name to William Goodrich.

The following year Hollywood was staggered by the murder of the aristocratic Paramount director William Desmond Taylor. It was rumored that Taylor had engaged in drug-enhanced homosexual orgies and a ménage à quatre with the actress Mary Miles Minter, Minter's mother, and Mack Sennett's girlfriend, Mabel Normand. Paramount studio executives were able to spirit away so much evidence that no one was ever charged.

To the extent possible, Hollywood moguls looked the other way at the sexual indiscretions of their stars as long as they were making money, but these back-to-back scandals were so extreme that they endangered the studios' reputations. Contracts with performers began to include morals clauses that set boundaries for their offscreen behavior. Careers were ended by the slightest hint of perversion, such as homosexuality.

The institution of marriage offered protection from suspicion. During the 1920s and 1930s it became almost a commonplace for homosexual men and women in the film and theater worlds to evade the morals clauses in their contracts by making calculated marriages. These arrangements took varied forms that were color-coded for conversational convenience: a "cranberry" marriage involved a homosexual man wed to a lesbian woman; a "lavender" husband was a tolerant fellow who knowingly married a lesbian wife (though he himself was plainly suspect); a "white" marriage was a completely sexless union (it is uncertain who outside the marriage was taking notes). A Boston marriage described two women who shared a home and a deep sentimental attachment to one another. The concept was popularized by Henry James in his novel *The Bostonians* (1885) and was inspired by the devoted friendship between his sister, Alice, and Katherine Loring. A Boston marriage originally described a chastely spiritual and economically practical arrangement, but it came to imply a lesbian alliance.

Having grown up in Boston's foremost social circle, aware of its guidelines and subject to its pressures to marry and raise a family, Eleo had seen how a poultice of pity and disdain was applied to the noxious condition of spinster-hood. Eleo had a wealth of opportunities to avoid that fate, but for her such an arrangement was fundamentally dishonest. It would have entailed, as well, a loss of independence that she found threatening. Mike Vanderbilt remained devoted to Eleo, even after knowledge of her sexual preference was un-avoidable, for the same reasons that had attracted him before—their shared enthusiasms made them compatible. Eleo had never been a clingy female desperate for marriage, nor to his relief was she ever fixated on his money, like so many other girls he had known. When Mike invented contract bridge in 1925 by refining the auction method of bidding and introducing the Club Convention, Eleo quickly learned the changes he introduced, and she contin-ued to be a welcome bridge partner. At the card table Mike's personality underwent a surprising transformation. Though he had always been addicted to speed, both on the roads, where drove his cars like a demon, and on the high seas, when playing bridge he was deliberate to the point of exasperating his partner and opponents. Each turn of the cards required exhaustive study, and he would frequently leave the table and walk around while calculating his options. This precision led Mike's mother to resurrect her childhood nick-name for him—Professor. Alva had never been fond of abiding by rules, and she made little effort to follow her son's revisions to the game. She drove Mike to distraction when she was his bridge partner. On the subject of mar-riage Mike was equally disinclined to be rushed, his ambivalence due, in part, to his and Alva's continuing affection for Eleo. He did not marry until after his mother died in 1933, when he was forty-nine years old. Mike married the thirty-two-year-old Gertrude Conaway, from Philadelphia, in a quiet cere-mony in his New York apartment. Mike's bride shared his passion for yacht-ing and she crewed aboard his ships, which he piloted to many America's Cup victories. They had no children.

Eva Le Gallienne was heartbroken when her first great love, Mary Duggett, left her in January 1921 for a marriage of financial convenience that fulfilled her family's expectations. Eva found solace in her work and on long Sunday drives in the country with the New York socialite Isabel Pell, a tall, cool, blonde rebel who dabbled in acting and adventures. Another of Isabel's friends, twenty-eight-year-old Mercedes de Acosta, invited Eva to dinner, and that meeting evolved into a passionate, obsessive, three-year romance. Mer-cedes was married to the sculptor and painter Abram Poole, but business kept him absent for long periods.

Mercedes yearned to be an important poet and playwright, though her tal-ent in those areas was marginal. She earned the lasting fame she craved by igniting passion in an illustrious gallery of women far more gifted than she. Mercedes' roster of romantic conquests, in addition to Eva, included Isadora Duncan, Alla Nazimova, Tallulah Bankhead, and Greta Garbo. Marlene

Dietrich was so smitten that she sent Mercedes roses and carnations by the dozens, sometimes twice a day. Truman Capote liked to say, when he played the game Six Degrees of Separation, which tracked the intersecting relationships among the theater and society elite, that he always used Mercedes de Acosta as his winning move.

Eva Le Gallienne fantasized about being married to Mercedes and proclaiming their love openly, but she confined her passionate declarations to paper, writing fevered letters to Mercedes when they were apart. Eva produced Mercedes' play about Joan of Arc, but the mediocrity of Mercedes' script, and Mercedes' continual lack of discretion in gossiping about her amours, caused Eva's ardor to cool. Eva rededicated herself to her own artistic goals and followed Eleo Sears's example by playing hours of tennis to work off her nervous energy. When Mercedes whined about Eva's diminishing affection, Eva counseled Mercedes on the benefits of staying active; she shared a lesson she had learned from Eleo, that "the glow of a body in action is a great healer for the mind that is torturing itself."[16]

Eleo's appreciation of the collateral benefits of physical activity began early in her life. The panorama of sport allowed her to express and define herself. Urged on by an impulse akin to an artist's to produce art, Eleo Sears rode, she swam, she played tennis, badminton, and squash, she ice-skated, sailed, played golf, practiced marksmanship, baseball, and boxing—and she did it all with style and uncommon skill. Training toward a competitive goal was satisfyingly consuming. During those intense and focused hours, quotidian concerns were crowded out, whether they were small, like an overcharge on a plumbing bill, or large, like a rupture in one's love life. Eleo's awareness of her own troubling sexuality had surfaced gradually. The prevailing belief during Eleo's formative years was that romantic love between women was improbable, and that schoolgirl crushes or "smashes" on attractive, daredevil peers were unremarkable. Many of the relationships that Eleo had with women over the years eventually became suspect, including those that were, in truth, quite innocent. It appears that Eleo and Eva Le Gallienne, for example, shared confidences and an enduring friendship, and nothing more.[17] For some in Eleo's circle, reevaluating her attachments to girls on the North Shore became a tempting game. Particularly suspect were those young women who had shared Eleo's athletic interests, most of whom eventually married, though a few did not. The number of women implicated grew with the evolving perception of a link between lesbians and girls viewed as tomboys and jocks. (This prism was inverted for male athletes, whose talent for sports protected them from being branded as gay.)

Eleo's involvement with Isabel Pell seemed to both women at the time to have been fated by the gods, because Isabel was born on Eleo's nineteenth birthday. Isabel Townsend Pell was a handsome girl, slender, tall, with a honey-blonde bob. She moved with a sophisticated slouch and often wore jodhpurs and riding boots and kept a cigarette dangling from her lips. Her friends called her Pelly. Pelly rode horses, played tennis, and showed dogs. She came from an athletic family. Her uncle was the tennis champion Theodore Roosevelt Pell, who on occasion was Eleo's doubles partner. Isabel's father, S. Osgood Pell, was an Arctic explorer and founder of a successful real estate company. The Pell family traced its origins to the de Pelles of France and to Thomas Pell, Esq., who, in the mid-1600s, owned the land that comprises the present-day Manhattan suburbs of Pelham, North Pelham, Pelham Heights, and Pelham Manor.[18] This ancestry entitled Isabel Pell to membership in the genealogically exclusive society the Colonial Lords of Manors.

Despite Isabel's blue-blood roots, her childhood had been unsettled and impoverished. Her parents were divorced in a highly public battle, after papa's adultery was discovered by his pregnant wife. Isabel was always aware of their constant wrangling over court-ordered child-support and custody arrangements. On her mother's behalf, little Isabel wrote to her "Daday dear," pleading with him to send money when his check was late. Throughout her childhood, Isabel mailed anguished notes to her father about her playmates who made fun of her because she didn't have nice things. "Dear dady, will you send me $35. I want to get a bicycle, all the other girls have one and I have not." She asked for a pony, and a cocker spaniel, and money for a train ticket so she could visit him. She got the idea that her father would have preferred a son, so at age seven she began to sign letters to him, "Lots of love & kisses from your loving boy, Isabel Osgood Pell."[19] When Isabel was thirteen her father was killed in a freak accident and her mother wandered off, leaving Isabel effectively an orphan. For years she was shuttled among relatives, until she landed finally in upstate New York, near Fort Ticonderoga, at the home of her devoted grandfather. Isabel made her social debut with the support of relatives. She began a brief theatrical career, taking a small part as a maid. She spent time in Paris, and in 1924 she became engaged to a West Virginia boy. The engagement was announced at a big party given by Isabel's aunt and uncle at the Ritz-Carlton in New York. A month before the wedding, Isabel abandoned the idea of marriage.

Eleo was crazy about Pelly and loved squiring her about. Often they were accompanied by Isabel's little dog, Pepe. By the time of their affair, Isabel was recognized as a notorious lesbian who had a nasty streak and a preference for playing the field. Isabel could be extraordinarily gracious and warm when she chose to be—children loved her—but in any adult relationship she liked to be the boss. One acquaintance called Isabel a "dreadnaught." Eleo, however, was so smitten that she dropped her habitual caution, apparently unconcerned about the impression they created. When Eleo and Isabel went out together, to a horse show or a tennis match, they looked like twins despite their age difference, each wearing a sports jacket and tie, jodhpurs and boots, and identical soft felt hats. One can imagine them coordinating their outfits, snapping on their hats in front of a mirror, and admiring the results. When they sat together in the back of one of Eleo's big autos with Tom Greene at the wheel, they would giggle like schoolgirls. But two such volatile people were not suited to stay together forever. Isabel moved on to a series of other women, including some on the North Shore whom she had met through Eleo. Her parting with Eleo appears to have been uncharacteristically tranquil. Another of Isabel's lovers noted bitterly after Isabel had moved on that she and her new amour were well matched in cruelty and "deserved one another."[20]

In August 1924, Freddy Sears, at the age of forty-four, did the most rebellious thing in his life. Eleo's brother traded his carefree bachelorhood for marriage to a twenty-one-year-old Canadian-born Ziegfeld Follies dancer, Norma Henderson Fontaine. The ceremony, which took place in Perth, Scotland, was brief and private. The years of happy sing-along fests at the home of the vivacious Vivian Cochrane Pickman had lit a spark in Freddy after all. Now that he was a married man, Freddy moved out of the Sears family home at 122 Beacon Street, which he had shared with Eleo and their father. Frederick Sr. looked increasingly distinguished as his hair and mustache whitened, but he maintained the habits of his youth. Every day, rain or shine, he could be seen plodding around Beacon Hill in his overshoes or riding his horse through the Fenway. Freddy Jr. bought a town home nearby for himself and his bride at 267 Commonwealth Avenue and a handsome country estate in Topsfield. Eleo had lost patience long before with her unproductive older brother, and she and Norma never developed much in the way of family feeling. The large extended clan of Sears and Coolidge relatives came to like Norma well enough, though they were surprised that Freddy's wife, considering her background in entertainment, was not an especially talkative woman. Freddy was devoted to her and he demonstrated his commitment by presenting her periodically with shares of blue-chip corporations. It was presumed within the family that Freddy and Norma rarely, if ever, shared a bed, but their lives seemed to flow contentedly enough, at home and on their extensive travels abroad.

The Prince of Wales thoroughly enjoyed his periodic visits to America. In the autumn of 1924 he came to the North Shore. When he wasn't chatting up the area's many pretty young ladies, he devoted himself to Eleo. She was a wonderfully entertaining companion, and she was one of the few women who could keep up with him. At a party given in his honor, the prince and Eleo twirled around the dance floor for eight straight hours. The prince returned to the North Shore the following fall and stayed at Savin Hill, Bayard Tuckerman's estate. Mrs. Tuckerman was Eleo's cousin, the former Phyllis Sears. Before the royal visit, the North Shore community was determined to remain aloof, but excitement built as state troopers and the Secret Service prowled the area. By the time the prince arrived with his entourage at the train station in Hamilton, the area was packed with mostly female welcomers. The dapper prince did not disappoint as he stepped onto the platform. He wore a bold black-and-white-checked suit over a light blue shirt and a bowler hat, an ensemble that would have been called loud if it had been worn by an American.

The prince was promptly whisked off to the Myopia Club to dress for a fox hunt. Elaborate preparations had been made for a drag hunt. Rather than leave the route to the chance decisions of a fox, an anise bag had been dragged over a scenic course beginning at Francis Appleton's farm. The course went past Nancy's Corner in West Hamilton (named for Nancy Astor, who lived there when she was Mrs. Bobbie Shaw), and from there across many of the finest estates on the North Shore. The route ended with a flourish at the Tuckermans' farm. Three hundred people watched the hunting party gallop off with the yelping hounds surging ahead. The Prince of Wales led the group, riding the Tuckermans' speedy Desert Queen. The Myopia-based riders, under the direction of M. F. H. Gordon Prince, included Major George Patton. The local riders looked more spectacularly English in their scarlet coats than their royal guest, who had chosen a muted riding habit in shades of brown. The Myopia riders did their best to conceal the fact that, as a horseman, the prince was outclassed. Several rest periods were prolonged on his account, and they held their breath when he threatened to lose his seat over some of the jumps. The prince was visibly fatigued at the finish, but his fellow hunters held back and allowed him to come first into view of the cheering crowd, which had swelled to two thousand. Eleo had opted, at the last moment, not to join the hunt, but when she attended the large posthunt party at the Tuckermans' home, she let it be known that her absence had sorely disappointed the prince. Criticism of the prince's riding ability sent Eleo galloping to his defense. "Slight accidents, that would never be mentioned were he not the Prince of Wales, are repeated over and over until people believe that he only gets on a horse to fall off. He is a daring rider and rides as if born to the saddle," Eleo asserted testily.[21]

Shortly before Christmas 1925, Eleo inaugurated a new national sport when she accepted a bet and began what would become a series of celebrated long-distance walks. Boston's First Families had been pursuing this mundane activity with Puritan regularity for generations, and Eleo was an heir to this tradition.[22] As a girl, Eleo had been happy to accompany her father on his treks around Beacon Hill. Later, during visits to California, she had often walked the thirty-plus miles between San Diego and Tijuana. In 1912 Eleo had made her valiant 109½-mile hike down the California coast. Thirteen years after that, Eleo's long-distance walks again made headlines.

Her timing was perfect. Stunts that strained human endurance were very much in vogue among Jazz Age youths. The marathon dance craze began then, sending drooping, glassy-eyed couples shuffling nonstop around a dance floor for months. On a dare inspired by the times, two Harvard boys, Paul Nitze and Brewster "Bruce" Righter, rode their bicycles from Boston, past the Righter family home in Greenwich, Connecticut, all the way to New York City. The triumphant boys didn't mind that the money they won from the bet was less than the cost of shipping the bicycles back to Boston.

The era's most bizarre test of endurance was flagpole sitting, a fad that lasted for about five years. In 1924 the Hollywood stuntman Alvin "Shipwreck" Kelly accepted a dare and took a seat atop a flagpole, where he remained for thirteen hours and thirteen minutes. Other men bettered his record and attracted growing audiences. Alvin Kelly ultimately recaptured his title as King of the Pole by sitting on a flagpole in Atlantic City for forty-nine days, above a crowd of twenty thousand people.

Eleo's supermarathon hikes drew national interest and acclaim and made her a household name. The press covered Eleo's walks in great detail, obviously rooting for this middle-aged woman who performed earthbound feats of physical and mental toughness that harked back to a fondly remembered, less self-indulgent time. Eleo's first big walk in 1925 was inspired by a thousand-dollar wager she had made the previous year in Paris with a friend, Howard O. Sturgis of Rhode Island. Sturgis had bet that she could not walk the forty-four miles between his home in Providence and hers in Boston in less than fifteen hours. Eleo trained for months, hiking around Boston and through the seven-thousand-acre Blue Hills Reservation in the southern suburbs. The hike began on December 14, after a blizzard had forced its cancellation on an earlier date. Eleo and the two young men who volunteered to be her pacers closely measured the planned route, using the mileage meter on her big Renault, as they drove from Boston to the start of the race in Providence. They determined that the actual distance was 47.8 miles. After a protein-packed meal of hard-boiled eggs, Eleo and her two companions left the starting line in front of Howard Sturgis's Hope Street home at one o'clock in the morning. Eleo looked almost delicate between her two strapping pacers, Roger Cutler, a noted member of the Harvard rowing team, and Albert Hinckley, class of 1924. Eleo had chosen a layered outfit for the hike, a dark woolen skirt and jacket, a wide-brimmed, soft felt hat, and sturdy, high-top shoes. She had bound up her ankles with gauze for support, and about her neck she loosely wrapped her faithful old black-and-white-checked muffler, the one she had worn when she drove ambulances in the war. The two men were hatless and had taken no special trouble with their footgear, planning to get by on their large, athletic physiques and their youth.

Up hill and down dale, through villages and towns, the hikers were trailed by Eleo's big, boxy beach wagon driven by Thomas Greene, carrying first-aid supplies, sandwiches, a thermos of steaming coffee, and another of chocolate milk. Behind him were automobiles carrying reporters. Eleo moved with the determined rhythm of a metronome, slightly ahead of the two men. The three walked mostly in silence, though occasionally Eleo was heard to comment on the passing scene, and sometimes there was laughter. At one point Eleo called out to the laggards behind her, "Boys, you're supposed to pace me, not chase me." Occasionally, the autos carrying the press shot to the front to quiz the walkers on how everything was going. "Great" was the only answer Eleo offered. The hikers paused three times en route to sip beverages, and they took a half-hour lunch break at the Dedham Community House. The lunch was served by one of Eleo's maids, Theresa Walsh, a petite Irish lass who had come along in the beach wagon. When the group neared Brookline, a police-man held up traffic with his white-gloved hand to let them pass. Reporters noted that Eleo still looked fresh, while Roger had torn open his jacket and developed a limp, and Albert looked haggard; but they continued on doggedly just behind her.

A light snow began to fall and made for slippery going as the hikers passed over the Charles River. "Thank God, there's no tide to set in against us," one of the exhausted fellows said.[23] The men were hard put to keep up with Eleo when she broke into a jog for the last mile. Traffic was jammed for blocks around Beacon Street as drivers stopped to watch Eleo and her pacers cover the final distance. Eleo bounded up the steps of her town house shortly after noon, eleven hours and six minutes after the start in Providence. Eleo noticed some schoolgirls standing in a doorway studying her shyly, and she gave them a smile and a wave. She grinned for the reporters, who besieged her for com-ments and begged her to pose for photographs. She said only that she was glad she had won the bet and that she could do it again easily, and she cut them off with a cheery "Me for bed. Bye-bye." Eleo's two pacers melted into the town house with little ceremony, offering few words beyond a round of congratulations. Once upstairs, the Irish maid Theresa massaged Eleo's legs and drew her a warm bath, adding seven special oils to her silver tub. Eleo and the men had dinner together, and then they went off for a night at the theater. A reporter stopped by in the evening to check on Eleo's recovery and was surprised to learn that Miss Sears had already gone out.

Eleo's artful demonstration of "pedestrianism" moved the *New York Times* to poetry in a pre-Christmas editorial that compared Eleo to the huntress Diana. Alexander Pope was quoted: "Those move easiest who have learned to dance"; so was Walt Whitman: "I think whatever I meet on the road I shall like. I think whoever I see must be happy." The *Times* editor invested Eleo's achievement with potential beyond the benefit to personal health. He saw pedestrianism as a panacea for roads and tunnels clogged by wheeled transport, and he called Eleo's record-setting hike "the one universal art to save the race from physical degeneracy."[24]

Congratulatory telegrams poured in from friends around the country. The *Pittsburgh Sun* said Eleo was proof that "the old saying about women being the weaker sex is more or less twaddle."[25] Eleo's walk gave birth to a mini–hiking industry, and scores of men and women took to the roads along the route she had popularized. Many of these new recruits contacted Eleo for details about the terrain and advice on how to prepare. Several men bettered Eleo's time, and a group of women in North Carolina served notice that they were planning to do the same. One woman wrote to tell Eleo that she would be celebrating her twenty-sixth birthday on the road in the hope of breaking Eleo's record. All the interest was gratifying, but the challenges called out for an answer.

Eleo improved her time dramatically on her next Providence-to-Boston jaunt shortly after Thanksgiving 1926, completing the trip in nine hours and fifty-three minutes. Eleo's companion for this effort was the tennis champion Bunny Ryan. "All you can do is play tennis," Eleo had teased the tennis star, until Bunny agreed to join her on a hike. After their doubles victory on the clay courts in Hot Springs, Virginia, where they defeated Molla Mallory and Katherine Porter of Philadelphia, Eleo spent six weeks training Bunny for long-distance walking. Five male pacers accompanied the two women on the hike and rotated in and out of the beach wagon. Bunny Ryan was exhausted at the end of the hike but beaming: "It was quite devastating, but a wonderful experience."[26] Eleo's pacers for this hike included her cousin Frederick Winthrop and Paul Nitze. Nitze was to earn his own time in the spotlight as a foreign policy advisor to presidents from Truman to Kennedy. He recalled Eleo and the hike with pleasure. "She was warm hearted, joyous, good-fun," he wrote of his experience; "it was a pleasure to be with her, never grueling."[27]

At the finish line, Clifton Church, a veteran hiker then seventy-three years old, met the group and handed over to Eleo the speed-walking crown he had earned in 1875 for covering the distance in ten hours flat.

The headline of the *Boston Herald* and the page 1 story in the *New York Times* for April 24, 1928, were about Eleo's seventy-four-mile hike from the Newport Casino to Boston. Eleo completed the distance virtually nonstop in 17¼ hours, in weather that ranged from a drizzle to a monsoon. News flashes on the radio tracked her progress. When Eleo and her three pacers reached the outskirts of Boston, a sizable crowd was standing in the rain to greet them. One of Eleo's pacers began playing to the spectators and cameramen. He pulled a "For Sale" sign off a lawn and, with a Sir Walter Raleigh flourish, laid it across a curb so Eleo could walk over a stream of water. He repeated this gallantry for about a quarter of a mile, until Eleo nearly tripped over the sign. Eleo was seen limping toward the end of the hike, and she admitted to being very tired, but she straightened up when they neared Beacon Street. While water ran off the brim of her hat, Eleo stood on the front steps of her town house and waved cheerfully to the several hundred people who packed the street.

The interest in pedestrianism that Eleo had sparked inspired a "Walkathon," a twenty-five-mile footrace from Laurel, Maryland, to Baltimore in October 1928. Among the seventy-four contestants were several women, including a sixteen-year-old girl. A 90-degree heat wave, almost unheard of so late in the season, felled some of the racers, and Eleo was injured when the fender of a passing automobile scraped her leg. She was the twenty-third person to cross the finish line and the only woman to finish the race.

Yet another sport that had little history of female participation piqued Eleo's curiosity when someone asked her if she played squash. "No," she said, "but I could." Eleo first tried the game in 1918. She beat the best male player in a match in Rye, New York, soon after, and she quickly earned a reputation as a clever player. In November 1918, at the Yale Club in New York, Eleo played an exhibition match with Walter Kinsella, the squash professional who had held the World Squash Racquets title since 1914. Their match was the featured attraction of a squash tournament organized to benefit the United War Work Campaign, and it drew several hundred people. Kinsella prevailed, as expected, though Eleo did not allow him an easy win in this predecessor of the 1973 "Battle of the Sexes" between the tennis stars Billie Jean King and Bobby Riggs. In the packed gallery at the Yale Club, a large contingent of women was able to watch Eleo play, marking the first time that females were allowed inside the club.

When Eleo first took up the game, women's efforts were regarded with "faint amusement," as Harvard's revered squash coach Jack Barnaby later acknowledged. Among the best squash courts in Boston at the time were the eleven courts in Harvard's Randolph Hall, which had been built by one of Eleo's uncles. The facility was named for Thomas Jefferson's granddaughter Eleonora Wayles Randolph, Eleo's great-grandmother. Eleo was the first woman permitted to play on those squash courts, and she persisted until she unlocked the courts for other interested women. When Harvard officially opened its courts to women during off-peak hours in 1928, grumbling was heard about dwindling male sanctuaries and how the ladies, not content with the right to vote, were invading still more territory.

Before Jack Barnaby became the head squash coach at Harvard, there was Harry Cowles, who taught Jack the game. Harry's teams went undefeated in intercollegiate play for fifteen straight years. Jack attributed his mentor's success to his perfect technique, his great footwork, and his understanding of "the power to deceive." Harry's instruction to players on cloaking their intentions and not telegraphing their shots appealed to Eleo. She followed his advice very literally at times by pulling her black bloomers out wide to cover up her shots into the corners. She developed a strong, reliable backhand shot and went on to win four Massachusetts state titles.

At the Union Boat Club, the longtime squash pro Jack Summers played with Eleo three or four times a week over several years. She gave him an education in the way upper-class business used to be conducted. Eleo never paid Summers for the time he spent with her, but one day she told him that her chauffeur would bring a new car over for him to look at, and if he liked the car it was his. Jack thought she was kidding. Of course, he loved the car that Tom Greene drove over the next day, even after Eleo prodded him, "Now, maybe you'll be on time." From then on, Eleo presented Jack with a new car every second year. "You had to know how to handle your blue bloods," Summers learned. "Some of them you couldn't send a bill to, but they'd take good care of you at the end of the year."[28] He never forgot Eleo's fury at another pro who once sent her a bill for seventy-five cents. Eleo saw no need to account for her dealings with the world penny by penny, but she did keep them in balance using her own measure of rough justice. She would never dream of violating an unwritten rule against borrowing anything from an employee. She once dispatched Tom Greene to the Union Boat Club to return a nickel to Summers. "What's this for?" he asked Greene after running down the three flights of stairs from the squash courts. "It's for the telephone call you made for her yesterday," Greene told him. Summers came to think of Eleo fondly, and he concluded that, all in all, she was a "good old scout."

Eleo organized the first women's squash tournament at the Union Boat Club in 1926. Two years later, at the age of forty-six, Eleo became the first female national squash champion. She beat forty entrants in the Round Hill Club Tournament in Greenwich, Connecticut, a contest that was dominated by strong players from Boston. Controversy accompanied this win, as it did with so much else in Eleo's life. Margaret Howe, a superb player and wife of the squash champion Bill Howe, always believed that the Round Hill tourney was not originally planned to be a national contest and became so only after Eleo had won it and insisted it be counted as the national championship. Eleo's title withstood the protest, however, and she retained the distinction of being The First. The following year, sixty-four players entered the national tournament, which was held in Boston. Margaret Howe won that championship in a terrific five-set struggle against Eleo in the finals. Eleo founded the Women's Squash Racquets Association and served first as its vice president and then as its president for a record thirteen years. She donated the first permanent squash trophy and provided generous financial support for all the association's activities. For five years she was also the captain of the Women's International Squash Team. Eleo remained a tough competitor well into her seventies. From time to time as she charged after a ball, she could be heard alerting a slow-moving opponent, "Get the hell out of the way!" For her groundbreaking work with the sport, Eleo is often cited as the "Mother of Squash." The designation is well earned, though the image it conjures has a sweetness that is misleading.

Eleo's deep involvement with squash did not lessen her devotion to tennis, which remained her first love. She donated a challenge trophy in 1927 to promote the sport among college-age women in the New England and mid-Atlantic states. The matches began in March 1928. Eighty years later, competition for the Sears Cup was still going strong.

Eleo was in London during the summer of 1928, where she shook up the venerable Ranelagh Club, one of England's premier polo venues, when she became the first female player on their men's polo team.

Eleo spent the early spring of 1929 in Burlingame, California, as a guest of Mrs. Whitelaw Reid. There Eleo was happily reunited with her friend of many years, Marion Hollins. The two women resumed their long golf rivalry at Pebble Beach and played polo together. Marion was another well-born, multitalented athlete who had been the Women's Amateur Golf Champion of 1921. Marion had become a golf instructor at Pebble Beach, and she helped to develop the course.

On the heels of her California trip, Eleo joined the professional squash player Walter Kinsella for a rematch of the game they had played eleven years earlier. Kinsella had run his string of consecutive world squash championships to twelve, from 1914 to 1926, and the rematch with Eleo ended with another win for him, but Eleo, loving the challenge, made it a rousing and memorable game.

May 1929 found Eleo in France, where she hiked 42½ miles from the Château Fontainebleau to Paris, spurred on by another bet with Howard Sturgis. The wager this time involved more than money, but the mysterious "something extra" was never disclosed. Eleo left Fontainebleau at five o'clock in the morning on a cool, windless day and, after eight and a half hours on the road, she arrived at the bar in the Ritz Hotel for a Brandy Alexander and a night of dancing. Eleo completed this hike nonstop, averaging a remarkable five miles per hour, faster than many of her Stateside hikes. Friends accompanied her by car and handed her a thermos of tea through the car window. When Eleo reached the Paris city limits she was met by three policemen, who did their best to clear a path for her through the formless Paris traffic. Eleo said that speed walking through the mad dash of cars added to the excitement. When asked how she felt, she was upbeat and, as ever, to the point: "Never felt better."

The mood was giddy too on the American side of the Atlantic. The stock market reached an all-time high on September 3, 1929. A share of stock in the radio broadcasting company RCA, the flagship of a new electronic age, was worth four hundred dollars. Three years earlier, that same share had fetched a then-lofty thirty-two dollars. Everyone knew the stories about telephone operators and waiters who had overheard an investment idea and retired with millions. Shoeshine boys hoped for a hot tip after they had polished and buffed, and even they knew the benefit of "buying on margin." Repairmen were encouraged to get homeowners interested in company stock while fixing their appliances. Shares of some companies were traded incestuously within preselected pools of investors to increase interest in the companies and drive up share prices. This manipulation was not even a secret. The activities and profits of the pools were reported in the financial newspapers. Far from being outraged, the average investor was reassured. To most people the stock market was an abstract, barely understood concept, whose bewildering ups and downs seemed random. So wasn't it fortunate that there were knowledgeable investors who kept it orderly! The public's only concern was to get in on the upward part of the swing. The financier Charles Schwab had worried that this freewheeling climate put the general public at risk, but he was no longer concerned. This boom, he was now convinced, was based solidly on the inventive energy and economic strength of the entire nation. "We must remember," he reasoned, "that today the United States is doing half the world's business and will continue to do so. Who can compete with us?"[29] Who, indeed, would not be convinced after seeing all the products pouring out of miles of factories, and the ideas for more flooding from research labs in every field—automobiles, aviation, power generation? Chicago boasted more telephones than existed in all of France. Germany barely used the amount of electricity needed by New York state alone.

The largest individual taxpayer in Massachusetts, according to records from 1926, was William Wood, the former president of the American Woolen Company. His fortune was reckoned to be $250 million. Eleo was not at all in the same league. She was comfortable with assets in the neighborhood of $10 million, roughly $119 million today. By 1929 Eleo had seen her holdings increase nicely, but compared to the high-flying stock market they had merely poked along. In the tradition of old-line New Englanders, most of Eleo's money was invested in stodgy, established industries that had stood the test of time, in companies that her grandparents would have recognized. There was no RCA in Eleo's portfolio, but there was General Electric, the New York Central Railroad, some oil, shares in the Winchester Repeating Arms Company, the Westbury Clock Company, and lots of unexciting, low-yielding bonds. Such prudence was common among Boston families and was less an investment strategy than the simple perpetuation of the attitudes and portfolios that were inherited, and they were looking as out of step with the times as corsets and high-buttoned shoes.

The stock market lurched downward on October 24, 1929, but it had dropped before. In the previous year or so it had dipped sharply, and after each salutary, cleansing retreat the market resumed its advance. On October 29, "Black Tuesday," the market's fall was stomach-turning. Over the next two months, stockholders lost nearly $40 billion, more than the country had spent fighting the Great War. We know now that was just the beginning. Then, however, investors gained hope from a market rally in December that added back some 20 to 50 percent to the lows of October.

The America that existed between 1920 and 1929 was so cinematic in its excesses that Cecil B. DeMille would have been proud to take a directing credit. He might have scripted the way the multitudes partied in wild pagan festivals and worshipped false gods, only to be destroyed with a mighty roar in the final reel. One might think that when the credits rolled at the close of the decade, there should have been some unmistakable sign, like a declaration of a war with a defined enemy, to announce the turn toward tragedy— but it would not be as simple as that.

CHAPTER 15

The Great Depression and the Changing of the Guard

AFTER YEARS SPENT studying the run-up to the Great Depression with the idea of determining its cause and fixing blame, the economist John Kenneth Galbraith reached the verdict that everyone had been responsible. The Crash occurred, he concluded, because hundreds of thousands of individuals, all exercising free will, were "impelled . . . by the seminal lunacy . . . of people seized with the notion that they can become very rich."[1]

The cascading collapse of that belief was painful to behold. By the spring of 1932, as the stock market rocketed down more than 53 percent, the New York Stock Exchange and the Chicago Board of Trade closed their doors with no announced restart date. Terrified depositors lined up outside their banks to retrieve their savings, only to have their worst fears confirmed when their banks, with no support from the Federal Reserve, had nothing to give them. Nationwide, nine thousand banks closed. By 1933 one-third of the nation was unemployed, and people were losing their homes to foreclosure or eviction at a rate of one thousand a day. Many of the great Newport mansions were boarded up while their owners struggled to raise cash. The gorgeous playthings of the rich, their customized automobiles and yachts, went on the auction block to be sold for pennies on the dollar. Boston was hard hit, despite its varied economy, when work in all its major industries—shipping, textiles, shoemaking, and glass manufacture—dried up.

As a group, Boston's risk-averse First Families were able to maintain an approximation of their pre-Crash lifestyles in homes that had been paid off by earlier generations. There were some, however, who could no longer afford the upkeep of their handsome Back Bay town homes and, to avoid losing them entirely, turned them into multifamily apartments or rooming houses.

People thought themselves fortunate when they were selected for jury duty because jurors were paid four dollars a day. In New York, "shoe-shine boy" was the fastest growing job category. Seven thousand men invested in shoe-shine kits in search of income from a new trade. Five cents a shine was half the going rate before the Depression, but the shoe-shine "boys" were better off than the apple sellers, because at least their investment didn't rot. The International Apple Shippers' Association sold boxes of surplus apples to unemployed men, who hawked them on street corners. With luck, they could sell the apples for ten cents apiece, but they would take less. Some six thousand apple sellers set up shop on the streets of New York, until their presence was deemed too demoralizing and disruptive, and they were shooed away.

The always quotable Will Rogers had it exactly right when he quipped, "We are the first nation to go to the poor house in an automobile." In 1929, the year the stock market crashed, four million Americans purchased cars, a level that would not be reached again for twenty years. Within the following ten years, one thousand car companies would vanish, many having been in business since the beginning of the century. Handcrafted, ultraluxury vehicles with storied names like Pierce-Arrow, Duesenberg, and the Stutz-Bearcat Speedster would live on only in memory. Gone too were classic plates with more mass appeal, such as the Stanley Steamer, the Auburn, Cord, Essex, and Reo. Though sales of General Motors cars dropped by two-thirds, its Cadillac brand became one of the most prestigious on the road and commanded premium prices of $5,000 to $15,000. General Motors' CEO, Alfred P. Sloan, managed to steer his company to a profit throughout the 1930s and never missed a dividend payment to stockholders. Fortunately for the privately held Ford Motor Company, its bookkeeping was so haphazard that it wasn't clear the company was broke and should have gone out of business.

It was reasonable to predict at the beginning of the decade, as President Hoover did, that "normalcy" would soon return and better days were just around the corner. When the economy continued to deteriorate, Hoover persuaded business leaders to pledge billions of dollars to the recovery effort, and he initiated programs to prop up wages, create jobs, and assist farmers and homeowners. These initiatives were truly radical, as they marked the first time the federal government had intruded so broadly in the peacetime economy. Hoover's programs addressed the same concerns as did Franklin Roosevelt's heralded New Deal, which followed shortly, but Hoover came out of the era looking like the goat and Roosevelt is remembered as the hero. Such is the power of appearances.

Herbert Hoover had seen the American dream operate in his own life. He had been born poor, worked hard, played fair, and become a millionaire. And he had grown up to be president. It was his misfortune to be president when all hell broke loose. Hoover had headed the relief efforts for a devastated

Belgium during the Great War, for which he was made an honorary Belgian citizen. When the Depression hit, President Hoover was more qualified than most to battle it. He believed that the entrepreneurial spirit of his nation's people was the source of America's magisterial prosperity, and he moved gingerly when awarding government handouts during the Depression because he was concerned that too much bureaucratic meddling would delay the recovery. Some economists were convinced, rightly as it turned out, that stopping the Depression was beyond the power of the federal government, but that hard fact was of little interest to the people who had lost so much. Hoover lacked the oratorical gifts to convey his concern for America's huddled masses, and they began to hold him personally responsible for their misery. The shanty towns and tent communities of the unemployed that sprang up around the country were angrily named "Hoovervilles," and "Hoover blankets" were the sad coverings of cardboard and newspapers that barely kept out the cold.

The presidential election of 1932 was a landslide for Franklin Roosevelt. Eleo Sears was not among the majority who voted for her old riding companion. Weeks before the election, the Massachusetts State Republican Committee announced with much fanfare that Eleo Sears was on the Hoover bandwagon. She did some last minute campaigning for Hoover, joined by two star athletes from Harvard who courted the youth vote. One of the young men, Charley Devens, had landed a glamorous job on the pitching staff of the New York Yankees and, in love with sporting metaphors, he announced that he was "keen in seeing [Hoover] stay on the field until victory has been assured." Eleo's declaration of support for her candidate was more nuanced. "Though I am a strong believer in free trade," she said in a prepared statement, "I think in the present state of unrest it would be safest to retain Hoover as President and I am going to vote for him."[2] Even on the campaign stump Eleo could not bring herself to advertise wholehearted agreement when she had private reservations. Eleo believed that taxes in almost every case did more harm than good, and that the protectionist levies that Hoover had placed on agriculture in 1930 were among his worst initiatives. The Smoot-Hawley Tariff fulfilled Hoover's campaign promise to protect American farmers from European overproduction, but the tariffs ignited a wave of retaliatory foreign levies. The resulting plunge in international trade beggared economies around the world and prolonged the Depression at home.

Nobody from Franklin Roosevelt's old crowd could have predicted that he would become such an instinctive and effective politician. When he first began to seek public office, many dismissed him as a patrician momma's boy, a "hothouse plant just set out among weathered and hardy rivals."[3] When this heir to a proud Republican legacy chose to run under the Democratic Party banner, it felt like a slap in the face. Franklin realized that as a Democrat he would be a unique and valuable commodity, while as a Republican he would be just another Roosevelt with political ambitions peeking from the shadow of his ebullient cousin Teddy.

In his Inaugural Address on March 4, 1933, Franklin Roosevelt made clear that he understood his role was to be the shepherd to a despairing flock. The voters had shown, he said, that "they want direct, vigorous action. They have asked for discipline and direction under leadership." The Depression had reached its most savage point and Roosevelt recognized that the American people were not looking for lessons in self-reliance. Like children who had stumbled and skinned their knees, they wanted the wound kissed and the pain to subside. Years later Eleanor Roosevelt was asked by Adlai Stevenson why it was that people like him and Herbert Hoover, men of modest beginnings, had failed to connect with the masses, while her husband, a product of wealth and privilege, had been reelected to four terms as president. Mrs. Roosevelt offered the astute observation that Franklin knew how to govern because "he was born into a feudal society."

Opinions about the president split along class lines. Roosevelt was not afraid to experiment, and he did not share Hoover's scruples about regulating banks and businesses and running up government deficits, all of which were anathema to the upper classes. Some of Roosevelt's policies, such as paying farmers not to grow crops, flew in the face of the nation's most cherished beliefs. Grace Vanderbilt, Mike's aunt, was a confirmed Roosevelt hater. During the Harvard-Yale boat races, she called out to Roosevelt as he watched the race from a neighboring yacht, "I don't like you, Mr. President. I don't like you at all." Roosevelt replied pleasantly, "Well Mrs. Vanderbilt, lots of people don't like me. You are in good company."[4]

Business leaders like Eleo's friend Alfred Sloan and the du Ponts, as well as many conservative Democrats, believed that Roosevelt's big government schemes were dragging the country toward socialist ruin. To them the federal government loomed like an octopus, its tentacles grasping ever larger portions of the people's business, and Roosevelt was its malevolently grinning head. When FDR took rhetorical and legislative aim at major corporate interests and railed against "economic royalists," the president's old acquaintances took those attacks personally. Franklin Roosevelt had a long memory, and the friends of his youth had equal powers of recall. They remembered how he had endured ridicule from his Harvard schoolmates and been rejected by the Porcellian Club. They were convinced that Roosevelt's decisions were motivated by these old resentments. Eleo's opinion of Franklin Roosevelt was far from benign and typically blunt: "He was a perfect ass, you know. He was not popular at college and if you're not popular at college, well, that tells a lot. . . . Then he got himself elected President and ruined the whole country."[5] And it was hard not to read at least a bit of "Look-at-me-now" swagger in the jaunty upward thrust of the president's cigarette holder, which he held in his teeth as he rode in his open car, acknowledging the cheering crowds like a Roman emperor.

On the other hand, Roosevelt did get people busy again in huge public works projects—four million people were recruited to rake leaves and paint signs. His goal was quantity rather than quality, as Eva Le Gallienne learned to her dismay when she approached the president for money to keep her foundering Civic Repertory Theatre afloat. FDR's only interest was in packing her theater with bodies regardless of their aptitude for stagecraft, a proposition that horrified Le Gallienne. Yet Roosevelt gave his frightened nation the direction it craved with a blizzard of new laws and federal programs. He soothed the battered populace with financial support systems and reassuring "Fireside Chats" on radio, which beamed into living rooms across the country.

The one narrow point on which Eleo and her friends did agree with the president was that the Eighteenth Amendment should be repealed. Congress began to roll back Prohibition as soon as the new administration took office. Enforcement had proven impossible and breaking the law was a national entertainment. John D. Rockefeller, an early supporter, threw in the towel after seeing that Prohibition had given rise to an army of lawbreakers that included many of "our best citizens." The Watchover Bible and Tract Society denounced Prohibition as the work of Satan. The "noble experiment" passed into history, and the liquor industry became an important source of employment and tax revenue as the country fought the Depression.

Aside from his opposition to Prohibition, Roosevelt had left his postelection plans vague, and in his inaugural address he sounded all the right, reassuring notes about the country having "nothing to fear but fear itself." In the first months after Roosevelt became president, Eleo was willing to give him the benefit of the doubt. She renewed her early friendship with FDR, and their shifting relationship spanned most of his four terms. Eleo initiated her correspondence with the new president in the unlikely role of worshipful citizen. "You are a very wonderful person," Eleo wrote to Roosevelt in the month after he took office, "just what this rudderless and drifting country has needed for years." Three weeks after his inauguration, Eleo was in Washington with another acquaintance of Franklin's, Frederick Prince Sr., and she decided to drop in on her old chum. She had followed Franklin's progress up the political ladder for years with considerable surprise, and now that he was the president, well, wasn't it always nice to know a president. Roosevelt was not at the White House when Eleo stopped by, so she left him a note, "You are a wonder—Take care of yourself—As Ever, Eleo Sears." Roosevelt immediately sent a friendly response, "Do run in the next time you are here. It would be grand to see you again." Eleo was immediately seized by an appealing vision of herself sleeping in the Lincoln Bedroom. She wrote again to Franklin, on behalf of "an old friend [who] is perishing for it," to ask for his photograph and his autograph on his "pretty" presidential note paper. She added, "Why don't you ask me to stay sometime next winter!!!!!" FDR appeared quite open to Eleo's request for a sleepover, and he replied with affection, "As they say in the Navy—'make it so.' "[6] And there the idea rested as Eleo and Franklin came to realize that they couldn't actually stand one another.

Throughout the Depression, everyone from every social stratum was affected financially and sought ways to retrench and conserve. In Eleo's case some of the pain was more psychological than real. The stodgy investments that made up her nest egg, which had looked so *yesteryear* in the go-go 1920s, saved her from the quicksand of the stock market in the 1930s, but this reprieve did not leave her untouched by the new realities. During the coldest months of the year, horse-related activities were always reduced. No horse shows were scheduled, and Eleo made little use of her beautiful collection of carriages. She began a seasonal practice that she maintained even after the Depression had passed. Eleo pared her stable hands down to a skeleton crew, sending the excess off with a small severance that didn't make up for the loss of their monthly wage. She hired most of them back in the spring. Some of her neighbors thought she should have tried harder to keep all the men on year-round.

During the winter of 1930, after much soul-searching, Eleo concluded the time had come to part with her splendid horse Radiant, who had been with her for most of his life and had made possible so many of her successes in the show ring. Radiant was twenty-one years old, a senior citizen now, but still grand to look at. Radiant had always been a handful, yet he had given Eleo his cooperation often enough, and she felt they had a special bond. Eleo was no longer able to ride him because he suffered recurring soreness in his front leg. Radiant had earned a life of leisure, but Eleo did not have stable facilities large enough or sufficient winter staff to devote to an old pensioner.

Eleo made an inspection tour of a farm for retired horses run by the New York–based Women's League for Animals and, after consulting with the caretakers and the veterinarian on call, she was satisfied that they would provide a good home for Radiant. The League was an admirable organization that, since its founding in 1910, had treated many thousands of creatures in trouble, including dogs, cats, horses, birds, and turtles. The League provided owner education and free veterinary care for low-income clients, such as emergency surgery for a tenement child's puppy that had swallowed an assortment of iron stove bolts, tacks, and nails. The Depression led to a surge in the number of sick and abandoned animals as their owners turned to other priorities, and the shelter's funding was strained to its limit. The League was ecstatic to have Radiant as a permanent guest. Along with the godsend of publicity from having the noted sportswoman Eleonora Sears judge their facilities to be worthy, Eleo provided a financial windfall for Radiant's care and sizable donations to the organization's general rescue work. For her own peace of mind, Eleo visited Radiant at the farm from time to time to see that he was settled in and content in his new home.

More than ever, horses were a luxury item. From 1931 to 1934 the polo fields at the Myopia Club saw little activity beyond casual matches because team members could no longer maintain the expensive string of mounts needed for high-level competition. There were no buyers for the surplus polo ponies, and many were turned out in the fields, "on the rough," to fend for themselves like horses in the wild.

The National Horse Show continued to attract equestrian society, but the show could no longer support Madison Square Garden, which had moved, in 1926, to bigger, less gracious accommodations on New York's West Side. Judge William Moore, who had sustained the National through the dark days of the Great War, had died in 1923, and no one had the funds and the inclination to take his place. In its diminished setting the National carried on, bucked up by the traditional cocktail luncheons and white-tie Saturday balls, in defiance of the clogged, noisy streets outside and the cramped, poorly ventilated basement stalls for the horses. The reincarnated Garden III was the largest indoor sports arena in the country, and to attract the admission fees it needed to survive, it hosted a jumble of other spectacles—basketball, hockey, ice revues, dance marathons, religious crusades, and roller derbies.

Eleo had in her stable a promising young horse, an Irish import named Barney Mor. Eleo engaged Henry Lee to assist in training her new jumper. Eleo and Henry had maintained their friendship during the nearly twenty years since their great hike down the California coast. Henry graduated from riding in steeplechase races to training horses, and some of his horses ran in the Belmont Stakes. Henry enjoyed playing polo at Myopia, but as a professional horseman he had little regard for the enthusiastic amateurs who rode in the Myopia horse shows. He liked to say that most of the riders fell off before the end of their event. Henry was married now with a son, Henry Jr., and a home in Beverly Farms, not far from Eleo. Beverly Farms was still a sleepy, friendly little community, and Henry Jr. could pick up the telephone and ask the operator what movie was playing at the picture show in town, or if she knew where his mother was. He was always surprised when Eleo arrived at their door and, after a sharp knock, barged into the front hall yelling for his dad, "Harry!!!" Eleo never stood on ceremony when dealing with old friends. Little Henry had never seen such a take-charge woman who didn't wait to be properly announced. Henry Jr. did appreciate that Miss Sears always remembered to bring him chocolates. His mother seemed upset that his father rushed downstairs the moment Eleo arrived or jumped in the car to meet her at the stable whenever she telephoned. Mrs. Lee knew her husband was not one to be pushed around and that he was not easily impressed. When he stayed with the Vanderbilts, he slept on the floor because he found their beds too soft. Henry Lee assumed that his wife was jealous of the bond he shared with Eleo and that she was in the dark about Eleo's sexual leaning. Henry reassured his wife cryptically, "It's not what you think. You don't ever have to worry." Eleo's sexuality, especially since her affair with Isabel Pell, was an open secret on the North Shore, the kind of general knowledge that was never discussed. The men who understood Eleo's secret assumed that the ladies were innocent about such matters, though most were not, and neither side planned to enlighten the other.

In 1930 Eleo was named Sportswoman of the Year. Nearing fifty, she continued to be a force on the squash court and a colorful advocate for the benefits of pedestrianism. Eleo was a familiar sight in her "knockabout mannish felt hat" as she swung rhythmically past the baseball field at Boston College, across the Harvard Bridge over the Charles River, and up through Cambridge, Lexington, and Concord. Eleo called her hikes of thirty-plus miles in the midday heat "just a little walk for exercise." On many hikes she carried hand weights with the grips wrapped in neatly ironed white handkerchiefs. In June 1932 Eleo was amused to read in the *Boston Post* that she had finished a thirty-three-mile walk looking "fresh as a daisy." During her outings thereafter, whenever a passing motorist or a reporter called out to ask how she was feeling, she would enjoy her reply, "I'm fresh as a daisy." The forty-seven-mile hikes through the night from Providence to Boston became an annual ritual. Each year on June 11 or 12 she set out with three or four college boys in tow. For them, often Brother Porcs with nicknames like Beebo, Peabo, and Tuck, surviving a hike with Eleo became a rite of passage. Thomas Greene would be there too, trailing the group in a sporty car, and a maid who rode along to dispense refreshments and tend to the lame. By 1934 the old Boston Post Road, once a carriage route, had become a four-lane highway. Policemen cautioned Eleo and her pacers to stay on the shoulder of the roadway as cars whizzed by.

Invitations to dinner or to Sunday brunch provided Eleo with a welcome social occasion and a pleasant focus for her day's exercise. She usually walked the thirty-five miles to the homes of her cousins Clara Endicott Sears and Emily Sears, the latter now married to Henry Cabot Lodge II and mother of two growing boys. Tom Greene met Eleo at her destinations with a change of clothes. Shortly before Eleo's 1934 Providence-to-Boston hike, she confounded observers with a "Mystery Hike" when she walked twenty-three miles dressed as a Girl Scout. Tom Greene explained to a puzzled reporter that Miss Sears's costume was the result of a dare and that she would be visiting Mrs. Louis Frothingham, widow of the congressman who had made an unsuccessful but game run for mayor of Boston in 1905. The unified support of the city's elite had not been enough to derail John "Honey Fitz" Fitzgerald, the charming rogue who was backed by the powerful Democratic machine. The Protestant Yankees who had built Boston and had run it since Puritan times were overwhelmed by the numbers, the entrepreneurial vigor, and the hunger for power of the legions of Fitzgibbons, Fitzpatricks, Fitzsimmons, and O'Tooles who migrated to their town. Beginning with Mayor Fitzgerald, Irish Catholics would dominate Boston politics for ninety consecutive years.

The relationship among the social classes changed radically during the twentieth century. Vincent Astor, who had taken on the role of family patriarch after his father went down with the *Titanic*, believed that the public had come to regard being rich as a character defect. Astor observed that the intentions of the well-to-do, no matter how sincere and selfless, were automatically "either discounted or misinterpreted." He decried the inaccurate and hurtful idea that the so-called "smart set . . . romp[ed] from orgy to orgy," a perception encouraged by society reporters still mining the famous Four Hundred and by the snooty "upper-crust" caricatures coming out of Hollywood. There was a Shakespearean majesty to Astor's indignation in behalf of his friends, who, he said, went about their lives with the "usual American tastes and held the usual American jobs." "They may have more money than the average American," Astor explained, "but they don't eat any more meals, they don't wear any more clothes, and they can't sleep in any more beds."[7] He also made the point that the average American was just as likely as those on the society pages to overstep the bounds of law and propriety. But such truth changed nothing. The masses had stopped believing that some classes were upper by divine right. Workingmen resented the "cocktail class" for their ready access to good liquor during Prohibition. They were no longer content to watch the Astors and Vanderbilts cavort in masked balls to show off their wit and good fortune. Now Average Joes wanted to be them, and they didn't much care if their elected leaders were crooks, so long as they were *their* crooks.

In the best First Family tradition, Eleo took her ongoing concerns about local politics and national policy directly to the top. She was incredulous that the corrupt and slippery politician James Michael Curley was reelected to his third term as Boston's mayor, despite a fraud conviction and a stay in prison. Eleo suggested in a note she sent to President Roosevelt that he could perhaps get rid of Curley by making him "a trappist monk." Curley was later elected governor of Massachusetts, and Eleo sent Roosevelt a series of newspaper articles to update him on Curley's nefarious plan to subvert the Boston postal system. Eleo also sought the president's help for a family of Chinese immigrants she had befriended who had fled the growing Communist threat in their country.

Eleo did not hesitate to let Roosevelt know that he was making her friends in the business community terribly unhappy when he targeted them with his

New Deal tax increases. Roosevelt's stated goal of balancing the federal budget was patently impossible to achieve this way because only 5 percent of the population paid any income taxes at all. It was Roosevelt's Gold Clause Acts, however, that provoked the greatest anguish among Eleo's business friends.

Roosevelt devalued the dollar by reducing the amount of gold that supported it, in the hope that this would reinflate prices of goods and services. The public was denied the right to sue the government over any resulting loss in value of their gold-backed bonds. To many people it looked like legalized theft. In June 1935 Eleo sent Roosevelt a commentary by the historian David Lawrence from the *Boston Evening Transcript*. Lawrence's article, "A Sovereign without a Conscience," questioned whether citizens would continue to lend money to a government they could no longer trust to maintain the value of their investments. Eleo wrote to Franklin, "I am terribly worried by the way the country is talking against you." She pleaded with him, "Why are you wrecking business everywhere—why kill the goose that lays the golden egg?" Roosevelt's personal secretary, Missy Le Hand, generally intercepted mail sent to the president, and sometimes it was she who handled Eleo's queries with a generic response. This time Eleo wrote to Franklin, "In whatever answer I get do please give me some sign that you have actually read this letter yourself." Roosevelt was surprisingly compliant. He suggested that Eleo spend an evening with him so he could explain his actions to her. He cautioned her "not to swallow what you read," and he recommended that she "ask the milkman, the butcher, the baker and the candlestick maker how specifically they have been or are being hurt. Then, finally, ask the poor working girl or any other worker whether they were helped or hurt."[8]

After Eleo received Roosevelt's reply, she marched off to interrogate an assortment of tradesmen. Two weeks later she dispatched her findings to the president. She had uncovered general displeasure with the way prices were heading up while the dollar was heading down. Her research, she told Franklin, took her to "movie theatres in little humble places, all a working audience—when your picture comes on—not a sound of applause to be heard, as once there was—." After her odyssey, Eleo's beliefs remained the same as the ones she began with. "It is terribly false economics to ruin producers and then to expect their employees to be well off," she wrote. "You are so splendid it is tragic to see your star declining and I hate to see it."[9] She included copies of what she identified as "pathetic letters from an intelligent but very poor and aged farmer." The letters lamented the payments being made to farmers to plow their crops under and to indiscriminately slaughter their pigs and cattle. The angry farmer claimed that this Roosevelt-sponsored initiative caused a formerly self-sufficient America to import pork and lard from overseas.

As Eleo recognized from her small sampling of the working-class mood, people did indeed feel at loose ends in a world that frightened them. It is highly doubtful, however, that the tradesmen who depended on Eleo's business would have engaged her in a truly searching discussion of economic policy. Roosevelt was shrewd enough to know that during this difficult time, America's butchers, bakers, and candlestick makers cared about broad results, not details, and they believed he had their interests at heart. Roosevelt repeatedly won reelection by margins in the millions, which made it clear that, whatever his flaws, the country at large believed that keeping him at the helm was better than the alternative.

Roosevelt's New Deal did not cure the Depression. The economy merely poked along and job growth remained anemic until the country geared up to fight the next world war. The international community had signed a pact in 1928 to outlaw war. Sixty-three nations pledged solemnly to settle their disputes through arbitration rather than by force of arms. The United States was in a mellow mood at that time and agreed to cooperate with the League of Nations. Despite such global harmony, there remained large pockets of discord. Japan occupied Manchuria in defiance of the League, then pulled out of the League altogether, and Hitler was beginning to demonstrate that German National Socialism was not a pretty thing.

An amusing story about the German problem circulated at Eleo's expense among the ladies of Boston's Chilton Club. The Chilton Club, headquartered on Commonwealth Avenue, was the female counterpart of the Somerset Club. It took its name from Mary Chilton, the only woman from the *Mayflower* to settle in Boston. The Chilton Club's carefully vetted membership devoted itself to gardening, debutante teas, and charity work. A feature of the club that pleased Eleo immensely was the requirement that members' male guests enter the building only through the side door. During a luncheon there in 1932 the ladies were discussing Adolf Hitler's recent election as chancellor of Germany. The ladies were surprised, so the story goes, that Eleo had no idea who this Hitler fellow was. "I can't be expected to know right off the bat the names of all the sophomores in the Porc," was her alleged excuse.[10]

England remained a bastion of civilization and in 1933 it strengthened its bond with America when its ladies began a cross-cultural squash competition. The Wolfe-Noel Cup series was named for the English team's captain, Elizabeth Wolfe, and its national champion, Susan Noel, who donated the permanent trophy. The two teams agreed to meet annually, alternating between Britain and America. The English ladies came to America for the first meeting. Immediately before the tournament, Eleo won an exhibition match against Susan Noel at the Harvard Club, but in the tournament itself, the English girls gave the home team a 4–1 beating.

Eleo was asked to be the captain of the American team and she became its impish mother hen. She drilled her girls and demonstrated shots and hosted tea parties for them at her Byron Street home before the matches. Eleo's standard outfit for squash was a cashmere sweater, black bloomers, and a crownlike crocheted hairnet that kept her hair out of her eyes. This last adornment may have influenced Susan Noel's pronouncement that Eleo was "a regal performer." A young woman coached by Eleo, Margaret Varner, went on to win four consecutive National Squash Championships, and she said that Eleo was her inspiration.[11]

In 1934 Eleo led the squash team to England, where she was greeted exuberantly by Lady Astor, "Welcome back to England, Eleo! Welcome back. . . . I have so much to tell you." Nancy Astor invited Eleo to a party she was hosting for that year's crop of Rhodes scholars. Though the Wolfe-Noel matches were uppermost on Eleo's schedule, she made time for her local friends and their horses. Eleo could count on a warm reception from many of Britain's premier titled houses—Mountbatten, Pembroke, Marlborough, Connaught, Northcliffe, Ravensdale—as well as other friends of long standing, such as Winston Churchill's mother, Lady Spencer Churchill, and David, the Prince of Wales. Eleo's fondness for the green and pleasant Anglo-Saxon isle was practically lyrical. "There is something about England—its sportsmanship, its sense of security, the atmosphere, the sure course of justice—they all make their appeal to me," she rhapsodized.[12]

London during the winter of 1934 offered a dreary venue for the squash competition. Fog and damp pierced the unheated courts at the Queen's Club, where an audience of more than one hundred sat huddled under blankets. Eleo was the nonplaying captain of her young U.S. team. She played only in the pretournament matches, which the American women dominated. By the end of the tournament itself, however, the Americans' spirits were as gloomy as the weather. The tough English lasses made the most of their home-court advantage and rolled over the visitors, 5–0. For the American team the lopsided score seemed terribly unworthy of the festivities that had surrounded their departure from home.

No trans-Atlantic crossing was undertaken lightly. Extensive presailing rites sent travelers on their four-day voyage to the Continent. During the last hours that an ocean liner remained at anchor in the Hudson River at New York's West Side Pier, friends and relatives bustled up the gangplank to help the traveler with the settling-in process. They explored the ship's amenities and saw that the steamer trunks were placed in the proper compartments. Ship stewards, dressed in crisp whites, jogged among the staterooms and cabins delivering baskets of fruit, flowers, and books sent by well-wishers. Previously delivered telegrams of bon voyage and Godspeed were read aloud. Eleo's stateroom filled with her girls and their families, who came in to share her cache of Champagne and chocolates. At noon, the fog-piercing blast of the ship's horn signaled a round of hugs and good-byes. Soon the ship drew majestically away from the dock. The passengers on board and their friends onshore strained for last glimpses and waved and blew kisses and got smaller and smaller.

England dominated the Wolfe-Noel series. The reason for that depended on which side was making the assessment. The British view was that the enthusiasm of the Americans could not overcome the more skillful shots and greater stamina of the English players. The American team framed the results quite differently. Their showing was lackluster because, they contended, they were actually better players than the English girls. The statistics, they believed, concealed that they played with more finesse, making it harder for them to adapt to the very different playing conditions in England than it would be for less skilled players. The American girls felt they had insufficient practice time on the English squash courts, which were wider by two and a half feet than those in the States, and they never got comfortable with the smaller, softer English squash balls.

In February 1935 Eleo's team was getting ready to host that year's Wolfe-Noel matches and they tuned up in a tournament in Atlantic City. During a break in the action, Eleo led the players and fans out to the beach. Looking trim and fit in her black bathing suit, fifty-four-year-old Eleo seemed barely older than her team of college girls. She plunged into the frigid ocean and frolicked in the waves, where she was joined after a bit by three girls from her team, who were hailed afterward as the newest recruits in the Polar Bear Club. Eleo toweled herself off and returned to the courts, where she beat a player twenty years her junior. In the Wolfe-Noel tournament, the American team prevailed, at last. Eleo was so delighted that she presented each of her girls with miniature sterling silver replicas of the trophy, which she had made by Cartier in Paris. Eleo also gave each team member a flip-top wristwatch in red, white, and blue.

Great Britain would ultimately win eleven of the sixteen Wolfe-Noel contests, which ran from 1933 until 1968, with a long break for the Second World War. Eleo revived the Wolfe-Noel matches after the war in 1949. Susan Noel said of Eleo, "She is one of those people who, by sheer force of character and generosity of nature, keep people together and make things go."[13]

It was obvious by the mid-1930s that Europe was again heading into dangerous waters, and the U.S. Congress busied itself passing neutrality acts. As life at home and abroad became increasingly unsettled and coarse, old-line Bostonians preferred to recall gentler times when amateur sportsmen, starched and spotless in white linen, played by the rules within prescribed boundaries. The Boston establishment had been present at the birth of such civilized competition, and their very own Eleo Sears was the epicenter. In 1936, as Eleo and her team made plans to cross the Atlantic to contend again for the Wolfe-Noel trophy, Eleo's admirers took the opportunity to celebrate the grand panorama of sport and its dauntless, multitalented practitioner. Eleo's friends launched plans for a tribute banquet, which they christened the National Sports Dinner.

Eight men formed themselves into the Sports Committee. An equal number of women became the nucleus of the Social Committee, and they booked the Crystal Room at the Puritan Hotel in Boston for February 10, 1936. The publisher of the sports magazine *Turf and Tanbark,* George Fergus Kelley, signed on as the event's chairman and sponsor. He was glad to associate his magazine with the person he called "the best-known, best-loved woman in the world of sports today."[14] The National Broadcasting Company agreed to carry a portion of the proceedings live on a nationwide radio hookup. At the Puritan Hotel, a black waiter who, after twenty-years there, knew Eleo well, offered his thoughts on the preparations, "Lan' sakes! How can that woman ever sit quiet long enough to enjoy that feed!"[15]

A fascinating mix of guests, numbering nearly two hundred, attended the black-tie evening. The *Boston Globe* editor Victor O. Jones described the gathering as "a perfect blend of the mink-and-monocle crowd with the dese-and-dem lads of the sports racket." The guests represented the fields of tennis, squash, football, fencing, polo, steeplechase, boxing, wrestling, figure skating, hockey, bike racing, and rowing. Each dinner guest received a handsome commemorative program that had Sargent's vivid charcoal portrait of Eleo on the cover under the Latin motto "MENS SANA IN CORPORE SANO"—"a healthy mind in a healthy body."

Eleo took her seat at the long head table, which was lined with floral displays. At her back was an enormous American flag. She was flanked by ten broad-shouldered athletes in tuxedos with stiff white shirtfronts. Eleo looked classically elegant in a low-necked gown of sapphire blue that was highlighted by a small diamond pin and a corsage of gardenias. The six-course banquet included green turtle consommé and filet mignon with béarnaise sauce. The dessert especially was worth waiting for—individual portions of ice cream molded in the shape of a horse on a grassy bed of green spun sugar.

The toastmaster for the evening, the radio commentator and *Boston Post* sportswriter Bill Cunningham, recalled the days when nice girls were not supposed to perspire. Eleo, he told the guests, was "a Modern Girl born into an old-fashioned era." He spoke poignantly of the times when Eleo could not find anyone to run with, so she ran alone along the edge of the Harvard track, pacing herself against the track team as it trained. Other guests popped up to salute Eleo and plug their sports. Hazel Wightman, Alice Thorndike, and the heavyweight champion Jack Dempsey took bows. Harry Cowles talked up squash as a fountain of youth and pointed to Eleo as proof. The Red Sox general manager and former second baseman Eddie Collins assessed the team's prospects for the season. Victor Jones hailed Eleo as having been more influential in emancipating women from the tyranny of low expectations than Carrie Nation, Helen Wills, and the English Channel swimmer Gertrude Ederle. Eleo took it all in appreciatively and smiled her famous smile. Bill Cunningham interviewed Eleo during the half-hour radio broadcast. Telegrams were read from Bill Tilden, Colonel Teddy Roosevelt (Alice's brother), Ina Clair, Lucius Beebe, and Mrs. August Belmont. From Ethel Barrymore came this salute: "To Eleo, long may she wave." The most touching telegrams came from two newspaper delivery boys who would surely have been invited to the banquet had anyone known of their existence. These lads had impressed Eleo with their work ethic. Without fanfare, she had picked them up by their blue collars and was putting them through college. Eleo liked to "adopt" people, but in the tradition of her grandfather Coolidge, who had declined to have his name carved above the door, she did not like to broadcast her charitable impulses. Eleo was old-fashioned enough to consider charity to be a private transaction that, if published, might embarrass the beneficiary. She was concerned too about being marked as a soft touch and having to fend off hordes of self-selected recipients. As the evening's celebration drew to a close, Eleo was called on to offer a few words and, as she rose to speak, the crowd broke into a spontaneous chorus of "For She's a Jolly Good Fellow." Eleo stood quietly for a moment and then she said in a small voice, "I don't deserve any of this. Thank you all from the bottom of my heart."[16]

Eleo's authentic modesty came as a surprise to people who had faced her blustery manner and who were unfamiliar with the temperament of a true sportsman. Eleo was always her own chief critic and competitor and never got lost in her momentary triumphs, ever aware that the next contest could have a different outcome.

Few in the room that evening were privy to an earlier drama involving the event's chairman, George Kelley, and President Roosevelt. Kelley had invited Roosevelt to contribute a written greeting to Eleo to be read during the radio broadcast. Kelley explained in a cordial letter that Eleo considered Roosevelt to be "a very great friend" and that she would be deeply honored to hear from him. Though Roosevelt was soon to face a reelection campaign, he likely assumed that the voters at Eleo's banquet would be Porcellian types who had never given him the time of day. He did not need to cater to them now. Nor had he any reservoir of affection for athletics in general. Having not made the football team at Harvard, which was held in much esteem by his cousin Teddy, he had had to settle instead for editing the school newspaper. And the president could not have been pleased that Eleo lectured him continually about economics and the needs of the business community. He did not want to encourage her. Roosevelt responded to Kelley through his assistant secretary, Stephen Early, saying that because he received many such requests to send greetings to old friends, he must be excused owing to "the great pressure of public business." The brush-off infuriated Kelley, and his reply to Early reveals how close to the surface the animosity toward Roosevelt was in certain circles. "The one thing that the President has been accused of constantly in the country," Kelley fired back, "is the 'selling out' of old friends."[17]

It is unlikely that Eleo ever learned about the president's snub, but if she did, she hid it well. She continued to correspond with Franklin, professing her affection for him and asking small favors. She contacted him whenever she was in Washington, and when he finally invited her to visit him in the White House she was genuinely pleased. In her thank-you note, Eleo referred to FDR's offhand comment that he enjoyed swimming and that she should join him sometime. She joked that on a future visit to the White House she might arrive in her bathing suit. To Roosevelt's staff, her jest sounded ominous. On the mantel in Roosevelt's study Eleo noticed a reproduction of the bust of the Egyptian queen Nefertiti, and she sent Franklin photos of the original sculpture, along with an account of its capture by the Germans during the Great War. She warned Franklin that the photos she was sending were "strictly copyright, so don't let anyone use them."[18] Eleo persisted in dealing with Roosevelt as though he were a once-pleasant child who had suffered a head wound and lost his way. Franklin's occupancy of the nation's most majestic office remained for Eleo a puzzling but potentially convenient accident.

In Hollywood the Depression wrought its painful changes, but on the sun-kissed West Coast the national economic collapse looked less dingy than elsewhere. A luxurious train trip was the preferred gateway to this paradise of palm trees and make-believe. Eleo went west on the Super Chief, the 1930s equivalent of the jet plane. The "Train of the Stars" left from Chicago for the forty-hour journey to Los Angeles. There was little left wanting on the swaying land-yacht, which was furnished with rare woods, deep carpets, polished brass, and crystal. Passengers were looked after by black porters who were all known as "George," after George Pullman, and by waiters who served with white gloves at linen-covered tables set with flowers and fine china. When travelers left their private Pullman Palace sleeping cars for the smoky club cars, they often found themselves hobnobbing with Hollywood's biggest celebrities.

The legendary film stars who had graced silent movies were ceding their places to a relentless crop of new and vocal performers. For those who worked in the movie business, the ravages of the Great Depression came as a second assault. The first was the revolution of talking pictures. High-paid film stars with squeaky voices or heavy foreign accents were suddenly has-beens, and caption writers joined the long lines of the unemployed now that their once-lucrative craft was wiped out. Many of Hollywood's tried-and-true publicity formulas no longer worked. During the Depression crowds still dutifully assembled to watch the stars and their entourages arrive in limousines for grand movie premieres, but the downtrodden public observed the glittering parade in sullen silence.

In the harsh light of serious times, moviegoers reassessed their naughty flirtations with on-screen sexual innuendo and concluded that their tastes had been hedonistic and unwholesome. Crusading religious groups rattled the sword of movie boycotts, and the major studios obligingly jettisoned controversial topics as they struggled for self-preservation. Between 1930 and 1933 movie attendance plunged by 20 million tickets, and the studios could not afford to take chances. Movie moguls humbled themselves before Will Hays, who ran the association of Motion Picture Producers and Distributors of America (MPPDA). The role of the Hays office in the 1920s had been mainly advisory. In the 1930s it was issuing seals of approval and shaping final scripts. The Hays office deleted scenes and plotlines that dealt with any type of sexual perversion, miscegenation, profanity, or childbirth. The censors insisted that scripts not romanticize criminality "such as banditry [or] daring thefts," and that there be no cleavage or on-screen lovemaking. The fade-out was born. The movie industry believed that this kind of "voluntary" self-censorship would save them from even more heavy-handed oversight by the federal government. The Production Code remained in effect until 1967.

Studio heads became convinced that the camera accentuated effeminate gestures and mannerisms and they cleaned house, ridding the back lot of "degenerates and fairies."[19] Vaguely androgynous personalities that excited adult moviegoers in the 1920s were losing their appeal. The pomaded magnetism of a John Barrymore, the foreign, smoldering Valentino types were now troubling. Unambiguously virile males were embraced, like Jack Armstrong, All-American Boy, and the cowboy Tom Mix and his gang of Straight Shooters. Tom Mix had been a real marshal in Oklahoma before becoming a hero to children on the radio and then graduating to movies.

In its search for inspiring role models, the public also idolized heroic animals, such as the great racehorse Seabiscuit, and Tom Mix's Tony, the Wonder Horse. The cowboy and his faithful mount were among the first movie stars to be immortalized on Hollywood Boulevard's Walk of Fame, where Tom's handprints shared the cement with Tony's hoofprints. In 1933, when the RKO Studio lost more than $10 million and was facing financial ruin, a mighty ape came to the rescue. King Kong captured the public's imagination and filled the theaters with his wrenching tale of unrequited love and death in a heartless, modern world.

Many of the biggest stars in Hollywood were bitten by the tennis bug, and they were thrilled when noted players visited the movie colony. Eleo played tennis and golf with many of the idols of the silver screen, and when those stars traveled east, they could count on her to throw them a big party with a fascinating guest list that brought together other luminaries from Hollywood and Broadway, performers from the Ice Capades, Harvard undergraduates, and members of Boston's police force. Clifton Webb, a tennis enthusiast, was the guest of honor at one of Eleo's Byron Street extravaganzas. The Harvard boys were rather startled by Cliff, who was so obviously and unapologetically "queer." Webb's career had begun on Broadway, where his effete style gave his characters the feel of fussy maiden aunts. In films that persona served him well in a series of endearing flustered-father roles. Webb was less concerned about being publicly identified as a homosexual than about being recognized for the working-class midwesterner he was, rather than the Yale-bred intellectual he and his devoted mother felt he should have been. The aging star marveled at his enduring on-screen popularity, and the stature gained by his work in the noir classic *Laura* and the 1953 version of *Titanic*. He would have been content to be appreciated simply as "the only man in Hollywood who knows how to hold a fish fork properly."[20]

The undisputed King of Tennis, Bill Tilden, was greeted like royalty when he arrived on the West Coast after turning pro in 1931. Chaplin, Gable, Errol Flynn, Douglas Fairbanks, and Joseph Cotten and his wife took tennis lessons from Tilden. Clifton Webb was a longtime friend of Tilden's, and he rented Constance Bennett's huge house in Beverly Hills, with its swimming pool and tennis courts. Every day between two and five, Tilden gave tennis lessons to Webb and other regulars—Garbo, Tallulah Bankhead, who was new to the game, the screen ingenue Katharine Hepburn, and the designer Valentina. After the lessons, they all migrated to Charlie Chaplin's courts to practice with Jean Harlow and Marlene Dietrich.

Bill Tilden had a knack for keying in on the strengths and weaknesses of the players he faced during his long career. Tilden ranked Eleo Sears as a "near great" when it came to tennis, and when he considered the breadth of her athletic skills and the totality of her pioneering exploits, he felt she had no equal. Eleo was, Tilden observed, "an outstanding exception" to the general rule that "high society's children too often lack the concentration and power of sustained effort essential to make the first-rate competitor." He also identified the intriguing dichotomy that was at the heart of Eleo's personality and appeal. Eleo possessed an "essentially dynamic nature" that existed in tandem with a core that was "quiet and aloof." This gave her, Tilden felt, "a provocative, almost alluring quality. She could have an earthy, small boy gamin quality when she wished, or she could be very much one of the Boston Sears."[21] He had opportunities to witness that other side, the haughty Boston Brahmin side. "There is no one who can cut you quite the way Eleo Sears can, when she has a mind to," Tilden observed.[22]

Bill Tilden's volatile temperament offered its own complexities. The Hollywood crowd chose not to examine the reason that Tilden was often surrounded by a harem of thirteen- and fourteen-year-old "ball boys." Many movie legends juggled delicate personal issues and were in no position to be judgmental. (An abortionist was accommodated by 20th Century Fox, and his services were available to players from all the major studios.)

Eleo got on fabulously with Tallulah Bankhead, who was a headliner at another of Eleo's Byron Street parties. Tallulah reveled in being the kind of bawdy broad likely to be banned in Boston. She was an Alabama-born belle who lived fast, drank hard, and was able to straddle the moral fault line of Hollywood's Production Code because she had talent, and because she really didn't give a damn. When Tallulah was in England at the same time as the Wolfe-Noel Cup matches, Eleo introduced her to her squash team. Tallulah greeted the team by doing a cartwheel and standing on her head, her version of a *veddy proper* English welcome. If you can believe Tallulah's extravagant off-the-cuff calculations, she loved "thousands" of men and women. Her male lovers were said to have included John Barrymore, Winston Churchill, and Edward R. Murrow. Among Tallulah's female conquests were Eva Le Galli-enne, Joan Crawford, Katharine Cornell, and, to prove she was no snob, Hat-tie McDaniel, the black actress who played a series of ladies' maids with gusto. Tallulah joined the throngs of men and women in pursuit of the icy Miss Garbo and, it is said, she was among the handful who were successful.

Katharine Hepburn made her film debut opposite Ethel Barrymore's brother John in *Bill of Divorcement* in 1932. Ethel said, "The face of Garbo is an Idea, that of Hepburn is an Event." Kate Hepburn and Eleo Sears met several times through the years and many people have noted their striking resemblance and how closely the athletic, trouser-wearing Hepburn cast herself in the Eleo Sears mold. Both women were well-scrubbed-looking New Englanders with crisp diction that had the snap of a tart apple, and both used quick, impatient dashes to separate their written sentences. Kate Hepburn also shared Eleo's devotion to sports, her determination not to be ordinary, and her preference for toning down her homosexual leanings for public consumption.

Hepburn's first starring role was as a glamorous British airplane pilot in the 1933 film *Christopher Strong*, in which her "Lady Cynthia" falls in love with a married man. The trajectory of the plot satisfied the censorship demands of the time. Hepburn's character switches from pants to dresses and gives up flying to win Lord Christopher Strong away from his feminine high-society wife. Hepburn's Lady Cynthia gets pregnant and chooses death in a plane crash over a life of dishonor. Despite the ending that made death the pathway to redemption, *Christopher Strong* is considered an early feminist film, and it was crafted by an all-female team. They gussied up the heroine's suicide to look like courage, as though she took ultimate control of her destiny. The National Conference of Catholic Churches gave the movie marginal approval with a "fair" rating.

The film's director, Dorothy Arzner, said the inspiration for the film's female pilot was the British aviator Amy Johnson, who had made a solo flight from England to Australia. Arzner wore her short hair slicked back and was the only female director to successfully make the transition from silent pictures to sound. She always tried to include scenes in her pictures that showed forceful women. Zoe Atkins, who adapted the script from a novel by Gilbert Fankau, had once written a love poem to Ethel Barrymore that appeared in an issue of *Vanity Fair*. True to form, Ethel had been more amused than scandalized by Zoe's tribute.

Eleo's very dear "Birry," Ethel Barrymore, was content to spend her time with Eleo quietly, away from crowds. Ethel had gotten a divorce in 1923 and had raised three children by herself, but she remained, as ever, an unflappable observer of the human condition. Even after the Shubert brothers honored Ethel by naming their new theater on West 47th Street after her, she saw mainly the humor in her iconic status. When asked how she got the audience to remain so quiet and attentive during her performances, the Queen of the Broadway Stage quipped, "I never let them cough. They wouldn't dare." The Ethel Barrymore Theatre survived the Depression, aided by the Shuberts' decision to air-condition the auditorium so it could compete with the new "air-cooled" movie palaces.

Throughout Eleo's life, she sought out people of accomplishment, whether in the theater, sports, politics, or law enforcement, and her admiration for excellence was egalitarian. A groom at her stable or a prime minister could earn her respect if he pursued his job with competence, speed, and an enlivening touch of humor. Eleo always considered her brother, Freddy, to be a slacker, and Eleo's lack of respect for him was at the heart of the friction between them. They disagreed often, usually about money. C. Z. Cochrane, the younger daughter of the vivacious Vivian Cochrane Pickman and the future Mrs. Winston Guest, stayed at Freddy Sears's house in Palm Beach when she was a teenager. C.Z. witnessed a typical confrontation between Eleo and her brother. Eleo was staying at the home of the Joseph Wideners, a few miles away, and early one morning she walked over to speak with Freddy. Her brother was still in bed when his French valet brought him the news that Eleo was downstairs. Freddy instructed his man, "Dites-lui que je suis malade." (Tell her that I am sick.) Eleo rolled her eyes when the message was delivered and charged up the stairs to Freddy's bedroom. Freddy hid helplessly under the covers while Eleo stood at his bedside, hands on her hips, and launched into the problem that she wanted settled.

As a child, C. Z. Cochrane loved watching Eleo. She admired Eleo's trim, suntanned looks, the confident way she moved, and the cut and quality of her tailored clothing. "Eleo was always so soignée," C.Z. noted approvingly. C.Z. also recalled that Eleo was strict about enforcing the rule at Myopia that prohibited children from entering the main clubhouse. Eleo would relent only if a child claimed a need to use the bathroom. In general, when it came to children, Eleo seemed unaware or unconcerned about the often-terrifying impression she made on them, though she was actually fond of well-mannered, well-spoken youngsters who didn't answer "Yup!" Eleo tended to treat boys, particularly if they were sons of friends, as though they were tough-as-nails barroom pals. It took laughably little effort to produce a startled, bug-eyed child, and it amused Eleo to provoke them. It was widely known that Eleo disliked being asked to make charitable donations, as she preferred to select her own causes on her own timetable. So when Phyllis Sears Tuckerman sent her son to visit "Cousin Eleo" on behalf of a local charity, it was an unenviable mission. Eleo exchanged a perfunctory "hello" with Cousin Phyllis's boy and then tossed a five-dollar bill down to him from her balcony. Eleo's shy visitor stood rooted in her front hall, crimson with fear and embarrassment, as he waited for the bill to slowly float down to him. Ben Bradlee, later the eminent executive editor of the *Washington Post,* never forgot his ordeal as Eleo's ball boy. Ben's father was an All-American football player known to his friends as "Beebo," and he had been one of Eleo's pacers during a Providence-to-Boston hike. He said the experience nearly killed him. He arranged for nine-year-old Ben to retrieve tennis balls for Helen Wills and Eleo at the Essex County Club. Eleo panicked Ben by banging balls at him and yelling, "Get a move on, damn you," whenever she thought he was daydreaming or not running fast enough. When Ben Bradlee grew to manhood he had opportunities to enjoy Eleo's hospitality, but as a boy he was convinced "she was as mean as a snake."[23]

The patience Eleo often lacked with people she could consistently summon for horses. When it came to horses and their needs, her Boston Puritan frugality evaporated. She had a sure eye for good horses, a willingness to spend whatever it took to obtain them, and definite, generally nonnegotiable ideas about how they should be cared for and in which shows they should be entered. Eleo's name recognition and her quality horses trumped her reputation for being a difficult owner, and she never had trouble recruiting talented riders who were eager to make their own reputations aboard her fine mounts. Eleo did not expect to pay top dollar for even highly skilled riders, nor did she need to. Labor has been a cheap commodity historically, and that was especially true in the lean years of the Depression. Good horses, on the other hand, could even then command a king's ransom. Eleo and her prizewinning horses attracted a number of exceptionally talented female riders who, to maintain their amateur standing, expected no payment at all. Instead, Eleo presented them periodically with thoughtfully selected thank-you gifts. During the early 1930s at the Country Club in Brookline, Eleo saw young Jimmy Rowe gallop Battleship, a son of the legendary Man o' War. She watched closely how Jimmy molded himself to the horse like a glove on a hand, and she knew she wanted Jimmy Rowe on her show jumpers.

Twenty-three-year-old James B. Rowe was Massachusetts-bred with English roots, but his twinkly, lake-blue eyes and ruddy cheeks gave him the look of an Irish country boy. He had grown up on his father's horse farm, a fun-loving kid who thought that time spent on book learning was time that could have been better spent on or around horses. Jimmy's boyhood plan was to be a jockey, but to his sorrow he grew to be a trim five feet six or so, not a big man but too tall to be a jockey. It was not in Jimmy's nature to be sorrowful for long, and he found he could make a reasonably good living as a show jumper and steeplechase rider. The overall impression one got of Jimmy Rowe was of a large, blue-eyed cherub, one you felt the urge to hug. In December 1934 Eleo offered the young horseman a chance to ride for her exclusively with a two-year guarantee. Accepting Eleo's proposal meant that Jimmy would have to quit the job he already had, jumping a nice horse that belonged to a "Mr. K.," who owned of a chain of clothing stores. That job was of uncertain duration, but Mr. K. was a likable, easygoing owner and he paid more than Eleo was offering. Both jobs had their attractions and, unsure which path to take, Jimmy appealed to his father for advice.

Fred Rowe responded to his son with a three-page letter that offered an intriguingly reasoned and beautifully written analysis of the situation as he saw it. Jimmy's obviously loving "Old Man" detailed his misgivings about Mr. K., prospect number one, because he was a businessman. Mindful of the many businesses laid low since the Crash, the senior Rowe saw little reason to have faith in the integrity of merchants engaged in a scramble for the Almighty Dollar. Though Mr. K.'s clothing stores were currently successful, that could change in these risky times, as Rowe knew all too well from his own struggling business. Rowe's customers included people with old family fortunes as well as the nouveau variety, and his experience left him contemptuous of the "new rich." He concluded that the newly moneyed "as a rule . . . have no honor when it does not pay, . . . they have no God but profit, and always break their word to save a loss." Fred Rowe's disillusion extended to his middle-class neighbors who got caught up in get-rich-quick schemes and "dumb" strategies to "debt themselves out of poverty." Jimmy's father speculated that Mr. K.'s "love for his horse and the horse game is determined from its advertising value" and that his interest could fade if it was not immediately successful—"a bubble blown quickly bursts suddenly."

Fred Rowe had far more faith in Eleo Sears, who "belongs to an old traditional family, who had the reputation of both peculiarities and honor." Her promise of a two-year contract could be relied on, and Mr. Rowe advised his son, "In these times you should consider security as a part of salary." Working for Miss Sears offered a unique advantage because she was "a social power of international standing . . . and a good recommendation from her will never be ignored," while a recommendation from a "new comer" like Mr. K. would mean little. Rowe acknowledged that "Miss S has her pecularities [sic] which you must expect from all Old Yankees, who in the final analayis [sic] put their soul or honor above everything else." Her employees remained with her for decades and this, Fred Rowe felt, spoke volumes. He put his faith in tried-and-true traditions and believed that the ascendancy of the johnny-come-latelies was temporary—"for a short while, they are in power, but their days are numbered, as progress is based on truth and honor."[24] Fred Rowe's uncomplicated faith in the triumph of man's better nature can, even now, wring tears from a stone.

Heeding his father's advice, Jimmy Rowe began riding for the Sears stable. He won blue ribbons in shows at Cohasset and Myopia. He joined Eleo for foxhunting at Myopia, where they galloped headlong across the valleys, jumping hedges, fences, and streams. Eleo confided her unease about jumping to Jimmy and he made suggestions that relaxed her. Eleo took Jimmy to Europe to ride in important shows in France. In 1936 Jimmy sailed to England with Eleo. Eleo's friend David was just beginning his abbreviated reign as king, following the death of his father, George V. Jimmy Rowe joined Eleo and the lords and ladies in her set on foxhunts. Eleo put Jimmy up in a suite at the Claridge Hotel in London, which she used as a home base when she was not at the country estates of friends. Jimmy was amazed to find himself seated in the hotel dining room among the marble columns, velvet brocade, and man-sized arrangements of fresh flowers, being served by the white-gloved staff as if he belonged. Jimmy had recently married his high school sweetheart, Virginia, and every day he wrote to Ginny to reassure her that, despite his adventures, he missed her. Eleo grew fond of Jimmy, and she became protective. When he got sick, she worried endlessly about his tonsils. She called the hospital to check on him when his tonsils came out. She presented Jimmy with a pair of gold cufflinks with exquisitely detailed horse heads that she had originally bought as a present for Alfred Vanderbilt. Alfred had perished on the *Lusitania* before Eleo could give him her gift.

Eleo was greatly disappointed when, at the end of 1936, Jimmy chose not to renew his two-year contract. Ginny wanted him home with her, and he had no shortage of other riding opportunities. The right people knew him now, and Jimmy had ambitions. He did not intend to stay a jump rider much longer and was working toward his trainer's license. Eleo, he knew, already had a trainer, her old friend Henry Lee. In July 1937 Eleo was thinking ahead to the fall when she wrote to Jimmy and asked, with a glimmer of hope, if he might "come back to the stable and help ride the horses etc—just for the hunting season." She had to send a second note before Jimmy replied, and she was deeply annoyed by his tardy response. Before they met finally at her house in Beverly Farms, she wrote again to Jimmy, "Please bring with you the sleeve links I gave you—I want to speak to you about them—."[25] She had been hasty, she decided, in awarding those particular links to someone who was no longer part of her immediate world. She was not embarrassed to ask for their return. She had a replacement pair for him, more appropriate really, ones that showed a scarlet-coated horseman going over a jump. They had gold backs, nice enough, and she had no personal attachment to them. Jimmy rode for Eleo a few more times, and then for a quarter century they parted company.

Another thing that Jimmy Rowe gave up when he left Eleo's employ was the opportunity to work out of one of the most imposing stables in the country. In 1936 Eleo took title to the property that had, for the longest time, been the object of her desire. Helen Frick sold her the noble-looking Tudor-style stable with the red roof and great arched entry that her father had built on a hill in Prides Crossing. The stone-and-stucco horse palace was an ideal setting for Eleo's growing stable of horses, and the building had an entire wing to house the collection of carriages and horse carts she had acquired through the years. The top floor of the stable held a complete apartment, with numerous bedrooms and a fully equipped kitchen. A stone retaining wall stood down the hill from the stable. A large cottage occupied the lower edge of the property. This substantial two-story house, dwarfed by the stable that rose up behind it, was divided to allow for occupancy by two families, making it suitable for the head groom and his family and the head gardener. The entire property was enclosed by Henry Clay Frick's grand wrought-iron fence.

While her horses were always Eleo's primary concern, she continued to invest much of her brimming energy in racquet sports. At the age of fifty-six, she was still a force on the squash court, and in January 1938 she defeated her younger sometime nemesis Mrs. William Howe to win, for the fourth time, the Massachusetts State Squash Championship. Eleo confined her competitive tennis to veterans' tournaments. In the summer of 1938 she reunited with her old friend and doubles partner Hazel Wightman at Longwood for the Women's Veterans Tennis Tournament, where they reached the final round. The warm friendship between Eleo and Hazel through the years revolved around their shared passion for sports. Hazel was a fine squash player as well, and she had won the national squash title in 1930. In a squash match she played against Eleo, Hazel valiantly stood her ground despite being half a head shorter than her opponent. Eleo charged toward the front of the court barking, "Get out of my way!" Hazel responded with equal vigor, "I can't. You're on my foot."[26] On the wall in her front hall at home, Hazel kept a framed copy of Sargent's charcoal portrait of Eleo.

For two days in September 1938 a monstrous hurricane laid waste to New England. Nothing more than rain had been forecast, and the storm caught the residents completely off guard. The last hurricane to trouble New England had struck in 1815, beyond living memory. The Storm of '38 came from the south and spun in the Atlantic, unseen and untracked, into a Category-Four killer. It slammed into the Hamptons on the tip of Long Island just before three o'clock in the afternoon on September 21. From there it galloped up the coast at sixty miles per hour in a tantrum of destruction, flinging aside cars, houses, and railroad tracks in its path. A tsunami-like storm surge consumed coastal towns in Connecticut and Rhode Island. Nearly 700 people lost their lives and some 63,000 were left homeless.

The storm's force left memorable disruptions farther up the coast. In New Hampshire, at the Rockingham Park racetrack, the day's racing lineup was running on schedule. A horse named Singing Slave was romping to victory in the sixth with Warren Yarberry in the saddle when a sudden blast of wind knocked Yarberry off his horse. Blessedly, Yarberry was not trampled as the other horses thundered past. Singing Slave crossed the wire in first place, but the riderless horse was disqualified. The track announcer, Babe Rubenstein, was calling the race until the moment his broadcasting booth was shaken loose from its moorings and sent crashing toward the stands. There was much luck at the track that day. Rubenstein and another man with him in the booth were able to crawl from the rubble to safety, and no one in the crowd was hit by the structure. The race card for the rest of the day was canceled.

Along the North Shore, centuries-old trees and power lines collapsed onto roads, and sections of roofs and chimneys flew from buildings. People later recalled being mesmerized by the sound of the storm, which came at them with a high-pitched scream as though from a wounded animal. In areas of the country familiar with big storms, wise horse owners go into overdrive when fierce weather threatens. Beyond the commonsense closing of stable doors and shutters, straw piles are removed or anchored down to keep them from blowing away. Horses that live outside wear halters marked with their name and address. Extra food and water is set out in big tubs where the horses can reach it. In paddocks across New England, the horses sensed the approaching storm before the people did, and they snorted in terror as the wind increased. Eleo's horses trembled and paced in their stalls inside the big Frick stable, but they were safe as trees crashed down around them.

Eleo was on Cape Cod on her way to have tea with Mrs. E. Atkins Baldwin when the hurricane made landfall there. At about four o'clock Eleo was walking toward Mrs. Baldwin's beautiful eighteenth-century house on the harbor in Cataumet when a tidal wave of water from Buzzards Bay washed over the lane. In some places the surge reached thirteen feet above sea level. The wave swept over Eleo and hurled her into a chain-link enclosure. After Eleo realized she was caught inside the Baldwins' tennis court, she swam in the swirling water, pushing debris aside until she found the gate and squeezed through.

Eleo kept swimming until she reached the Baldwins' home, arriving at their second floor window in time for tea. For years afterward, Mrs. Baldwin enjoyed retelling this story, always with gales of laughter.[27]

Long after the storm departed, cast-off bits of civilization littered miles of roads. A section of road along the North Shore was still blocked by a large downed tree when the mother of Eleo's cousin John Sears set out in her car on an errand. At almost the same moment, an acquaintance arriving from the opposite direction was stopped by the same obstacle. The two women quickly hit on a practical solution. They exchanged car keys, climbed over the tree, and continued on to their destinations, each driving the other's car.

In the immediate aftermath of the storm, newspapers in America called the hurricane of 1938 "the wind that shook the world," so gravely was the most populous section of the country affected by lost lives and damaged property. In the larger world, the stars were aligned for a still greater catastrophe as Europe spun out of control, and soon this natural disaster moved to the back pages. Within days of the hurricane, Britain, France, and Italy agreed to let Adolf Hitler amputate parts of Czechoslovakia following his summer invasion of Austria, in the hope that these new morsels would satisfy the wolf. Despite this, the Duke and Duchess of Windsor traveled to Germany and spent part of their honeymoon with Hitler at Berchtesgaden. They also enjoyed a yachting excursion with Axel Wenner-Gren, the Swedish industrialist who was a close friend of the Luftwaffe commander, Hermann Göring.

Eleo was dismayed to see the duke, her darling David, wasting himself with such dubious and boorish companions, but then lately he had been doing many inexplicable things. The most unimaginable thing he had done was to give up the throne of England after less than a year to marry the hard-faced American divorcée Wallis Simpson. Before his marriage, David had had an agreeable mistress, Lady Furness, the former Thelma Morgan, whose identical twin sister, Gloria, married Eleo's old pal Reggie Vanderbilt. But Thelma lost her heart to the playboy prince Aly Khan and followed him to the United States, clearing the deck for Mrs. Simpson. After David's abdication, his brother George VI replaced him on the English throne and sent him packing to a minor post as governor of the Bahamas. David was not even allowed to return to England without first getting his brother's permission. Though many of Eleo's friends thought the duke was a "twit," Eleo did not abandon her royal dance partner, who had dazzled her with his attention. His autographed photo remained in its honored place on Eleo's piano at Byron Street, though the image now had a distinctly sorry look.

International troubles, amplified by the usual political song and dance, came in for comic treatment in the musical satire *Leave It to Me*, which moved into Boston's Shubert Theatre in October 1938. The show's plot deals with the uncertain art of offending an audience and prefigured Mel Brooks's hit with a similar premise, *The Producers*. The story line of *Leave It to Me* involves an American ambassador who is unhappy and cold in Stalinist Russia. He tries to get himself recalled by insulting his Communist hosts and the German ambassador, actions that only endear him to the congressmen back home. Reversing course, the American diplomat succeeds in losing his job by speaking in favor of peace and a unified world. The second act, set in Siberia, featured the newcomer Mary Martin, who did a chaste striptease while singing Cole Porter's delightful "My Heart Belongs to Daddy." The number brought down the house, and Mary Martin made the cover of *Life* magazine. Eleo invited the whole cast of the show to a party at Byron Street, and that was when, as Mary Martin exuberantly described it, "I came into HER fabulous life." Eleo and Mary met often through the years in Boston or New York as Mary starred in a succession of hits—*South Pacific, Peter Pan, The Sound of Music*. Mary said that Eleo captured her heart because of her "warmth, her wit, and down-to earth qualities. She was as chic in muddy boots and jeans as in her sables and Mainbochers."[28] Mary classified Eleo with Isak Dinesen and Katharine Hepburn as "real women, with courage, and a lust for life."

The show *Leave It to Me* played for nearly a year on Broadway and began a road tour in October 1939. By then Germany and Russia had signed a friendship pact, and the musical about Hitler and Stalin and dancing peasants lost its appeal. Some seven decades later, bartenders who consulted *Mr. Boston's Bartenders' Guide* could still find the recipes for two versions of the Leave It to Me cocktail, both Russian red, one with grenadine in a gin base, and one with a splash of raspberry syrup.

When it was announced that the king and queen of England would visit the White House before going to New York for the 1939 World's Fair, Eleo had a brilliant idea. More than a decade earlier, she had been formally presented to their royal predecessors. She had ongoing friendships with the best families in England, and she was a great friend of their former king. She had also ridden horses with the president of the United States and was giving him advice on managing the national economy. Surely, she reasoned, all this entitled her to hobnob with the current king and queen. Eleo shared her conviction with President Roosevelt. "Wouldn't it be rather nice to have ME as well!! I am quite serious about this so please think it over," she wrote to the president. Eleo offered to arrange for Their Majesties to attend the International Polo matches at the Meadowbrook Club as a respite from their official duties. Even in the midst of her "humble petition" to the president, Eleo could not bring her dislike of his leadership to heel. She told Franklin that she had just returned from London and Paris, where everyone thinks he is wonderful. She added, "I would agree, except for the New Deal in your heart! I hope this piece of frankness won't ruin my chances of the visit I have planned!!!"[29] The president instructed his secretary to advise Eleo of the impossibility of her plans, putting her gently but firmly in her place.

Franklin Roosevelt was the first president to appear live on television when he opened the World's Fair in Flushing Meadows on April 30, 1939, though the broadcast was limited to receivers located at the fairgrounds and at Radio City Music Hall in Manhattan. That night Albert Einstein threw a switch that turned on floodlights around the fairgrounds. The next day television sets became available for purchase in department stores across the nation. The 1939 World's Fair was styled as a showcase of modernity and innovation, and the fairgrounds had a self-consciously modern look. The buildings, all sharp angles and unadorned surfaces, represented the latest in architectural thought, but they were no match for the "White City," which had stunned visitors to Chicago's Columbian Exposition almost fifty years earlier, coincidently during another economic depression. General admission to the 1939 World's Fair was only seventy-five cents, but adding food and souvenirs could cost a family as much as seven dollars. The event had been proposed as an antidote to the Depression, but less than half of the paid admissions promised by the fair's promoters actually materialized.

Crowds did flock to the RCA building that demonstrated television for the first time. They watched news broadcasts and boxing matches on a small screen mounted in a transparent Lucite cabinet that showed off the inner workings of this mysterious technology. David Sarnoff, head of RCA, hailed television as a new art form that would benefit all mankind, but long after its debut in 1939 its influence remained limited. Television screens, the largest of which was all of nine inches, were set like jewels in meticulously crafted art-deco cabinets that were sized as either floor or table models. The least expensive table model cost $199.50, and top-of-the-line floor models with built-in radios cost $600—an impressive $3,000 to more than $9,000 at today's prices. Sales promotions were aimed therefore at the very wealthy, and advertisements pictured viewers in tuxedos and ball gowns smiling in front of the lacquered cabinets. Few sales were made. The economy was shaky and talk of war filled the radio airwaves. Little broadcasting content was available for television's five channels. Eleo had been curious to see the flickering images coming from the Lucite box, but she could think of no compelling reason to sit in front of a cabinet to watch other people at play. Radio provided all the canned entertainment she needed, and evenings spent conversing with friends about horses and politics or winning money from them playing bridge and backgammon passed pleasantly enough. She did not bother to buy a television set until 1963, when she was eighty-two years old, and then, after it arrived, she didn't turn it on for weeks.

The scene in the fair's international section was jarring, like a painted grin that masked a mouth of decaying teeth. The pavilions of hostile nations circled a central promenade called the Court of Peace, in front of which sat an oddly named water feature, the Lagoon of Nations. King George and Queen Mary formally opened the British pavilion. The German government, which now controlled Czechoslovakia, sent Professor Ladislav Sutnar, a Czech artist, to retrieve for the Reich the valuable arts and crafts that were on display in the Czechoslovak pavilion. Neither the professor nor the artwork returned to Germany. In the Polish pavilion an excellent restaurant served up national dishes and visitors could enter an essay contest with the theme "I would like to visit Poland because . . . ," this despite the problem that in August the Nazis had begun their invasion of Poland and the world was plunged, once again, into war.

For Eleo too an era ended when her father died on New Year's Eve 1939, a few weeks short of his eighty-fourth birthday. Age had only made Frederick Sr. more eccentric. For years he had insisted that the domestic staff at 122 Beacon Street wear rubber-soled shoes so as not to wear out the hardwood floors. Eleo said of her father, "He did everything in one way and nothing in another way, except give himself a grand good time."[30] She said it without bitterness. She had resigned herself to his shortcomings long before. Still, he was her father, part of many good childhood memories, a link to her mother. It all had gone by so fast that it took her breath away. After Frederick died, Eleo found an oil painting in a closet that he had worked on and never shown to anyone. It was a self-portrait, surprisingly well done. Eleo hung it in her living room.

CHAPTER 16

Love and War on the North Shore

◦

THE "BEST" STORY ABOUT how Eleo ended up with Rock Edge, her handsome Georgian mansion on Paine Avenue in Prides Crossing, has her winning the nearly three-and-a-half-acre oceanfront property in a backgammon game. A Michigan-based politician, Frederick Alger, inherited Rock Edge and lived there for a year. According to those most likely to know, Fred Alger was looking to unload the property to pay the death duties owed on his grandfather's estate. Beyond that, details vary. On Eleo's side of the wager, it is said that she staked the large steam-powered yacht that she used for summer trips between Bar Harbor and Newport, a yacht given to her by Mike Vanderbilt. No one disputes the fact that Eleo was a crackerjack backgammon player and that she played with creditors and solicitors who were willing to let payment of their claims ride on the double-or-nothing outcome of a game. Eleo was regularly seen boarding the 10:00 A.M. train from Prides Crossing to New York with a backgammon set under her arm, confident of finding someone on board willing to try his luck against her.

It appears that Eleo came out of the high-stakes backgammon game as the big winner, getting the house and all its furnishings. Fred Alger, so the story goes, left the table with the title to Eleo's yacht. The Alger family signed Rock Edge over to Eleo in May 1940. The stately redbrick country house had been built in 1909 with a formality that would have made it more at home on a city street. The house came with thirty-seven generously sized rooms surrounding a grand staircase, and it included fifteen bathrooms. Visitors drove past a grass tennis court framed by two small Victorian-style pavilions and cascading roses before reaching the front steps and the four granite columns that guarded the front door. At the rear of the house, the grass ran to the edge of a boulder-packed retaining wall that gave the house its name. The boulders sloped dramatically down to a 335-foot strip of private beach with a steel pier.

A classically styled bathhouse shared the panoramic view across the water of the small islands and wandering coastline beyond Prides Crossing. Rock Edge became Eleo's joy. The steam yacht that went home with Frederick Alger was commandeered for use by the navy soon after war was declared.

One of Eleo's first houseguests after she was settled in at Rock Edge was Mrs. George Balanchine, the lovely Vera Zorina. Zorina had a flourishing stage and film career and was, for the most part, enjoying her high-profile marriage as Balanchine's second wife. Her Broadway vehicle at the time, Irving Berlin's *Louisiana Purchase,* was choreographed by Balanchine. Zorina saw no reason to maintain the caution toward Eleo that her mother had insisted on earlier. Zorina had first met Eleo in April 1938, during the Boston tryouts of the Rodgers and Hart musical comedy *I Married an Angel.* Reviewers raved about the show's spectacular choreography, music, and sets, which were concocted by the dream team of Joshua Logan and George Balanchine. Eleo attended the sold-out opening-night performance. She was so taken with the production that she returned the following night and every night thereafter during its three-week run. Eleo could not take her eyes off the lead dancer, the twenty-one-year-old Vera Zorina. Zorina was the white-winged angel that came down to earth and won the heart of a man who had vowed to remain a bachelor. Zorina had the long-limbed grace of a filly and soulful eyes that warmed her Nordic looks, and Eleo was entranced. Across the footlights Zorina began to expect the dependable presence of the striking-looking, blue-eyed woman in a black dress seated in the front row, left of the aisle. One night Zorina's agent, Dwight Wiman, took Eleo backstage to meet the dancer. Eleo invited Wiman and the entire cast to a party at her Byron Street *garage* (accent on the first syllable). The evening was lively with music and Champagne and pleased everyone. Wiman was less thrilled later when Eleo sailed her yacht to New York and visited Zorina backstage after her Broadway debut in *Angel.* Eleo invited Zorina and her mother to visit her on the yacht, and Zorina, who was intrigued by her wealthy, "marvelous-looking" admirer, longed to accept. She had grown restless with the constant company of her mother and her agent. Wiman, however, had a serious talk with Zorina's mother. He alerted her to the lesbian gossip surrounding Eleo and the negative influence such talk would have on her daughter's budding career. Zorina's mother insisted that she refuse Eleo's invitation. Two years passed before they met again.

"Vera Zorina" was a name that its owner was never comfortable with. She had been christened Eva Brigitta Hartwig by her German father and Norwegian mother. In 1934, at the age of seventeen, she joined the Ballet Russe de Monte Carlo, where the director of the company insisted, as he did with all foreigners, that she select a Russian name from his list so as not to dilute the essential Russian character of the ballet. She chose "Vera Zorina" because it was the least difficult to pronounce. Her friends always called her Brigitta.

Zorina was often lonely while she traveled with the Ballet Russe, though she met a memorable assortment of people. She and her company were introduced to Tallulah Bankhead, who astonished the dancers with her trademark headstand. Zorina never forgot how Tallulah's beautiful evening dress fell away, revealing her to be "utterly and entirely naked." One night after a party, Marlene Dietrich cornered Zorina and made advances. Marlene was another star who treated sexual relationships with men and women as an equal opportunity enterprise, and she was especially taken with Zorina because they both spoke German. Zorina reacted to Marlene's overtures first with amazement and curiosity, and finally with "acute embarrassment." Zorina and Dietrich remained friends, however, and they shared screen time in the patriotic war movie *Follow the Boys*.

After Eleo and Zorina reestablished contact, Eleo's neighbors noted with keen interest that Eleo often drove her station wagon to the salmon-trimmed train depot with the sign that read simply "Prides" to collect Zorina and her luggage. The nature of the relationship between the dancer and Eleo was widely presumed. After Eleo bought Zorina a maroon Duesenberg, the suspicion of impropriety hardened into certainty. Several of Eleo's friends, such as Mabel Storey and Vivian Cochrane, maintained their equilibrium and gladly joined Eleo and Zorina for tea at Rock Edge. Vivian brought along her daughters, Nancy and C.Z., who were thrilled to know such a glamorous couple. Zorina was well aware of the suspicion in the air. Her insistence that her friendship with Eleo was totally devoid of sexual drama changed few minds. Zorina said that in all the years she knew Eleo, "She never even held my hand."[1]

As a child Zorina had loved riding horses, but she had to give that up because an injury to her legs would threaten her dancing career. Zorina was happy just to watch the horses in the National Horse Show at the Garden from Eleo's box, along with Eleo's Boston friends who traveled with her in her private railroad car. Eleo's horses rolled into Grand Central Station in their own specially equipped car. Zorina got to ride an elephant in a pachyderm ballet called the "Circus Polka" in the 1942 Ringling Brothers and Barnum and Bailey Circus. Balanchine created the choreography for the fifty performing elephants, and Igor Stravinsky composed the music. Doubtless, Eleo agreed that Zorina looked magnificent sitting on the lead elephant, Modoc, the largest Indian elephant in America.

At Rock Edge Zorina declined to join Eleo on her daily swim in the ocean because she found the water too cold, but it was heaven for her to stretch out on a towel on Eleo's beach and lose herself in a book. Zorina admitted to being "a passionate reader." The hypnotic sounds of the surf were shattered from time to time when Eleo discouraged would-be trespassers with a shout, "Get the hell off my beach!" Still, Rock Edge was the place where Zorina sought refuge to regroup and refocus whenever she faced career setbacks or had a serious argument with Balanchine.

Zorina's professional life took a stinging turn after she was cast opposite Gary Cooper in the movie based on Hemingway's novel *For Whom the Bell Tolls*. Zorina was on location in the mountains of Spain, her luxuriant hair already cut short to resemble the character Maria, when she noticed that the director Sam Wood and members of the crew suddenly turned cool and uncomfortable in her presence. Wood had decided that Zorina's cropped hair made her nose look too prominent, and the producer, David Selznick, wanted Ingrid Bergman for the part, now that her work on *Casablanca* was finished. Zorina was replaced. Bergman was reported to have remarked ungenerously, when her fellow Scandinavian and rival was first picked for the coveted role, "What the hell do they know. . . . She can't act."[2] Balanchine did not offer Zorina the emotional support she needed after this body blow, so she fled to Rock Edge. Zorina poured out her anger and embarrassment to Eleo on long, soothing carriage rides. Eleo gave her the courage to return and fight for the next part she wanted.

Zorina often accompanied Eleo when she drove around Boston in her immaculate maroon Lincoln with her initials on the door. Zorina enjoyed the way every policeman they encountered gave Eleo a respectful salute, "Good morning, Miss Sears," and held up oncoming traffic so she could make her turn. Often they would point out to Eleo, in an amused and friendly way, one of her more questionable driving maneuvers. Zorina recalled a curious encounter while shopping for sweaters with Eleo at Jordan Marsh. Eleo approached a young man whom she thought looked familiar. "Do I know you?" Eleo demanded. When he gave his name, Eleo thought for a moment and said, "Never heard of you," and turned abruptly and walked away.

Eleo could be imperious too with her household staff. She insisted on maintaining standards that were in line with those of the great households she had known all her life. Eleo's staff dressed in white uniforms in the mornings and black in the evenings, and the women wore hairnets. The staff was on duty fourteen hours a day and responded promptly to call bells, the intercoms of the time. Eleo had no tolerance for slackers. Eleo expected "her people" to work unobtrusively and to speak only when spoken to. She was angered one day to see a maid standing around and talking with Zorina instead of cleaning her room. In Eleo's view, the maid exhibited lazy behavior and a lack of respect for both the guest and her employer. Thomas Greene was responsible for Eleo's cars and pursued his calling with skill and quiet dignity. Zorina liked him very much. Everyone who came to know Thomas considered him a rare gem. He had been trained in the old ways when he worked for Alfred Vanderbilt. The burly chauffeur was always immaculate in his uniform and he knew not to chitchat. When he drove Eleo to a dinner party at a friend's home, he waited outside with the car, even in the pouring rain. He did not expect to be invited inside and it never occurred to Eleo to do so. Still, across the class divide, Thomas and Eleo were devoted to each other. She might get annoyed with him about small things, or criticize his driving and warn him, "If you don't shape up, I'll have to take over." Most of the time when she spoke of him, she called him "My Darling Thomas."

Though American servants were never so rigidly stratified as their English counterparts, they could be bigger snobs than their employers, and they equated their own status with that of the household they served. Eleo's staff was proud to work for her. Most felt she treated them fairly, and they did not resent her. They understood that Bostonians of her generation had particular standards and long-held traditions, and Eleo and her eccentricities were part of that mystique.

Women of Boston's First Families could easily convince themselves that they were only steps away from the poorhouse. Eleo was constantly appalled by the outflow of funds needed to maintain her increasingly complex lifestyle, but she never contemplated scaling it down in any meaningful way. Her sporadic attempts to save money were often absurdly petty. To reduce electric bills she supplied only twenty-five-watt lightbulbs for the service areas of the main house and the stable, and she patrolled the house for lights left burning in unused rooms. Yet she regularly returned from European trips with trunks full of beautiful gifts, cashmere sweaters and gold watches, for the seven or eight members of her household and grounds staff, as well as an equal number of grooms.

Theresa Walsh was in her teens when she began to work for Eleo, not long after she arrived from Ireland. During Eleo's first Providence-to-Boston hike, Theresa served the lunch and ministered to Eleo and her pacers. One morning when Theresa was still fairly new, she forgot to draw Eleo's bath. Eleo growled at her, "Goddamn you," and Theresa cowered on trembling legs, longing to be back in County Galway. Theresa recalled another time when she was tasked with retrieving a specific fur coat from a big, dark closet hung with several similar-looking coats. She needed a flashlight to search for it. When Theresa emerged nervously with the right coat, Eleo complimented her, "You're a lot smarter than I thought." Early on, in her excessive zeal to clean the living room, Theresa managed to crack five of Eleo's crystal door knobs, and she ran in terror upstairs to her bedroom and fell sobbing onto her pillow. Eleo sent her personal maid, Hannah Brown, upstairs to comfort Theresa. When Theresa offered to quit, Eleo told her to stay and gave her a raise. Most of Eleo's staff would have acknowledged that the pluses of working for her far outweighed the minuses. In an era when workers did not routinely expect health insurance, Eleo's people knew that she would pay for doctors' visits and operations that they, or their families, needed.[3]

Zorina saw Eleo act defensively toward her staff only once. As dessert was being served during a beautifully set luncheon at Rock Edge, a heavy quart bottle of cream appeared incongruously on the dining table. After all the guests had poured the cream awkwardly onto their dishes of strawberries, Eleo marked the level of the remaining cream in the bottle with a pencil before it was taken back to the kitchen. During the war cream was expensive and hard to get, and Eleo suspected it was being siphoned off by the kitchen help.

Next to the military draft during the Second World War, the rationing of food and materials had the biggest effect on the home front. Sugar was the first commodity to be rationed, in April 1942, and it remained in short supply throughout the war. In November coffee was rationed. The supply of silk for ladies' stockings was diverted to making parachutes. The public was left to juggle a devilishly complex government-designed system of ration books. The coupon books came in red and blue and "A" thru "F" and entitled different groups of people, the young, the old, doctors, ministers, and mail carriers, to different amounts of meat, cheese, shoes, and gasoline. There were total monthly allotments to be calculated, plus individual point values—steak used up twelve points, ground beef only seven. Shoe purchases were limited to three pair per person per year. It was reported that a man came home to find that his house had been robbed, but he was elated because the thieves had not discovered the family's ration books hidden in the linen closet. "Thank God," said the relieved burglary victim, "they took only the silver, my wife's jewelry, and my Phi Beta Kappa key."[4] Between 1942 and the war's end in 1945, it was estimated that about 25 percent of all rationed products were bought and sold on the black market.

Throughout the war years, the public's cooperation was enlisted in a series of national drives, to buy bonds, save scrap metal, and reclaim fat drippings. The comedians George Burns and Gracie Allen loved to close their radio shows with pleas to housewives to support the "Fat Drive." The idea was for women to bring their waste cooking fat to local food markets and other fat collection stations for eventual use as glycerin for explosives.

Metal was especially critical to the war effort, and foods that came in metal cans were rationed. The War Production Board banned outright the use of metal in hair curlers, cocktail shakers, dog identification tags, and asparagus tongs. The metal conservation drive forced changes in the popular board game Monopoly. The game first appeared in the middle of the Depression, when the allure of real estate empires and stacks of paper money sold thousands of sets. During the war the Parker Brothers Company substituted wooden game pieces, as in the original 1935 version, for the ten die-cast metal tokens—the Scottie dog, the wheelbarrow, the horse, the shoe, and so on. The wife of General George Patton recalled with gratitude how Eleo dismantled the grand wrought-iron fence that surrounded her stable in Prides Crossing and shipped it off to support the scrap metal drive.

Before America entered the war, Eleo wrote to Winston Churchill to express her admiration for him and for the courage of the British people as they faced the Blitz. Eleo included a contribution for canteen trucks and supplies for the British army. Her contribution was significant enough to draw a personal thank-you note from Churchill, along with a treatise on the important role the trucks were playing in the British war effort.

When the war came to America's doorstep after the bombing of Pearl Harbor, air-raid drills became common practice across the nation. Civilians enlisted as "spotters" to scan the skies for enemy aircraft, and military authorities complained that these overzealous volunteers reported "every damn blackbird they see as a Messerschmitt."[5] The shining gold dome of Boston's State House was hidden under a coat of gray paint to reduce its visibility to enemy bombers. Americans covered their windows with blackout curtains, but the requirements of homeland security did not mean that homemakers needed to let down their fashion guard. *House and Garden* magazine advised making blackout shades seem cozy by stitching fabrics that matched the interior decor to the blackout backing.

Eleo's wartime activities included work for Bundles for America. She volunteered at the canteen in the Bundles headquarters on Newbury Street in Boston and handed out coffee and doughnuts to the soldiers. She was a major sponsor of the Christmas Bundles Ball, which funded the Massachusetts Rehabilitation Program and honored the theater people who volunteered at the canteen. Broadway and Hollywood were fully involved in the war effort. Film stars enlisted in the military, entertained troops in the war zones, and made movies that saluted the bravery of the soldiers and the rightness of the cause. Winston Churchill said that the film *Mrs. Miniver,* which depicted the courage of ordinary Londoners during the Blitz, was worth more to England's war effort than a flotilla of battleships. Eleo was delighted when Hollywood agreed with Prime Minister Churchill and awarded her good friend Greer Garson an Oscar for her performance in the title role.

As it had been in the First World War, the content of radio shows and movies was designed, both via spontaneous private impulse and government censorship, to promote a single patriotic point of view. Reporters did not dwell on the horrors and mistakes of the battlefield. The public was spared the daily body count and the number of "our boys" killed by friendly fire, though such deaths ultimately reached the thousands.[6] Likewise, the home front was insulated from the fact that large numbers of bombs dropped from our airplanes and torpedoes fired from our submarines failed to explode. Doubt and dissent were peacetime luxuries. Draining away national resolve only made it harder to bear the costs of what needed to be done. Posters displayed iconic images of heroism and sacrifice, such as the poster showing a GI holding a cup of coffee with the caption "Do with less—so they'll have enough." As a result, Americans dutifully saved their fat drippings for their country.

In 1941 the Women's Association named fifty-three women as America's foremost leaders. In the field of politics they selected Eleanor Roosevelt; from the world of cinema they chose Mary Pickford; and in sports they selected Hazel Wightman and Eleo Sears as joint honorees. As the years advanced, Eleo had lost none of her grit and zest, as a player, coach, and pedestrienne. She was the sentimental favorite in numerous squash tournaments, where she battled against players half her age. She was a regular entrant too in veterans' tennis matches at Longwood, the Essex County Club, and the Country Club. The U.S. Women's Squash Racquets Association elected Eleo to be their permanent honorary president. The lifetime honor that touched Eleo most deeply, however, came from a member of Britain's Wolfe-Noel team. Margot Lumb, the winner of both the British and the American National Singles Championships, was often Eleo's squash partner in doubles matches, and they developed a close friendship. When Margot gave birth to her first child, she named the girl Eleonora and asked Eleo to be the baby's godmother.[7]

Rock Edge became a home base for many out-of-towners who played in local tournaments. In his "bread and butter" note to Eleo, the tennis player Ashmead Seabury thanked her for his weekend stay at Rock Edge and included a check "on account" toward paying off his backgammon losses to her. Eleo was at her best when Rock Edge was filled with guests. The large house could feel empty and inhospitable with only herself and the help in residence. Though extra guests meant extra work, Eleo's staff too welcomed new faces. Then Rock Edge took on a festive air and Eleo was sure to keep the vases throughout the house bright with fresh flowers. When Eleo was busy with hostess duties, she was less annoyed by details like a new dent in the silver teapot.

The twenty-year-old golfer Betty Hicks won the USGA National Championship in 1941 and celebrated her victory with a trip to Rock Edge in Eleo's limousine.[8] The victory party included a mutual friend, Charlotte Glutting, a Curtis team member, and Betty Hicks's sixteen-year-old sister. Eleo hustled Tom Greene into the back of the limo and she drove. The championship luncheon at Rock Edge was typical of Eleo's menus for company—a lobster chunk appetizer, fresh fruit salad topped with sherbet, and vermouth-simmered veal stew. Eleo's guests washed down the courses with bottles of Dom Pérignon that she opened with a dramatic pop.

Eleo actually had little interest in food. Her own preferences were spartan, and close friends and family who dropped by at mealtime would be served a bit of meat, boiled vegetables, and vanilla ice cream. Eleo did insist on fresh orange juice at breakfast because it seemed a healthy way to start the day. She rarely drank more than a glass of wine with dinner, and for her a good cup of coffee was mostly sugar with cream. She was convinced that the sugar boosted her energy, and she never cut back on that ingredient, despite war rationing.

When Eleo visited Washington, D.C., she often stayed with Evalyn Walsh McLean, the heiress of a great mining fortune. Evalyn was acclaimed at the time as an extravagant hostess, but she is now remembered primarily for the diamonds she owned. The 95-carat Star of the East was a notable part of her collection, but Evalyn is linked principally with the Hope Diamond. Though comparatively petite at 45.52 carats, the Hope Diamond is the most perfect blue diamond in existence. The diamond's mystery and its perceived value were enhanced by the jeweler Pierre Cartier, who embellished its exotic history with tales of murder, Turkish sultans, King Louis XIV—and a deadly curse.[9]

Cole Porter had many friends in the Boston area, and when he stayed at Rock Edge, Eleo had her Steinway grand piano carried out to the bathhouse so that he could compose in a convivial setting. Porter walked painfully with the aid of a cane and had to be helped out to the bathhouse. He had been left crippled by a horrific riding accident in 1937, when his horse slipped down a muddy hillside at Long Island's Piping Rock Country Club and rolled on him. In the years that followed, Porter endured more than thirty operations and almost constant pain, but his physical limitations did not dampen his sense of humor or his creative spark. His Boston friends were tickled when he slipped references to their town's baked beans and genteel Back Bay into his polished lyrics.

In November 1947, Greer Garson spent five days at Rock Edge with Eleo while recuperating from some minor surgery she had had at nearby Beverly Hospital.

Sooner or later during any visit to Rock Edge, the time came when Eleo would say to her guests, "I suppose now you would like to see the horses." It was not a question. A phone call would be made to the stable, which mobilized the grooms. Bridles were put on the horses designated to be "presented." The horses' stall bedding was tidied, and the braided straw mats between the stalls were straightened. Everything was checked for dust. Then Eleo would be there, glowing, thrilled to share her greatest pleasure with her friends. A newcomer's attention was captured first by the noble proportions of the Tudor stable, and then by the fine, gray gravel in the front yard that was combed into delicate lines and swirls, giving the walkway the serene look of a Japanese garden. The five-star horse palace was a sanctuary, a sparkling horse heaven, so clean you could almost eat off the floor. Its hallway was paneled with gleaming white tiles. Above the tiles hung original Currier and Ives lithographs depicting quaint country lanes and horses pulling sleighs through the snow. The stable help attended to the building and its contents from dawn to dusk on an unvarying schedule. Tuesday was Brass Day, explained John Brotchie, a former stable boy, when "every bloody piece of brass in there" was polished to a warm luster. Thursday was Carriage Day, when Eleo's several dozen antique and modern carriages in the west wing of the stable were meticulously cleaned. Her collection of vehicles included a horse-drawn fire engine and the 1912 Simplex she had acquired from Mike Vanderbilt. Eleo frequently treated the stable boys to special lunches, and they got a daily break between three and four o'clock for high tea, but woe to them if the stable failed her very literal white-glove test. As far back as 1910, Eleo had explored strategies to bring optimum care to horses and their surroundings. For the Coronado Country Club, which in those early years housed as many as three hundred polo ponies during the polo season, Eleo devised a contest and awarded prizes to grooms who excelled in maintaining the horses in their charge.

At her Prides Crossing stable, all that Eleo could imagine a horse might want she provided. Rubber was a scarce commodity during the war, but she managed to get rubber mats for the horses to protect them from slipping. Each horse occupied a large, immaculate stall that held a varnished wooden water bucket with its inside painted an unblemished white. The water was changed twice daily. Eleo's horses were given breakfast at seven o'clock, and after breakfast the feed buckets and tubs were removed and scrubbed. In the afternoons, treats and a substantial snack were served. Every horse was alert to Eleo's voice and thrust its head forward for an affectionate rub. Carrots and apples were nibbled. Some of the horses could delicately snatch a sugar cube that Eleo held out to them between her teeth. Eleo revealed to her visitors a bit of the special history of each horse, its achievements, and the endearing habits or quirks that set it apart from others in the equine world. Over there, that's Reno, the gorgeous chestnut mare that Eleo's cousin Fred Winthrop rode to victory in Myopia's Challenge Cup for three years in succession; and this here is good old Caviar, who, in his youth, had also won the cup three times. Pike's Peak too was a phenomenal jumper with a wall full of ribbons. Don Juan stood patiently in the end stall. Many of Eleo's friends loved to ride him because he responded to the softest touch and looked out for his rider's welfare.

Outside the stable, once again on the Zen-swirled gravel, grooms and horses emerged from the arched doorway in an elegant parade of form and movement for Eleo's guests. Eleo might then ask Shasta to do his tricks, but the brown and white pinto pony was not always in the mood. Eleo had rescued Shasta from a western roadside circus. He was so thin, Eleo said, that "you could hang a hat on his hips." Eleo had quizzed his owner, "How much does a bushel of hay cost?" The circus owner had no idea and Eleo knew the pony wasn't getting any, so she bought him. Shasta could shake hands, bow, and spin in a circle, but sometimes he preferred just to nuzzle and get his ears scratched, or stand still and study the clouds and the birds. Eleo said that ever since the pony had gotten used to the good life, living on the fat of the land, so to speak, he had become lazy. When Shasta was ready, he gave a charming demonstration of his accomplishments, and Eleo beamed as proudly as if he had composed a symphony.

Eleo dreaded saying a final good-bye to any horse that had served her well. Only irreversible pain could induce her to have a horse put down. After a large burial pit had been dug, Eleo laid her friend to rest gently and with honor, covered with a new bedsheet, a pillow under its head. Eleo was not a particularly religious person. She rarely went to church anymore, though as a child she had gone weekly at her mother's insistence. Eleo said she still "had enough in the bank on that account." Yet she liked to believe that her departed dear ones would be comfortable until the next time they met. Eleo's stable men observed, quietly among themselves, that the buried sheets and pillows would have done nicely on their beds at home.

When Katharine Hepburn was given a tour of Eleo's stable, she admired the horses, of course, but her most lasting impressions were of the large tack room, colonized by row upon row of saddles, boots, bridles, all polished to a soft luster. Hepburn recalled Eleo and the atmosphere at Rock Edge as "thrilling . . . wonderfully distinguished . . . the *Real Thing*—."[10]

Judy Garland recharged her shattered spirit at Rock Edge on carriage rides with Eleo and naps on the warm sand on Eleo's beach after reaching one of the many low points in her turbulent life. Thin and frail, strung out on pills and liquor, Garland arrived at Peter Bent Brigham Hospital in Boston on May 29, 1949, directly from Hollywood, for what her publicist called a "check-up." The self-destructive star had unraveled after her recent separation from husband number two, Vincente Minelli, and her firing from the movie version of *Annie Get Your Gun* nineteen days earlier. She was treated at Peter Bent Brigham until the end of June, and she visited friends in Boston and Eleo at Prides Crossing until the end of August. When Garland returned to California, she was plump, relatively stable, and a new fan of the Boston Red Sox.

The staff at Rock Edge was always glad that Gretchen Warren stayed for long stretches during each summer and fall. She was the sweetest lady and easy to please. Gretchen had been Nora Sears's dearest friend, and she transferred her affection to Nora's daughter, coming to regard Eleo "like one of my own." As Gretchen herself put it, she had "taken over" the mother role in Eleo's life, and Eleo adored her equally. Gretchen was now in her mid-seventies and widowed but as keen as ever. She continued to write poetry and read eclectically. Eleo described her "second mother" lovingly, as having "the delicacy of a shell, the endurance of an elephant, the knowledge of Aristotle, the wit of Rabelais and the grace of Fra Angelico's Madonna."[11]

Eleo and Gretchen Warren often traveled together, but whenever Gretchen sailed off alone, Eleo anxiously awaited her return. "Mrs. Warren is back from Ireland and is with me—Thank Heavens—," she wrote to their mutual friend Morris Carter, who was hoping to time his visit to Rock Edge to coincide with Gretchen's arrival. Morris Carter was the director of Fenway Court, that grand legacy of Isabella Stewart Gardner. Eleo and Gretchen had taken a special interest in Morris's career and they encouraged him like doting stage mothers. The two women were infuriated when Morris was on the brink of losing his position with the Gardner Museum. Morris considered giving up his post without a fight until Eleo sent him an impassioned directive: "You cannot behave this way. No one will go near Fenway Court unless you are there—You are just perfect . . . —you are to stay on 'till I tell you that it is all right for you to leave— . . . don't upset me so terribly—it is really bad for me— . . . Please be good—."12 Bolstered by his friends' fervent confidence, Morris stayed on at Fenway Court. When Morris took his wife, Beatrice, to a luncheon at Rock Edge, the couple was thrilled to discover that Ethel Barrymore was already there to share the invigorating view from Eleo's terrace.

Gretchen Warren had always been a romantic with a weakness for causes. During the war, her sympathies were engaged by a Massachusetts doctor who treated patients suffering from arthritis, high blood pressure, and circulatory problems. The doctor began experimenting with electrical stimulation to supplement his standard use of massage and skeletal realignment. Owing to a war-inspired directive, the doctor could not obtain the electrical equipment he needed. Gretchen's enthusiasm for the doctor persuaded Eleo to bring the plight of this medical "lone eagle" to Franklin Roosevelt's attention. Eleo had no alternative but to appeal again to Roosevelt because her preferred presidential candidate and friend, Wendell Willkie, had lost the election of 1940.

Neither Eleo nor Gretchen was shy about calling their doctor friend "possibly the greatest living biochemist." Both women knew that Roosevelt understood the consequences of polio, and they stressed the possible benefit of the doctor's research for infantile paralysis. Eleo recoiled from the harshness of the affliction and the very concept of paralysis. In her written plea to Roosevelt she referred to the condition delicately as "the infantile." The president's people linked the doctor up with people on the War Production Board, and through them he was able to secure the equipment he needed. This result was the high-water mark of Eleo's efforts to enlist the president's help for friends who suffered from war-related maladies. On a matter that deeply affected Eleo herself, she was left empty-handed.

Given the wartime restrictions on purchasing automobiles and tires, it was inevitable that Eleo would run afoul of Rationing Order no. 2A. This rule, devised by the War Production Board, was the most disliked and most flouted law since Prohibition. In 1941 the Dutch East Indies fell to the Japanese and the supply of rubber was reduced as a consequence. The U.S. government responded with the "Idle Tire Purchase Program," which mandated all unused tires be turned over to the government. The public was soon forbidden to purchase new tires. Then gasoline sales were restricted, and the national speed limit was lowered to thirty-five miles per hour. Automobile production was diverted to war-related vehicles. No private passenger cars could be purchased between 1942 and 1945. Well in advance of the announced March 1942 deadline for new car purchases, Eleo ordered two Ford beach wagons, built to her specifications and painted in her exact shade of maroon. Eleo left no deposit with T. C. Baker and Company because she always sealed such transactions with a handshake. Eleo returned home from travel abroad in January 1942 to find that the ban had taken effect early and that her order could no longer be filled because she had not sealed it with a deposit. Eleo's efforts to dislodge her cars proved fruitless, so she appealed the injustice of her predicament to the president. "I am sunk," she wrote to Roosevelt, explaining that she owned two old cars with tires so bald they could not be retreaded. "Have I got to walk everywhere?" the Great Pedestrian lamented.[13] Eleo received in response a treatise on supply and demand from the administrator of the Automobile and Truck Section of the Price Board. He explained that she was but one among some four million car buyers who were at the mercy of local rationing boards, which had few nonemergency vehicles to distribute. Eleo was not used to being lost in a crowd, and this lack of presidential assistance contributed to her final unsparing judgment of Roosevelt, that "he kept everything for himself and nothing for anybody else."

Anger over a car led Eleo's former amour Isabel Pell to become a legend of the Second World War. Pelly had always been addicted to novelty and adventure. She had found plenty of both on a foggy flight from Copenhagen to southern Norway in 1933, when the seaplane she was sharing with the chic wife of the banker Henry Fleitmann crashed into the Baltic Sea. The two women were rescued by a passing freighter and suffered only minor injuries from their frigid dunking. Isabel then spent some years with an older woman in Paris, and when the war started she was living with the daughter of a prominent French family. They kept house in a *moulin,* an exquisitely renovated old mill, in a small village on the Riviera, midway between Grasse and Cannes. Among the few constants in Isabel's nomadic life were her perfume, a Tabac Blanc called Always, and her automobile. Isabel owned a succession of Duesenbergs, and she named each one Olga. When a German commandant traveling near Grasse commandeered Isabel's Duesenberg, she began working for the French resistance to avenge Olga.

Isabel stored guns and ammunition for the resistance and, after being questioned by the Gestapo, and by Italian agents, and by the Vichy police, she spent two months in the Puget-Thénier prison, along with her maid, who was also involved with the underground. There Isabel saw firsthand the brutality of the Germans. During daily walks that Isabel was permitted to take around the prison, she was contacted by men who feared being shipped off to labor camps in Germany, and she helped them to organize a Maquis cell. On the day the Italian armistice was announced, the Italian soldiers who were minding the jail slipped away quietly while the prisoners were celebrating, and Isabel and her maid simply walked out the front gate and went home. Later Isabel disguised herself as a peasant and, using the code name Fredericka, she journeyed to the mountain hideaway of the chief of the Free French, whom she knew only by his code name, Joseph. She worked with Joseph until he was killed by the Gestapo. Isabel was credited with many acts of bravery, among them shepherding sixteen American paratroopers to safety around German lines after they landed far from their target. Isabel became an unofficial "chief of staff" to an American general as his troops fought their way eastward along the Riviera. The general called Isabel "an amazing woman," and he noted, "She keeps going day and night. . . . The French are crazy about her and do anything she tells them."[14] At the end of the war, France awarded Isabel the Légion d'Honneur. A French comic book told the tale of Fredericka of the Maquis, "la femme à la mèche blonde," "the woman with the blonde streak" (a reference to a lock of ivory hair that flashed from Isabel's dark blonde bob).

Allegations surfaced after the war of complicity and double-dealing that tarnished the legend of Isabel Pell. A cousin of Isabel's, Stephanie Pell, married a Frenchman and relocated to the south of France. Isabel welcomed her cousin Stephanie warmly when she first arrived in France. Stephanie asked Isabel to be godmother to her first child. Isabel attended the baptism looking utterly disheveled, but when she saw that the other guests were a more upscale group than she had expected, she borrowed a curling iron. Isabel then borrowed two thousand francs from Stephanie's mother-in-law and presented the money to Stephanie as her gift for the baby. Stephanie's mother-in-law never saw those two thousand francs again.

Isabel's cousin gradually discovered that her maiden name, Pell, was a source of embarrassment in some parts of France, where Isabel had a terrible reputation as a collaborator who worked for whichever side could advance her interests. Townspeople who had been with the French underground believed that Isabel "had played both sides of the field."[15] They blamed Isabel for the deaths of several neighbors who were caught and executed. Isabel was undeniably accomplished in the art of negotiation and accommodation. During her impoverished childhood, she had been forced to navigate the treacherous shoals of warring parents and stepparents and a shifting lineup of relatives on whom she depended for support. France was in turmoil both during and after the war, as the Vichy French, the Nazis, and the Allies jockeyed for control, and later when the Communists came in and battled the anti-Communists. For Isabel, staying on the winning side was second nature.

Eleo never learned about any of the accusations against Isabel. When

Isabel returned to New York, Eleo was thrilled to have her on the same side of the ocean. Eleo and Isabel made up for lost time, spending weeks together in New York, Boston, and Prides Crossing. Eleo took Isabel with her to the homes of friends, where Isabel wore her medal dangling from a wide ribbon around her neck. Isabel was by then a far cry from the trim, athletic-looking young woman of their first meetings, but Eleo did not seem to notice. Eleo's friends observed that, in Isabel's presence, Eleo seemed almost deferential.

Though Eleo's high regard for Isabel Pell blunted her impulse to take charge and dominate, Eleo remained hypervigilant on matters that involved her property, her territory, her personal space. Eleo was determined to let no one take advantage of her. A sad lesson that was learned by all wellborn children at a tender age was the need to guard against pretenders who expected to profit from their friendship. It was a lesson learned by the Vanderbilt children when they noticed that shopkeepers routinely inflated their prices by 50 percent when sending goods to the Vanderbilt mansion on Fifth Avenue. Eleo was aware that as a wealthy single woman she was especially vulnerable, and she needed to prove that she was not. Eleo employed financial people to manage her business affairs, but she was a well-informed gatekeeper. She knew how much came in, and she signed the checks, so she knew what was going out and where it went.

Eleo's household staff understood that the most serious offense they could commit was to be caught stealing or getting any kind of kickback from suppliers. Such infractions were inevitable and unstoppable in upper-class households, but on Eleo's properties they were rare, because she gave no second chances. Eleo dismissed any suspected culprit without a backward glance, and such a servant found that, once tainted, the only work available would be far away, among strangers.

Eleo often attended public auctions, which attracted her with their lure of undiscovered treasure and contests of cunning and money. Eleo acquired much of her art and furnishings at auction, and often she concealed her interest in a particular lot by using a friend as a "beard" to bid for her, thus avoiding the run-up in price that her interest would unleash. Eleo bought a second town house a few doors down from 4–5 Byron Street, where she stored the extra rugs, tapestries, and furniture she had won. Byron Street was blessed with a desirable central location, but that attribute came with problems. Eleo was routinely infuriated when drivers ignored her "No Trespassing" signs in their quest to find parking near Beacon Street. These intruders clogged the little street, and their bumpers often extended in front of Eleo's garage doors. Thomas Greene and a Byron Street neighbor copied down the license numbers of five of the worst offenders, and Eleo filed complaints against them in Municipal Court. One errant parker pleaded guilty to trespass and was fined five dollars, but the judge dismissed the remaining four cases because, technically, neither Eleo nor her neighbor had seen those defendants commit the alleged violations. Not long after the unsatisfactory verdict, the offending autos returned to Byron Street. Under cover of darkness, Eleo sent Thomas outside with an ice pick to administer vigilante justice to the tires of the outlaw autos. Problem solved . . .

Eleo was on guard too against trespassers at Rock Edge. Six townspeople regularly used the lane alongside her house on Paine Avenue as a throughway to the beach, and they proved impossible to discourage. Paine Avenue was clearly posted as a private road, and Eleo and her neighbors hired Beverly policemen to prevent public access. The six interlopers claimed that they had squatter's rights because, for twenty years, long before Eleo owned the property, they had been using the path. The battle heated up after Eleo installed a chain-link fence topped with barbed wire across the narrow lane. Eleo petitioned the court in Beverly for relief. In a letter she wrote to Morris Carter, she mentioned her "land court thing." "I always seem to be in hot water one way or another," Eleo told him.[16] After the judge visited the "Paine enclosure," he ruled in Eleo's favor.

The merits of Eleo's case did not endear her to the Beverly locals, especially after it was learned that among the people denied access to the ocean were the parents of a boy killed at Guadalcanal, who was posthumously awarded the Silver Star for heroism. The broad outline of the conflict—rich landowner versus dead war hero's parents—was a ripe target, and several college boys were inspired to parody the episode in a parade float they built for the annual Fourth of July celebration in Beverly Farms. In a makeshift jail they corralled the world's three greatest "Horribles"—"Adolf Hitler," "Emperor Hirohito," and "Eleo Sears," played by a lad from the Farms wearing a man's suit. Eleo was not amused.

Over the years, Eleo's relations with business owners in Beverly Farms were quirky and abrasive and, quite often, perversely entertaining. Eleo frequently visited the plumbing store in the Farms to place an order or to complain about substandard parts or service. She always took her problems straight to the boss, Augustus Callahan. When Callahan had heard all he cared to from Eleo, he turned down the volume on his hearing aid. Eleo countered this gambit by raising her voice. Callahan reduced the volume further, and then for his final move he turned the hearing aid off completely. When Eleo resorted to shouting, Callahan would just look at her and shrug with a contented smile. Eleo always left the shop defeated but well satisfied with her visit.

Eleo's habit of command became more ingrained with time, as she lived on her own and had only herself to answer to. She readily bulldozed meeker souls, but if you stood your ground and asserted your own dignity, you could earn her respect. Matthew "Gus" Smith was Eleo's head groom, and she valued his judgment about horses. The Irishman had worked for Henry Clay Frick, and he had since trained horses at Myopia and polo ponies for Frederick Prince. One day Eleo visited Gus at his home on Hale Street. She came on horseback and jumped the row of hedges that bordered his property, snapping a bush in the process and trampling his front lawn. Gus was furious and ordered Eleo off his place. Eleo was contrite. She had the damage repaired promptly and they remained cordial.

The outcome was similar with Eddie Hogan, the husband of one of Eleo's most elegant jump riders, Joanie Walsh Hogan. Eddie owned an automobile dealership, and he sold Eleo a maroon Chrysler convertible with wooden sides, the paint custom-mixed in Germany. Eleo told Eddie that she was about to leave for Europe and would pay him for the car when she got back. Eddie said to her, "Miss Sears, when you look over the stern of the boat, you're gonna see a lawyer in a speedboat following you." Eleo chuckled and paid him before she left. Eddie knew that with Eleo, "You had to stand up or get buried."[17]

A teenage girl taught Eleo a touch of humility. Eleo had remained close to the family of the late Judge Moore, and in the evening she often joined them for a game of bridge or backgammon. The Judge's son was embarrassed one evening when his daughter Pauline returned home and pointedly refused to greet Eleo. Pauline explained to her father that she used to say, "Good morning, Miss Sears," whenever they met, but Eleo never responded, so Pauline decided to ignore her, too. Paul Moore related his daughter's principled stand to Eleo, and from then on Eleo never failed to give Pauline a hearty greeting whenever their paths crossed. No hard feeling remained through the years, and Pauline and her husband were often Eleo's guests for suppers and parties at Byron Street.

Shortly after New Year's Day in 1947, Eleo's brother, Freddy, did a most unexpected thing. After a short illness, at the age of sixty-six, he died. Freddy and Eleo had not been close for a long time, but his sudden passing left her nostalgic for their early years, when she had dragged him along on her escapades. It was an odd and lonely feeling to know that now only she was left, the last of the line. Freddy's wife, Norma, petitioned the Somerset Club for widow's privileges so she could continue to use the club's facilities. In a bizarre twist, within a few months she, too, was gone. Norma's and Freddy's estates passed to the Sears and Coolidge cousins. They had chosen to leave nothing, not even a button, to Eleo. Eleo was galled as well to see in the obituary for her brother in the *New York Times* that her name was spelled wrong: "Mr. Sears, also, leaves . . . a sister, the prominent sportswoman Eleanora (Eleo) Sears."

Boston's elite families have not ranked at the top of the nation's wealthiest in more than a century, but their offspring continue to benefit from a financial cushion that allows them to avoid "shirtsleeve" work if they choose. The family trust is the vehicle that makes this option possible. As explained by *Fortune* magazine in 1933, the trusts stand "between the Bostonians and the activities of contemporary life like the transparent but all too solid glass which separates the angel fish of an aquarium from the grubby little boys outside."[18] Eleo was a beneficiary of trusts from both the Sears and Coolidge sides of her family. Her brother's death threatened her interest in the Coolidge trust. Thomas Jefferson Coolidge set up his trust in 1913 for his grandchildren and their issue. For the next thirty-seven years the trust distributed the income from this fund, which by 1950 had grown to approximately $8 million. The number of T.J.'s descendants had also grown. More than thirty-five people were now eligible to receive distributions.

After Freddy's death, the Fiduciary Trust Bank of New York, administrator of the Coolidge trust, decided that the trust was no longer enforceable because it violated the rule against perpetuities. The bank insisted that future dispersals from the trust be governed by a later will that T.J. had executed, and the bank held up all distributions pending this outcome. Not for an instant did Eleo consider bowing down before an interfering bank. She argued that her grandfather's later will had been written when he was in a less robust state of health and mind and did not represent his truest intent. It surely mattered to Eleo that her financial interest would be reduced under the terms of the newer will, which mixed her brother's share of the money into the general pot, rather than its being paid to her in its entirety. Eleo petitioned the Probate Court to uphold the original version of T.J.'s trust, and her action met with unified opposition from her Coolidge cousins. William Appleton Coolidge, who at age fifty was the youngest of T.J's surviving grandchildren, issued a stern appeal to Eleo to keep the family conflict out of the public eye. He laid out the grave consequences he foresaw if she persisted in airing family matters in open court—the financial hardship to some of the beneficiaries, a reexamination of her grandfather's suggestible mental state in his final years, the details of T.J.'s compromising involvement with a Miss Payson, and the revelation that one of the trust recipients was, in all likelihood, T.J.'s illegitimate son. Eleo assured her cousin that all these and other delicate issues had received her "solemn attention," but she stood firm against the family. She explained, "The spirit to compromise with the demands made with the Fiduciary Trust Co, now so prevalent, just does not appeal to me at all, legally, morally, or from the family viewpoint."[19] Though the Probate Court ruled against Eleo, she was not so easily quashed. Eleo eventually won her case in the Massachusetts Supreme Court, thereby preserving her percentage and, presumably, her grandfather's blessing.

CHAPTER 17

The 1950s: Worlds Still to Conquer

~

ELEO LOST AN EARLY-ROUND squash match at the New York Women's Invitational in February 1954, winning only one game of four against the tournament's top seed, but she kept the score close in all the games. This was one of Eleo's rare appearances outside veterans' tournaments, and a sportswriter noted that the indomitable seventy-two-year-old still had all the shots, if not the legs. Eleo turned in a very respectable performance even though three weeks earlier she had been knocked down by a car during one of her walks, and she had to admit that her back was still "pretty lame." "I got to play, though," Eleo said; "I've had so much athletic activity in my life that I've got to keep going. If I don't I'll simply die."[1]

Eleo gave no ground, either, in her continuing and largely hopeless war against the invading detritus of modern life. She launched crusades against encroaching utility poles and sewage pipes that tried to cross her North Shore property, even when the result was imperfect service for herself and her neighbors. To keep the property surrounding Rock Edge out of the hands of developers, she bought up neighboring parcels from Helen Frick, Nackey Loeb, and J. Wigglesworth, whose family had settled the land in the 1600s. Eleo was upset when Frederick Prince gave his estate, with its outstanding bridle paths, to Gordon College. Prince reminded Eleo that if she had married his eldest son, as he had hoped she would, those bridle paths would have belonged to her.

Plans were in the works to enlarge Route 128 to accommodate the daily charge of commuter cars and big rigs between Gloucester and Boston. The four-lane expansion would slice across properties with bridle paths that Eleo and her friends had used for generations. Eleo conceived the idea of an underpass that would let horses and riders cross safely beneath the highway to the trails on the other side. This solution mattered enough to Eleo that she was willing to pay for its extra design and construction costs, and it is probable that she lined up like-minded neighbors to chip in. Eleo took her proposal to the former governor of Massachusetts Joseph Ely, who now headed a private law firm and had represented Eleo in her action to preserve the Coolidge trust. Eleo asked Ely to present her plan to his great friend Bill Callahan, commissioner of the Department of Public Works, who owed his job to the former governor. Ely decided against spending his political capital on Eleo's idea for an underpass, so he delegated the job to a young associate who recalled feeling like "a sacrificial lamb" as he described Eleo's offer to the commissioner and two Turnpike engineers. The three public servants, "men of the people," good Democrats all, thought the idea of a special tunnel for use by the horsey set was one of the funniest things they had ever heard. North Shore residents actually did have a long history of using private funds for public improvements. In 1912 a group of residents had banded together and raised $30,000 to construct a graceful arched bridge over the railroad tracks at Norton's Point in Manchester. They had contributed some $375,000 over twenty-five years toward gypsy moth control and construction and maintenance of roads in their area. But, that was no longer how things were done. Ely told Eleo that, though he had tried mightily, he was simply unable to convince the Department of Public Works of the merits of her underpass.[2]

Eleo frequently relied on the legal services of Governor Ely's firm, Ely, Bartlett, Thompson and Brown. When she had business pending at their office, she would stop by late in the afternoon as she hiked around Boston attending to errands. Her unannounced arrival was always fraught with drama. The freshman associates could be forgiven, the first time, if they mistook the fabled lady for a member of the building's cleaning crew when she charged in wearing her "work clothes." Her standard outfit for walking or puttering around the stable was an oversized man's cardigan, a plain khaki skirt, and heavy brown shoes with thick white socks. Wisps of windblown gray hair straggled from under her well-worn felt hat. In cool weather, Eleo added a wool scarf and a shapeless tan canvas coat, reminiscent of the old-time automobile dusters, its pockets stretched out of shape from carrying apples and carrots for the horses. She had eased into that stage of life familiar to generations of women from Boston's First Families who entered their later years with relief, excused at last from the fashion race. They let their hair go gray, and, when out doing the day's chores, they dressed for efficiency and low-heeled comfort. At Ely, Bartlett, Thompson and Brown, if their frazzled-looking visitor, deeply suntanned and her eyes electric blue, directed a sharp question to any of the fledgling lawyers, he snapped to attention. It was an involuntary response to the tone of someone used to getting immediate answers. The entire office staff was on notice that if they carelessly mailed Eleo a document that had her name misspelled, she would either throw it out unopened or send it back marked "person unknown."

George Hopkins, an attorney who had worked intermittently with Governor Ely, became Eleo's favorite advocate and business advisor. Hopkins, like Eleo, was in his mid-seventies and, though he was semiretired, the effort he put into maintaining his relationship with Eleo made it very nearly a full-time job. Eleo affectionately called him "Hoppy," and he called her "Miss Sears," but they had an extraordinarily close, trusting association. Hoppy ensured his coveted position by resorting to highly creative solutions to Eleo's problems. A case in point was the lawsuit against Eleo by the Railway Express Company, which had shipped a horse for her from California to Boston. She paid the bill, but she balked when the company sent an additional bill because they had, inadvertently, charged her less than the rate posted for that service. By law, to prevent kickbacks to favored shippers, freight companies were prohibited from charging a customer less than the posted rates. The added freight charge was not large, but Eleo refused to pay the second bill on principle, and Railway Express sued her. Research into the quirky statute revealed that the rule governing freight charges was clear and that Eleo had no legal defense to the suit. Hoppy knew that Eleo had little tolerance for failure, so he paid the bill himself and told her that he had won the case.

During the 1950s the federal government was on a tax-and-spend tear. After income taxes were increased by 20 percent to fund the Korean War, Eleo took up the fight against government waste of public money. Some economists agreed with her that the war was a pretext, and that the money would actually be spent on cost overruns for a variety of government projects. Eleo set to work rousing public outrage over "the criminal spending in Washington." She wrote and published a manifesto, "An Open Letter from One Taxpayer to Another," which cited the findings of the Hoover Commission that hundreds of millions of dollars were being wasted by federal agencies through duplication and inefficiency. In August 1950 Eleo opened the Boston headquarters of the antitax "Eleonora Sears Committee," which left no doubt as to who was leading the charge.

Eleo called her tax revolt "a second Boston Tea Party," an apt marketing strategy for this descendant of revolutionaries. "Action must be taken," Eleo declared as she stood in the doorway of the campaign office, "—by the people—to reduce wasteful Government spending and to lower taxes, so that we are not all reduced to poverty."[3] Eleo's goal was to attract ten million voters, each contributing one dollar to fund an antitax lobbying effort in Washington. She was convinced that such a groundswell of indignation would sway Congress. Her Boston office was to be the first among a nationwide network of branches. Eleo designed and printed brochures with a registration coupon for people to send with their dollar to her committee. For the cover art of the brochure, she chose her Sargent charcoal portrait.

From the earliest days of the republic, income taxes had never affected more than a small fraction of the nation's wage earners. By the end of World War II, the tax rolls had ballooned from 4 million souls to more than 43 million, and rates were hiked by a supplementary "Victory Tax." The Korean War renewed the call for more revenue, and the Truman administration broadened the tax base and pushed up the rate. For those few taxpayers in the top bracket, the rate was an astonishing 94 percent. Eleo believed that this confiscatory rate could "wipe out" those relative few who had to pay it, but it was the waste of all that money that moved her to action. Though most of her countrymen lived light years away from the top bracket, Eleo was convinced that there were millions of taxpayers as angry as she was about the careless way their money was being spent.

Americans tended to believe, down to their Puritan roots, that work, thrift, and entrepreneurial risk taking were virtues. Even Treasury officials within the Truman administration worried that siphoning off so much of the fruit of people's labor would destroy their incentive to work. Eleo sounded the alarm that "the day . . . of a youth hoping to become a millionaire by hard work has passed."

Eleo's organization initially attracted some seven hundred supporters. Her Steering Committee, by design, was composed entirely of men. The world of business and finance was completely a male preserve, and Eleo felt her mission would be perceived as more serious with an all-male cast. She presided with self-satisfaction over the strategy sessions of her committee, which included former Governor Ely, her attorney George Hopkins, William McCormick Blair, the administrative assistant to Illinois's Governor Adlai Stevenson, and Frederick C. Dumaine, the shrewd, abrasive president and chairman of the New Haven Railroad. Federick Dumaine was known among Eleo's extended family as the illegitimate son of her grandfather T. J. Coolidge.

Eleo tried, without success, to enlist the public support of former President Herbert Hoover, who would have been a valuable headliner for her organization. She knew Hoover slightly and she sent him a copy of her "Open Letter to Taxpayers," which was based on his own committee's report to Congress. The Korean War made it awkward for the ex-president to campaign against the current administration, and Hoover declined to join Eleo's group.

Unintentionally, Eleo herself undercut the antitax mission of her committee when she broadened her political activism to advocate the impeachment of President Truman. For her, the final straw was Truman's dismissal of the charismatic but insubordinate general Douglas MacArthur. Eleo circulated petitions calling for Truman's impeachment and collected signatures. Erroneously but quite understandably, the *Boston Globe* linked her pronounce-ments against Truman with the Eleonora Sears Committee. Eleo's forlorn committeemen dispatched a telegram to the *Globe*'s editor that insisted awk-wardly that Eleo's political opinions did not reflect the views of her epony-mous organization. Eleo's antitax campaign never managed to attract more than a thousand or so contributors, far from her stated goal of ten million. It took another decade, until President Kennedy used tax reductions to lift the national economy, for federal income tax rates to begin any meaningful retreat.

The Cold War world of the 1950s presented threats more appalling than rampant government waste and high taxes. When Eleo was asked by a *Sports Illustrated* columnist at the National Horse Show whether horses might someday vanish because of their diminishing role in the modern world, Eleo's thoughts turned apocalyptic. Such an awful prospect was no longer incon-ceivable in an era of "assured mutual destruction." Eleo offered her opinion that "the world would be so much better off with horses instead of people. For one thing, there'd be no wars." And she offered her idea of an alternative future, "If humans do obliterate themselves through nuclear warfare, the horse may survive because he can live off the land."[4]

The year 1952 marked the seventieth anniversary of the Vincent Club vari-ety shows, and for that year's lighthearted nostalgia fest Eleo was a featured performer. Between the scheduled acts, the conductor Ruby Newman handed the baton with great ceremony to Mrs. William Stanley Parker, who had led the orchestra in earlier years. As Mrs. Parker commanded the orches-tra, Eleo came onstage wearing a white V-neck tennis sweater and clasping two tennis racquets to her chest. She began pestering Mrs. Parker, "Come on, let's get out of here and play some tennis." Mrs. Parker declined the invita-tion, telling Eleo testily, "Can't you see I'm conducting?" They bantered back and forth until Mrs. Parker said to Eleo, "Listen here, I'm very busy with the orchestra. You'll just have to find something to do until I'm finished. Why don't you take a little walk to Providence in the meantime?" The two old friends brought down the house.

In the fall of 1952 college football fans were focused on the annual rivalry between Harvard and Yale. Eleo never missed this seismic match, and she never went alone. When the game was in New Haven, Eleo often took along a railroad car full of friends. Winning a place on Eleo's coveted passenger list involved an element of luck. If you met her on the street or telephoned her at the right time, you were invited. Riders on the football train included the teenage ice skating phenom Tenley Albright, Henry Cabot Lodge and his family, several branches of Saltonstalls, the newspaperman Ben Bradlee, who had done time as Eleo's terrified ball boy, Mabel Storey and her children, and many assorted spouses. Mabel Storey had been one of Eleo's closest friends for a long time. Tall, blonde, and opinionated, Mabel shared Eleo's love for horses and appreciation of good jewelry. Mabel kept the accounts for the Carpet Club at Myopia, which provided funding to repair horse trails and jumps. The money came from penalties paid by riders who fell off their horses during fox hunts. They were fined five dollars for the first fall and three dollars for a second fall that occurred within the same week. Eleo made her contributions to the Carpet Club fund on occasion.

As Eleo's football-bound train rumbled along, she roamed the aisle, chatting and joking with her guests and ensuring that everyone had an ample supply of Champagne and snacks. At the New Haven station, a bus with a motorcycle escort waited to transport the group to the Yale stadium, where they had reserved seats straddling the fifty-yard line, courtesy of Eleo's friends in the Porcellian Club. For Eleo, the most emotional games were those in which Jeff Coolidge Jr. took the field. To Eleo's delight, the handsome grandson of Eleo's late Uncle Jeffie was voted Harvard's Most Valuable Player. In one of the games against Yale, Jeff was tackled so hard that he was knocked unconscious. The team doctor determined he had not suffered any permanent damage, but Jeff still had to survive Eleo's follow-up care. She insisted on taking him home with her in the railroad car. Jeff was carried on board like a prince fallen in battle and laid out across the seats. Eleo and her friends hovered over him, fluffing his pillow, patting his shoulder, and nearly drowning him with concern and liquid refreshments.

Eleo reeled from a blow that she never saw coming when Isabel Pell dropped dead in June 1952. Isabel toppled off her chair in a Madison Avenue restaurant where she was having dinner with a friend. Fifty-one-year-old Isabel had a history of health problems, and there was talk that alcohol was involved. Eleo was devastated. After Isabel's funeral, Eleo negotiated with Pelly's relatives over the disposition of her ashes. Eleo was adamant that her bond with Isabel surpassed any claims of blood kin. Eleo took Isabel, in a bronze canister, and placed her in the brick basement vault at Christ's Church Longwood that held the remains of her family. For Eleo, Isabel would always be the great heroine of World War II.

Barely noticed among the tide of European immigrants that came to America after the Second World War were a half dozen former cavalry officers from Hungary. During their long and varied careers in America as riders, trainers, coaches, course designers, and judges, these Hungarians would help to revolutionize the art of horsemanship in their adopted country. They were an appealing group, smart and ambitious, with a becoming shyness about their stumbles in a new language. These onetime soldiers had been classically trained in a riding academy in Budapest that was the equestrian equivalent of West Point. Several of these men found their way to Eleo. Gabor Foltenyi came to her first, and he was soon joined by another brilliant rider, Bertalan de Némethy. Their methods for training horses and riders remained controversial until, after repeated success in competition, they could no longer be overlooked. Eleo was their first convert.

American ideas of working with horses had been shaped by the rowdy spirit of the Wild West. The Hungarians arrived with a different thought, that you did not have to "get tough" with a horse to control it. They spoke instead of "winning his confidence" and being "gentle but firm," concepts that sounded sensual, almost mystical, and fit exactly with what Eleo wished for her "babies." Gabor Foltenyi believed that the key to being a great rider had little to do with intellect and everything to do with "feel." The best riders could send and receive signals through the backs of their mounts, which, like the pliant middle of an accordion, formed the connecting bridge between the front and rear ends of the horse. Gabor's method of training horses and riders was based on the art of dressage, which relies on nearly undetectable signals, a slight shift of balance or pressure from the seat bones and legs, a subtle technique that, to the uninitiated, is like watching grass grow. Gabor learned that most American horsemen in the 1950s considered dressage a dirty word, if they had heard of it at all. The name, of French origin, means "training." The European military developed the technique of directing a horse without reins to free a rider's hands to use weaponry.

In competitive show dressage, a horse demonstrates the gaits of the walk, trot, and canter. At higher skill levels, horses seem to float as they perform dancelike flying lead changes, *piaffes,* and pirouettes. The basic abilities that underlie this fancy work have universal application. A horse that carries itself properly is prepared to jump or work on the flat. Gabor spoke with surpassing tenderness of the harmony that was possible between a horse and a rider: "Through the activity of the hind end and through the arched back and neck, he comes into your waiting hands."[5] Gabor felt that women generally were better riders than men because they lacked brute strength and the instinct to conquer. Gabor's preference for females extended to horses. "Once you get the mares on your side, and they understand they are not going to be forced or crucified, you can count on them," Gabor said. "I love those sensitive mares! I wore spurs for decoration. I didn't need spurs on those mares, I'll tell you!" Eleo grew to love Gabor like a son.

Gabor was about to join the Hungarian National Equestrian Team when his hopes were dashed by the Second World War. Instead of riding in the Olympics, he fought across Poland and the Pripyat Marshes in eastern Russia with Hungary's First Cavalry Division. Gabor participated in one of the last cavalry charges of the war against the Russian army as it marched on Budapest.[6] After the war, Gabor was trapped behind the Iron Curtain and spent the next three years making his tortuous way through border crossings until he arrived in New York in May 1951. Gabor found work at a series of stables doing what he knew and loved best, training and showing horses. He became very fond of the refined American Thoroughbreds, which tended to be more sensitive and responsive than the European warmbloods he had grown up with. Gabor won his first American jumping competition at the Devon Horse Show near Philadelphia. His breakthrough victory, in terms of personal recognition, came on the opening night of the National Horse Show in Madison Square Garden. Not long after that success, Gabor was warming up a horse before an event at Piping Rock, cantering around an out-of-the-way part of the show grounds, when he nearly ran into Eleo. That introduction marked the beginning of his relationship with Eleo Sears and her "wonderful" horses, a meeting that Gabor considered to be one of the pivotal events of his life. It brought him opportunities that assured his future.

Eleo made Gabor a job offer too good to refuse, and he began his life with her in October 1953. Gabor was a perfectionist, and he never gave up until he had unlocked the potential of each of Eleo's horses. They responded beautifully to his quiet, thoughtful approach. Soon Eleo invited Gabor to move into Rock Edge. By day they worked together at the stable with the horses. On some mornings he joined Eleo for an ocean swim and then they rode together. In the evening they went to the theater or the club, or Eleo invited friends to dinner at Rock Edge. Gabor and Eleo enjoyed wide-ranging discussions of current events, his boyhood experiences, and his training philosophy. It pleased them both that, always, talk came back to horses.

For Gabor, so recently a refugee with little he could call his own, his life with Eleo filled him with wonder. She spoiled him unabashedly. Gabor mentioned that he enjoyed using English lavender soap for his bath, and within days he had it by the case. After Gabor said that he liked Champagne, Eleo bought up all the Coronation Champagne she could find (which had been used for the coronation celebration of Queen Elizabeth II), and for the next two and a half years, every evening meal at Rock Edge began with Champagne. But beyond all the sweet luxuries, which included a handsome new tuxedo, Gabor's greatest pleasure came from working with Eleo's horses, which were of overwhelming quality, and he could do that to his heart's content. If he decided that something extra was needed for the horses, anything for their comfort, new leg wraps, or a visit from the vet—Presto! it appeared. If the grooms ran low on saddle soap, they had only to mentioned it to Eleo, and the next day cases of saddle soap arrived at the stable. This must be, Gabor thought, what heaven was like. Eleo did not get angry with Gabor when he exchanged the pitiful twenty-five-watt lightbulbs she supplied for the stable with stronger ones. She protested that the brighter light was blinding, but she did not insist on removing the bulbs.

Eleo's appreciation of fine horses and her competitive instinct drove her to try to own the best. Her splendid Reno was one of the most celebrated show hunters on the East Coast. Eleo admired the fiery mare Sidonia and offered to buy the chestnut beauty, but Sidonia's owner, Bill Summer, would not sell her. Summer's resistance whetted Eleo's appetite even more, so she sent him a blank check, and Sidonia moved to Prides Crossing. Taking Gabor's advice, Eleo bought Diamant, a German-owned champion that had impressed Gabor with his confident jumping ability, and Diamant proved to be a big winner for Eleo's stable. Eleo bought Ksar d'Esprit after Gabor fell in love with the majestic gray horse, which was a key member of the Canadian jumping team. Ksar d'Esprit measured a huge 17.2 hands, and his bravery and talent matched his size and power.

Eleo demonstrated to Gabor every day, through her generosity and respect for his judgment, how deep her affection for him was. She seemed to be always smiling. The comforts of life at Rock Edge helped soften the ache Gabor felt for distant family and homeland. Eleo began calling him "Öecsi" (pronounced ou-stee), "little brother" in Hungarian, which was his family's fond nickname for him. Gabor grew to love Eleo and to think of her as his second mother.

During the long New England winter, Eleo traveled with Gabor in her private railroad car to Southern Pines in North Carolina. Her intention was to spend the coldest months in the sunny horse country near Pinehurst, where she had bought a farm known as The Paddock. While there Eleo had the pleasure of seeing a horse she had imported from Ireland, Golden Loch II, win the hotly contested Sand Hill Cup. She developed a new circle of acquaintances who flocked to her parties, drawn by her intriguing persona as the eccentric Boston socialite and sports legend. Yet Eleo stayed in Southern Pines for just a fraction of the time that was planned. After only a few weeks in February, she packed up and returned to the cold and snow of Boston. She refused to discuss the illogic of her early return or the impracticality of the lightly used southern farm. She missed her horses at Prides; that was the main thing. She missed being there for their afternoon meal. Eleo liked rolling up her sleeves, straddling the big food barrel, mixing bran, molasses, and hot water into a mash with a wooden paddle and adding cut-up carrots. She loved the way the horses stomped impatiently in their stalls and whinnied to her while she worked. They pushed her with their heads to hurry as she scooped their portions into their feed buckets, and then they plunged their noses in and ate with contented crunches the food she had prepared. There was nothing quite so satisfying to Eleo as knowing she was contributing to their well-being, making them happy.

In her seventy-third year, Eleo embarked on an adult version of a childhood dream. As a little girl she had dreamed of riding the winning horse in the Kentucky Derby. Her grown-up wish was to breed and own that horse. Eleo was acutely aware of the gulf between aspiration and achievement. She knew many people who were seduced by the dream of a Derby win, but precious few who had been in the winner's circle at Churchill Downs with their horse wearing a blanket of roses. And only eight of those winning horses had been owned by women during the Derby's seventy-nine-year history. Eleo was always restless without new worlds to conquer, but in choosing to build a breeding and racing stable from the ground up, she began with a big strike against her. She was no longer young, already late out of the gate. Having made her decision, Eleo plunged in with total commitment. She placed a call to Gabor's friend in California, Hartmann Pauly, who had arrived in the United States four years before Gabor. The fifty-eight-year-old horseman had formerly been a major in the Hungarian army. Major Pauly combined expertise in horse breeding with a valuable twenty-year friendship with His Highness the Aga Khan, the thirty-eighth Imam of Iran, whose Thoroughbred empire contained many of the best bloodlines in the world. Major Pauly quickly became an indispensable part of Eleo's racing plans. Eleo called him "a wonderful fellow," and on his advice she bought Kincsem Acres, a ranch adjoining his property near Santa Barbara, for use as a year-round training facility and stud farm.

Eleo studied bloodlines and began assembling her foundation stock. She announced her entry into the horse-racing fraternity with a headline-making purchase at the Saratoga horse sales in August 1954 that left no doubt of her intention to be a serious contender. Four planeloads of horses from the Aga Khan's stables in Ireland, flown in under the supervision of his son Prince Aly Khan, added cachet to the thirty-fourth edition of the famous horse auction. The Aga Khan's mystique was enhanced when his subjects presented him with his weight in platinum—243 pounds—during his birthday celebration. For another birthday, he received his weight in diamonds.

Eleo arrived at Saratoga Springs with her Hungarian contingent in tow, Hartmann Pauly and his wife, Bert de Némethy, and Gabor. They were among two thousand buyers and spectators who traveled to this elm-shaded resort town in upstate New York for the annual yearling sales, where top horse enthusiasts enjoyed a week of dinner parties, dancing until the wee hours at the Saratoga Golf Club, and early morning breakfasts at the track to watch the horses work out. Spotted among the crowd were the philanthropist and former ambassador to Cuba Harry Guggenheim, Singer Sewing Machine heir F. Ambrose Clark, radio and television personality Arthur Godfrey, boxer Jack Dempsey (who declared, "It's a hell of an education . . . this sales stuff!"), and cosmetics queen Elizabeth Arden.

During the weeklong auction 272 horses were sold. The young horses were led, one at a time, by white-jacketed attendants onto an elevated platform. The dirt-topped platform was roped off like a boxing ring, and each horse bore a prominent tag on its rump with an identifying number. The nervous yearlings watched the crowd as intently as they were being studied. Their prospective owners, cradling dog-eared auction catalogues like Bibles, sat in rows of white folding chairs that surrounded the ring on three sides and stretched to the back of the large pavilion. Many of the yearlings on display were frightened by the noise and the lights and produced steaming piles of manure that were quickly scooped away.

At a long table on the opposite side of the ring, Humphrey Finney, the auction president, sat facing the audience and acted as master of ceremonies. The jovial, fast-talking auctioneer George Swinebroad moved the proceedings along at a brisk clip. Excitement grew as the final horse was led in on the last night of the auction. Finney spoke: "This colt, ladies and gentlemen, should need no introduction. Hip No. 284 is a half brother to Tulyar. He is by Tudor Minstrel out of Neocracy. I don't have to remind you that I think he's one of the grandest colts we've ever been privileged to offer."[7] Swinebroad started the bidding at $10,000. Within a minute, by $10,000 increments, the bid had leaped to $60,000. Then $65,000. It was big money in 1954, nearly $530,000 today, and the crowd grew quiet in respect. President Finney caught the eye of the white-haired lady in the third row. Eleo looked regal, formidable, in a slim black dress with a mandarin collar and a single strand of pearls. Finney mouthed a silent question, "Seventy-five?" Eleo gave him a barely perceptible nod. Tension hung heavily as the auctioneer waited for another bid, until the yearling in question let out a whinny, like a long giggle. The auctioneer addressed the youngster, "Shut up, you. I'm doing all I can for you." Then Swinebroad brought the gavel down. Eleo had paid the highest price of the auction, and the second-highest price for a yearling in U.S. history. Eleo's bid became known as the "$75,000 Nod." Because of the rapid-fire patter of the auctioneer and their imperfect command of the language, some in Eleo's Hungarian entourage thought the bidding for the colt had climbed to $7,500. When the actual price was explained to them, they nearly fainted.

Eleo also brought home from the sale a second yearling and a three-year-old filly, all from the Aga Khan consignment. Eleo's eyes sparkled like a child's on Christmas morning when she talked about her new gangly-limbed bay yearling, which she named Tudorka, and her other acquisitions. They were so full of unknowns and promise. Eleo readily acknowledged the risk: "Those baby horses are wonderful, but they're a great gamble. You never can tell how they will turn out."[8]

If some corner of the racing world was still unaware of Eleo's entrance into the sport, she punctuated her arrival in October when she presented the winner's trophy to the du Pont family at the prestigious Suffolk Downs "Yankee Handicap." In November 1954, at the Lexington sales, Hartmann Pauly purchased two broodmares for Eleo's stable, both from the Aga Khan's Nearco bloodline, which were already in foal to top sires. Usumbura and Rivaz were sent to Kincsem Acres to await their time. Eleo authorized Major Pauly to purchase France's top two-year-old filly, Soya, and a three-year-old brother of Tudorka. Eleo's foundation purchases for her opening year in the racing business were estimated to be over $700,000 (more than $5.5 million today). Eleo chose white and royal blue as the colors for her racing silks, and though she was not a patient soul, she understood there would not be much racing action until the "children" were older. Eleo's racing stable now had fourteen horses for running and breeding. It was a modest-sized operation compared to others in the horse game, but "just enough," Eleo said, "to have a lot of fun."[9]

Eleo was increasingly unhappy about being an absentee owner. Her racing operation at Kincsem Acres put three thousand miles between her and her four-legged brood. In December 1954 Hartmann Pauly came east and joined Eleo on a tour of Burrland Farm in Middleburg, Virginia, and the following month Eleo purchased the 460 acres of rolling bluegrass pasture. Burrland Farm was like a small town. Accommodations for people, in clusters across the land, included a twelve-room manager's cottage, a large guesthouse, and two tenant cottages. Horses were housed in a stable with twenty-eight gracious box stalls. There were additional barns for broodmares, for weaning and stud activities, and a polo stable and indoor and outdoor exercise tracks. The pièce de résistance was the formal main house, a white-pillared brick colonial that had been built by Major Burr Noland in the late nineteenth century. At one point in its history, the property had been a summer boarding school for girls. The renowned horseman William Ziegler bought the place from Air Force General Billy Mitchell in the late 1920s and raised some of the country's top horses there.[10] William Ziegler's daughter was married to Eleo's friend Bill Steinkraus, famed as the first American jump rider to win an individual Olympic gold medal.

For Gabor Foltenyi it was love at first sight when he met his fellow Hungarian Elizabeth Baer. Bert de Némethy introduced Gabor to the pretty twenty-eight-year-old during the 1952 National Horse Show at the Garden. Elizabeth was amazed by the huge indoor stadium, its scale unknown in Europe at the time, and by the crowds dressed in evening gowns and tuxedos. She was charmed by Gabor, who was still basking in the glow of his jumping successes on opening night. Elizabeth was bright and enthusiastic, with happy hazel-green eyes, and she could match Gabor's wartime experiences with harrowing escapes of her own. Soon Elizabeth agreed to share Gabor's life in America, but her husband back in Germany was a complicating factor. She was married to a former lieutenant in the German army. The German officer had many times come to the aid of Elizabeth and her family as they hid from rampaging Russian soldiers in remote mountain cabins and refugee camps. Hungary had sided with Germany during the war and the Red Army exacted brutal revenge on Hungarian civilians. When the war ended, Elizabeth married her German soldier and moved in with his family in Frankfurt. Their comfortable home was one of the few left standing after the war. Elizabeth's in-laws had been careful to conceal their profound contempt for Hitler, the "house painter," and his Nazi henchmen. But the chemistry between Elizabeth and her husband, Sonny, seemed to vanish after he exchanged his uniform for everyday clothes, and Elizabeth saw that gratitude was not enough to sustain her marriage. Their relationship was further strained by the death of their infant son. Gabor agreed to wait for Elizabeth while she returned to Germany to end things with Sonny.

Eleo welcomed Elizabeth with open arms when she arrived in Boston in October 1954. Eleo intended to gain a daughter when Gabor married his "Little Erzsebet," not lose a son. Eleo agreed to be Elizabeth's American sponsor and she affirmed to the immigration authorities that Gabor's fiancée would not be a burden to the country. Eleo installed Elizabeth in a bright bedroom at Rock Edge overlooking the ocean. For weeks after, Elizabeth awoke to the sounds of the surf outside her window with the not-unpleasant conviction that she was still in her gently rolling cabin on board the S.S. *Queen Elizabeth* en route to America. It tickled Eleo when Elizabeth described her onboard encounter with the Queen Mother and her lady-in-waiting while they strolled on the Promenade Deck. Elizabeth had made a formal curtsey and chatted with the Queen Mum about the blustery weather at sea. Elizabeth arrived in Prides Crossing not long after the Hurricane of '54 had washed away Eleo's dock and flattened all the trees behind her stable. Along the North Shore, hundreds of trees lay splintered on the ground. Gabor and Elizabeth looked out on the blasted landscape and saw the bomb-devastated countryside of Eastern Europe.

Gabor and Elizabeth were married on December 13, 1954. Eleo wanted to organize a big wedding, but after the couple considered the logistical problems, they decided that a small, simple ceremony was more appropriate. Most of their family and friends were still stranded behind the Iron Curtain and the rest, fellow immigrants, were scattered across Europe and California. None could afford to make a trip to Massachusetts. Eleo had wedding announcements printed so that the Foltenyis could, at least, notify everyone they cared about. Eleo was now living at 148 Beacon Street, a town house a few doors west of her childhood home, once owned by her grandfather T. J. Coolidge and next door to the double town house where Isabella Stewart Gardner had lived. For the Foltenyis' wedding Eleo filled the town house with flowers and hired a justice of the peace. In her parlor Eleo gave Gabor away, and Elizabeth's brother stood with her. Eleo presided over an elegant wedding dinner and the happy couple was toasted with Gabor's favorite Champagne. After dinner, Eleo suggested that they all go up to Prides so that Elizabeth's brother, a former cavalry officer, could see her horses. Eleo insisted on driving, and she confined Tom Greene to the passenger seat. Eleo was more tired than she realized after the daylong celebration and she could barely keep her eyes open, but she would not consider allowing Thomas to take the wheel. The group arrived safely only because they were able to come up with enough conversation and songs to keep Eleo awake. Eleo's wedding gift to the Foltenyis was waiting, a beautiful maroon Mercedes, which she knew was Gabor's favorite car. For the Foltenyis the gift represented freedom from the financial burdens that weighed down their friends, who struggled to meet monthly car payments and repair bills on secondhand jalopies.

Gabor and Elizabeth moved into the unoccupied half of the head gardener's cottage, down the hill from the stable in Prides Crossing. Their new home was sun-filled and spacious, and Elizabeth planted flowers. All the watering and weeding was attended to by one of Eleo's six gardeners, so that Elizabeth had, in effect, her own staff. Eleo and Elizabeth discussed furniture arrangements and picked colors, and within short order a new bedroom set arrived, along with kitchen equipment and new carpeting for all the rooms. Because of Eleo's generosity, the Foltenyis could put almost all Gabor's salary away for their future. They paid nothing in rent and practically nothing for food because they ate lunch and dinner at "the big house" with Eleo. With the Foltenyis Eleo was at her most charming, and their time together was always entertaining and often joyous. In the evenings they played cards and talked about politics and horses, hers and her competitors'. They went to the theater together, and concerts, and dinners at the homes of friends.

When Gabor was out of town at horse shows, Elizabeth did her best to keep up with Eleo on some of her "little walks," often ten-mile jogs that left Elizabeth drained. Elizabeth did not really ride horses, but she once got to sit on Ksar d'Esprit. She was intimidated by the horse's great size and strength and acutely aware that she would be helpless to stop him if he suddenly decided to take off. But she tried not to seem anxious in front of Gabor and Eleo.

Gretchen Warren continued her regular visits to Rock Edge. Now in her eighties, she had written about Eleo with motherly pride to Mrs. Morris Carter at Fenway Court, where Morris remained as the venerable director. Gretchen shared with Beatrice Carter her latest insight into Eleo's rarely publicized good works: "I've found secretly to my amazement that really only the *poor* know what Eleo does with modesty & humility & tact & silence. She simply pours help to the needy and always as if the privilege were hers not theirs." Gretchen cited Eleo's recent donation of eighteen cars, in a single year, to struggling senior citizens who had to continue working to make ends meet. Gretchen's own advancing age prompted her to confide in Beatrice Carter, "I *must* tell a few—to let them understand a very conscientious rare noble being—Don't forget this when I go."[11]

The Foltenyis found Gretchen Warren to be an "adorable, old-fashioned lady," and they grew enormously fond of her. Gretchen engaged the young couple in detailed analyses of postwar Europe. She was intrigued to hear about their childhoods and their strategies for evading Russian roadblocks. Mrs. Warren gave Elizabeth grandmotherly scoldings about her smoking and her too-short new hair cut, and she presented her with an autographed copy of her published poems.

Eleo invited Gabor and Elizabeth on a kaleidoscope of adventures. At the Myopia Hunt Ball, Eleo came in on Gabor's arm and she enlisted her long-time hunting companion John Lawrence to be Elizabeth's escort. Lawrence was a widower in his seventies, still handsome, with youthful, twinkling eyes. The oddity of the pairings that Eleo devised for the evening actually added to the fun. Eleo took the Foltenyis backstage to meet Sarah Churchill when the talented thespian daughter of Sir Winston was in a play in Boston. On New Year's Eve, Eleo, Gabor, and Elizabeth dined at the Ritz and went to the Ice Capades. The figure-skating star Tenley Albright came to Rock Edge for tea, and Gabor and Elizabeth were fascinated to learn about the exacting training regimen required of an Olympian. Tenley had won the silver medal in the 1952 Winter Olympics. She was training at the Boston Skating Club, under the guidance of Eleo's good friend Maribel Vinson Owen, for the 1956 Olympics.

When the Foltenyis' compatriot Bert de Némethy was invited to be the coach for the U.S. Olympic Equestrian Team, Eleo was reluctant to part with him, but it was a grand honor and she gave him her blessing. Then she let Bert persuade her to lend her two best jumpers to the team. He appealed to her patriotism, explaining that the fledgling American team was blessed with some of the most talented riders in the world, the likes of Bill Steinkraus, Hugh Wiley, Arthur McCashin, and John Russell; if they were ever to beat the top European teams, however, they had to have mounts of equal ability. In short, Bert told Eleo, they needed Diamant and Ksar d'Esprit. Eleo shipped her two beauties to the team's headquarters in Gladstone, New Jersey, for as long as Bert wanted them.

One morning Eleo mentioned to Elizabeth Foltenyi, so casually that Elizabeth almost missed it, that Prince Aly Khan and his son would be joining them for lunch. In America the prince was known mostly for his stormy marriage to Rita Hayworth, Hollywood's copper-maned temptress. Movie magazines and gossip columns occasionally mentioned sightings of Aly Khan cavorting with this or that beauty aboard a yacht in the Mediterranean, or in France at the horse races in Deauville. The European news media, in contrast, were totally obsessed with the life and revolving passions of the playboy prince. Aly Khan loved women on a global scale. He loved the way they talked, the way they dressed, they way they thought. And they were magnetized by his dark, attentive, hungry eyes. The German tabloids, which Elizabeth had followed avidly for years, provided an ongoing frenzy of detail about his every dalliance.

In accord with strict Muslim doctrine, Aly Khan neither smoked nor drank, but no one's pretty wife was safe. During the war Aly had served in France under Eleo's cousin Lieutenant Colonel Henry Cabot Lodge. Lodge was frustrated that the prince directed so much of his energy to intrigues with officers' wives, and finally a job was found for Aly that suited his talents. He was tasked with procuring fresh chicken and eggs for the troops. Aly proved resourceful in this line of work, apparently able to find an ample supply of French farm girls willing to give up their poultry to him. For his military service during Allied operations in southern France, Aly was awarded a Bronze Star for gallantry. The prince's father, the Aga Khan, had never approved of his son's sexual preoccupations and bypassed him when he chose his successor. The Aga Khan designated his grandson Prince Karim, a Harvard student-athlete, to succeed him as the forty-ninth Imam of the world's Shia Ismaili Muslims. His son Prince Aly was given a harmless job as Pakistan's ambassador to the United Nations.

Aly Khan visited his son at Harvard and took the boy to Prides Crossing to meet one of his best customers. Eleo gave the princes a royal tour of her stable, and they stayed for lunch at Rock Edge, where everyone chatted with them as if they had known them for years. Sitting next to Aly Khan, Elizabeth was spellbound. Finally, she got up the courage to ask him about some starlet he had just started seeing. The prince seemed a bit startled. "How in the world did you know about that?" he asked Elizabeth, who explained that it had already been reported in the German newspapers. Elizabeth could scarcely believe the glamorous life that she and Gabor had drifted into.

This lovely interlude at Prides Crossing, with Gabor and Elizabeth as Eleo's surrogate children, could not last indefinitely, however much Eleo might have wished it so. Having spent the first year and a half of their married lives with Eleo, Elizabeth and Gabor decided the time had come to strike out on their own. They had accumulated enough money to buy a small home, and Gabor had made excellent contacts and could be sure that his skills were in demand. Their move was fueled by Elizabeth's increasing unease about their situation. She was profoundly grateful to Eleo for all her kindnesses to them, but the feeling of obligation was not a light burden. The Foltenyis began to chafe under the subtle, and sometimes not so subtle, restrictions on their movements. Most of their activities and friends came through Eleo. They had made a few friends of their own; Elizabeth had enjoyed working in a boutique owned by an acquaintance in nearby Salem, but because their daily lives were so intertwined with Eleo's, socializing without her felt secretive and uncomfortable. Several of Eleo's younger friends would have liked, on occasion, to invite the Foltenyis alone for cocktails or dinner, but no one wanted to risk offending Eleo. Eleo was great company, full of energy and often very funny, but her presence changed the dynamic of a gathering because she had an opinion on everything and some deference was expected. Eleo was hurt when she wasn't included. She loved being with the younger generation, with their unlined faces and bubble of ideas for the future. Her own, more sedentary age group could be too depressing for words. They had aches and pains and needed time to rest. There would be time enough for that after you were dead, Eleo had decided long ago.

For the Foltenyis there was also the not insubstantial matter of the furniture for the cottage. No sofa or chairs for the living room ever came. If the Foltenyis wanted to entertain their friends at home, they either had to sit on the living room carpet or take their guests up to the big house to be with Eleo. Was the empty room a result of miscommunication, a simple oversight, or a deliberate omission? Elizabeth was too shy to ask, but the vacant space grated. Gabor had worked for Eleo for four years, and during all that time he had always felt basically content. He traveled to competitions, met interesting people, and rode all those splendid horses, and his affection for Eleo never wavered. Men are simpler souls. As Elizabeth came to see it, they were living in "a gilded cage."

Consciously or not, by making it awkward for Gabor and Elizabeth to have a life separate from hers, Eleo insulated them from gossip about her private life. Gabor and Elizabeth learned about Eleo's sexual leaning only later, long after they had left Prides Crossing. But by being overprotective, by holding Gabor and Elizabeth so close, Eleo hastened the very thing she dreaded. After they told Eleo of their decision to leave, the Foltenyis packed their few belongings into the maroon Mercedes and headed west, feeling once again like refugees. Eleo was too deeply hurt to be gracious about their departure. She had been welcoming and generous, and now they no longer needed her. She still needed them. Gabor went on to become a highly respected trainer, dressage coach, and show judge. He and Elizabeth started a family. They kept in touch with Eleo. They remembered her at Christmas and on her birthday with cards and flowers, but it was never the same again.

Gabor's friend Hartmann Pauly oversaw Eleo's racing stable at Kincsem Acres in California for less than five months, but it took several years of litigation before Eleo fully disentangled herself from him. Major Pauly claimed that when he had talked to Eleo about drawing up a formal employment contract, she had assured him, "You and Mrs. Pauly will be taken care of for life. You won't have a thing to worry about."[12] It was the type of impulsive, expansive statement that Eleo was fond of making. Eleo's attorney George Hopkins visited Pauly in California and they settled on a salary of $1,000 per month, plus 10 percent of any race winnings. In December 1954 Eleo stayed at Kincsem

Acres for several apparently pleasant weeks with Major Pauly, and he joined her in her private box at the track at Santa Anita. Pauly then traveled east to tour Burrland Farms with her before she bought the property. He received a letter telling him that he was fired a few weeks later, on January 31, 1955.

Shocked by Eleo's sudden turn, Pauly brought suit against her for breach of contract and claimed damages totaling $361,014, which included a hefty chunk of assumed future earnings. His claim was later reduced to $165,000. Pauly testified that he had never been paid any of the salary that Eleo had agreed to. On the witness stand, Eleo told the jury that she did not involve herself with such matters. Contract issues, she said, were left to her accountant and others to deal with. She also hid behind a memory lapse concerning any long-term promise to Pauly. Amid the flurry of charges and counter-charges, it emerged that there was a problem with Tarjoman, one of Pauly's highly touted purchases for her from the Aga Khan. Bought for $83,000, the three-year-old full brother to the famed Irish horse Tulyar had a deformed foot, a detail that Pauly had not mentioned to Eleo. Pauly had also received a gift from his friend the Aga Khan, a colt named Mizban that was valued at $45,000. The gift aroused Eleo's suspicion of a kickback, and she took Mizban with her when she moved her racing operation to the East Coast. Pauly wanted the horse back. Though Eleo's legal team never accused Pauly directly of financial impropriety, Eleo clearly drew that conclusion. It took only a whiff of disloyalty for Eleo to write someone off, and once her trust was shaken, regaining it was like trying to unring a bell. The jury, and then an appeals court years later, found Hartmann Pauly's version of events more credible than Eleo's. He was awarded $85,000, but Eleo was allowed to retain custody of Mizban.

With her racing stable now relocated to Burrland Farms, Eleo made a fresh start. She hired a new trainer and changed her racing colors to maroon with cerise hoops on the jockey's sleeves. Her horses' winnings up to that point did not amount to much, but George Hopkins got into the habit of sending her the purse money, instead of just depositing the checks in her bank account. Receiving this bit of concrete evidence of success gave Eleo outsize pleasure.

To handle the training of her jumpers at Prides Crossing, Eleo hired Nancy Sweet-Escott, an English horsewoman who was one of the first professional female trainers. Among Sweet-Escott's quirks was her unshakeable faith in a special liniment that she rubbed on a horse's ailing legs. Everyone assumed it was a powerful curative: it stank so badly that it had to be good for something.

The truism that "events seldom work out as planned" is especially apt in dealing with horses. Eleo had high hopes for her recently purchased jumper, Mr. Linnett, who was being trained by Sweet-Escott. Though the eight-year-old horse didn't like to run in mud, he was entered in the world-renowned, usually muddy Grand National Steeplechase Race in Aintree, England. Eleo arrived in Aintree only to learn that Mr. Linnett had gone lame and would not be competing. Still, Eleo got on well with Sweet-Escott. During a dinner party that Eleo hosted, the trainer bet that Eleo couldn't hit a spot on the ceiling with a popping Champagne cork. After a couple of tries, with a couple of bottles, Eleo won the bet.

The combined expenses of Eleo's revenue-eating racing business, her stable of jumpers, the upkeep of far-flung homes and properties, each with its own staff, and continuing gifts of money and automobiles to people in need left her hemorrhaging money. Yet, when Eleo's longtime friend and tennis partner William Clothier presented her with an intriguing proposition, it was not the financial component that gave her the most pause. The National Lawn Tennis Hall of Fame opened its headquarters in 1954 at the Newport Casino, site of the first U.S. Championships, and Bill Clothier was chosen as its first president. As Bill explained in a lengthy letter to Eleo, "Its sponsors have been foolish enough to ask me . . . and I have been foolish enough to accept."[13]

The Hall of Fame's new president was the logical person to approach Eleo. They had a half century of shared history and an ongoing friendship. Eleo regularly found herself in Bill's neighborhood in the Philadelphia suburbs, where she attended squash tournaments and horse shows and where they had many mutual friends. Eleo shared the Clothiers' box at the Devon Horse Show when she had horses entered. Eleo and the Clothiers dined at Androssan, the grand Main Line mansion of Edgar and Hope Scott. Edgar Scott was the fellow who, without Eleo's intervention, would have been "splattered" in a fall from a hotel window. Eleo could count on a hearty welcome from Edgar's charming wife, the former debutante Hope Montgomery, who was the inspiration for the heroine of *The Philadelphia Story*.

In Bill Clothier's initial letter to Eleo, he outlined a plan for a "memorial room" in the Hall of Fame that would commemorate Eleo's uncle Richard Dudley Sears, America's first national lawn tennis champion, and would recognize Eleo's own pioneering athletic achievements. In Eleo's case, the envisioned memorial would not be limited to lawn tennis, but would act as a repository for the hundreds of trophies and photographs from her remarkable range of sporting interests. Bill wrote, "I am not exaggerating when I say that your activities have exceeded those of any other woman athlete in this country." Bill ended his typewritten letter to Eleo stiffly, "Yours very sincerely," a closing that reflected his certainty that his correspondence would be reviewed by other, "official" eyes.

Eleo was beyond surprised to receive a "typewritten letter!!!" from Bill. Impersonal typed documents were exchanged in court cases, as Eleo had ample opportunity to observe, or mailed to overbearing government agencies like the IRS, not something that friends sent friends. Despite that, Eleo was at first "bowled over" by Bill's concept, "really overcome about the whole thing—." Her initial pleasure with the unexpected honor was tempered by her habitually harsh self-assessment. Eleo told Bill that she doubted she was worthy of such a memorial: "of all people I should say that I was the one that can't do anything and never really have done anything—." Any hint that she was being flattered always made her bristle, and though Bill had studiously avoided mention of any expected financial commitment, Eleo hadn't been born yesterday. She anticipated that the honor would involve some cost. "If my family should be asked to give money for such a thing, I feel sure they would just laugh," Eleo advised him. Eleo ended her reply to Bill with characteristic warmth, "Much love dear Bill, ever Affectionately."[14]

Over the next several months, Bill Clothier worked diligently to overcome Eleo's modesty about her achievements. He pointed out how, by her example, she had inspired so many young athletes, and that her "all-around career in sports . . . has been unsurpassed." Bill promoted the Hall of Fame not just as a museum of tennis history, but as a positive influence on the character and physical well-being of future generations of sportsmen and -women. The Sears Memorial Room, as Bill envisioned it, would be a social venue for the organization, decorated by life-size photographs of Eleo and her uncle, displays of their trophies and memorabilia, and Sargent's charcoal portrait of Eleo. Despite Eleo's unease with the idea of a shrine to herself, she seriously considered the $100,000 donation Bill requested to cover some of the start-up costs of the Hall of Fame, and to furnish and maintain the memorial space. Eleo referred the funding logistics to George Hopkins. Hopkins was not encouraging when he told Bill Clothier, in confidence, that the Hall of Fame's tax-exempt status would be of no use to Eleo because her racing stable was losing so much money that her tax liability was already next to nothing. Bill left the meeting with Hopkins lamenting that Eleo's advisor was neither a horseman nor a tennis buff. Nor was Hoppy a totally disinterested observer. Strapped for cash himself, Hopkins had recently appealed to Eleo for a loan, and she had given him $595,345 in bonds. She made him a gift of most of the money and took his promissory note for $200,000 to be repaid in eight years, at 2 percent interest semiannually.

Eleo was also shouldering the budgetary troubles of the Boston Mounted Police. She routinely made up the difference between what the city budgeted for its horses and the actual cost to buy and maintain them. In 1956 her maternal interest in "the boys" and their horses at the Back Bay station led her to step in when municipal cutbacks left the mounted division short of horses for its thirteen officers. Eleo obtained Justinson, one of the finest registered Morgans in New England, and gave him to the city. She subsidized the purchase of two American saddle-bred horses, which allowed the city to spend only $700 for $1,600 worth of horses. Officer Ben Donahue was brokenhearted over the death of a horse he had ridden for years. Eleo invited Officer Donahue to visit her at home. She told him to pick out the best horse he could find and she gave him a signed check, the amount left blank for Officer Donahue to fill in. At Christmastime Eleo made a ritual of visiting the station house and handing each of the men an envelope containing a five-dollar bill, a practice she had begun when five dollars was a good wage. She explained to the shyly appreciative men that the gift was her way of sharing the spirit of Christmas. Over the years Boston policemen reciprocated Eleo's friendship and affection. They extended to her chauffeur, Thomas Greene, the same driving and parking latitude that Eleo enjoyed, holding up oncoming traffic and waving him through intersections. The patrolmen gave Eleo's Beacon Street town house special scrutiny as they rode by, particularly after a break-in there in 1954 when Eleo was out of town.

The negotiations between Eleo and Bill Clothier concerning her expected donation to the Tennis Hall of Fame dragged on for years and introduced a strained note to their friendship. As the Hall of Fame gained recognition and donors, a contribution from Eleo became less critical; however, Eleo's old doubles partner continued his quest to wring a sizable donation from her. Bill Clothier was spurred by his admiration for Eleo's pioneering role in women's athletics, as well by his interest in maximizing the funds for the organization he led. Eleo attended the induction ceremonies in Newport in 1955 for the first players enshrined in the Tennis Hall of Fame, a list headed, to her great pleasure, by her uncle Richard Dudley Sears.

By 1957 Bill Clothier had invested three years in cultivating Eleo and combating her skepticism about a memorial room, and he scaled down his expectations. He proposed that she donate only $50,000, or give the full amount as a bequest in her will. That way she could, as Bill put it, "enjoy her room now" and pay for it later, an idea Eleo found uniquely distasteful. What was stopping Eleo had never been about parting with a huge chunk of cash during a time of extraordinary personal expenses. She had proven herself to be impulsive and stubborn enough to do as she pleased, when she pleased, and leave the worry about affording it until later. Despite Bill Clothier's dauntless efforts to persuade her, Eleo was never in love with the idea of a memorial room. It seemed too much blatant self-promotion, very un–New England. She knew it would have been anathema to philanthropists of her grandfathers' generation. Yet because Bill was such a dear old friend and so earnest about it all, she never had the heart to say no unequivocally. She continued to give him reason to hope that money would, eventually, be forthcoming until shortly before Christmas 1957, when she wrote to him, "Well I am very much afraid that there won't be all that [money] going to you—so hadn't you better throw me out. Mr. Hopkins died the other day, so I am left on a limb just now."[15] Bill Clothier chose not to take this as Eleo's final word on the matter either, and he alerted his attorney in New York that he had recommended him to Eleo as Hopkins's replacement.

George Hopkins had been more than just Eleo's lawyer; he had been her financial consultant, a gofer, a confidant. The extent of the bond between them became clear after his death. He had originally intended to divide the bulk of his $400,000 estate among three women, whom he identified as "my friends of many years." A codicil that Hopkins wrote in April 1955 (at the time of Eleo's extraordinary gift and loan to him) directed that $300,000 go to "my revered client of many years, Eleonora R. Sears." Hopkins left his son, George Jr., only one dollar.

There were many lawyers, bankers, and investment advisors keen to take up the mantle of the fallen George Hopkins. They converged on his funeral in New York City toward the end of December 1957. William Miller, a certified public accountant, went to the funeral pay his respects to George Hopkins. He had worked on several projects with Hopkins and had grown to like him. Someone introduced Bill Miller to Eleo and they talked for a long while, about Hoppy, about her business problems, about his investment philosophy. Bill Miller was a youngish man, in his early forties and presentable looking, reminiscent of a less-chiseled William Holden. He seemed knowledgeable and solid—maybe it was the way his lips hardened into a thin determined line when he was deep in thought, or his clear blue eyes, a much milder version of Eleo's, which made him look trustworthy. His relative youth was a plus; she wasn't likely to outlive him, and he had no expectations. He was a sole practitioner, a nobody really. He had, at that point, only a handful of substantial clients. The day after the funeral, Eleo telephoned Bill Miller and said she would like to speak with him about taking over the management of her financial affairs. It was his turn to be "bowled over."

CHAPTER 18

A Far Kingdom

⁓

BILL MILLER WAS enchanted by Eleo. Though he was inclined to be intimidated by the large footprint her forebears had left on history, Eleo's firm handshake, her decidedly improper sense of humor, and her unadorned manner of getting right to the point were squarely within his comfort zone. Bill and Eleo discussed her business troubles and her plans, and they batted silly jokes back and forth. Over time, their exchanges took on a clearly affectionate tone. Bill was enchanted by the idea of Eleo—the lone woman who had dared and endured and surmounted all manner of challenges—the championships, the horses, the early experiments with race cars and airplanes. She was a person who would be remembered, and now he was a part of it all. Bill appreciated women in general—he was a thoughtful husband—but he was regularly heard to express disdain for women drivers, and he was always pleased to point out that practically all the best chefs were men. He recognized that Eleo was more than his match in most arenas, and it made him proud to know her. Later he would confess to her his "deep affection and admiration such as I feel for few people on earth."[1]

Working for Eleo was as relentless as it was thrilling. Though she was only one person, Bill quickly discovered that an industry's worth of documents required his attention on a weekly basis. Before Eleo, Bill had been able to handle his small roster of clients by himself from his home in a suburb of New York City, with an occasional typing assist from his wife. Now he needed full-time help, and he hired a male secretary-assistant, a Mr. LeCount. Besides a place to put LeCount, Bill needed a more businesslike setting to send and receive Eleo-related correspondence. He rented office space, two cubicles and a waiting area, in the Chanin Building in Manhattan, a sober setting conveniently across the street from Grand Central Station, and he had new stationery printed.

Bill scrambled to get up to speed on Eleo's continuing courtroom dramas, in which he began to play a background role. The Hartmann Pauly business was still not settled, as far as Eleo was concerned. She was convinced that Pauly had gotten the better of her, and she wanted him held accountable for overcharging her for horses of dubious quality. Another legal squabble erupted after Eleo purchased the three-acre estate of her next-door neighbor in Prides Crossing, the retired banker Cornelius Wood, and then proceeded to demolish the thirty-seven-room house on the property. An infuriated Wood went to court to have the transaction declared invalid and the sale of his property rescinded. The initial asking price for the property had been $60,000, but when Eleo expressed interest Wood refused to sell it to her for less than $80,000. Wood explained to his real estate broker, "There is one person in the U.S.A. to whom I will not sell at the lower figure. . . . I can hardly endure the thought of her possessing this beautiful property."[2] Their mutual animosity had been stoked when Wood neglected to close the gate across the lane to the beach that he shared with Eleo. In court Wood admitted that he and his uncle had ignored Eleo's directive to close the gate. Wood said that Eleo then threw some large rocks at them. Eleo said, "If I had thrown the rocks, I probably would have hit them." What galled Wood most was that Eleo had made an end run around him. She had acquired his property for only $51,500 by using a straw buyer, one of George Hopkins's friends of long standing, Eulalia Schultes, a New York nurse. Schultes had kept secret Eleo's involvement. Still another of Eleo's property disputes involved the boundaries of her farm in Southern Pines. Eleo's legal battles had now become Bill Miller's battles, and he testified on her behalf in a North Carolina courtroom. Opposing counsel congratulated Bill on his eloquent and winning defense of Eleo's position. "You could be a senator or, failing that, ambassador to the Court of St. James," the attorney told the inwardly beaming Miller.

Bill coordinated the work he did for Eleo with advisors at her banks, but she gave Bill sole control of a small pot of money to invest for her. The funds came from five years of accumulated winnings from her racing stable, a paltry $33,023.86. This was the purse money George Hopkins had been sending to her, and it was lying fallow in her Boston checking account, earning no interest. Bill invested the money in shares of Royal Dutch Petroleum, and six months later he was able to report to Eleo, with what he hoped seemed like modesty, that the investment had increased by $9,000 after the dividends were figured in.

Bill's role expanded from devising and executing a game plan for Eleo's personal taxes to include the general oversight of her racing business. Eleo appointed Bill the vice president and treasurer of the E. R. Sears Racing Stable, Incorporated, and he suddenly found himself negotiating the price per ton of the straw and hay required at Burrland Farm and Southern Pines, and the cost of a time-share for one of Eleo's mares with the virile stallion known as Cohoes. Bill's prior acquaintance with horses consisted of watching cowboy movies and seeing out-of-towners rolling through Central Park in horse-drawn carriages. Bill studied books packed with charts, black-and-white photographs, and line drawings that unraveled a range of equestrian mysteries—judging, breeding, feeding, management, selling, racing, riding, and recreation. Since childhood, Bill had been the poster boy for the self-help era. He had taught himself swimming technique, tennis, and boxing using books he borrowed from the library. He purchased the books he needed to work through Eleo's horse matters. Before long, he learned to ride and he bought himself a cowboy hat.

Bill joined Eleo in her box at Piping Rock, always one of her favorite horse shows, and she introduced him to the influential people she knew, C. Z. and Winston Guest, the du Ponts, the Whitneys, the Phipps, and the Marshall Fields. "I'd like you to meet Mr. Miller, My Man of Business," Eleo always put it, and Bill felt taller. Bill escorted Eleo to a cavalcade of events. They had front-row seats for the comedy *Critic's Choice* at the Ethel Barrymore Theatre. After the performance Eleo took Bill backstage to meet its star, Henry Fonda, and they all chatted together about "old times." Bill and Eleo had dinner at Sardi's with her cousin John Winthrop Sears, who was in town during a break in his studies at Oxford. Sardi's was the hangout for Broadway performers who came to meet and greet and read the first reviews of their shows. From across the dining room, Ethel Merman called out in her grand, booming voice, "Eleo! How the hell are you!" and she pulled up a chair at their table and joined them for a drink. Bill and Eleo went to the Stork Club, a former speakeasy that was storied for its rich and prominent clientele—the Rockefellers, the Duke and Duchess of Windsor, Bogie and Bacall, DiMaggio, and J. Edgar Hoover. According to Ethel Merman, who was romantically linked to the Stork Club's owner Sherman Billingsley, the club's exclusive reputation thrived "by selling the assumption that not everyone was equal," Billingsley, a former bootlegger, would banish a guest if he didn't like her hairdo.[3] During a pre-Christmas dinner at the '21' Club, known to longtime patrons as "Jack and Charlie's place," Bill handed out crisp five-dollar bills from Eleo to all the waiters and busboys who wandered by their table. Bill ordered a beverage with his dinner that was brought out on a silver tray, and it looked creamy white and gorgeous in its crystal goblet. A woman at the next table was intrigued. She leaned toward Bill and asked, "Pardon me sir, but I simply must know—what is that delicious-looking drink?" "Milk," said Bill. "Milk??!!!!" his inquisitor repeated blankly. Alcohol made Bill sleepy, and he was driving.

On many occasions it was Bill who drove Eleo around New York and Boston, to Piping Rock, and to the yearling auctions and races at Saratoga. It gave him great satisfaction when Eleo commented on the smooth way he handled his car. Keeping his speed consistent through turns and up hills and down was a little game he liked to play with himself, which in the years before automatic cruise control required a sensitive touch. Bill owned a 1956 DeSoto when he met Eleo. DeSotos were positioned as a mid-level vehicle for the working man, but it was a terrific-looking car, vanilla colored with chrome-edged blue wedges that streaked across the sides. In his second year with Eleo, Bill traded in the DeSoto for a Cadillac with swept-back tailfins that, with its suggestion of estate homes and country club memberships, seemed like a more appropriate conveyance for his client. Bill ordered the sleek Cadillac in maroon, not as striking as Eleo's shade, but not bad for an off-the-rack color. The bench seats of the Cadillac were upholstered with rose damask and matching leather trim. Maroon was the color Bill would also choose, many years later, for the very last car he ever owned.

Bill and Eleo liked to practice frugality in small things, which was a legacy of their very different backgrounds. Both were willing to drive a good distance out of their way to avoid paying a quarter toll. Neither thought that was strange. Money was money, and outsmarting the toll collectors was a small triumph against oppressive bureaucracy. There was a tollbooth that stood between Bill and a pretty beach in Connecticut where he took his wife and children on summer weekends. That toll could not be avoided, in either direction. Toward the end of the season, Bill passed through the tollbooth yet again and announced to the attendant as he handed her his quarter, "One more payment, and I'll own the road."

Prince Aly Khan took Bill Miller to lunch at '21' to discuss the financial terms of Eleo's purchases from the Khan stable. Bill emerged from their meeting feeling triumphant. The negotiations had gone well, but Bill's elation came from his newly won insight into the source of the prince's legendary appeal to women. The prince had mastered the ability to listen. He made you feel, Bill discovered, that *your* conversation and *your* interests were the most original, the most fascinating topics in the world, and that you were to him, at that moment, the single most important person in the world. "By the time the coffee was served," Bill confessed, "I was half in love with him myself."

When Eleo dined at home alone, she preferred to eat very simply—foods that seemed healthy and rich in energy. When she entertained, however, nothing pleased her more than adding zing to the meal by introducing her guests to something new and unusual, such as zabaglione, which was tasty and fun to say. Her heartfelt invitations, like her urgent telegram to her cousin John at Harvard, were hard to resist: "PLEASE COME TO DINNER SATURDAY EVENING SEVEN OCLOCK NO DRESSING JUST DRINKING DONT FAIL ME."[4] For Bill Miller, the happy result of Eleo's hospitality was the opportunity to meet many noteworthy people, such as the multifaceted Dick Button, a law school graduate and figure skater who was the first American to win back-to-back

Olympic gold medals and the first to perform a double axel in competition. Eleo was also very fond of William Steinkraus, captain of Bert de Némathy's U.S. Equestrian Team and winner of multiple Pan American and Olympic medals. Bill Steinkraus competed with great success on Ksar d'Esprit, and he had formed a bond with Eleo's magisterial dapple-gray horse. Steinkraus was amused that Ksar always paused to study the crowd before focusing on the course, and he noticed that the horse's heart beat faster after he had "counted the house."[5] One meal that Bill Miller had with Eleo was interrupted so she could take a long-distance phone call from Greer Garson.

Ambassador Henry Cabot Lodge Jr. was a frequent luncheon guest at Rock Edge. He had married Emily Sears, one of Eleo's favorite cousins, and his political career in the Senate and as a vice presidential candidate always stirred Eleo's vigorous support. Bill Miller was relieved to find that Ambassador Lodge was a very approachable man with an inclusive smile. Henry Lodge always took it as a compliment when people said that he didn't seem "like a Lodge" at all. His patrician grandfather, the first Senator Henry Cabot Lodge, had been renowned for his air of condescension. Alice Roosevelt Longworth quipped about her father's friend and political ally, "He never lets you forget that his family has been reading books for generations."

Eleo was in the habit of turning up at the junior Lodge's home on major holidays—Thanksgiving, Christmas, Easter—for what the family jokingly referred to as her "ceremonial visits." Eleo grew close to the Lodges' two sons, George and Harry. Harry was touched to discover that Eleo saved all the trinkets he had given her through the years, the linen handkerchiefs and such. A visit from "Cousin Eleo" that Harry remembered with particular pleasure came when he was nineteen years old and a sophomore in college. Eleo drove up in her new 1932 Lincoln convertible, a twelve-cylinder experimental version with a flamboyantly long body by Le Baron. After watching Harry walk admiringly around the sweeping automobile and caress its deeply lacquered maroon finish, Eleo told him that Tom Greene would return the next day to give him the keys to the car. When Harry got married, Eleo's wedding gift was a pair of giant crystal chandeliers, each of which would have been a comfortable fit in Blenheim Palace.

Whether Eleo was receiving visitors or paying a call, she was a stickler for punctuality, which she considered an indicator of good faith and seriousness of purpose. Beyond that, it was simply good manners to arrive on time, a mark of good breeding, like sending thank-you notes. Eleo was unfailingly pleased and surprised that Bill Miller managed to ring her front doorbell precisely at the appointed moment every time, even though he faced a five-hour commute from New York to Prides Crossing. His trick was simple. He left his apartment in the suburbs north of the city early enough to surmount any assortment of routine difficulties—traffic, bad weather, road construction, a flat tire. If things went smoothly, he arrived with time to spare and could linger at the coffee shop in Beverly Farms, a short hop from Rock Edge.

The nibble of apprehension spawned by these business trips to Prides Crossing heightened the pleasurable rush that Bill felt as he drove through the iron gates at Rock Edge and around Eleo's rose-draped tennis court, before parking in front of the tall columns of her stately brick home. It was an expansive feeling to know that he was expected, to know that the staff would work efficiently and discreetly to ensure that his stay was comfortable and trouble-free. There would be meals served on the terrace, where the sun glinted off the ocean and the breeze smelled of sea salt and roses. There would be walks on Eleo's private beach. Eleo assigned Bill a room overlooking the tennis court. The furnishings in the room, and throughout the house, were not new. They had the worn patina of age and looked as though they had been in the family for generations. It was all as it should be. Like a tourist in a distant and exotic country, Bill brought along his cameras, the slide camera and the new Polaroid that took instant pictures. He photographed the flower-encircled tennis court and the steep rock wall that separated the house from the sea. He took pictures of the noble Tudor stable, and of Eleo shaking hands with her pinto pony, Sugar Plum. Eleo posed for Bill, leaning against a column at the front of the house. She even let him snap her in her brown bathing suit, towel in hand, as she headed for her morning laps in the ocean. After a few days in Prides, Bill returned home with life lessons for his children about the importance of conversing without fidgeting, the significance of eye contact and good posture, and the polite way to eat soup.

Bill had grown up in a large, boisterous, working-class family. He always thought of them, his family, as consummately good, generous people who would give you the shirt off their backs. For reasons he never understood and could never articulate, he had always felt dissatisfied, at odds with the stained, bustling sidewalks outside his window. The Great Depression scarred his teenage years. He was thirteen when it began.

Bill idolized his father, a strong, handsome man who had found work for his large hands in a butcher shop. Even during the darkest days of the Depression, there was always meat on the family table. Scarce funds were invested in a violin and a series of lessons that Bill wanted. The burden of justifying this expense was lightened when Bill won a medal in a music contest and played his violin on a radio program. In school he was inspired by the sixteenth-century philosopher Michel de Montaigne, who argued in favor of intellectual freedom. At home in the shower, Bill sang arias from *Rigoletto* and *La Bohème,* and he brooded and yearned for something beyond.

One day while heading home, Bill turned a corner and saw a man selling apples from a carton on the sidewalk. It was a banal sight during those hard times, but this particular apple seller would haunt him for decades. The man was about his father's age. He wore a carefully pressed suit with a clean white shirt and a spotless tie. His fedora was neatly brushed and creased at the top just so, and his shoes had a fresh coat of polish. He might have worked in an office once, or in a nice store. Maybe he had a wife who had washed and ironed his shirt and had straightened his tie before sending him into the street to sell apples. Perhaps he had children, maybe a boy. . . . The man stood gallantly beside the carton with a hand-lettered sign that read, "FRESH APPLES, 10¢," in his good clothes, prepared by these small acts that preserved his dignity, and he tried to look welcoming, not tired or needy, as people hurried by.

Bill worked at a series of jobs throughout his teenage and college years because he needed the money. He rather liked the job he had one summer as a waiter at a mountain resort, though it was demanding work. Bill always placed a premium on efficiency, on economy of movement that produced maximum results, and that summer he took enormous pride in being able to clear off a crowded dinner table in one trip. He practiced over a bed until he could make a bouquet of six or eight dinner plates, which provided a stable base for the cups and silverware he piled into the center. Two female guests at the resort that summer slipped their room keys into his pocket. He was flattered, but he swore that he never took them up on their offers. Some of the jobs Bill had were numbing. Machinery was expensive and people were cheap. He froze while wrestling giant packing crates into and out of trucks at a loading dock during a subzero winter. It got worse during long stretches of the Depression when no one was hiring. Bill knocked on doors and asked to do whatever work was available. He stood in a shop office, which was dangling a job he didn't want that paid pennies an hour, where the boss looked him over like a slab of beef and told him to turn around before saying, "No." Many times Bill was told he was too young, too old, too inexperienced; there was nothing for him. He longed for a day when he could tell them to go to hell. More than once, after a fruitless day of job hunting, too demoralized to go home, Bill took refuge at the movies. A dime bought the cool darkness of a movie palace and a double feature. Bill's favorites were the westerns, the great Tom Mix and Tony, the Wonder Horse, who came when Tom whistled. Tom Mix wore a white hat, and when battling bad guys, he let his guns do the talking. Mix jumped on Tony's back from a rooftop to escape a trap, and he could rely on his horse to pull him to safety as he dangled precariously over a cliff.

Bill majored in psychology in college, which is how he met his wife, Evangeline, "Vangie." During a class that gave students practice in giving and taking psychological tests, Vangie administered the "Wiggly Blocks" test, and Bill was one of her test subjects. Vangie's mother saw no promise in her daughter's future with Bill, who had little to offer then beyond good looks and a blue suit. It was Vangie's father who noticed that his new son-in-law had a facility with numbers and suggested a career in accounting, rather than psychology, as a more likely path to a decent living. To a remarkable degree, Bill's accounting practice was built on serendipity, on being in the right place at the right time, as he was with Eleo, which was fortunate because Bill retained a lifelong abhorrence of asking for work.

Many of Bill's earliest clients gave him increasing roles in their business affairs and, owing in large measure to Vangie's knack for relationships, became family friends. But Bill's association with Eleo was of a different order of magnitude. As thrilled as Vangie was by his new horizons, and even though she knew her worries were entirely unfounded, she could not resist worrying that among the irresistible attractions at Rock Edge was the presence of the ice skating star Tenley Albright. Vangie's imagined rival was at that time training to be a surgeon, and was, as Vangie was acutely aware, much younger, with an athletically toned body, and a history of triumphing over adversity that Bill was sure to find appealing. All this had led Eleo to single Tenley out.

When Tenley Albright was a child, she persuaded her father to flood their backyard so she could try out the new skates she had received as a Christmas present. Doctors encouraged Tenley's interest in skating as a form of rehabilitation after she was stricken with nonparalytic polio at the age of eleven. Tenley began to skate regularly at the Skating Club in Boston, and, for a while, she was indistinguishable from the other little girls who glided around the huge rink. But gradually her perseverance and artistic flair separated her from the pack. The hard-driving, gravel-voiced skating coach Maribel Vinson Owen noticed that when Tenley tried new moves on the ice, like sit spins or jumps, repeated falls only made her work harder. Maribel supervised Tenley's training and coached her to multiple U.S. and World titles, and to the silver medal in the 1952 Olympics. It amused Eleo to hear her friend Maribel roar, "Smile!!!!" as Tenley gravely practiced her figures and free-skate program. Tenley was able to combine skating practice at four in the morning and after-school ballet lessons with a full academic schedule, and later with a premed curriculum at Radcliffe. Ten days before the 1956 Winter Olympics in Cortina, Italy, Tenley hit a rut in the ice during an outdoor training session and her skate blade cut a two-inch gash in her right ankle. Tenley's father, Dr. Hollis Albright, a Boston surgeon, flew to Italy and found his daughter in bed, barely able to walk. For both father and daughter it was a highly charged moment when, after the figure skating competition, Tenley stood spotlighted on the top of the medal platform with the Italian mountains in the background as her national anthem played. For the U.S. Olympic Team, Tenley's victory was a sorely needed bright spot in an otherwise dismal showing. America's Cold War rival, the U.S.S.R., participating in its first Winter Olympics, had out-medaled all thirty-two of the nations that competed. Tenley's win represented half of America's entire gold medal count in the 1956 Winter Games.[6]

Following her Olympic victory, Tenley retired from amateur figure skating and entered medical school to work on her next goal, to become a surgeon like her father. Tenley's floral lab coat stood out brightly from the drab standard-issue coats that her colleagues at Harvard Medical School wore as they made their rounds. Eleo's friendship and financial generosity smoothed out bumps along Tenley's chosen path.

Tenley left her upper-middle-class life to begin a dazzling new chapter when she moved into Eleo's house in Prides Crossing. There were dinners at the top restaurants in Boston and New York and evenings at the theater. There were excursions on Eleo's private train to the Harvard-Yale football games in New Haven. There was travel to England, where Prince Aly Khan joined them in Eleo's box for the Grand National Steeplechase races and flirted with Tenley. Eleo took the whole Albright family under her wing. A good word from Eleo eased the entry of Tenley's brother into Harvard and the Porcellian Club.

Tenley treated Eleo and a group of Eleo's friends to a performance of her winning Olympic program that was choreographed to the barcarole from Offenbach's *Tales of Hoffmann*. Her original performance had inspired the Olympic audience to hum along to the music. Eleo could barely contain her admiration for her protégé when she discussed Tenley's performance with her cousin John Sears. "She is wonderful," Eleo told John, "way above everyone else, and such a darling—."[7] Eleo's affection came as a torrent of gifts, clothes, and jewelry, including a diamond necklace made from a cross that had belonged to Eleo's mother. Eleo told Tenley that one day she would have the prized ruby ring that Eleo had been given by Isabella Stewart Gardner. Eleo assured Tenley that her future would be secure.

Though Tenley's determination and competitive drive were beyond dispute, Eleo's friends were interested to notice that around Eleo, Tenley often appeared deferential and shy. Before Eleo, Tenley had little experience with horses and she was ill at ease among horse people, whose jargon-laced conversation combined a layer of snobbery with an unexpected egalitarian streak. Horse people shared a bond that cut across class lines—they all stepped in the same horse manure and hit the same hard ground when they fell. Eleo gave Tenley a gift that to Eleo was beyond price, the ownership of a soon-to-be-born foal. Tenley could name the baby and watch it grow and, Eleo hoped, develop into a great racehorse. Eventually Tenley came to appreciate the link shared by Olympic contenders and racehorses. Both were propelled out of the gate time after time by a similar rush of adrenaline.

At Rock Edge, Eleo and Tenley often talked together long into the night, and when Eleo had difficulty falling asleep, Tenley sat by her bedside and read to her. For Eleo sleep rarely came easily. She told Bill Miller that she was regularly awakened during the night by a jittery feeling in her legs and that the discomfort was worse when she hadn't gotten enough exercise. The symptoms Eleo described are consistent with "nocturnal myoclonus," restless leg syndrome. The irony did not escape her. She had made exercise a cornerstone of her life, and now she wasn't able to stop even if she wanted to.

Eleo rewrote her will to leave nearly her entire estate to Tenley. Tenley's athletic skill and her tenacious pursuit of her goals made her seem like a reincarnation of Eleo's youthful self. Eleo had come to love Tenley as a daughter, as a graceful and desirable young woman, and as a sliver of immortality. Eleo included her "Man of Business" in her hopes for the future. She asked Bill Miller to promise never to leave her, and to stay on for ten years after her death to administer her estate and to look after Tenley. For that service, and for acting as cotrustee with Tenley of her charitable Eleonora Randolph Sears Foundation, Eleo arranged to leave Bill a bequest equal to 5 percent of her estate. This snapshot of the future, the promise of financial security for his family and a continuing role in Eleo's legacy, left Bill breathless. He advised Eleo to open her foundation with a tax-advantaged gift of appreciated shares from her holdings of IBM stock.

Bill had learned a variety of lessons from his youth, the main one being the importance of constructing a stable core, both emotional and financial, that would see him securely through an uncertain future. To build his financial base, Bill studied books on investment philosophy. He was always conscious of the need for a margin of safety, though he enjoyed placing large, risky bets—he liked to say that the difference between a good investment idea and a great idea, between a hundred shares of a stock and a thousand shares, was just a zero. He had done quite well for himself on balance. Eleo entrusted Bill to watch over her finances and he took that mission very much to heart. Eleo was a forceful advocate, in theory, for frugality and conservation of her assets, but her definition was very different from her accountant's, and it became a source of friction between them. The conflict came to a head over a horse named Mitochondria. Nancy Sweet-Escott had taken charge of training Eleo's race horses after Hartmann Pauly and a successor had left the picture. Her results were not inspiring. Bill Miller quickly lost patience with her quirky methods and ideas, which seemed to him, from a business standpoint, frivolous and impractical.

Mitochondria had recently been gelded and Sweet-Escott thought the horse seemed depressed. She decided that shipping Mitochrondria from Burrland Farm in Virginia to Southern Pines, for the change of scene and the marginally warmer climate, might improve his mood. The farm manager at Burrland took the extraordinary step of telephoning Bill, long-distance, on a Sunday morning in March 1959, to ask if Bill would authorize the expense of shipping the horse. Bill told him flatly, "No!" Bill learned later from Sweet-

Escott that exactly the opposite was done—the horse had been shipped, and Eleo had agreed to pay the trucking charges from her personal account.

Bill erupted. He mailed a three-page tirade to Eleo, written in his neat, compact script, that began with the warning "RUN FOR SHELTER, THERE'S A STORM COMING!" "Why," he demanded, "was I bothered on the telephone Sunday morning if no one was going to pay attention to me anyway?!!! Can we afford to play practical jokes long-distance?" Eleo had put *him* in charge of her racing business, Bill reminded her, and he had been made to look like an "idiot" before her employees. She had made him "boss" and instructed him to pull everything together and ensure "that we do not throw our capital to the four winds." He had not sought such authority, but had it "thrust" upon him, and, therefore, he had a right to expect that his decisions would be honored: "If I say we go off the cliff, we go off the cliff. *That* is what being a boss means." Bill told Eleo that once she placed her people in a position of author-ity, she should "*back us up or fire us.*" "Fortunately," Bill continued, "I have the courage and confidence and the financial resources to enable me to speak plainly and to the point. And—that I'm doing. . . . I will not stay with you only to see you torn apart by well-meaning employees." As Bill saw it, he was busy down in the engine room ensuring clear sailing for the racing business, while "you two girls are having so much fun on top deck. . . . [You] will blissfully dance along until we smack into a reef." Next he took on Sweet-Escott directly, venting his frustration with Eleo's horse trainer while obviously iden-tifying with the horse in question. "All this about the horse feeling better in S. P. [Southern Pines] is a lot of hogwash," he told Eleo. "Why the hell didn't we send him there before he was gelded. All these people running around with knives cutting horses and then being kind to them! . . . I am not in love with her,—you are, and so far, she is just another so-called trainer."[8]

For Bill, being treated as a mere figurehead threatened more than his self-respect. Eleo pounced on weakness. Bill understood that if he allowed him-self to be stepped on, to look weak in her eyes, the wound was mortal. He did not understand something far more delicate.

"Dear Mr. Miller," Eleo wrote back immediately, "I have never in all my long life received such a letter as I received from you to-day—How dare you say that I am in love with Mrs. Sweet-Escott." Eleo went on to explain curtly that she had decided to pay for the horse van because of a misunderstanding of his plan for allocating funds. "I do not understand what you mean about being 'Boss' no one has asked you not to be—," and she concluded coldly, "Sincerely E.R.S—."[9]

Bill was stunned. He had let his emotions spill over and could scarcely recall the specifics of what he had written. He had, accidentally, touched a nerve he hadn't even realized was there. He comprehended only that Eleo had taken grave offense and given him "a blow on the head" for using "some language that I've heard you use time and again." As to the main point of his letter, hadn't she herself told him, "'Guard my capital for me.' . . . Where do I stop guarding it? . . . I know exactly how a well-trained dog must feel after being punished for doing exactly that which he has been trained to do." Bill was contrite: "Had you really believed me about my being so fond of you, you could not have interpreted my letter so harshly and been so hurt by it." He begged Eleo to return his letter so he could burn it, as he was returning hers and hoping for the same. He saw, too late, that he had been carried away with his own dream of seeing Eleo's racing stable surpass all the other great names in racing. He had let his zeal "blot out the fact that it is all your money, your horses, and your show . . . and that my fifty reasons are unimportant next to your one big reason—namely, that you want to have fun and are not concerned primarily with cost, as I am." He ended, "Please sign your letters 'As ever' again. I'm sorry. . . . Always idiotically yours, *WBM*."[10]

And so the storm passed, and the sailing was calm once again.

Despite Eleo's Herculean outlays, the results of her racing enterprise were depressingly lackluster. Wins were rare and her patience was running out. Only Sizzling, a two-year-old bred by the Sears stable, was showing any real promise, with a victory in the Jeanne d'Arc Handicap at Narragansett. Overall, the Sears Racing Stable was having no luck, and even worse, Eleo's efforts seemed stalked by bad luck—"stinking luck," Eleo called it. The five-year-old Tudorka, the $75,000 yearling she had bought with so much hope, had returned only a pitiful $4,580 during his racing career. Tenley's foal was born sickly and did not survive. Eleo had understood that racing was a gamble when she got into it, and she was philosophical, saying, "Just because you lose a match doesn't mean you quit playing the game."[11] But she knew a jolt was needed. Eleo decided to let bygones be bygones and she turned to Jimmy Rowe, the smiling redhead who had ridden for her in the 1930s and then had left her.

Jimmy Rowe was by this time a well-respected horse trainer with an admirable record of success, though early on he had run into some lean years. He wrote to Eleo then, to ask if she had an opening at her stable. Her reply was brief, but not unkind—she had "*no* vacancy at present." "Best of wishes to you," she signed off—she still had a soft spot for him.[12] In the winter of 1960 Eleo dispatched Tom Greene to reestablish contact with Jimmy, who was working for one of Eleo's cousins, Mrs. Quincy Shaw McKean, the tennis champion and former Kay Winthrop. Tom Greene arranged for Jimmy to meet Eleo at Madison Square Garden, and he gave Jimmy a heads-up that Eleo would invite him to be the new trainer for her racing stable, and that the starting salary would be $12,000. The job had tremendous appeal, but the salary was barely adequate to support Jimmy's young family. Jimmy asked

Tom if he thought Miss Sears might sweeten the offer. "Talk to her," Tom advised. "You might as well. . . . She's got it."13 Eleo was in a marvelous mood during the eight-day National Horse Show. Five of her horses were entered and all five won ribbons. Reno, Sidonia, Radar, and Among the Stars were then, and would be for many years, practically unbeatable in the Working Hunter division. Her phenomenal Pike's Peak also took the Conformation Hunter Championship. Jimmy Rowe too left the Garden happy. Eleo had agreed to a base salary of $15,000, plus 10 percent of all race winnings.

Jimmy Rowe was delighted with every aspect of his new situation. Eleo was "a grand lady to train for," Jimmy recalled. "She never asked you about anything, about bills or anything, training bills—*What had to be done, had to be done*."14 Eleo hoped that Jimmy would be able to bring her horses "back to life" after Nancy Sweet-Escott's poor showing with them. And Eleo offered her new trainer some motherly advice, "Take care of yourself and don't drink too much beer—you look better when you are thin—!!"15 Within less than a year, Jimmy had Eleo's horses in the best condition of their lives, and during a two-month stretch at Suffolk Downs, six of her horses won nine races. People in the business started to take notice. For years, they had been pleased to add up all the money Eleo was spending, and now they started to tote up the wins. The best was yet to come.

Spicy Living was a home-bred yearling, and the youngster was showing incredible speed. She had some of the Thoroughbred world's finest blood coursing through her veins. Eleo had purchased her mother, Rivaz, sired by the great Nearco, from the Aga Khan stables. Rivaz had been a champion runner in Europe, and she was a full sister to Nasrullah, upon whom the Aga Khan line had been built. The Sears stable mated Rivaz with the long-distance champion Gallant Man. The culmination of Rivaz's eleven-and-a-half-month pregnancy was awaited with the anticipation that attended a royal birth. After the filly princess was born, Bill Miller sat with a legal pad at his kitchen table, writing down names and scratching them out. He wanted to come up with a name for the new arrival that was fitting and unusual enough to register with the Jockey Club. He tried various combinations of syllables in the names of her sire and dam. There were such high expectations wrapped up in this youngster. Then he had it: "Spicy Living"! The E. R. Sears Racing Stable had spent so many years in the wilderness—didn't they deserve that?

Eleo's racing operation at Burrland Farm was in the heart of the high-rent district of Middleburg, Virginia, where, it was said, there were more millionaires per square mile than in any other section of the country. The Paul Mellon family entertained Queen Elizabeth and Prince Philip and the Crown Prince of Japan at their sumptuous Little Oak Spring farm. Middleburg was also a part-time home for a number of Eleo's Boston friends, including Eleo's great favorites C. Z. and Winston Guest. Eleo broke her own rule about keeping outsiders off her place and let Winston use stall space at Burrland to house his two-year-olds. Foxhunting was the neighborhood passion, and slackers were not welcome. "I saw a boy riding with his coat unbuttoned the other day," a Middleburg matron complained, "and I wanted to throw up."[16]

The newest arrivals in the Middleburg neighborhood were the John F. Kennedys. They rented the tastefully appointed Glen Ora estate south of the village, down the road from Eleo's farm. The presidential entourage commuted between Washington, D.C., and Middleburg and wreaked havoc in the tranquil horse community. "We really have a time with the yearlings when the president and his family fly in with three helicopters," Jimmy Rowe grumbled. "They fly right over the training track and the young horses really go crazy."[17] Jackie was often seen riding Bit of Irish on the paths bordering her property, with little Caroline alongside on her pony. Jackie could not avoid disrupting the peaceful enclave of seven hundred horse lovers. A Secret Service detachment trailed her, and reporters from across the United States and Great Britain camped out at the rustic Red Fox Tavern in the village. Yet the First Lady managed to charm even her husband's most vehement opponents. She was invited to join the neighborhood Orange County Hunt, though her doctor advised her to limit her jumping until she was fully recovered from the caesarean section she had undergone during the birth of her son, John Jr. The president was not included in the invitation to join. "He doesn't hunt," said Thomas F. Furness, president of the Hunt, without any hint of regret. "He's too busy."[18]

Most of Eleo's property in Virginia was low-tax farmland, but Burrland's main dwelling, the elegant Georgian brick mansion, entailed a significant tax liability. The house was one of the jewels of the property, but Eleo had never bothered with it. In the five years since she purchased the farm, the main house had stood empty. Eleo never furnished it, and when she visited Burrland she stayed in one of the cottages on the property, or in town at the Red Fox Tavern. Eleo resented the tax burden of the house, and the presidential election of 1960 spurred her to poke a stick in the eye of the tax dragon. President-elect John Fitzgerald Kennedy, who had snatched the Massachusetts Senate seat from her cousin Henry Cabot Lodge in 1952, had now quashed her cousin's bid to be vice president. In Eleo's view, Kennedy, the rascally son of a rascally Irish father and grandfather, was poised to run the whole country into the ground. That dismal prospect left her in no mood to pay taxes of any kind, and certainly not on a place she never used. Eleo contracted with a young realtor in the Middleburg area, John Talbot, to demolish the Burrland house. Talbot concluded that the most efficient, cost-effective way to accomplish that was to burn it down. Anything that could be salvaged, the decorative hardware, the doors, the slate from the roof, was removed, and the boxwood maze at the back of the house was dug up. All the salvaged parts found new life on other buildings in Middleburg and the surrounding counties. On Inauguration Day 1961, while a light snow fell and the town's fire chief looked on, a group of hired men filled the closets inside the house with straw and doused the building with diesel fuel. Then they ran around outside the house throwing lighted matches through the windows. The sturdy old building, dampened by the snow, took three hours to catch fire, leaving Talbot ample time to worry that if it didn't burn and Eleo didn't pay him, he would loose his shirt after all the money he had laid out. The blaze, when it finally caught, was spectacular and could be seen for miles. The four Doric columns that stood two stories high at the front entrance to the house did not burn, and they proved too big to bury in the rubble. The columns were rescued and reused by their previous owner, William Ziegler.[19]

As Bill Miller and Jimmy Rowe worked in their different spheres for Eleo's racing business, they developed great respect for one another and came to feel like comrades in the same cause. Bill concluded that Eleo's latest trainer was that hoped-for combination—a true professional who was knowledgeable and honest and always tried to do his best. Bill got on well with most of Eleo's employees: Mrs. Slowe, keeper of the household accounts; Tom Greene, now semiretired but still in charge of the mechanics who kept Eleo's cars running and the wooden sides of her Mini-Morris varnished; and Jessie, Eleo's personal maid, who, after decades with Eleo, knew where everything was and when it was needed. Jessie laid out Eleo's clothes and kept her confidences. Eleo had come to depend on her maid's calming, competent presence. For nearly anything a visitor might need, Eleo would say with enormous warmth, "Ask Jessie, my Jessie will know." It was a blow to Eleo's entire household when Jessie announced tearfully that it was time for her to retire. She hoped to spend her final years with what remained of her family in Ireland. Finding a replacement for such an irreplaceable person was a daunting task. Eleo was always extremely cautious before she hired anyone to work in her home. During one National Horse Show, Eleo summoned Mrs. Walter Devereux, the wife of the show's president, to her box. "Bunnie" Devereux was a shy woman and she waited uncomfortably as Eleo rummaged through her purse and retrieved a crumbled bit of paper. Reading from the paper, Eleo questioned her, "Do you know Molly O'Hare?" After a bit of thought, Bunnie could not recall her. Eleo was incredulous, "Well, she cooked for you. Is she a good cook? Does she drink?"

The men working at Eleo's stable in Prides thought that Eleo had hired Jessie's replacement, Marie Gendron, during a trip to Europe, because the new housekeeper just seemed to show up one day. Eleo had actually found her through an employment agency recommended by her cousin Mrs. Robert Winthrop. Marie Gendron came with good references. She had been a seamstress and had taught French, and, at one time, she had been a sort of a governess-chaperone to the daughter of a New York attorney when the girl was traveling through her native France. Just by being French, Marie Gendron's qualifications for the job were assumed. The most fashionable households were staffed by French help. Eleo's new housekeeper, Madame Gendron spoke very competent English, but the point was to speak French to the help if one had traveled widely and been properly educated, and Eleo was fluent. Bill Miller thought Gendron seemed rather cold, but Eleo liked her, and it was none of his business anyway. He knew only menu French.

America woke up on February 15, 1961, to the incomprehensible news that an airplane had crashed in Belgium, four miles from the Brussels airport, and all on board, including the entire U.S. World Figure Skating Team, had perished. The team, its coaches, officials, family members, and friends, had been headed to the World Championships in Prague. The flight had taken off the previous day, Valentine's Day, and before boarding the small Sabena Boeing 707, the team had posed for a group photo, smiling on the stairway up to the jet. Twice the plane circled the airport before it fell suddenly out of a blue, cloudless sky, striking a grove of trees at a 70-degree angle. Shrapnel from the explosion killed a young farmer in his field and tore off the leg of another. The seventy-three people on board the plane were incinerated as flames and smoke mushroomed above the trees. The only survivor of the inferno was a German shepherd dog who had been in the cargo hold, but the dog was so badly injured that a police officer shot him. On the plane, in addition to the crew members and international passengers, was Tenley Albright's coach, Maribel Vinson Owen, and her two daughters, both skating champions, twenty-year-old "little" Maribel and sixteen-year-old Laurence. Also onboard were two U.S. Ladies Singles medalists, three North American Men's medalists, two brother-and-sister teams, three pairs of dance medalists, the husband-and-wife dance team of Patricia and Robert Dineen, who had decided at the last minute not to take their nine-month-old son along, three international judges, and Dan McMinn, the team manager. They had all known that disaster was coming. Many of the charred bodies were found in the crash position.[20]

As news of the tragedy filtered back home throughout the morning, skaters from the greater Boston area were pulled as if by a magnetic force to the Boston Skating Club. Nobody ventured onto the newly groomed ice. A shaft of sunlight stretched down through the window of the hangerlike building and turned the huge space into a cathedral. Just past seven o'clock in the morning, eighty-year-old Gertrude Vinson, matriarch of the First Family of Figure Skating, mother of Maribel and grandmother of Laurence and "little" Maribel, was visited by Dr. Hollis Albright and two of Mrs. Vinson's friends. Wanting to soften the blow, they arrived early, before she had heard the news bulletins flashed over the airwaves. Tenley's father administered a sedative to

"Grammy" Vinson under the guise of giving her a flu shot, and her two friends began speaking about the hazards of air travel. Grammy understood. Before she knew about the fate of her close-knit family, she said, "If one's gone, I hope they're all gone, because one can't live without the others."[21]

Eleo and Tenley had known everyone on the team. After the bodies were identified and flown home, Eleo and Tenley joined the families on the heartbreaking round of funerals and packed memorial services, where telegrams of condolence were read from President Kennedy and Secretary of State Dean Rusk. The distraught families returned home to sort through the belongings of their vanished members, cancel appointments on their calendars, bring home their dry cleaning, and cry over their trophies. The most commonplace items took on magical significance, and each new find brought fresh pain as though from a phantom limb—a blouse with a missing button, an orphaned sock, a comical tennis-sized ball made of scraps of tin foil that was forgotten in the back of a kitchen drawer. No one wanted these things now, but discarding them felt like a betrayal.

Within days after the crash, the U.S. Figure Skating Association established the World Figure Skating Team Memorial Fund. The fund was to be a "living memorial" that would award skating and academic scholarships to the promising athletes of the future. Eleo anchored the fund with a large gift. Tenley and Dick Button were the headliners of a memorial ice skating show held at the Boston Garden. During the intermission, the twelve-year-old U.S. Novice Champion, Tina Noyes, went among the audience with a tin can, which was quickly filled with donations.

Chilled by this lesson of mortality and random fate, Eleo and Bill Miller fine-tuned her will. Two desirable goals, avoiding the large estate tax and enhancing Eleo's historical legacy, could be made to coincide, as Bill explained to Eleo in what he called "one of the most important letters I have ever written to you."[22] After considerable study, Bill endorsed the idea of bequeathing one million dollars to the Eleonora Randolph Sears Foundation, rather than give it to Tenley outright. Bill reasoned that federal and state taxes would eat up more than two-thirds of the money if Tenley received it directly. As a trustee of the E. R. Sears Foundation, Tenley could control the entire tax-free amount and would reap, Bill said, "great influence and power that will do her more good than the $270,000 she would get from the $1,000,000 after taxes." Bill also recommended that Tenley direct the foundation's money to build "the Eleonora Randolph Sears Clinic for Children, or whatever else Tenley thinks is most helpful to needy, sick people." Marshaling all his powers of persuasion to assure this outcome, Bill invoked Eleo's revered ancestor. Bill told Eleo that Thomas Jefferson "always worked for the public good and I want the world to keep remembering you not only as a great athlete . . . but as the generous person that I and your friends know you are." As to his own financial interest in her will, Bill acknowledged that, if these proposals were carried out, he would be a net loser. None of the foundation's money, nor the money in another trust planned for Tenley, would figure into his percentage. He asked that his percentage be raised slightly on this "*radically*" lowered base, which would still result in a loss for him. "I am giving up my money for the idea," Bill told Eleo, "so you know how much it means to me."[23] Bill was a romantic at heart, and burnishing Eleo's legend for posterity meant more to him than a cold calculation of dollars and cents. He was highly conscious of the accident of fortune that had brought him to his treasured place with Eleo Sears, as her trusted advisor, as the vice president of her racing stable, and, within hierarchical social limits, as her friend. Beneath his dark business suit and tie, Bill was a knight defending the interests of his lord, both then and into the hereafter.

These days death was often on Eleo's mind. It was impossible not to sag after the loss of so many dear friends. Ethel Barrymore was gone, from a heart attack, and Gretchen Warren from graceful old age. Eleo took Mabel Storey along with her when she went to Charlie Geigan's funeral. Charlie had managed Eleo's stable in Prides. Originally, he had come east from California and, when he interviewed for the job, Eleo had sent him away, complaining that he was too expensive. She reconsidered and hired him the next day. After Charlie developed heart trouble and had to stop working, Eleo had Tom Greene take his check to him at his daughter's house on the first day of every month. To honor Charlie, Eleo and Mabel attended their first Catholic wake at St. Mary's Church in Brookline. Charlie's relatives wondered about the two ladies sitting in the back of the church who had arrived in the chauffeur-driven maroon Rolls Royce.

Outwardly, through it all, Eleo seemed to remain as she had always been, defiantly vigorous and handsome, her skin fissured but glowing and firm like a well-cared-for saddle. Rather than surrender to the ravages of age, she appeared to keep her focus on the future. Her delight in her horses was undimmed, the racing stable was now a source of pride, and she still swam and rode nearly every day. She rode her golden palomino with a western saddle, making sure he was not lazy about doing his tricks. For a while Eleo researched the breeding of quarter horses. To the resounding shock of a friend's young son, this elderly, white-haired lady borrowed his quarter horse, and for a week she reveled in its speed and hairpin spins. While in Southern Pines, Eleo tried out a newly acquired polo pony, Rosinda, but she was not impressed. Eleo wrote to Jimmy Rowe about her, "She is just exactly what I don't like—slow and not cheerful going," and she shipped Rosinda to Burrland, where Jimmy put her to use as a lead pony for the race horses.[24]

Eleo was blessed also in having friends who knew enough to take her growling with a grain of salt. The years had not increased Eleo's tolerance for insincerity or softened her handling of nincompoops who crossed her path. A new man on staff at Myopia greeted her erroneously and far too effusively for her taste. "Good morning to you, *Mrs.* Sears," he gushed with a big toothy smile. Eleo practically flew over to Mabel Storey, who was on the Myopia hiring committee. "Who is that Ipana commercial you've got working here?" Eleo demanded, referring to a popular toothpaste brand. "Fire him!" she commanded dramatically, knowing full well that Mabel would do no such thing.

Eleo continued to take almost childlike pleasure in surprising her friends. At a Wine and Food Society event, Eleo sipped Château Mouton Rothschild and chatted with Mabel Storey's daughter, Ruthie, Ruthie's husband, and some friends of theirs. They all savored the expensive nectar, and the two giddy young couples decided it would be really swell to drink it on a regular basis. Laughingly, they asked Eleo to see what she could do about that. The following afternoon, an astonished Ruthie and her friend were on the telephone with each other, exclaiming, "You'll never believe what was just delivered to my door!" Both had received an entire case of the Château Mouton.

September 28, 1961, was Eleo's eightieth birthday, and Mabel Storey hosted a luncheon for her. It came seven months after the plane crash, but it was not a melancholy affair. If anything, the recent tragedy made the gathering sweeter. Mabel had rallied the staff, and there was much good food and cake and fine Champagne for the toasts. Tenley made a lovely speech about her gratitude to Eleo for all her help and support, and she echoed the sentiments in the room when she recalled how Eleo's enthusiasms and sense of fun had embraced them all through the years.

Nobody gave much thought to Marie Gendron, who busied herself in the background.

CHAPTER 19

Endgame

ANY PEOPLE MADE substantial efforts to penetrate the shroud that Marie V. Gendron slipped over the details of her life. They hoped to uncover some fact that would derail her or might explain her. Marie Gendron lived to be one hundred years old.

Only this much is known:

She came from France, from an area not near Paris.

She had been married to a Mr. Shank when she was seventeen, though that was not discovered until much later, and would, most likely, have changed nothing.

She was a devout Roman Catholic. She became a U.S. citizen and registered to vote as a Republican.

She was in America during the war years, leaving behind in France a mother and a brother named Victor, who may have died during the war.

In her last years she fantasized about returning to them.

She was, as she believed herself to be, a shrewd judge of people and a capable steward of her inheritance.

She grew increasingly silent during her long, final decline. Her last intelligible words were, "La guerre, la guerre . . ."

She died, remembered by few, loved by no one.

When she was in her prime, she did great damage.

At one stage of her life, Madame Gendron was known simply as Marie. Eleo called her "Vicki," a play on her middle name, Victorine. Most people referred to her as "Madame," and using the American pronunciation, which accented the first syllable, brought a quick, stern rebuke. When Eleo met her, Marie Gendron was middle-aged and thickset, with a prominent Roman nose, dark eyes, and straight, chin-length, salt-and-pepper hair: not someone who would normally rate a second look.

Within a startlingly few months of her arrival, Madame Gendron planted herself in Eleo's home and began to peel away Eleo's attachments of a life-time. Madame's icy presence became an increasingly lethal repellant. Eleo accepted fewer and fewer invitations and only those that included her new companion and friend, Madame Gendron. Eleo's household staff was reduced in number as Madame found fault with one worker after another and dismissed them.

Mabel Storey visited Rock Edge one evening to have dinner with Eleo, and she was astounded when Madame joined them at the dinner table. After the meal Eleo began to clear away the dirty dishes and Mabel expressed her shock. A clearly annoyed Madame explained to Mabel that since she had pre-pared the meal, it was only fair that Eleo clean it up. Mabel had never been bashful about sharing her opinions, and she was characteristically blunt in advising Eleo, "Get rid of her!" Mabel's continuing insistence on this point caused Eleo to turn on her with fury and, after years of devoted friendship, to sever all contact with her. Mabel's daughter, Ruthie, had spent the summer in Maine with her in-laws and had not heard of the "big falling-out" between her mother and Eleo. Ruthie greeted Eleo affectionately when she saw her standing next to her car at the Myopia Horse Show. As Ruthie was walking away, she heard Madame ask Eleo gruffly, "Who's that? Who's that?"

Mabel's husband and son were also struck by Eleo's sudden alteration. They had been among Eleo's favorite people over the years, and she had always been extremely welcoming to them, but when they visited Rock Edge after Madame arrived, they found Eleo oddly detached. Eleo barely spoke to either of them, and they wondered uncomfortably, if she possibly had been drugged. Soon after, they received a note from Madame telling them that Eleo did not to wish see them again.

Another unsettling visit to Rock Edge was made by Richard Thorndike, who had known Eleo since he was a boy. Richard had grown up on the North Shore. His grandparents, the Neal Rantouls, were longtime residents and knew Eleo well. Richard was twelve or thirteen when he began hanging around Eleo's big stable, willfully ignoring the No Trespassing signs that Eleo had posted because he enjoyed seeing the horses and was fascinated by the meticulous way the stable was kept. He examined all the details, the gleam-ing brass trim and the carefully placed half moons of straw matting outside each stall door. The stable hands permitted this neighbor's boy to wander at will, but they worried that Eleo might discover their indulgence. If Richard was there when Eleo made an unannounced visit to the stable, the grooms quickly stashed him in the hay chute. The day came when Eleo caught Richard at the stable and she came after him with a buggy whip. Richard instinctively began to run, but then he turned and grabbed the end of the whip, and he told her that he intended to own her stable one day, after she had passed away, and he wanted to learn how to keep it looking so nice. His audacity stopped Eleo in her tracks and made her smile, and through the years Richard remained on excellent terms with her. Then Madame arrived and, as was widely noted, "Everything came to screeching halt."[1] Madame Gendron told Richard that Eleo would not be able to see him when he telephoned one day for an appointment. Richard went anyway and Madame refused to let him in the front door. He pushed it open and insisted on having tea with Miss Sears alone. Madame permitted that, though her eyes narrowed and she slammed the door loudly on her way out of the room. Richard had the distinct impression that Madame pulled up a chair on the other side of the door and listened to his amiable conversation with Eleo for the entire forty-five minutes they were together. It saddened him profoundly to see what had been inconceivable only a short time before, a reversal where the general had become a foot soldier. Such a shift in power from the stronger to the weaker is seen in nature, where even a deeply rooted tree can be strangled by a vine.[2]

Madame Gendron wrote to Eleo of her passion for her, using images that were poetic, spiritual, soaring. She folded the note and left it for Eleo to find. It was addressed in a way that leveled the ground between them.

E.R.S. from M.V.G.

Mon âme soeur, grande
Chère âme qui fut trouvée au plus
bizarre et inattendue moment de
ma vie.
Elle existe cette âme, elle est réelle,
elle me transporte à la plus
haute cîme.
Oh Chère âme soeur, ne me laissez
jamais tomber dans les abîmes.
Ensemble nous pourrous
atteindre les plus hauts sommets
où seuls resident les aigles.

My soul's sister, great
Dear soul, who was found at the most
bizarre and unexpected moment of
my life.
It exists this soul, it is real,
it transports me to the
highest summit.
Oh Dear sister of my soul, never let me

fall into the abyss.
Together, we will
reach the highest peaks
where only eagles live.[3]

That Madame's feelings were reciprocated was evident in a letter Eleo sent to her. Madame had not been well and Eleo attended the races in Saratoga Springs without her during the summer of 1962. It was one of the rare occasions when she and Madame were apart. Eleo wrote to Gendron of her concern, "Darling Madame, You frighten me so when you feel ill. Please do not do it anymore. I love you so very very much and we could have such fun together. Please take care of yourself. I want you to be happy all the time."[4]

In her own venomous way, Marie Gendron did come to love Eleo, or at least to feel for her a glimmer of understanding and warmth. They were two lonely women, and they believed they were each other's last chance for happiness. They confided in each other their fears and disappointments. Tragically, Marie Gendron brought to the equation an attachment that was devouring and cruel. She had arrived at a sour, unattractive middle age, a time of life when most people begin to think of retirement. She was a maid in other people's big homes with nothing to show for her trouble, no money, no dear friends. It was not the life she felt she deserved. But now—against all the odds—she had stumbled on a treasure. Marie Victorine Gendron intended to hold on to it with every ounce of strength she possessed.

Rumors and accusations surrounding the relationship between Eleo and her housekeeper flew among family and friends who pooled their observations about Marie Gendron's increasingly effective psychological and, conceivably, chemical manipulation of Eleo. Visitors to Rock Edge were surprised to see that when Madame came down late for meals, as she often did, Eleo waited for her and refused to begin eating until she was seated. Frequently Madame appeared wearing something new and expensive, a necklace, a ruby ring, a fur wrap. There were reports that Eleo appeared nervous when Gendron was nearby, and that once she said something that Madame objected to, and Madame "shushed" her. A story circulated that one night Eleo had been found in town sitting on an orange crate. She was bruised and disoriented and was escorted home. Belatedly, this came to be seen as an attempt to escape. But Eleo was quick to refute any idea that she and Madame were other than inseparable. Eleo's insistence on this point became more vehement the more it was challenged. Many of Eleo's alarmed relatives consulted Bill Miller about their options for putting a stop to the relationship. A private detective was hired in the hope of uncovering something incriminating in Madame's background that could be shown to Eleo, but the investigation got sidetracked following a possibly different Marie Gendron from

Quebec who had spent time in Rio de Janeiro, and nothing useful was ever turned up. Various plans were floated for removing Eleo from her house-keeper's pernicious influence. Bill Miller knew that Eleo liked and trusted Jimmy Rowe, and he telephoned Jimmy with a desperate, impractical thought. "Jim," he said, "take her home with you before it's too late." Jimmy told Bill, "You know I got two bedrooms. The wife and I are in one and the kids are in the other. Where am I goin' to put her?"[5] It was crystal clear to everyone who worked for Eleo what was going on and what Marie Gendron was after. Thomas Greene discussed the scandal with Jimmy Rowe. Both men disliked having the proper order of things upset, and they were incensed to see Eleo being "chased by that lesbian bitch." Tom Greene asked Jimmy with dark humor if he couldn't find someone more appropriate for Eleo. Eleo's cousin Catherine Coolidge met with Helen Frick and a third friend to discuss mounting a rescue mission. They considered inviting Eleo to join them for lunch, alone, and then kidnapping her. But they recoiled from the specter of what was sure to be an appalling scene and the myriad difficulties that would follow. The plan never got past the talking stage.

In truth, by the time Eleo's friends had absorbed the shock of her light-ning transformation and regrouped, it was already too late. The bonds necessary to ensure Eleo's total, unshakable commitment to Marie Gendron were in place, and the astonished North Shore community could do little but watch from the sidelines as events played out and left behind the riveting car-nage of a train wreck. Marie Gendron had given Eleo the promise of abiding love in place of the distracted attention of her relatives and friends. Madame worked unceasingly to isolate Eleo from those relatives and friends, whom she painted as being guided entirely by self-interest and, therefore, unwor-thy of Eleo's love and trust. Madame consolidated her power over Eleo's emo-tions, over Eleo's finances, by alternately offering and withholding affection, by alternating outbursts of anger and jealousy with moments of great tender-ness, in a cycle designed to keep Eleo off balance. Those are precisely the techniques employed with devastating effect by all successful cult leaders. The people closest to Eleo could never comprehend how she, who had always been on guard against insincerity and double-dealing, could be so completely taken in. They worried that if Eleo was prey to such manipulation, might not their less vigilant, aging parents be at the mercy of their designing servants or nurses. Eleo had the misfortune to meet a person of uncommonly malevolent intent, with the skill to exploit her fears and resentments, just when she had reached a critical crossroads in her life. Though Eleo appeared to have kept old age at bay, it was clearly on her mind long before she met Marie Gendron. Eleo had alluded to her concern about it for years, signing fond letters to her cousin John Sears, "Your poor old doddering Cousin Eleo."[6] To an athlete like Eleo, an aging body was not a joke; it was a thief that made her feel vulnerable, and reaching the age of eighty was an unsettling milestone. Marie Gendron offered Eleo physical comfort, massaging away the inevitable aches of her hard-worked muscles and joints. She offered Eleo safe harbor in a world that was devious and treacherous, a world in which planes could fall out of the sky and vaporize your friends. She offered Eleo rock-solid devotion in place of the beloved girl Tenley Albright, who was getting married and leaving Rock Edge.

Because Eleo's deepest attachment was to Tenley, that extraction was the bloodiest and left the biggest scar. For all that, it was surprisingly simple. On New Year's Eve 1961 Tenley married Tudor Gardiner, a son of Boston's other noted Gardner family, the clan of the "one-eyed Gardiners." Tudor Gardiner was divorced, but he was otherwise superbly credentialed: college wrestler, Phi Beta Kappa, Porcellian Club, Somerset Club, a law degree, an M.A., and soon a Ph.D. in classical philosophy from Harvard. Eleo had met Tenley's prospective mate on several occasions and she halfheartedly approved of him. Tudor Gardiner was quite a bit older than Tenley, but he was not someone she really could object to. The wedding ceremony that joined the Albrights and the Gardiners was attended only by members of the two families. If Eleo had been there, the occasion would have taken on a far larger dimension, but Madame Gendron had already seen to it that Eleo would stay away. Eleo had dared to believe that Tenley would always be there for her, an adult child to supply the caring and companionship that enriched the homes of neighboring families. But the twenty-six-year-old Tenley would be starting her own family now, and however reasonable Eleo knew that prospect to be, it left an ache of abandonment and ingratitude after all that Eleo had given to her, and all that she was prepared to give. It made room for Madame's drumbeat of whispered doubts, especially the most crushing one, that Tenley had stayed with Eleo only for the money. In the months leading up to Tenley's wedding, Gendron had searched for and found a pile of bills for gifts that Eleo had bought for Tenley. Madame rifled through a desk drawer and found love letters that Tenley kept there. Their author may have been a neighbor of Eleo's, a journalist. Madame showed these letters to Eleo as proof of Tenley's secret life and duplicity.

Less than a month after Tenley's wedding, Eleo signed a new will, a will that, as only Bill Miller and Eleo's attorneys knew at the time, no longer included Tenley. Bill had recommended to Eleo at first that she proceed slowly and cautiously before drawing up any new will. He hoped that Eleo would relent during a cooling-off period. Once it was clear to Bill that Eleo would not be deterred, he worked with her to shape the new document to her satisfaction. He assured Eleo that regardless of what anyone else thought or did, she had the right to dispose of her money and property as she saw fit. "Tenley is well taken care of," Bill wrote to Eleo. "You have been kind to her and she appreciates everything you have done for her. After all, she is a decent person." Bill saw that he was powerless to save Tenley. He was saddened by that fact, but he mentally cut her loose and turned his attention to saving himself. The large bequest he was to get from Eleo for looking after Tenley was also gone, but he still had his job. He told Eleo that he understood that she was feeling "a bit troubled and confused by the actions of people around you." He assured Eleo, "*When the going gets tough, you can count on me. . . .* I want your respect and trust more than anything."[7]

Marie Gendron was included in Eleo's new will with a bequest of $50,000. What most distressed Bill was Eleo's directive to begin closing down the Eleonora Randolph Sears Foundation, which he had daydreamed about directing, in tandem with Tenley, and which in his most cherished fantasy became the agent of some important medical advance. Instead, over the next months, heeding her accountant's always tax-conscious instructions, Eleo distributed the last of the foundation's moneys to Massachusetts General Hospital and Beverly Hospital.

Madame meanwhile was calculating how best to separate Bill Miller from his control over Eleo's finances. She saw him as an opposing force who divided Eleo's loyalty, and he was proving to be an unexpectedly tenacious rival. Miller was making every visible effort to accommodate Eleo and to convince her that he remained in her corner. Madame, however, was convinced that despite his apparent reasonableness, he was still in league with the "Boston group," the plotters. Marie Gendron prided herself on having an infallible nose for deception, and to her Bill Miller smelled deceitful. Gendron was a dictatorial tigress with other women, but her instinct was to be more polite and circumspect in dealing with men. She had considered and quickly discarded the possibility that Bill might be useful to her. He liked to think of himself as a real Boy Scout—he was always going on about needing to face himself in the mirror each morning when he shaved. Bill had confided to Eleo that his most enduring wish was "to be guided at all times, regardless of temptation, . . . by a love of honor, decency, and integrity. . . . More than anything else, I want to leave for my young son and daughter the memory of a man, their father, who had set an example of living that will give them strength and courage when the going gets tough."[8] But Gendron believed that everyone, however much he or she might protest, had something to hide. Her opportunity to undermine Eleo's "Man of Business" came just weeks after Tenley's wedding, when Bill and Eleo went to dinner in New York. Madame joined them in the chauffeured car as far as the restaurant, but she was to continue on without them to Eleo's hotel. The car stopped in front of the restaurant, where Bill hopped out and waited to give Eleo a gentlemanly assist. He decided the weather wasn't cold enough for the topcoat he brought, so he tossed it in the backseat and took Eleo's arm. They went on to enjoy a very pleasant dinner. Bill was rocked by the next day's phone call from Eleo, who berated him for his thoughtless treatment of Madame. The carelessly tossed topcoat had landed partly on her. Who the hell did he think he was, treating Madame Gendron like his servant—it was an insult, an outrage, and neither of them would stand for it! Bill protested and apologized, to no avail, that it was purely an accident, that his attention had been diverted because he was so focused on seeing Eleo safely out of the car. Madame bided her time.

Bill was offended to the core by the unfairness of the accusation. He had worked in service trades himself and would never dream of insulting anyone who toiled for a living. The assault crystallized a thought he had had for some time, that he was not being adequately compensated for all he was doing, and certainly not enough to take such abuse. And he had absorbed the lesson that Eleo admired an attack far more than a retreat. He asked for a raise. Bill had been working for Eleo for four years at a salary of $40,000, (about $290,000 at current values). Eleo balked at Bill's request for an increase to $50,000, and she demanded an explanation. Sounding weary, Bill recited his litany—the ever-increasing cost of his overhead and the fact that practically his entire office was given over to her affairs. When Eleo protested that never before had she paid anyone so much money, Bill countered that he was not "anyone," and that she had in fact paid George Hopkins $44,000 per year, and had given him a gift of $600,000 besides, on which she paid the gift taxes. "Unlike Mr. Hopkins," Bill assured her, "I will never approach you for a penny." He pointed to all the tax refunds he had obtained for her and lamented, "The shortest thing in life is one's memory of the good deeds of others." Finally, he reminded Eleo of what her situation had been when he first took over, "You were on the verge of bankruptcy. Your attorneys . . . advised you to sell Burrland at once, to get rid of your racc horses, to cut down everywhere and on everything. . . . You had problems—land, money, people—everywhere, in all directions people were annoying you. I got them off your back." Bill pointed out that now Eleo was richer by $4 million and Burrland and her racing business were prospering. Bill asked Eleo to consider, "Has it been luck—all luck? Was it your luck or mine?"[9] Filled with righteous indignation that was stoked by his perception of ingratitude and injustice, Bill made his stand. At this point he was fully prepared to quit, if Eleo had not, grudgingly, agreed to his demand.

Madame had no intension of letting the incident with the topcoat die so easily. It continued to fester and cast a pall over Bill's relationship with Eleo. Bill's wife, Vangie, counseled conciliation, and she typed his surrender note. In contrast to the thousands of words he had written to Eleo over the years, the few typed sentences to Madame Gendron had all the enthusiasm of a man being led to the gallows:

Madam Marie V. Gendron   April 20, 1962
Hotel St. Regis
5th Avenue and 55th Street
New York 22, N.Y.

Dear Madam Gendron:

I have just returned to my office after having met Miss Sears at the
hotel. From my conversation with her, it is evident that I was rude to
you last January. I wish to apologize. I was stupidly thoughtless then,
and I hope you will forgive me.

I do hope that you and I will be friends. Nothing would please me
more.

> Sincerely yours,
> William B. Miller[10]

Within and peripheral to the North Shore community were "well-meaning" individuals who took it upon themselves to inform Eleo of all the eyes
prying into her private life, and all the suspicions, slurs, and half-baked
schemes that were circulating. Eleo was kept up to date about alleged infight-
ing among her inner circle, including rumors of backstabbing between Tenley Albright and Bill Miller. The effect of all the scattershot accusations was
to bind Eleo more tightly to Madame. The terrible impropriety of her attachment to her housekeeper drove Eleo to defend it all the more fiercely, and she
issued a remarkable declaration meant to answer the charges against Madame.
She sent the document by registered mail to everyone who she thought
needed enlightenment:

> I wish to make a statement concerning rumors heard lately about
> Mme. Marie V. Gendron that she keeps me a prisoner in my house,
> that I am under her will and cannot do as I wish, also the rumors
> stated that she gave me drugs etc etc—I wish to say now that I have
> not been a prisoner in any way shape or manner, that I have come
> *and* gone as I wished. . . . Madame Gendron is my companion and
> friend—she is a very wonderful person and has done everything to
> make me happy—and she looks after my welfare at all times, and
> takes all responsibility for me—I am saying all this of my own free
> will, as it is the truth and nothing but the truth— . . .
>
> Eleonora Randolph Sears[11]

The uproar was heard as far away as London, where Tenley's family was
vacationing. Tenley's father wrote promptly to Eleo in an effort to reassure
and defuse her. Dr. Albright ignored the substance of Eleo's declaration and
told her instead of the appreciation that the Albright family felt "every day"

for all she had done for them. His peace offering had no effect. Weeks later Eleo sent a poisonous, hateful note to Tenley, accusing Tenley of "crooked schemes" to separate her from Madame and of an "evil design" to have her committed. Eleo accused Tenley of slander and of being mercenary and called her terrible names. "I have given orders," Eleo raged, "not to answer your telephone calls, etc.—in short I do not want to see you or your family— my doors are closed and do not come down to my beach."[12] Through her lawyer, Eleo demanded and got the return of the diamond jewelry and her mother's cross that she had given to Tenley.

Bill Miller responded angrily to his copy of Eleo's declaration. While he did not care, he wrote to Eleo, about her relationship with Madame Gendron, he resented Eleo's recent "unwarranted rudeness" to him: "The injustice of it appalls me. . . . You seem to enjoy hurting people, and lately me especially." Eleo had also begun to hint that his services might no longer be needed, and he cautioned her that if, as she had stated in her letter, she was still completely in charge of her own affairs, then "agreements you and I have entered into, oral as well as written, are fully binding."[13]

To the extent possible, Bill kept his distance from the fireworks that were bursting around him. He continued doling out funds to meet the payrolls for Eleo's staff and handling the day-to-day concerns of running the racing stable. He gathered the necessary financial information from all the nooks and crannies of Eleo's life to prepare her tax returns. He bought stock for her account on his own authority, as he had always done, and when for the first time Eleo questioned his purchases, Bill offered to reimburse her for the shares and keep them for himself. She let the purchases stand. The racing business, which was in Bill's charge, was flourishing, and he was still thrilled to be part of it. He fervently hoped that by continuing to do what he had been hired to do, he could stay under the radar and ride out the storm. That was not the plan Madame had in mind, but for the time being she allowed him to think he had played her to a draw in his quest to retain Eleo's favor.

Bill's business trips to meet with Eleo in Prides Crossing went smoothly. Bill and the two women were on their best behavior, and at breakfast they all laughed more than necessary at a joke that was made when they ran out of bananas. In a letter to Eleo following one such visit to Rock Edge, Bill reported that Jimmy Rowe had returned from the horse auctions at Keeneland without making any purchases for the racing stable. Jimmy thought many of the horses appeared to have been "doctored." Bill called Jimmy a "Good Man" and agreed that they didn't want horses that were kept together "with glue and prayers." Bill showed Eleo how well he had learned his lesson at Madame's hands, telling her, "I had a most delightful time with you and Madame Gendron. You are both great fun to be with. . . . Perhaps the three of us can have dinner together the night you come into New York."[14]

Throughout much of this convulsive and sad time, there were heartening oases of normalcy that offered glimpses of the old Eleo and rekindled hope that this aberration might yet end well. When the Boston Mounted Patrol was again being threatened by bureaucrats who wanted to eliminate the unit's thirteen horses and transfer their riders to foot duty, Eleo returned to the barricades. She countered the city's position that the mounted patrol was too expensive and no longer necessary in today's fast-paced world. Eleo spoke on behalf of the many Bostonians who supported the mounted division, explaining to reporters, "It will be a terrible thing if they do take [the horses] away. We have worked hard to get the right horses for the policemen. It is the most difficult thing in the world to get a good horse for police duties."[15] Her outcry aided the Mounted Patrol in winning a reprieve, and through the years it went on to earn the respect of city planners for its value in crowd control and the ability of an officer sitting eight feet off the ground to spot trouble at a distance and respond quickly.

Eleo's inspiring feats of physical endurance were recalled after President Kennedy challenged the Marines to improve their training so they could hike fifty miles in twenty hours. The *Boston Globe* dismissed the military's puny goal and declared, "Miss Sears Would Have Left Marines in Dust."[16]

Continuing a tradition of many years as Thanksgiving approached, Eleo sent Tom Greene to the homes of her stable manager, gardeners, head grooms, and groundsmen to deliver all the ingredients for a complete Thanksgiving dinner, from the freshest turkey to the most luscious corn pudding and cranberry sauce. Tom drove the maroon Volkswagen minibus, normally used only on Wednesdays for the laundry run, which for this mission was stacked to the roof with carefully labeled boxes of delicacies from S. S. Pierce.

Eleo's horses continued to win praise and top honors in the show world, and they gave her tremendous pleasure. At the National Horse Show at the Garden in the fall of 1962, Eleo watched six of her horses compete successfully, including Ksar d'Esprit and Diamant jumping for the U.S. Equestrian Team. At the show, Eleo was greeted by a friend whose family she had known for three generations, and he found her in a playful mood. Eleo introduced her fifty-year-old visitor to her companions with a flash of her accustomed humor, "This boy's mother is the most beautiful girl in New York."

On the pastures at Burrland Farm, 135 head of cattle grazed contentedly, an ideal-sized herd for the property, and cattle sales were providing a useful supplement for the upkeep of the farm. Eleo had started the herd eight years earlier with twenty cows and a bull. The big dream that began it all, of owning a successful racing stable and breeding champions, had caught fire at last and the E. R. Sears Racing Stable sparkled with accumulating successes. During Jimmy Rowe's three-year tenure as trainer, Eleo's horses won sixty races. When Eleo strode to her box at a racetrack, Bill Miller noticed how the crowds parted and the handicappers watched her closely, hoping to gauge her level of confidence before they placed their bets. They watched Bill Miller, too. He was by her side and was probably important. Even the huge bet that Eleo had placed on Tudorka, the high-class $75,000 yearling, was paying off. He was a failure as a racehorse, but he was proving his worth as a stud. Tudorka sired Tune-Swept, and his home-bred daughter was fulfilling his promise of speed and earnings. Eleo's horse Sizzling was still sizzling, and Stylish Urchin was doing the same. Eleonora Sears was chosen to be the guest of honor at a red-carpet, black-tie dinner hosted by the Eastern Racing Association, and the date of their dinner in October 1962 was adjusted to accommodate her schedule. On a single day in that same month, Eleo had two huge wins at the track in Narragansett. Three-year-old Rough Note poured on the speed late in the backstretch and scored a big upset in the featured race, and earlier two-year-old Spicy Living had won her third straight victory. Spicy Living had led the field by ten lengths and would have won by more if the race had been longer.

On racing forms every horse in each race is summed up with a phrase that paints a portrait as concise and pregnant with meaning as a line of haiku: "Showing promise"; "Improves in mud"; "Hardly there."[17]

Spicy Living put the racing world on notice with a string of impressive victories as a two-year-old, and by age three she was called "the Sears buzz bomb," the "sensation of the nation," and simply "Wow!" A sports reporter noted that "names are often meaningless, yet 'Spicy Living' has a genuine tingle."[18] Because she was on the small side, 15.2 hands, with a mushroom brown coat, the handlers at the track called her "Mousy." At Eleo's stable, her full-time groom, Leo Hall, and the other stable men affectionately called her "Mary Ann," though Leo had no idea how that got started. Leo had begun looking after Spicy Living when she was a yearling and he was only seventeen. He saw her with stars in his eyes and exulted with the enthusiasm of a love-struck teenager: "She is the best three-year-old mare in the world!" Spicy had been wild as a youngster. She got the temperamental gene from her surly mother, Rivaz. Jimmy Rowe said that Spicy Living gave the entire stable crew "more than our share of trouble. . . . No one will ever know the work that's been put into her, right from the beginning."[19] During the year that Spicy raced as a two-year-old, Jimmy dropped from 169 pounds to 149 pounds. Though he worked with thirty-eight other Thoroughbreds in Eleo's stable, he attributed the weight loss all to Spicy Living. She got spooked by a noisy crowd and a band that played before the Jeanne d'Arc Stakes in Narragansett and ran last. Before the race at Gulfstream Park a photographer with a big flash camera got too close, and Spicy took off over the paddock fence and gashed her leg. When a horsefly landed on her, she bucked and kicked and developed a quarter crack in her hoof, which required a four-month layoff.

Leo Hall analyzed Spicy's problem as a tricky mixture of distrust of humanity and a hatred of being alone. He talked to her softly and sang to her, and for several nights before a big race he slept next to her. Jimmy Rowe was relieved to see Spicy start to settle down and mature as a three-year-old. Leo noted with pride that she was getting as calm and contented as an old mule.

Spicy Living, with the outstanding jockey Jimmy Combest on board, conquered the first two legs of the 1963 Triple Crown for Fillies, which one turf writer dubbed the "suffragette series." Spicy beat strong fields in the Mother Goose Stakes and the Acorn Stakes at Aqueduct. If she pulled off a win in the $120,000 Coaching Club of America (CCA) Oaks, she would earn a $25,000 purse sweetener and be the first filly in history to win the fillies' Triple Crown. There would be no denying her, then, the honor of being named Filly of the Year for 1963. Oddsmakers for the Oaks contest sent Spicy off as the 2–1 favorite. Her two top challengers among the field of ten were the always dangerous Smart Deb from Chicago and Lamb Chop, owned by William H. Perry of Middleburg, Virginia. Both Smart Deb and Lamb Chop had finished just behind Spicy in the two previous Triple Crown matchups. Lamb Chop was also in contention for the coveted Filly-of-the-Year designation and, like Spicy Living, she boasted a golden pedigree. She was by Bold Ruler out of Sheepsfoot. Her grandfather was the 1943 Triple Crown winner Count Fleet. The smart money looked for Smart Deb again to place second to Spicy and for Lamb Chop to come in third. The race proved to be the thrilling contest that the crowd of 51,000 had come to see. Spicy Living and Lamb Chop fought a head-to-head duel in the final eighth mile, before Lamb Chop surged ahead and crossed the wire in front by three and a half lengths.[20] Smart Deb finished third, a length and a half behind Spicy Living.

Eleo was not at Aqueduct in June to see Spicy Living run in the climactic Triple Crown race, nor had she witnessed Spicy's previous triumph in the Mother Goose Stakes. Nor was Eleo on hand for Spicy's next race on an overcast afternoon in July, when Spicy "annihilated" the field and won the Delaware Oaks Stakes by six lengths. During much of the 1963 racing season Eleo was in Europe with Madame. Before they left, Jimmy Rowe had asked Madame if Miss Sears would be back in time to see her filly run. "Mind your own goddamn business," Madame told him. On a whim during their travels, Eleo and Madame acquired a small white poodle, and they named her Caprice. They doted on Caprice as they would a child and rarely disciplined her. They took Caprice with them to Southern Pines, where Eleo spent most of the winter season. Madame preferred the climate there to the temperature in Boston. For her the improved atmosphere involved more than weather.

Questions about Bill Miller's loyalty resurfaced, and he reported to Eleo that no one from the Boston crowd contacted him any more about her relationship with Madame. "The fact is," he told Eleo, "that none of your 'friends'

give a damn about me and never did, and I am happy to be rid of them."
Though Bill knew full well that the concern shown by most of Eleo's friends
and relatives for her and for her good name had nothing to do with any
thought of personal gain, he parroted Eleo's sentiments that they were interested only in her money. He called them "Vultures." He suggested that they
might now consider him "a traitor [who had] gone over to the side of the
enemy (Madam, of course) or some such nonsense. They probably believe
that Madam and I are old friends and that we have cooked up a plan between
us on how to get all of your money away from you."[21] Bill had abhorred Gendron from the start and privately bemoaned the tragic mischief she had
wrought, but he chose to cling to the foundering ship. His weakness was due
not merely to the fine salary Eleo paid him, though it was more than he had
dreamt of earning from a single client, and college tuitions for his children
loomed.[22] And it was not just that he couldn't face dismantling the infrastruc-
ture he had developed around Eleo, the New York office and his assistant,
LeCount. And it was not only the still flickering hope that something for
Eleo's legacy might yet be salvaged from the ashes. More than all these
things, his weakness came from the fear that, once this experience was over,
his life would feel smaller.

But if Bill Miller, who was as incapable of subtlety as a bull elephant, imagined that by dusting off his psychology books he could lull Marie Gendron into
seeing him as an ally, he greatly underestimated her. At every turn Madame
encouraged Eleo to doubt her advisor's sincerity, and she counseled Eleo to
launch an investigation into Miller's handling of her affairs. Madame suggested the New York law firm of Bisco, Winkler and Higgiston for the job.
Twenty years earlier, Gendron had chaperoned Leonard Bisco's daughter during her visit to France. On October 3, 1963, Bisco, Winkler and Higgiston submitted their report. The firm had been told to "proceed cautiously . . . to
ascertain whether there was anything of an improper or irregular nature in Mr.
Miller's administration of [Miss Sears's] affairs." Eleo had signaled the type of
accusatory report she was looking for and the firm did its best to oblige. The
investigators reported that they could not give Eleo assurances that "mistakes
in judgment may not have been made or that an expense account . . . may not
have been padded, or that an improper disbursement of a minor nature may
not have been made, for we made no effort to check on these items." Not until
the closing paragraphs of their summation did the firm offer its "general
impression" that "Mr. Miller . . . has been administering your affairs capably
and, so far as our examination discloses, with complete integrity." The report
even went a step further and recommended that Eleo avoid upsetting her present arrangement with Mr. Miller in order to ensure his "fullest cooperation"
until her current tax problem was resolved. The IRS was challenging the
tax losses taken by the E. R. Sears Racing Stable for the 1955–60 reporting

periods, claiming that the entity was actually a hobby and not a business. The government was looking to collect $1.3 million in back taxes, and Bill was fighting the reclassification. He contended that, far from owing back taxes, the racing stable deserved a refund of $13,000. Even Madame Gendron acquiesced in leaving Bill Miller alone until the "hobby question" was settled.

In November 1963 Eleo was the unanimous choice of the New England Turf Writers Association as the Horse Breeder of the Year, the breeder who had done the most for New England racing, and they presented her with a hand-illuminated scroll. Many sports reporters took the opportunity to recall Eleo's trailblazing history and laud her as a pivotal force in the emancipation of women. The racing establishment looked to Eleo's horses to set the pace for the future. Most of her stable's proven winners were still sound and eager to run, and Jimmy Rowe had high expectations for their current crop of two-year-olds. Everyone, from Eleo's trainer to her business manager, from the farm managers to the exercise boys, agreed that the 1964 racing season would be a golden time for the E. R. Sears Racing Stable.

Bill Miller's presentation to the IRS on the "hobby question" gained traction, and instead of having to pay back taxes, it appeared likely that the racing stable would receive a refund of more than $20,000. Despite this positive outlook, by January 1964 Bill was again under pressure to reassure Eleo of his loyalty and discretion. Madame was impatient to break the stalemate and had been busy backstage turning him into a villain. Bill insisted to Eleo, "I see *no one* and speak to *no one* that knows you. . . . I am not so weak and disgusting as to lie to you. . . . I am like a clam. I do not talk to anyone."[23] In March Gendron came to Bill's office and handed him a letter from Eleo: "I expressly wish that you do not try to stay in the house where ever she [Madame] may happen to be and not annoy her in any shape or form. I asked her to have this wish of mine fully, fully protected by law if necessary . . . in order that her existence be fully and peacefully protected. I am in full possession of all my mental faculties. ERS"[24]

Bill had begun to notice when he was with Eleo that during the day she seemed alert and in control, but in the evenings, especially after a glass of wine with dinner, her attention wandered and her conversation turned hazy. Bill called it "sun-downing." He had no good words for the miasma of paranoia that Madame was churning up.

Madame and Eleo began to explore the idea of moving to Florida permanently. Eleo had spent many winter seasons in Palm Beach at the homes of friends. She enjoyed the summery atmosphere and the intimately sized shops on Worth Avenue, where the sales ladies greeted her by name. The shops and the social clubs were patronized by people of breeding who lived in grandly scaled Moorish-style homes painted the color of warm sand and crowned with orange barrel roof tiles. The State of Florida was also quite civilized in its gentle tax treatment of large estates. Madame reminded Eleo that up north she supported scores of people, people who made demands on her, people who had to be watched and paid. Palm Beach offered an inviting retreat, distant from those cares and complexities and far from those whom Madame repeatedly characterized as her grasping relatives. Madame assured Eleo that she had already accomplished all that anyone had expected of her, more than anyone expected, and now, at the age of eighty-three, it was time for her to lay down her burdens.

Eleo began her incremental move to Palm Beach with the purchase of a house at 200 El Bravo Way. El Bravo is a quiet street of well-kept homes that is within a hearty walk of the center of town. The street extends across the narrow waist of Palm Beach Island, between the ocean and a large bay studded with boat docks. The house that Eleo bought had been built in 1930 in a neat Spanish style. Above its front door hung a narrow wooden balcony carved in a lacy fretwork design. The house itself was built to withstand the violent storms that periodically lash the Florida coast. Recessed windows on either side of the fireplace in the large living room revealed that the walls were nearly two feet thick. The ceilings in the main rooms were spliced by thick, dark wooden beams. Eleo and Madame debated in French where to hang pictures. Eleo took Madame shopping on Worth Avenue for white mink jackets and jewelry, and they walked Caprice along the Worth Avenue amusement pier. The hundred-foot-long pier hosted a chic restaurant and a variety of shops. From the end of the pier fishermen cast their lines into the Atlantic, and you could watch retirees swim in rhythmic slow motion. Caprice was not permitted to romp on the beach because her fluffy white coat got full of sand and made a mess in the house, but she strolled with Eleo and Madame along El Bravo Way, past the hedgerows of Australian pine and eucalyptus and bougainvillea that guarded the big homes from prying eyes. At sunset the sky over the bay turned a satin pink, and the clouds took on the color of plums. In the evenings Eleo and Madame saw shows at the Palm Beach Playhouse and dined at the exclusive Everglades Club, where people talked about them after they left.

In the summer of 1964 Eleo attended the races in Saratoga, where she announced that she was quitting the racing business and would begin closing down her racing stable. Over the next several months, most of the thirty-nine horses at Burrland were sold at auction or taken in claiming races, and many, like Rough Note and Gold Frame, went on to win for other stables.[25] Spicy Living raced a few times during 1964 in Eleo's maroon and cerise colors and either won her races or placed, but her suspensory joints got so bad that Jimmy Rowe decided she would have to be retired. Mrs. Allaire du Pont bought Spicy Living for $25,000 as a broodmare with the hope she would pass on her elite breeding and speed. Eleo began the hunt for a buyer for Burrland Farm itself. The eventual new owners offended Eleo with an initial offer that she considered insultingly low. They then purchased the property using a straw buyer, a tactic Eleo had used many times. The new owners changed the name of Burrland Farm to Hickory Tree Farm.

Each man who worked at Burrland dealt with the demise of the racing stable in his own way. Most began the mad scramble to find work at neighboring barns. Bill Miller sorted through the array of accounting issues that came in the wake of the dissolution of the business, and he met the continuing payroll needs at Eleo's homes in Boston and Prides Crossing. His main worry was for his friend Jimmy Rowe. Jimmy and his family could not live on the small fixed stipend Eleo paid him. He supported his family with his percentage of the purses that the horses won from racing, but he had been instructed to sell the horses. As Jimmy understood it, he had not been fired, but his main source of income was to stop at the end of September 1964. Bill wrote an urgent letter to Eleo. He explained that Jimmy "was frantic because he had no connections of any kind and was completely without work." Bill had taken it upon himself to discuss the trainer's predicament with one of Eleo's lawyers and had suggested that Jimmy be given a salary increase to tide him over until he could find a new position. Bill also asked Eleo, with the shyness of an outcast, if she might let Jimmy keep a few of the more minor horses, "a few horses that were cripples [either] as sort of a gift . . . for nothing or just for a token payment. . . . I can tell you from first-hand experience with him, he was your friend and deserves your loyalty. Please forgive my interference. I know you want to help Jimmy, and so I spoke up. I meant no harm."[26]

By that time, the fall of 1964, when it came to matters involving Bill Miller, Eleo had moved beyond reason. Gendron had panicked Eleo with her certainty that both Bill Miller and Tenley Albright Gardiner would make trouble for her after Eleo was gone. Eleo's lawyer confirmed that Miller held Gendron responsible for interfering in his affairs. As Eleo read Bill Miller's appeal in behalf of Jimmy Rowe, her fears for the future twisted its sentiments beyond recognition. Eleo saw it as a "long tirade" and she withdrew into the fortress of social class erected long ago by her Brahmin ancestors. Eleo reminded Bill loftily, "You have no business to tell me how and when to sell my horses—I do as I please being the sole owner—. . . So Mr. Miller, why do you talk thus? You are in my opinion only reflecting your own aspirations and your own image— . . . you do not have to place yourself on a pedestal of moral virtues to tell me how to treat my old friend Jimmy Rowe." Eleo asserted that she had already "gladly given" Jimmy the horses he wanted, and she told Miller pointedly that she had referred Jimmy to "an old friend of mine of a substantial respected and old family." As Eleo saw it, her accountant had presumed above his station. She was done with him and she turned him back into a frog. Eleo concluded her letter with a final slap: "Your information about horses is absolutely no good to me."[27] Eleo terminated Bill's services in a follow-up notice that was mailed the same day. Bill had come to expect that the axe would fall, but when it finally was there before him in black and white he stomped through his house, cursing Madame and mumbling about the insanity of it all, much as he had done on other occasions. But his tone with Eleo when he responded to his formal dismissal was measured and conciliatory. "By abandoning me as you contemplate doing," Bill explained to Eleo by certified mail, "I am left with an expensive office, useless furniture, and no clients. At my time of life, to start from scratch, to build again from the very bottom like a boy just out of school is a bit too much. . . . I feel certain that the friendship and respect we have for one another will lead us to a satisfactory solution."[28]

Bill Miller painted a dire picture of his future, one that was not entirely true but that he expected would help in the final bargaining process. He had retained a few loyal old clients and his own portfolio of investments was substantial and growing. He would certainly never have to sell apples on a street corner. Nonetheless, at the moment he wrote it, the bleak assessment felt true. Bill explored the possibility of contesting the revised version of Eleo's will that had cut off both Tenley and himself, which he believed was a product of Gendron's "undue influence," but he had no stomach for a vicious, protracted court battle. In the end, Bill settled for a modest severance check, and he signed a general release to Eleo and Madame of all future claims, and for him the drama was over. Bill acknowledged, much later, that for most of the nearly six years he had spent with Eleonora Sears, he had had a marvelous time. It had been a great ride.

In the summer of 1965 there was a break-in at Rock Edge. The culprit was never caught, and Eleo was frightened into hiring protection from the Boston-based Central Secret Service Bureau. For twenty-four hours each day, at the cost of $2.15 per hour and $18,782.40 per year, a man in a brown suit and brown fedora, armed with a gun and a large German shepherd dog, walked around the perimeter of the house, patrolled up and down along the beach, and checked all the visitors who came to the front gate. The constant presence of a security guard and his big dog was concrete proof that the world was an insecure and alarming place. Given how ideally this development enhanced the claustrophobic, paranoid atmosphere that was so useful to Marie Gendron, one could suspect that she orchestrated the break-in. The surveillance team further restricted the flow of visitors to Rock Edge and kept alive Eleo's thought to relocate permanently to Palm Beach. A few months after the break-in, Eleo signed a formal power of attorney that gave Marie Gendron the authority to manage and operate all her homes, pay her bills, endorse checks, and withdraw funds in the event of Eleo's illness or incapacity.

Eleo visited the Myopia Hunt Club during the summer of 1966, where she met many formerly close friends. She was pleasant to all of them, even Mabel

Storey. When Gendron was out of earshot, Eleo was asked why she no longer saw her old friends and why she did not kick Madame out. Eleo is reported to have said, "I can't. I'd like to, but it's too late, and I'm hooked."[29] And some time later Eleo was heard to say with a flicker of regret, "Helen Frick doesn't like me any more," but no one thought that Eleo seemed particularly unhappy with her situation or showed any real desire to be rid of Madame. A cousin of Eleo's observed that she no longer looked as smartly groomed as she once had, that she no longer looked soignée.

Eleo was now nearly eighty-five years old, and she was having trouble with her eyes. Age and a lifetime in the sun had taken their toll. As Eleo's macular degeneration progressed, Gendron consolidated her hold on the details of running the household. She could now officially, out of necessity, read the mail that Eleo received, and she began to answer Eleo's correspondence, writing out what Eleo dictated and incorporating her own thoughts. Nudged by Madame, Eleo began to jettison the layers of her attachments to Boston and the North Shore, but Eleo approached this retrenchment from the life she had built with reluctance, in stages. She bought an expensive new horse, a three-year-old jumper named Among the Stars. Star had earned the title of Horse of the Year in 1965 and again in 1966. In November 1966 Eleo attended the National Horse Show at the Garden, where she had two horses entered, Among the Stars and Up in Smoke. Both were to be ridden by Dave Kelley, one of the foremost jump riders on the show circuit. As Kelley was preparing to enter the ring with Up in Smoke, Eleo told him that she would like to lead Smoke into the ring herself. With great reluctance, Kelley handed Eleo the reins. He stayed behind her, fearing harm to this frail-looking lady with limited vision who walked erectly beside the keyed-up, dapple-gray horse. Smoke tensed and snorted as he got nearer to the action in the ring and heard the noise of the audience. The big horse jerked his head back nervously but Eleo was unfazed. She gave the reins an authoritative yank and talked to Smoke in the firm, kind voice that her horses knew so well, and Smoke quieted and walked docilely beside her. The people in the nearby boxes applauded when Eleo came into view, saluting the gallant white-haired lady and the era that was ending. Dave Kelley was thrilled to bring home two winning rides for Eleo during the show. Among the Stars won the Hunter Championship, and Up in Smoke was the Reserve winner. Kelley called the double win for Eleo on that day a "golden moment." Eleo made her last visit to the National the following year, when she relinquished her box, number 72, which she had held for generations.

Eleo refused to consider selling her town house on Byron Street, which had been a gift from her grandfather Frederick Sears and had been the scene of so many memorable parties. Thomas Greene was living there now with his wife, Mary. Eleo wrote a new will in 1966 and in this version, her faithful old chauffeur and his wife were to receive title to the entire furnished property upon her death. The couple was also to receive a bequest totaling $100,000, an amount that included the generous gifts Eleo had been giving them in recent years. Apart from a few much smaller bequests that Eleo planned for her stable managers, her goddaughter, the two Lodge brothers, and the Sears family chapel, Marie Gendron was to get everything else.

Eleo was in Palm Beach during the winter season in 1967, and there she drew up a formal list of her eight most troublesome enemies. The document was witnessed and notarized by her lawyer and it gave Madame Gendron "complete authority" to prevent those persons named from ever seeing Eleo or contacting her: "Dear Madame Gendron: From time to time during the past few years these persons have interfered in my personal life causing me great periods of unhappiness and constant mental turmoil. . . . I implore you to protect me in every way from these persons listed above."[30]

Occupying the first two places on Eleo's list were Tenley Albright Gardiner and her husband. Mabel Storey and her husband were named, as was William Miller. None of them had taken any overt action against Eleo in years.

In the spring Eleo was diagnosed with leukemia, and she began in earnest to settle the affairs she had hesitated over for so long. She walked the streets of Boston with long strides and a tall, stout walking stick. She visited the police stables for a final check on the horses. Sargeant Paul Simonetti was there when she came in. He had known Eleo since he was a rookie and he saw that the horses recognized her immediately. At the sound of her step they turned to her and whinnied before she spoke. Eleo could no longer make out the sergeant's face, but she smiled her still lovely smile when he greeted her. Simonetti echoed the sentiments of all the men in the mounted division who considered Eleo to be "the sweetest, loveliest person in the world."[31]

Then Eleo and Marie Gendron went to Prides Crossing to close up Rock Edge. They stayed nearly a week at a local hotel and dined several times at the King's Grant Inn on Route 128, where Eleo raised hell about the poor service and threatened to buy the whole goddamn place if that's what it took to get what she ordered. John Brotchie had no trouble recognizing Eleo's distinctive voice and colorful vocabulary. During previous summers, he had worked long hours at her stable. John's twin brother, Jim, and their uncle had all worked for Eleo at various times, and she had called them all "Jimmy" for convenience. John was waiting tables at the inn during his summer break from college, and he went over to Eleo's table and reminded her, "Miss Sears, it's Jimmy. I worked for you." Eleo greeted him affectionately and advised him, "I'm blind as a bat." The restaurant's owner was relieved to have a waiter able to satisfy his difficult customer, and he put John in charge of Eleo's table. Eleo and John reminisced about her wonderful horses, particularly the massive chestnut champion, Tenor-Riff, that she had brought home from Ireland.

This Grand National Champion had been raised on the short grass of the Emerald Isle, and when he was first put out in the longer grass in Eleo's paddock, the horse stood frozen with fear. John Brotchie did not tell Eleo the nickname the grooms had given to her prize horse—"30Gs," because of the $30,000 that he was rumored to have cost and the additional $30,000 they figured would be needed to train the timid fellow. Tenor-Riff began his American jumping career at a minor horse show nearby in Milton. John was sent along to look after the horse, and he recalled the humorous events of that stiflingly hot day. Tenor-Riff was showing far more interest in eating flowers off the ladies' hats than in doing any jumping. The horse's exalted reputation as Dublin's Grand National Champion attracted the amused interest of the other grooms at the show, most of whom also hailed from Ireland. They demanded proof that Tenor-Riff was truly an Irish champion. Several of the lads poured beer into their tweed caps and offered the beverage to the horse. Eleo was waiting at her stable in Prides as the horse van pulled into the courtyard after the show. Tenor-Riff came weaving down the ramp, burping beer fumes from both ends. "Jimmy," Eleo exploded, "what the hell have you done to my horse? He smells like a brewery!"

Eleo never tipped John for the meals that she and Madame ate at the King's Grant Inn, but on her last day in the area, Eleo took his hand. "You probably won't be seeing me again," she said to him, and she pressed a folded $100 bill into his palm. "For old time's sake," Eleo told him.[32]

Eleo and Madame stayed in Palm Beach for the winter season in 1968, as her illness worsened. They walked Caprice along El Bravo Way and attended a comedy at the local playhouse. In the afternoons they sat in the sun on wrought-iron chairs in their enclosed garden and chewed over old resentments. Their small tropical backyard was protected on all sides by the house, a detached garage, and a concrete fence that was lushly lined with palm trees. The servants' quarters were in the apartment over the garage, and at night through the open windows the help could hear the unmistakable sounds of physical abuse coming from the main house. If anyone asked Eleo about her new bruises the next day, she said, "I fell." Gendron directed a revolving cast of cooks, housekeepers, part-time chauffeurs, and gardeners who consistently disappointed her and were quickly shown the door. Gendron spoke French with her preferred housekeeper, Lorette Jenart, who had recently arrived from Belgium, but she shared no details of her past. Gendron became jealous when she saw Lorette talking with Eleo, and she warned Lorette to leave Miss Sears alone or she too would be fired. Lorette reminded Madame that she had a good job waiting for her in New York, so it was fine with her if she was told to leave, and Madame backed off. Eleo came into the kitchen often during those last months and asked anxiously about the time, but she couldn't seem to keep the number in mind after Lorette told her.[33]

It is not a rare thing that people beset by the increasing powerlessness of age begin to fixate on controlling their earthly finances. They use their holdings to settle old scores and reward a shifting list of the deserving. Eleo became one of those people. She was buffeted too by her need to appease her companion and keep her possessions out of the hands of those she believed wished Madame harm. Eleo was convinced there would be trouble after her death from the people in Boston who hated Madame and would prevent her from getting any part of Eleo's estate. Gendron had already done quite well for herself. In the six and a half years that she and Eleo were together, Eleo made numerous gifts to her of stock, valued at the time above $360,000, and an equal amount of cash. During those years Eleo signed at least five versions of her will, and she edited the instructions further in many codicils. Most of the changes gave Gendron new funds and new powers. One codicil voided any suggestion that Eleo may have made that Isabel Stewart Gardner's ruby ring would eventually go to Tenley Albright. The ring was redirected to Madame, together with a large ruby and pearl pendant that Eleo had bought from the Gardner estate. Before Eleo signed any of the new documents, Marie Gendron made a point of walking out of the lawyer's office so that the witnesses who signed the papers could attest in good conscience that Madame did not know of or coerce the changes.

Eleo set in motion the process of selling Rock Edge and closing her Prides Crossing stable. She placed her remaining nine horses in the temporary care of Dave Kelley, and she made another decision that she had been delaying. She contacted an agent to find a buyer for 4–5 Byron Street. Eleo informed Thomas Greene that his home would be sold, but she reassured him that she had left him $30,000 in her will to buy a new house, and he would also get title to his favorite car, her Mercedes Benz. The vastly reduced bequest to Tom Greene was the unhappy result of a war Eleo had with herself. She had always felt kindly toward Thomas. He was a last link to her colorful past, and he had served her loyally for more than half a century, ever since Alfred Vanderbilt drowned on the *Lusitania* in 1915. In her final months, Eleo met more than twenty times with her lawyer and contacted him almost daily by phone, and she often touched on her concerns about Tom Greene. One time she would be disposed to give him a lot of money—$200,000 or so, and a week later she would say, "Well, Tom and his wife are real old, they are older than god, like me, and they don't need that money because all they are going to do is die, and it will go to his no-good son."[34]

Eleo was admitted to Good Samaritan Hospital in West Palm Beach in March 1968. She was a difficult and highly agitated patient. After two weeks, on March 26, at the age of eighty-six, Eleo found, at long last, rest and peace. Madame Gendron would claim that during that final stay in the hospital, Eleo laughed and joked with the nurses and called out for her, "Vicki, Vicki."

None of that was true.[35] The funeral service took place as Eleo had planned it, in Boston at Trinity Church in Copley Square, and the hymns that Eleo had selected were played. As Eleo had directed, Marie Gendron took her place in the first row with members of the Sears family, who, having practiced for generations to maintain their composure, greeted her with cool civility. They were glad that they would not need to concern themselves with Madame's funeral arrangements at some future date, as she had declined Eleo's offer to join her, in due course, in her family's vault with Isabel Pell. The service at Trinity Church was packed with relatives and friends of long standing who spoke only of happier days, when Eleo had taught their children to play backgammon and became part of their families. They remembered the time when a circus came to Boston and Eleo invited all the clowns home for lunch. The rector offered the final prayer, "Praise be to thee, O God, for all people like Eleonora Sears who take life in their stride and face it with enthusiasm and zest."

Lined up outside the church in Copley Square, four police officers sat at attention on Domino, Holiday, King, and Pete, horses that Eleo had helped bring to the unit. They followed the funeral cortege a short way as it headed toward the Sears family chapel.

Epilogue

THE RUMOR THAT Eleo was buried alongside her favorite horse intrigued Boston, as did speculation about how much she had been worth. The official value that was placed on her investments and properties was $13,133,857.51, a magnificent sum at the time.[1]

As Eleo had predicted, trouble did erupt over her will, but it came from a different "Boston group" from the one she had imagined. Six Boston area hospitals, which usually competed with each other for patients and funding, joined forces in a tug-of-war with Marie Gendron for their portion of Eleo's estate. In 1963 Eleo had drawn up a will that named the six hospitals, Massachusetts General, New England Deaconess, Boston Lying-In, Peter Bent Brigham, Children's, and Beverly hospitals, as her ultimate beneficiaries. The version of Eleo's will that emerged in May 1965, however, effectively cut out the hospitals when it gave Gendron the right to determine her own beneficiaries, and it was that change that set the stage for battle.

In accordance with Eleo's wishes, Gendron hand-delivered several of her silver trophies and a brass hunting horn to friends whom Eleo had thought would appreciate them, and she saw to the distribution of Eleo's other token bequests. Then she hunkered down to fight for the rest. Madame wielded Eleo's name as a sword and a shield, telling anyone who questioned any action she took, "Miss Sears would have wanted . . . Miss Sears told me many times . . . Miss Sears warned me against . . ." Eleo's housekeeper-companion had already lost in the court of public opinion. Bostoners who vacationed in Palm Beach returned home with enigmatic reports that down south "they're saying Madame did her in."[2]

Gendron prepared a fifty-one-page journal for her lawyers to assist them in defending her against charges of fraud and undue influence. The journal presented Madame's version of Eleo's conflicts over the years with cousins and friends. Madame Gendron's defense attorneys took depositions from bankers, insurance salesmen, and acquaintances who had known Eleo in the years since Madame joined her. Many of them affirmed Eleo's continuance as a gracious hostess and her grasp of the financial consequences of her actions. A tradeswoman who had done work for Eleo within a year of her death recalled her as having been "sharp as a tack."

The other side had witnesses, too. Eleo's doctors offered a convincing alternative view of her debilitating illness and declining competence. Statements were taken from discharged chauffeurs and maids and the security guards who had patrolled Rock Edge, who all attested to Gendron's dark side. One of the former security guards testified that Eleo had once asked him, "How can I get rid of her?"[3] Witnesses who had once been Eleo's close friends, including Tenley Albright Gardiner, detailed their suspicions concerning drugs and offered evidence that a brawny butler in the household may have acted as Madame's accomplice. In 1970, after two years of brutal charges and countercharges, Gendron's counselors were able to convince their steely client to agree to a Solomon-like settlement. Eleo's money and properties, substantially diminished by legal expenses and estate taxes apportioned among Florida, Massachusetts, and the federal government, were divided in half, between Madame and the six hospitals.

Madame Gendron then took two actions that Eleo would never have sanctioned. Eleo had explicitly entrusted Madame with the welfare of her horses, only two of which remained unclaimed by the end of the legal fight. Radar, many times a champion jumper at Madison Square Garden and Myopia, had developed a bad ring bone above his hoof. He was also, unfortunately, a "cribber" and nervously chewed the wood of his stall, a habit disliked by horsemen. Radar had become a drain on Madame's economic resources, but she had to obtain a court order to compel the stable manager to shoot him. She needed another court order to overcome resistance to putting down Eleo's gentle giant, Ksar d'Esprit. The old Olympic medalist had outlived his usefulness. After the gunshot, the large dapple-gray horse crumpled to the ground and the grooms stood around him and cried. William Steinkraus, who had ridden Ksar with so much success, was pained when he learned what had been done. He would have gladly let Ksar d'Esprit live out his days on his farm in Connecticut.[4]

For many years, Madame used the El Bravo house in Palm Beach as her home base, and from there she launched herself and Caprice on extended overseas travels. Every September found Madame in Paris and visiting the "Royal town" of Pau, where Eleo had stayed as a girl with her grandfather T. J. Coolidge. Despite her travels, Madame kept a watchful eye on her business affairs and investments in the States. From Spain, Portugal, and the Swiss Alps she sent jovial updates to her lawyers with travel news and investment instructions, letters that began "Greetings from La belle dame de l'Europe."[5] When she was in her eighties, Marie Gendron moved to a comfortable condominium on a golf course in Clearwater, Florida, where she was known as "Mrs. G." or "Vicki." She placed photographs of Eleo around the apartment. There was one of Eleo holding a trophy and standing beside Madame at the front gates to Rock Edge. All the furnishings in Marie Gendron's apartment came from what remained of Eleo's vast inventory. In the living room Madame hung an oil portrait of Eleo that had been painted in Palm Beach, and the lovely Sargent charcoal sketch. Madame also displayed the oil portrait she herself had painted of Caprice, whom she continued to mourn long after the poodle's death. With every passing year, Gendon stashed more Bibles in random corners of her apartment. When Madame was in her nineties, a kindly neighbor bought groceries for her and took her to doctors' appointments. Gendron's benefactress found "Vicki" to be moody and intensely private. Despite the many favors done for her, Vicki treated her thoughtful neighbor with disconcerting unpredictability, seeming to like her one minute and not the next. Occasionally Gendron would speak about Eleo and gaze at her portraits. She would explain with tears in her eyes that Eleo was "a beautiful lady" and that she had loved her very much.[6] In time, Madame packed her trunks with linens for a visit to her deceased mother and brother in France. She began to wander and she was moved to a nursing home in St. Petersburg. There, in 2004, a few months short of her 101st birthday, Marie Gendron slipped away in silence.

Eleo's passing sparked a resurgent appreciation of her teeming, precedent-setting life and her personal quest to redefine a woman's place in the world order. In a long-delayed ceremony in Newport in 1968, shortly after her death, Eleo was elected to the Tennis Hall of Fame, finally joining her uncle Richard Dudley Sears. Over the next thirty-five years, Eleo's name was added to the rolls of the Horseman's Hall of Fame, the International Women's Sports Hall of Fame, the Show Jumping Hall of Fame, the United States Squash Hall of Fame, and the National Horse Show Foundation Hall of Fame. Recognition came too for Eleo's greatest race horse, Spicy Living. At Rockingham Park in New Hampshire, where Spicy had won impressive victories, they named the richest race for fillies after her, the annual Spicy Living Stakes. As a broodmare, Spicy Living gave birth to twins, a rare occurrence for a horse. Neither of her offspring had her speed or her level of success.

A group of Eleo's friends and relatives, led by Mabel Storey, overlooked the troubles of the past and took up a collection for a commemorative bronze plaque that was sculpted with Eleo's image. The memorial found a home in Beverly Hospital, on the North Shore, which had received many contributions from Eleo over the years and was among the winners in the contest for her estate.

After those legal conflicts were resolved, a work crew was dispatched to clean out her wine cellar on Byron Street. The workmen went through the iron gates of the large, tiled underground storage room and brushed aside years of cobwebs. Someone opened a bottle of champagne and decided it didn't have the proper pop and that the entire collection, its labels obscured by layers of dust, was spoiled. Nearly three thousand bottles, many containing rare vintage wines, ports, gins, and aged whiskeys, were loaded onto trucks and driven to the dump in Milton. By the end of the following day, residents from the surrounding towns had liberated every bottle.

Notes

CHAPTER 1: THE BATTLE OF BURLINGAME

1. *San Francisco Chronicle,* August 27, 1911.
2. *Boston Post,* April 9, 1909.
3. *New York Times,* August 14 and 16, 1910.
4. Newspaper fragments, probably *San Francisco Chronicle,* March 30, 1910, and March 30, 1912, unattributed.
5. Ibid.
6. Newspaper fragment, probably *San Francisco Chronicle,* March 30, 1910.
7. *Burlingame Advance,* March 29, 1910.
8. *New York Times,* March 12, 1912, 1, 6.
9. *Burlingame Advance,* March 29, 1912.
10. Henry Lee Jr., interview by author, March 12, 2001.
11. Newspaper fragment, probably *San Francisco Chronicle,* March 30, 1912; *New York Times,* April 1, 1912. Newspaper accounts agree on the principal incidents of the walk, but they vary slightly on the specifics of time and total distance. An average has been presented.
12. Probably *San Francisco Chronicle,* March 31, 1912.

CHAPTER 2: BACK BAY BEGINNINGS

1. Angela Forbes Winthrop, interview by author, March 11, 2000.
2. Mary Caroline Crawford, *Famous Families of Massachusetts,* vol. 2 (Boston, 1930), presents the early spelling as "Sayres." John W. Sears, the family historian, backs the one I have used.
3. Cleveland Amory, *The Proper Bostonians* (New York, 1947), 172. Massachusetts General Hospital had a two-tier system for pricing its accommodations. Baker Memorial was for people with annual incomes under $7,000, who paid a maximum of $150 regardless of the type of operation or the number of visits. Those better off, with incomes greater than $7,000, would go to Phillips House; they had to pay whatever doctors thought they could charge. This pricing structure lasted into the mid-twentieth century.
4. Colonel Robert Gould Shaw recruited free blacks from New England for the 54th Massachusetts Volunteer Infantry. After he was killed leading a charge against the Fort Wagner Battery in North Carolina, he was buried by Confederate soldiers in a common grave with his men. An imposing granite monument to Colonel Shaw stands at the Beacon Street entrance to Boston Common.
5. Dorothy B. Wexler, *Reared in a Greenhouse* (New York, 1998), 407n18, quoting Dorothy Winthrop Bradford.
6. Amory, *Proper Bostonians,* 88. Captain John Codman felt, at the age of seventy-five, that he was "going soft." He rode a horse from Boston to New York in the middle of winter to prove to himself he could still manage it.
7. Geoffrey Blodgett, *The Gentle Reformers: Massachusetts Democrats in the Cleveland Era* (Boston, 1966), 29.
8. Samuel Hornblower, "Fifteen Minutes: The Old Boys' Clubs," *Harvard Crimson* Online, www.thecrimson.com/article.aspx?ref=100719.
9. Marie C. La Franz, "The 'Queen' and I," www.equijournal.com/equijournal/mc14.shtml.
10. Crawford, *Famous Families,* 2:213. T. J. Coolidge's father, Joseph Coolidge IV, married Eleanora Wayles Randolph on May 27, 1825. She was Thomas Jefferson's favorite granddaughter, born of his daughter Martha.
11. T. J. Coolidge, *The Autobiography of T. Jefferson Coolidge* (privately printed, 1902; Boston, 1923), 8, 10.

12. Joseph E. Garland, *Boston's North Shore* (Boston, 1978), 276.
13. Amory, *Proper Bostonians*, 67.
14. Coolidge, *Autobiography*, 76.
15. Crawford, *Famous Families*, 2:170–71. Thomas Gold Appleton, lawyer, painter, and raconteur, was the first man in Boston to cultivate a mustache (a point made in Michael West, *Transcendental Wordplay* [Athens, Ohio, 2000], 17).

CHAPTER 3: A BOSTON STATE OF MIND

1. The original toast was made at a Harvard class dinner in 1880 and was revised and recited by Dr. Bossidy at the annual midwinter dinner for alumni at Holy Cross College in 1910.
2. Amory, *Proper Bostonians*, 18.
3. Ibid., 31.
4. Wexler, *Reared in a Greenhouse*, 46–47. Mrs. Winthrop was living on New York's Fifth Avenue at the time, but she took her New England First Family attitudes with her.
5. Sears family archive, courtesy of John W. Sears.
6. Wexler, *Reared in a Greenhouse*, 34.
7. Marian L. Peabody, *To Be Young Was Very Heaven* (Boston, 1967). The particular incident described occurred in the spring of 1893, when Eleo was eleven. In response to inhumane treatment of working horses, the ASPCA had been formed in New York in 1866 by Henry Bergh. The Massachusetts SPCA had been founded in Boston by George Angell in 1868.

CHAPTER 4: DIPLOMACY AND FASHION

1. Coolidge, *Autobiography*, 87.
2. The maximum salary of consular personnel through 1895 was $2,500, equivalent to about $60,000 in 2005.
3. Kristina Harris, "The Bridal Trousseau," *Victorian Decorating & Lifestyle*, 1990. Available at www.vintageconnection.net/BridalTrousseau.htm.
4. Cleveland Amory, "Bostonian Unique—Miss Sears," *Vogue*, February 15, 1963.
5. Their concern was well founded. On June 25, 1894, Carnot was assassinated by an Italian anarchist.
6. By Executive Order in 1895 President Cleveland required high-level consular positions to be filled by persons who passed an examination on consular regulations and language proficiency.
7. Henry F. Graff, ed., *The Life History of the United States*, vol. 8, *Reaching for the Empire, 1890–1901* (New York, 1964), 94.
8. Ibid., 98.

CHAPTER 5: COMING OF AGE IN A NEW CENTURY

1. Editors of Time-Life Books, *The Golden Interlude: 1900–1910* (Alexandria, Va., 1991), 29.
2. Walter Lord, *The Good Years: From 1900 to the First World War* (New York, 1960), 2–3.
3. "Social Sets of Other Cities," *Washington Post*, December 31, 1912, records the boyhood recollections of Henry Cabot Lodge.
4. For a delightful account of the life of a Boston debutante, see Abigail Adams Homans, *Education by Uncles* (Boston, 1966), 99–109.
5. Louise Hall Tharp, *Mrs. Jack: A Biography of Isabella Stewart Gardner* (Boston, 1965), 28.
6. Amory, *Proper Bostonians*, 282, quoting a *Boston Globe* article from 1938.
7. Florence Howe Hall, *Memories Grave and Gay* (New York, 1918), 89.
8. Peabody, *To Be Young Was Very Heaven*, 34.
9. Crawford, *Famous Families*, 2:84.
10. Fiske Warren was the U.S. Court Tennis Champion of 1893.
11. Tharp, *Mrs. Jack*, 14.
12. Douglass Shand-Tucci, *The Art of Scandal: The Life and Times of Isabella Stewart Gardner* (New York, 1997), 151.
13. Morris Carter, *Isabella Stewart Gardner and Fenway Court* (Boston, 1925), 161.

CHAPTER 6: TENNIS QUEEN OF NEWPORT

1. Frank Phelps, one of the great scholars of early lawn tennis, has done extensive research on this point.
2. James Dwight is quoted in Garland, *Boston's North Shore,* 246. The lawn tennis set first used by Fred Sears and Jim Dwight was imported by Arthur Beebe, T. J. Coolidge's brother-in-law.
3. H. Roper Barrett, five-year-member of the British Davis Cup Team, is quoted in E. Digby Baltzell, *Sporting Gentlemen* (New York, 1995), 46.
4. In 1881 James Dwight organized the United States Lawn Tennis Association, the precursor of the USTA, to standardize the way the game was played. He was also its president for twenty-one years.
5. Susan K. Cahn, *Coming on Strong: Gender and Sexuality in Twentieth-Century Women's Sports* (New York, 1994), 91, quoting Mary Porter Beegle, "Hygiene and Physical Education in Trade Schools for Girls," *American Physical Education Review,* February 1914.
6. Joseph P. Garland, *Boston's Gold Coast: The North Shore, 1890–1929* (Boston, 1981), 207, quoting the *Boston Reminder.*
7. Ibid.
8. "Miss Eleonora Randolph Sears," *Boston Globe,* September 25, 1910.
9. Garland, *Boston's Gold Coast,* 229, quoting Talbert's *Playing for Life,* upon his visit to the Merion Cricket Club in Philadelphia in 1938.
10. "Miss Eleanora [sic] Sears of Boston Takes Newport by Storm by Her Skilful Tennis Playing," *Boston Globe,* July 26, 1903.
11. Editors of Time-Life Books, *The Golden Interlude,* 204.
12. Michael Teague, *Mrs. L.: Conversations with Alice Roosevelt Longworth* (Garden City, N.Y., 1981), 142.
13. Ellen Micheletti, "The Gilded Age," www.likesbooks.com/gildedage.html.
14. Arthur T. Vanderbilt II, *Fortune's Children: The Fall of the House of Vanderbilt* (New York, 1989), 87.

CHAPTER 7: OF MOTORCARS AND MILITANTS

1. *San Francisco Chronicle,* August 27, 1911.
2. The most significant event in the history of the modern oil industry occurred on January 10, 1901, with the discovery of oil at the Spindletop oil field near Beaumont, Texas. The bountiful success of this oil well accelerated the development of the internal combustion engine and, with it, automobiles, railroads, ships, and airplanes.
3. The winning driver was George Heath in a French Panhard; www.hickoksports.com/history/autorace03.shtml. The bronze trophy cup for the Vanderbilt Cup races stood thirty-one inches high and was engraved with a picture of Willie Vanderbilt in his favorite auto. The Vanderbilt Cup races continued intermittently until 1917, when America entered World War I. Willie K. Vanderbilt also funded the construction of the Long Island Motor Parkway, America's first expressway, which was the site of subsequent Vanderbilt Cup races. It was popularly referred to as "Willie K.'s Speedway."
4. "Athletics the Love Cure," *New York Times,* November 6, 1909, 2.
5. Alva E. Belmont, *One Month's Log of the "Seminole"* (New York, 1916), 48.
6. Carrie Chapman Catt and Nettie Rogers Shuler, *Woman Suffrage and Politics: The Inner Story of the Suffrage Movement* (New York, 1923), introduction.
7. Lord, *The Good Years,* 276.
8. Cynthia Crossen, "Déjà Vu," *Wall Street Journal,* March 5, 2003, B1, quoting Priscilla Leonard's 1897 comment.
9. Lady Constance Lytton, *"No Votes for Women": A Reply to Some Recent Anti-Suffrage Publications* (London, 1909), 6.
10. Margaret Kineton Parkes, *Why We Resist Our Taxes* (London, 1911) .
11. Winston Churchill was born at Blenheim Palace when his mother, Jennie Jerome Churchill, was attending a weekend party there and went into labor. Jennie was the first of "the marrying Americans" who went to Europe to seek high-end, titled husbands.
12. *New York Times,* October 13, 1909, 1.

CHAPTER 8: WEDDING BELLS AND PORCELLIAN BLUES

1. That sister, Irene Langhorne, later married the illustrator Charles Dana Gibson and became the real-life inspiration for the Gibson girl.
2. Teague, *Mrs. L.,* 129.
3. Editors of Time-Life Books, *The Golden Interlude,* 61.
4. McKinley was taken to the home of John Milburn, whose son Devereaux was one of polo's greatest players.
5. Teague, *Mrs. L.,* 129.
6. Many sources make this point, including Kenneth S. Davis, *FDR: The Beckoning of Destiny* (New York, 1972), 156; Blanche Wiesen Cook, *Eleanor Roosevelt* (New York, 1992), 1:149; Geoffrey Ward, *A First-Class Temperament: The Emergence of Franklin Roosevelt* (New York, 1989), 46.
7. "She Walks, Runs, Rides, Swims, Plays Tennis, Baseball and Polo," *San Francisco Examiner,* March 7, 1909.
8. The lobby of the Waldorf-Astoria featured the two-ton marble and bronze clock that was first displayed at the Chicago Columbian Exposition in 1893. The hotel provided the young Astors with an income supplement of $200,000 annually, worth more than $4 million today.

CHAPTER 9: THOROUGHBREDS, YACHTS, AND AEROPLANES

1. The weather vane now resides in the Philadelphia Museum of Art as the centerpiece of its Great Hall.
2. An exception to the sidesaddle rule had been made for very young girls who were allowed to ride astride beginning in 1907, though few ever did.
3. *Boston Sunday Globe,* October 28, 1962, 30. Mrs. J. Marion Edmunds has also been credited with that feat, when she road astride at the National in 1913.
4. Eleo particularly admired Margaret Carey of Buffalo and Mrs. Herbert Wadsworth, who rode sidesaddle all the way from Washington, D.C., to Genesco, N.Y.
5. *Boston Herald,* April 23, 1904, 3.
6. Henry Lodge, interview by author, March 2000.
7. F. W. Glasier, Brockton Fair Official Souvenir Program (1910).
8. Garland, *Boston's Gold Coast,* 125.
9. Ibid., 151.
10. Edward Weeks, *Myopia: A Centennial Chronicle* (Hamilton, Mass., 1975), 66.
11. Teddy Roosevelt was an ex-president when he was a passenger in a Wright biplane on October 11, 1910. The first president to fly in a plane while in office was Franklin Roosevelt in 1943.
12. Claude Grahame-White flew for the British Royal Air Force. He was the first pilot to fly at night and the first to carry airmail packages.
13. Graham Wallace, *Claude Grahame-White: A Biography* (London, 1960), 107.
14. Ibid., 110.
15. Ibid., 128.
16. Quoted in *The Lucius Beebe Reader,* ed. Charles M. Clegg and Duncan Emrich (Garden City, N.Y., 1967).
17. "Eleanor [sic] Sears Told 'To Stay On Earth,'" probably *San Francisco Examiner,* October 26, 1910.
18. By the time the Wright brothers disbanded their team, a year after Johnstone's death, only four of the original nine aviators were still alive.

CHAPTER 10: A TITANIC YEAR

1. *New York Times,* September 25, 1911, 1.
2. Ibid.
3. Newspaper clipping, probably *San Francisco Chronicle,* August 27, 1911.
4. *New York Times,* November 27, 1911, 1.
5. From 1908 until 1914, when the moving assembly line was introduced, Model T's also came in green, blue, and red. Fast-drying black was the only color that didn't hold up the line.
6. *New York Times,* February 19, 1912, 5.

7. "Miss Sears's Latest Fad," *New York Times,* February 8, 1912, 9.

8. Ibid. The Skating Club of Boston became the home of most of America's figure skating champions for nearly half a century.

9. "Walk Exhausts Miss Sears," *New York Times,* April 1, 1912, 13.

10. Kevin Bonsor, "Augusta Resident Famed for Rescuing Passengers on Titanic," Morris News Service, www.onlineathens.com/1997/122097/1220.a2titanic.html.

11. Walter Lord's carefully researched account, *A Night to Remember* (New York, 1955), suggests that the final song played by the orchestra may have been the Episcopal hymn "Autumn," which contains the verse "Nearer, my God, to thee." A letter sent by Elizabeth Nye, a survivor, to Walter Lord in 1955 describes the cold, starry beauty of that night and the ten young musicians who stood knee-deep in water and played. A copy of the letter is displayed in the National Maritime Museum, Greenwich, England. For that voyage on the *Titanic,* a first-class suite cost $5,000. Third-class passage was $30.

12. *San Francisco Chronicle,* May 29, 1912.

13. "Women's Horse Show," *New York Times,* June 9, 1912, C6. The Devon Horse Show ran from May 29 to June 1, 1912.

14. News clipping from the scrapbook of Mrs. Tilly Tuckerman Cutler, daughter of Phyllis Sears Tuckerman.

15. *American Lawn Tennis* 6, no. 3 (June 15, 1912): 75.

16. Eleo would win the national mixed doubles championship four years later, in 1916, with her partner Willis Davis.

17. "Two Titanic Survivors," *American Lawn Tennis* 6, no. 2 (May 15, 1912): 57.

18. James Chace, *1912: Wilson, Roosevelt, Taft & Debs—The Election That Changed the Country* (New York, 2004).

19. Newspaper fragment, probably from the *Boston Globe,* February 1936.

20. Lord, *The Good Years,* 117.

21. "Woman of Charities," *Boston Globe,* December 26, 1912.

CHAPTER 11: WARRANTS AND WAR CLOUDS

1. David Sears's church is at Colchester and Chapel Streets in Brookline.

2. Amory, "Bostonian Unique—Miss Sears," 82.

3. The first Form 1040, in 1913, allowed deductions for losses from fires, storms, and, because of the *Titanic* disaster the previous year, shipwrecks.

4. Clipping from unidentified newspaper, October 2, 1913.

5. Clipping from unidentified newspaper, October 3, 1913.

6. Lord, *The Good Years,* 341.

7. The Wasbash paper is quoted in www.washingtonpost.com/wp-srv/national/2000/allen/allen2full.htm.

8. John A. Krout, *United States since 1865,* 14th ed. (New York, 1963), 133.

9. "Spray from Summer Tides of Society's Ebb and Flow," *Washington Post,* August 4, 1914, 7.

CHAPTER 12: THE GREAT WAR

1. Words by Alfred Bryan, music by Al Piantadosi.

2. "The Lusitania Resource: Mr. Alfred Gwynne Vanderbilt, Saloon Class Passenger," www.rmslusitania.info/pages/saloon_class/Vanderbilt_ag.html.

3. Ibid.

4. *American Lawn Tennis* 9, no. 7 (August 15, 1915): 301.

5. Molla Bjurstedt and Samuel Crowther, *Tennis for Women* (Garden City, N.Y., 1916), 17–18.

6. *American Lawn Tennis* 13, no. 9 (September 15, 1919): 394.

7. The territory was shared by foxhunters from the Strawbridge family. The Strawbridges joined Bill Clothier's father, Isaac, to found the Strawbridge & Clothier department store chain that for many years was synonymous with Philadelphia.

8. The complete text of the prayer was still part of the Thanksgiving Day Blessing of the Hounds that was held on November 22, 2001, which my daughter and I attended with William J. Clothier II. This was the last of some thirty years of observances that Bill II was able to attend.

9. Henry Lodge, interview with author, March 2000.
10. J. Stanley Reeve, *Radnor Reminiscences: A Foxhunting Journal* (Boston, 1921).
11. Rupert Brooke's poem "The Dead" is quoted in Paul Fussell, *Great War and Modern Memory* (New York, 1975), 22.

CHAPTER 13: DRY SOCKS AND AMBULANCES

1. Belmont, *One Month's Log,* 14.
2. Ibid., 54.
3. Ibid., 41.
4. Garland, *Boston's Gold Coast,* 227.
5. Morton Harvey was the first singer to record a blues song, "Memphis Blues" (1914).
6. From the diary of an ambulance driver, William Yorke Stevenson, *At the Front in a Fliver* (Boston, 1917).
7. "Our Colored Heroes," poster produced by E. G. Renesch, Chicago, ca. 1918.
8. This photo was reprinted in the *Boston Evening Transcript Magazine,* February 8, 1936.

CHAPTER 14: ROARING TWENTIES

1. The modern four-way, three-light traffic signal was developed by William L. Potts, a Detroit policeman, in October 1920, not the often-credited African American inventor Garrett Morgan, who received a later patent for a related device. See www33.brinkster.com/iiiii/trfclt.
2. Marc McCutcheon, *Writer's Guide to Everyday Life from Prohibition through World War II* (Cincinnati, 1995), 161.
3. "A Horseless Lady Paul Revere," *Literary Digest,* January 16, 1926, 58.
4. See "Women's Fight for the Vote: The Nineteenth Amendment," www.law.umkc.edu/faculty/projects/ftrials/conlaw/nineteentham.htm.
5. Harry G. Levine and Craig Reinarman, "Alcohol Prohibition and Drug Prohibition: Lessons from Alcohol Policy for Drug Policy," CEDRO, 2004; Murray L. Pfeffer, "The Wonderful Nightclubs: 'That Glamorous, Fabulous Era!' " www.nfo.net/usa/niteclub.htm.
6. Coolidge, *Autobiography,* 281.
7. *American Lawn Tennis* 12, no. 14 (February 15, 1919): 392.
8. Harold Kaese, "Eleonora Paid with New Cars," possibly from the *Boston Globe,* March 29, 1968, 51.
9. *American Lawn Tennis* 13, no. 14 (July 1, 1919): 149.
10. *American Lawn Tennis* 16, no. 6 (August 1, 1922): 271.
11. This story is recounted by Mildred L. Young in *Cape Cod Genealogical Society Bulletin,* March 1991.
12. This restriction at the Somerset Club endured through the late 1950s.
13. Neil Miller, *Out of the Past: Gay and Lesbian History from 1869 to the Present* (New York, 1995), 193–95, quoting Quentin Crisp's "Four Bohemias."
14. This was determined by Eva Le Gallienne's biographer Helen Sheehy.
15. William J. Mann, *Behind the Screen: How Gays and Lesbians Shaped Hollywood* (New York, 2001), 87, quoting a comment made to the New York Herald.
16. Helen Sheehy, *Eva Le Gallienne: A Biography* (New York: 1996), 122, quoting a letter from ELG to Mercedes de Acosta, June 28, 1924.
17. This is the conclusion of Helen Sheehy.
18. The original land grant from the English governor of New York to Thomas Pell was 9,160 acres, made on October 8, 1666. Land that Pell bought from the Siwanoy Indians became the present-day town of New Rochelle. By royal grant in 1687, John Pell, a nephew, was the first lord of the manor of Pelham.
19. Isabel Pell to S. Osgood Pell, September 12, 1907. The author is indebted to Honor Moore for sharing her superb research on Isabel Pell.
20. Honor Moore, *The White Blackbird* (New York, 1996), 175–76. Honor's grandmother Margarett Sargent was one of Isabel Pell's conquests.
21. Garland, *Boston's Gold Coast,* 271. Garland's account (261–72) was drawn from the scrapbook compiled by Phyllis Sears Tuckerman, courtesy of her daughter Tilly Tuckerman Cutler.

22. During the nineteenth century many women gave walking exhibitions that attracted thousands of paying customers. These Pedestriennes garnered praise for their endurance and scorn for their vulgar self-promotion. They were marginalized and remembered only dimly as "brazen and immoral burlesque entertainers." See Dahn Shaulis, "Pedestriennes: Newsworthy but Controversial Women in Sporting Entertainment," *Journal of Sports History* 26, no. 1 (Spring 1999): 29–50.

23. "Wins Wager in 44-Mile Hike," *Boston Globe,* December 14, 1925.

24. "Walking" (in a series of editorials on assorted topics), *New York Times,* December 16, 1925.

25. Quoted in "A Horseless Lady Paul Revere," *Literary Digest,* January 16, 1926, 58.

26. *Boston Post,* November 30, 1926. Jean Bassis, a North Carolina factory worker, may have walked the route in nine hours and twenty-six minutes in September, but her claim was never verified.

27. Paul H. Nitze to the author, February 23, 2000.

28. Kaese, "Eleonora Paid with New Cars."

29. Warren Sloat, *1929—America before the Crash* (New York, 1979), 29.

CHAPTER 15: THE GREAT DEPRESSION AND THE CHANGING OF THE GUARD

1. Louise I. Gerdes, ed., *The 1930s* (San Diego, 2000), 15–16.

2. "Eleo Sears on Hoover Wagon," *Boston Herald,* October 21, 1932.

3. Robert H. Jackson, *That Man* (New York, 2003), quoted in a review of the book by Jeff Shesol in *New York Times,* November 2, 2003, 14.

4. Cornelius Vanderbilt, *Queen of the Golden Age: The Fabulous Story of Grace Wilson Vanderbilt* (New York, 1956), 294, 296.

5. Amory, "Bostonian Unique—Miss Sears."

6. ERS to FDR, April 28, 1933, and FDR to ERS, May 3, 1933, FDR Library.

7. "Society Is Not 'High,' Vincent Astor Says," *New York Times,* December 16, 1925.

8. FDR to ERS, July, 11, 1935, FDR Library.

9. ERS to FDR, July 28, 1935, FDR Library.

10. David Wieneke, "Boston History and Architecture, 1997–2002," www.iboston.org/mcp.php?pid=sears.

11. Margaret Varner Bloss, interview by author, October 18, 2001.

12. Newspaper fragment, possibly by Victor O. Jones, *Boston Globe,* 1936.

13. James Zug, *Squash: A History of the Game* (New York, 2003), 67.

14. From the program of the National Sports Dinner, February 10, 1936, courtesy of Richard A. Hillway.

15. Ibid.

16. Victor O. Jones, "174 at Banquet to Miss Sears," *Boston Globe,* February 11, 1936.

17. George Fergus Kelley to Stephen Early, February 4, 1936, FDR Library.

18. ERS to FDR, January 18, 1937, FDR Library.

19. Mann, *Behind the Screen,* 127.

20. Ibid., 256

21. William Tilden, *My Story: A Champion's Memoirs* (New York, 1948), 145–46.

22. Tilden's comment from October 1922 is from quotes compiled by Burt Goldblatt for the Sears family archive, courtesy of John W. Sears.

23. Ben Bradlee, interview by author, October 12, 2000.

24. Frederick Rowe to his son, James, December 10, 1934, courtesy of James Rowe.

25. ERS to James Rowe, July 23 and July 24, 1937, courtesy of James Rowe.

26. Zug, *Squash,* 302n68.

27. Mr. T. P. Spencer shared this account, which he had heard from his mother, a friend and close neighbor of Mrs. Baldwin.

28. Mary Martin to Burt Goldblatt, August 9, 1981, Sears family archive, courtesy of Burt Goldblatt and John W. Sears. James Mainbocher was the first American fashion designer to find success in Paris. The Duchess of Windsor chose him to design her wedding dress, ensuring his popularity.

29. ERS to FDR, May 18, 1939, FDR Library.

30. Amory, "Bostonian Unique—Miss Sears," 82.

CHAPTER 16: LOVE AND WAR ON THE NORTH SHORE

1. Eva Brigitta Hartwig, interview by author, June 5, 2001.
2. Paul Henreid, Bergman's costar in *Casablanca,* is quoted in Otto Friedrich, *City of Nets* (Berkeley, 1986), 166–67.
3. Theresa Walsh, interview by Honor Moore, October 9, 1986.
4. McCutcheon, *Everyday Life,* 85, quoting an article in the *Ladies' Home Journal,* December 1944.
5. Ibid., quoting *Time* magazine, July 1943.
6. Historically, wartime casualties from friendly fire have been substantial. During World War II they included more than 600 soldiers during the fighting in Normandy, 100 paratroopers during the invasion of Sicily, and 1,200 on U.S. ships from Allied gunfire. It is estimated that one-third of the nearly 60,000 Allied POWs in Japanese custody were killed by Allied bombs.
7. Eleo's namesake has never been fond of her name because people never spell it properly. Eleonora Carson (Margot Lumb's daughter), interview by author, October 27, 2008.
8. Betty Hicks won the USGA Championship at the Country Club over Helen Sigel on September 13, 1941.
9. The curse of the Hope Diamond did seem to afflict Evalyn McLean. Her alcoholic husband dissipated the family fortune and ran off with another woman. She suffered the loss of her nine-year-old son to an accident and her twenty-four-year-old daughter to suicide. The family newspaper, the *Washington Post,* went through bankruptcy. On several occasions Evalyn had to hock the diamond to finance her lavish lifestyle. Evalyn herself died relatively young, at the age of sixty-one.
10. Katharine Houghton Hepburn to Burt Goldblatt, March 23, 1981, Sears family archive, courtesy of Burt Goldblatt and John W. Sears.
11. ERS to Morris Carter, June 10, 1944, Morris Carter Collection, MC194, box 1, folder 3, Schlesinger Library, Radcliffe Institute, Harvard University.
12. ERS to Morris Carter, March 11, 1948, Morris Carter Collection, Schlesinger Library.
13. ERS to FDR, February 5, 1942, FDR Library.
14. "U.S. Unit Saved by N.Y. Woman, a Maquis Chief," *New York Herald Tribune,* September 7, 1944, 7.
15. Stephanie Pell-Dechame, interview by Honor Moore, February 1990.
16. ERS to Morris Carter, June 10, 1944, Morris Carter Collection, Schlesinger Library.
17. Edward and Joan Hogan, interview by author, Myopia Hunt Club, August 1, 2001.
18. Amory, *Proper Bostonians,* 34.
19. ERS to William Coolidge, August 1950, Sears family archive.

CHAPTER 17: THE 1950S

1. Harold Rosenthal, "Miss Sears, Now Past 70, Loses Squash Match Here," *New York Herald,* February 16, 1954.
2. I am indebted to Norman Byrnes for sharing this story of his unsuccessful mission to the Department of Public Works, as well as for the Railway Express story that follows.
3. "Boston Heiress Proposes 2d 'Tea Party' on Taxes," *New York Times,* August 18, 1950. Quote from Eleo Sears, "An Open Letter," 1950.
4. Jimmy Jemail, "Hotbox," *Sports Illustrated,* November 21, 1955, 7.
5. Gabor Foltenyi, interview by Lucie Bouchard, "On the 'Feel'ing of Dressage."
6. In the winter of 1943 Russian Cossacks, mounted on ponies, fired machine guns and threw grenades in a successful attack on a column of German tanks frozen in place in Ukraine. See "Legacy of the Horse," the International Museum of the Horse, www.kyhorsepark.com /museum/history.php?chapter=104.
7. Joe Estes and Whitney Tower, "The $75,000 Nod," *Sports Illustrated,* August 23, 1954, 8–11.
8. Tap Goodenough, "Love to Have Derby Winner, Says Eleonora," *Boston Evening American,* May 9, 1955.
9. Arthur Stratton, "Fabulous Eleonora Sears, 73, Trys Hand at Horse Breeding," *Boston Herald,* November 20, 1954.
10. Brigadier General William Mitchell was court-martialed for insubordination because of his

unorthodox view of the crucial military role of air power. His prediction that a Japanese attack on Hawaii would be the catalyst for America's entry into World War II was made fifteen years before the attack occurred. Posthumously, General Mitchell was awarded the Congressional Medal of Honor. Gary Cooper played him in the movie *The Court-Martial of Billy Mitchell.*

11. Gretchen Fiske Warren to Mrs. Morris Carter, April 27, 1953, Morris Carter Collection, Schlesinger Library.
12. "Didn't Pay Stable Manager, Eleonora Sears Testifies," *Boston Globe,* January 29, 1958.
13. William J. Clothier to ERS, January 10, 1955. Correspondence between ERS and WJC, January 10, 1955, to January 6, 1958, relating to the Tennis Hall of Fame is courtesy of Richard A. Hillway.
14. ERS to WJC, January 16, 1955.
15. ERS to WJC, December 21, 1957.

Chapter 18: A Far Kingdom

1. WBM to ERS, April 20, 1961, author's collection.
2. "Miss Sears Threw Rocks at Me, Plaintiff Charges," *Boston Globe,* May 5, 1961.
3. Ethel Merman, with George Eells, *Merman: An Autobiography* (New York, 1978), 94.
4. ERS to John W. Sears, telegram, September 18, 1957, Sears family archive, courtesy John W. Sears.
5. Bill Steinkraus and Sam Savitt, *Great Horses of the United States Equestrian Team* (New York, 1977).
6. The only other American gold medal from the 1956 Olympic Games was won by Hayes Jenkins, for Men's Figure Skating.
7. ERS to JWS, Easter Sunday [April 21], 1957, Sears family archive, courtesy John W. Sears.
8. WBM to ERS, New York, March 23, 1959, author's collection.
9. ERS to WBM, The Paddock, Southern Pines, March 25, 1959, author's collection.
10. WBM to ERS, New York, March 27, 1959, author's collection.
11. "Events & Discoveries," *Sports Illustrated,* August 22, 1955, 14.
12. ERS to James Rowe, January 19 [ca. 1940s], courtesy of James Rowe.
13. James Rowe, interview by author, Fort Lauderdale, February 12, 2005.
14. Ibid.
15. ERS to James Rowe, November 23, 1960, courtesy of James Rowe.
16. Huston Horn, "A Rampart of Pedigree," *Sports Illustrated,* February 11, 1963, 74.
17. Russ Harris, "Clicks for Miss Sears' Stable," *Miami Herald,* January 1963.
18. Virginia Bohlin, "Two Boston Brahmins Near Kennedy Estate," probably *Boston Globe,* March 20, 1961.
19. John Talbot, interview with author, May 10, 2001.
20. The Sabena Boeing 707 that crashed was among the five planes that had made sixty-two round-trips the previous summer between Belgium and Africa to evacuate refugees from the war zone in the Congo.
21. See www.boston.com/sports/packages/usfigureskating/stories/122900_shattered_dreams.
22. WBM to ERS, April 20, 1961, author's collection.
23. Ibid.
24. ERS to James Rowe, February 23, 1962, courtesy James Rowe.

Chapter 19: Endgame

1. Ruth Storey Felton, interview by author, November 2, 2000.
2. Richard Thorndike, interview by author, August 3, 2001. Thorndike made good on his ambition to own Eleo's stable. For a short while he ran a riding academy there. The relationship between Gertrude Stein and Alice Toklas is an example of a similar rebalancing of power and control. See Janet Hobhouse's *Everybody Who Was Anybody: A Biography of Gertrude Stein* (New York, 1975), 71, quoting Mabel Dodge on the reaction of Gertrude's brother Leo.
3. Marie V. Gendron to ERS, undated note (translation by Louise Roy Doucet).
4. ERS to MVG, from the Gideon Putnam Hotel, Saratoga Springs, N.Y., August 1962, author's collection.

5. James Rowe, interview by author, February 12, 2005.
6. ERS to J. W. Sears, January 10, 1961, Sears family archive, courtesy John W. Sears. Similar expressions can be found as far back as 1957.
7. WBM to ERS, February 28, 1962, author's collection.
8. WBM to ERS, April 20, 1961, author's collection.
9. WBM to ERS, January 24, 1962, author's collection.
10. WBM to MVG, April 20, 1962, author's collection.
11. ERS, registered letter, May 6, 1962, author's collection.
12. ERS to Tenley Albright Gardiner, June 24, 1962, author's collection.
13. WBM to ERS, May 14, 1962, author's collection.
14. WBM to ERS, October 19, 1962, author's collection.
15. Arthur Stratton, "Eleonora Sears Leads Protest—No Mounties? Foes Saddle Up," *Boston Herald,* November 20, 1962.
16. "Miss Sears Would Have Left Marines in Dust," *Boston Globe,* February 6, 1962.
17. *Boston Traveler,* July 22, 1964, 36.
18. Tap Goodenough, "Ex-Hinghamite May Have Champ," possibly *Boston Globe,* June 1, 1963.
19. Joe Hirsh, "Monmouth Park," *New York Morning Telegraph,* July 1, 1964.
20. Kentucky-born Lamb Chop was named Filly of the Year for 1963. Jimmy Rowe always believed that Spicy Living was more deserving, but that the southern-based committee did not want to see the honor go to a New England breeder. During a race at Santa Anita the following year, Lamb Chop shattered her ankle and was buried in the track's infield.
21. WBM to ERS, March 4, 1963, author's collection.
22. In 1963 an Ivy League education cost $4,000, about $44,000 in 2009.
23. WBM to ERS, January 24, 1964, author's collection.
24. ERS to WBM, March 16, 1964, author's collection.
25. Horses entered in claiming races can be bought for a predetermined amount before the race by anyone filing a claim slip in that amount with the racing secretary. Any purse money won by that horse in the race belongs to the original owner.
26. WBM to ERS, September 30, 1964, author's collection.
27. ERS to WBM, October 4, 1964, author's collection.
28. WBM to ERS, October 5, 1964, author's collection.
29. Quotes are from notes of conversations with friends, including Alice Coffin, Mabel Storey, Mrs. Quincy A. Shaw, from 1964 to 1967; Sears family archive, courtesy of John W. Sears.
30. ERS to MVG, January 1967, author's collection.
31. Sgt. Paul Simonetti, interview by author, July 19, 2000.
32. John Brotchie, interview by author, July 25, 2001.
33. Lorette Jenart, interview by author, June 13, 2000.
34. Gustave Broberg, the lawyer who drafted Eleo's last will, apparently made this statement in an interview in preparation for litigation establishing Eleo's will, May 29, 1968, From the files of Caldwell, Pacetti, Barrow, and Salisbury, Palm Beach, Fla.
35. This conclusion is based on author's review of hospital records.

EPILOGUE

1. At present values her estate was worth approximately $82 million.
2. Letter from Louise —— to Richard Dudley Sears, April 1968.
3. Case notes from the files of Caldwell, Pacetti, Barrow, and Salisbury, Palm Beach, Fla.
4. William Steinkraus, interviews by author, April 2001 and June 2004.
5. MVG to Robert Salisbury, Esq., September 24, 1972, and September 1974.
6. Rose Caso, interviews by author, July 11, 2001, and September 10, 2001.

Selected Bibliography

Amory, Cleveland. "Bostonian Unique—Miss Sears," *Vogue*, February 15, 1963.

———, ed. *Celebrity Register*. New York: Harper and Row, 1963.

———. *The Proper Bostonians*. New York: E. P. Dutton, 1947.

Balsan, Consuelo Vanderbilt. *The Glitter and the Gold*. New York: Harper and Brothers, 1952.

Baltzell, E. Digby. *Puritan Boston and Quaker Philadelphia*. New York: Free Press, 1979

———. *Sporting Gentlemen: Men's Tennis from the Age of Honor to the Cult of the Superstar*. New York: Free Press, 1995.

Barrymore, Ethel. *Memories: An Autobiography*. New York: Harper and Brothers, 1955.

Beebe, Lucius. *Boston and the Boston Legend*. New York: D. Appleton-Century, 1935.

Belmont, Alva E. *One Month's Log of the "Seminole."* New York: Privately printed, 1916.

Bjurstedt, Molla, and Samuel Crowther. *Tennis for Women*. Garden City, N.Y.: Doubleday, Page, 1916.

Bradlee, Ben. *A Good Life*. New York: Simon and Schuster, 1995.

Bradley, Hugh. *Such Was Saratoga*. New York: Doubleday, Doran, 1940.

Bret, David. *Tallulah Bankhead: A Scandalous Life*. New York: Robson Books, 1996.

Brough, James. *Princess Alice*. Boston: Little, Brown, 1975.

Bryant, Jennifer O. *Olympic Equestrian: The Sports and the Stories from Stockholm to Sydney*. Lexington, Ky.: Blood-Horse, 2000.

Cahn, Susan K. *Coming on Strong: Gender and Sexuality in Twentieth-Century Women's Sports*. New York: Free Press, 1994.

Caroli, Betty Boyd. *The Roosevelt Women*. New York: Basic Books, 1998.

Carter, Morris. *Isabella Stewart Gardner and Fenway Court*. Boston: Houghton Mifflin, 1925.

Carter, Tom. *First Lady of Tennis: Hazel Hotchkiss Wightman*. Berkeley, Calif.: Creative Arts, 2001.

Catt, Carrie Chapman, and Nettie Rogers Shuler. *Woman Suffrage and Politics: The Inner Story of the Suffrage Movement*. New York: Charles Scribner's Sons, 1923.

Clarke, Gerald. *Get Happy: The Life of Judy Garland*. New York: Random House, 2000.

Collier, Peter, and David Horowitz. *The Roosevelts*. New York: Simon and Schuster, 1994.

Condon, R. J. *Great Women Athletes of the 20th Century*. Jefferson, N.C.: McFarland, 1991.

Conley, Kevin. *Stud: Adventures in Breeding.* New York: Bloomsbury, 2002.

Cook, Blanche Wiesen. *Eleanor Roosevelt,* vol. 1. New York: Viking, 1992.

Coolidge, Thomas Jefferson. *The Autobiography of T. Jefferson Coolidge.* [1902.] Boston: Houghton Mifflin, 1923.

Cooper, Barbara. *The Manual of Horsemanship.* Warwickshire, U.K.: Pony Club, 1993.

Crawford, Mary Caroline. *Famous Families of Massachusetts.* 2 vols. Boston: Little, Brown, 1930.

Curtis, Caroline Gardiner. *Memories of Fifty Years in the Last Century.* Boston: Privately printed, 1947.

Davis, Deborah. *Strapless: John Singer Sargent and the Fall of Madame X.* New York: Penguin Books, 2003.

Davis, Kenneth S. *FDR: The Beckoning of Destiny.* New York: Putnam, 1972.

Editors of Time-Life Books. *The Clamorous Era, 1910–1920* (series: This Fabulous Century). Alexandria, Va.: Time-Life Books, 1970.

———. *The Golden Interlude, 1900–1910* (series: This Fabulous Century). Alexandria, Va.: Time-Life Books, 1969.

Felsenthal, Carol. *Alice Roosevelt Longworth.* New York: Putnam, 1988.

Fenno, Virginia Chapman. *Past Times: Intimate Tales of Our Illustrious Ancestors.* Privately published, ca. 1993.

Fox, James. *Five Sisters: The Langhornes of Virginia.* New York: Simon and Schuster, 2000.

Fussell, Paul. *The Great War and Modern Memory.* New York: Oxford University Press, 1989.

Galanter, Marc. *Cults: Faith, Healing, and Coercion.* New York: Oxford University Press, 1989.

Gallico, Paul. *The Golden People.* Garden City, N.Y.: Doubleday, 1965.

Garland, Joseph E. *Boston's Gold Coast: The North Shore, 1890–1929.* Boston: Little, Brown, 1981.

———. *Boston's North Shore: Being an Account of Life among the Noteworthy, Fashionable, Wealthy, Eccentric, and Ordinary, 1823–1890.* Boston: Little, Brown, 1978.

Gerdes, Louise I., ed. *The 1930s.* San Diego: Greenhaven Press, 2000.

Green, Martin. *The Mount Vernon Warrens.* New York: Charles Scribner's Sons, 1989.

Hall, Florence Howe. *Memories Grave and Gay.* New York: Harper and Brothers, 1918.

Halpert, Stephen, and Brenda Halpert, eds. *Brahmins and Bullyboys: G. Frank Radway's Boston Album.* Boston: Houghton Mifflin, 1973.

Harper, William A. *How You Played the Game: The Life of Grantland Rice.* Columbia: University of Missouri Press, 1999.

Himes, Cindy L. "The Female Athlete in American Society: 1860–1940." Ph.D. diss., University of Pennsylvania, 1986.

Hines, James R. *Figure Skating: A History.* Urbana: University of Illinois Press, 2006.

Homans, Abigail Adams. *Education by Uncles.* Boston: Houghton Mifflin, 1966.

Horowitz, Helen Lefkowitz. *The Power and Passion of M. Carey Thomas*. New York: Alfred A. Knopf, 1994.

Jones, Howard Mumford, and Bessie Zaban Jones, eds. *The Many Voices of Boston: A Historical Anthology, 1630–1975*. Boston: Little, Brown, 1975.

Keylor, William R. *The Twentieth-Century World: An International History*. 4th ed. New York: Oxford University Press, 2001.

Lambert, Gavin. *Nazimova: A Biography*. New York: Alfred A. Knopf, 1997.

Langtry, Albert P., ed. *Metropolitan Boston: A Modern History*. Vol. 3. New York: Lewis Historical Publishing, 1929.

Lash, Joseph P. *Franklin and Eleanor*. New York: W. W. Norton, 1971.

Le Gallienne, Eva. *At 33*. New York: Longmans, Green, 1934.

———. *With a Quiet Heart: An Autobiography. 1953*. Reprint, Westport, Conn.: Greenwood Press, 1974.

Longworth, Alice Roosevelt. *Crowded Hours: Reminiscences of Alice Roosevelt Longworth*. New York: Charles Scribner's Sons, 1933.

Lord, Walter. *The Good Years: From 1900 to the First World War*. New York: Harper and Brothers, 1960.

———. *A Night to Remember*. New York: Holt, 1955.

Lytton, Lady Constance. "No Votes for Women": A Reply to Some Recent Anti-Suffrage Publications. London: A. C. Fifield, 1909.

Maher, James T. *Twilight of Splendor*. Boston: Little, Brown, 1975.

Mann, William J. *Behind the Screen: How Gays and Lesbians Shaped Hollywood*. New York: Viking, 2001.

Maxwell, Elsa. *R.S.V.P.: Elsa Maxwell's Own Story*. Boston: Little, Brown, 1954.

McCutcheon. Marc. *Everyday Life from Prohibition through World War II*. Cincinnati: Writer's Digest Books, 1995.

McLellan, Diana. *The Girls: Sappho Goes to Hollywood*. New York: St. Martin's Press, 2000.

Merman, Ethel, with George Eells. *Merman: An Autobiography*. New York: Simon and Schuster, 1978.

Miller, Neil. *Out of the Past: Gay & Lesbian History from 1869 to the Present*. New York: Vintage Books, 1995.

Moore, Honor. *The White Blackbird*. New York: Viking, 1996.

Mount, Charles Merrill. *John Singer Sargent: A Biography*. New York: W. W. Norton, 1955.

Noverr, Douglas A., and Lawrence E. Ziewacz. *The Games They Played: Sports in American History, 1865–1980*. Chicago: Nelson-Hall, 1983.

Peabody, Marian L. *To Be Young Was Very Heaven*. Boston: Houghton Mifflin, 1967.

Press, Petra. *The 1930s*. San Diego: Lucent, 1999.

Rector, Margaret Hayden. *Alva, That Vanderbilt-Belmont Woman*. Clarkson, Me.: Dutch Island Press, 1992.

Reeve, J. Stanley. *Radnor Reminiscences: A Foxhunting Journal*. Boston: Houghton Mifflin, 1921.

Roger, Susan Fox. *Sportsdykes: Stories from On and Off the Field*. New York: St. Martin's Press, 1994.

Roleff, Tamara L., ed. *Domestic Violence: Opposing Viewpoints*. San Diego: Greenhaven Press, 2000.

Schanke, Robert A. *"That Furious Lesbian": The Story of Mercedes de Acosta*. Carbondale: Southern Illinois University Press, 2003.

Schneider, Elizabeth M. *Battered Women and Feminist Lawmaking*. New Haven: Yale University Press, 2000.

Shand-Tucci, Douglass. *The Art of Scandal: The Life and Times of Isabella Stewart Gardner*. New York: HarperCollins, 1997.

Sharp, Harold S., ed. *Handbook of Pseudonyms and Personal Nicknames*. Vol 2, first supplement. Metuchen, N.J.: Scarecrow Press, 1975.

Sheehy, Helen. *Eva Le Gallienne*. New York: Alfred A. Knopf, 1996.

Slater, Kitty. *The Hunt Country of America Revisited*. New York: Cornwall Books, 1987.

Smiley, Jane. *Horse Heaven*. New York: Alfred A. Knopf, 2000.

———. *A Year at the Races*. New York: Alfred A. Knopf, 2004.

Sprague, Kurth. *National Horse Show: A Centennial History, 1883–1983*. New York: National Horse Show Foundation, 1985.

Steinkraus, Bill, and Sam Savitt. *Great Horses of the United States Equestrian Team*. New York: Dodd, Mead, 1977.

Stuart, Amanda MacKenzie. *Consuelo and Alva Vanderbilt*. New York: HarperCollins, 2005.

Teague, Michael. *Mrs. L.: Conversations with Alice Roosevelt Longworth*. Garden City, N.Y.: Doubleday, 1981.

Tharp, Lousie Hall. *Adventurous Alliance: The Story of the Agassiz Family of Boston*. Boston: Little, Brown, 1959.

———. *Mrs. Jack: A Biography of Isabella Stewart Gardner*. Boston: Little, Brown, 1965.

Tilden, William T. *My Story: A Champion's Memoirs*. New York: Hellman, Williams, 1948.

Tomkins, Calvin. *Living Well Is the Best Revenge*. 1971. Reprint, New York: Modern Library, 1998.

Vanderbilt, Arthur T. *Fortune's Children: The Fall of the House of Vanderbilt*. New York: William Morrow, 1989.

Wallace, Graham. *Claude Grahame-White: A Biography*. London: Putnam, 1960.

Ward, Geoffrey. *A First-Class Temperament: Franklin D. Roosevelt*. New York: Harper and Row, 1989.

Weeks, Edward. *Myopia: A Centennial Chronicle, 1875–1975*. Hamilton, Mass.: Myopia Hunt Club, 1975.

Weisberger, Bernard A. *The Life History of the United States*. Vol. 8, *Reaching for the Empire*. New York: Time, 1964.

Wexler, Dorothy B. *Reared in a Greenhouse*. New York: Garland Publishing, 1998.

Zorina, Vera. *Zorina*. New York: Farrar, Straus and Giroux, 1986.

Zug, James. *Squash: A History of the Game*. New York: Scriber, 2003.

Acknowledgments

This book's long journey from conception to completion was like the recipe for preparing stone soup. Many extraordinary people shared their recollections, insights, photographs, and letters with me in their homes, by phone, at their clubs, and in a parked car alongside the polo fields of Myopia. An army of draftees combed through scrapbooks and photo albums and checked facts with other family members. They treated me to coffee and lunches. They graciously responded to follow-up queries and pointed me to other fertile areas for research. Without their bountiful contributions, there would be no soup.

The manuscript and I could not have done without J. Linzee Coolidge and his delightful and essential lists of "Findings," or John W. Sears and his unflagging interest and goldmine of family lore. I had the benefit of Bill Steinkraus's tough but fair critique that moved the prose from a trot to a canter. Thank you, Gabor Foltenyi and dear Elizabeth, for the charm of your memories and the warmth of your friendship. I am indebted to Honor Moore for sharing her research and her interviews with Pell family members and Theresa Walsh. Jonathan Winthrop offered crucial early assistance. William J. Clothier II maintained his parents' open-door policy and allowed me the run of his tennis library. Patricia States excavated the files of the Vincent Club when I began my research and did it again seven years later. I am grateful to Pamela Zauss and Michael Bove for their hospitality and the beautiful way they preserved and enhanced 200 El Bravo.

Color and light were added by Charlotte and Jack Barnaby, John Brotchie, Norman Byrnes, Esq., Clarence "Honey" Craven, Tilly Tuckerman Cutler, Burt and Kathy Goldblatt, who were inspired by Eleo first, Edward Hogan and Joan Walsh Hogan, Dottie Wightman Hood, Lorette Jenart, John Lawrence, Henry Lee Jr., Henry Sears Lodge, the Right Reverend Paul Moore Jr., Pauline Moore Nickerson, Paul H. Nitze, the dedicated tennis historians Frank Phelps and Richard A. Hillway, Volney "Tuck" Righter, James Rowe and his daughter Emmy Lou, Robert Montgomery Scott, Sergeant Paul Simonetti, Mabel Storey's children, Dr. Bayard Storey and Ruth Storey Felton, John Talbot, Richard Thorndike, Herbert Tuckerman, Angela Forbes Winthrop, and Brigitta Hartwig Wolf.

My sincere thanks also to Frederick M. Alger, Ken Benner, Ben Bradlee, Gustave Broberg, Esq., Donald Bruce, Francis "Hooksie" Burr, Manley Caldwell Jr., Esq., and his helpful staff at Caldwell & Pacetti, Eleo's goddaughter, Eleonora Carson, Rose Caso, Arthur "Bud" Collins, Betty Howe Constable,

Gladys Craven, George Fanning, Sherry Flax, Esq., at Saul, Ewing, LLP, Alexander Forbes, Eileen Joyce Fuller, C. Z. Guest, Thacher Longstreth, Dr. Keith Merrill, Stephen Nonack, Joanne Holbrook Patton, Louise Roy-Doucet for her French translations, Professor Brooke Smith, T. P. Spencer, Scott Steward, Margaret Vernon, and Patricia Yeoman.

Edgar Driscoll and Lisa Tuite arranged entry to the files of the *Boston Globe*. Marvelous Martha May of the Burlingame Historical Society turned up gems. Aaron Schmidt at the Print Department of the Boston Public Library made photo acquisition a pleasure. Welcome assistance came from Verity Andrews at the Library of the University of Reading, U.K., Christine Donovan at the Hotel del Coronado, Anne Farrell and the Unites States Squash Racquets Association, Richard Johnson at the Sports Museum of New England, Jennifer Krafchik at the Sewall-Belmont House and Museum, Julie Ludwig at the Frick Art Reference Library, Shawn Middleton with the Northeast Health System, and Alycia Vivona at the Franklin D. Roosevelt Library. The book also benefited from the cooperation of the Arthur Ashe Youth Tennis and Education Center, the Beverly Historical Society and Museum, the San Diego Historical Society, the Schlesinger Library at the Radcliffe Institute of Harvard University, and my hometown library, the Tredyffrin Public Library in Strafford, Pennsylvania.

It saddens me to have to add that not all those among this grand assemblage of contributors are still here to see how their gifts enriched the finished project. When I last spoke with them, they were in fine spirits and told entertaining stories, and that is how they remain in my memory.

This project was well served by my editor, Ann Twombly, who presided over the big picture with great efficiency and with an eye for detail that is second to none. Webster Bull and his staff at Commonwealth Editions brought this account of the remarkable Eleonora to light with gratifying enthusiasm.

I was blessed to have had the benefit of key insights and encouragement from my brother, Bill, the Renaissance man. My husband, Spencer, performed masterfully as a jack-of-all-trades and as an agreeable traveling companion. A final nod of appreciation goes to my children, Christopher and Kelly, who transcribed interview tapes with minimal complaint.

Index